C000246556

EX

Brian Winch

The Old Rectory, Knapton Green, Norfolk NR28 ORU

NAPOLEON AND IBERIA

NAPOLEONIC LIBRARY

Dedicated to the memory of
my parents,
F.J. and Selena Horward

NAPOLEON AND IBERIA

THE TWIN SIEGES OF CIUDAD RODRIGO AND ALMEIDA, 1810

Donald D. Horward

Greenhill Books, London
Stackpole Books, Pennsylvania

This edition of *Napoleon and Iberia – The Twin Sieges of Ciudad Rodrigo and Almeida, 1810* first published 1994 by Greenhill Books, Lionel Leventhal Limited, Park House 1 Russell Gardens, London NW11 9NN and Stackpole Books 5067 Ritter Road, Mechanicsburg, PA 17055, USA

British Library Cataloguing in Publication Data
Horward, Donald D.
Napoleon and Iberia; Twin Sieges of Ciudad Rodrigo and Almeida, 1810 - New ed
I. Title
940.27

ISBN 1-85367-183-5

Library of Congress Cataloging-in-Publication Data available

Publishing History
Napoleon and Iberia was first published in 1984 (University Presses of Florida) and is reproduced now exactly as the original edition, complete and unabridged, with the addition of new prefatory and bibliographic material.

Printed and bound in Great Britain by Bookcraft (Bath) Limited, Midsomer Norton

Contents

Maps

Illustrations

Acknowledgments

R ESEARCH ON THIS book has continued over a period of several years so there are many to whom I am indebted. In France, I owe an unusual debt of gratitude to the late Prince and Princess d'Essling who opened their family archives to me. Each day for months, I went to their apartment early and left late, having pored over Masséna's papers, surrounded by constant reminders of his campaign in Portugal. Similarly, I am indebted to their son, Victor André Masséna, seventh prince d'Essling; our talks over a period of years have given me valuable insights into the Marshal's character. At the Archives de la Guerre, I am pleased to acknowledge the director of the Service historique de l'armée "Terre," General J. Delmas, who has upheld the high tradition established by Pelet when he was director of the archives between 1830 and 1850. His interest in my research and his collaboration at Villenoy-Meaux, when we shared the platform and unveiled the plaque to Pelet, are deeply appreciated. Also at the Service historique, I am pleased to recognize my longtime friend Lieutenant Colonel Jacques Vernet, who shared his knowledge of the archives with me. M. Bernard Favre, a valued friend for more than two decades, introduced me to the collections at the Service historique and has been of considerable aid ever since. I would like to acknowledge the aid of the director and his staff at the Archives Nationales, especially Mme Chantal Tourtier-Bonnazzi, conservateur, who is responsible for the vast Napoleonic collection there.

In Portugal, I am equally indebted to many for their efforts in facilitating my research. Without both the morale and financial sup-

ix

port of the Calouste Gulbenkian Foundation in Lisbon, it would have been extremely difficult to complete my numerous research trips to Portugal, Spain, England, and France. I am pleased to acknowledge the support of the directors of the International Department, Dr. José Blanco and Dr. Pedro da Cunha, and more particularly, the enthusiastic support of the adjutant director, Senhora Maria Clara Farinha who always took time from her busy schedule to meet and talk with me about my project. In addition to the Calouste Gulbenkian Foundation, I would like to acknowledge the aid and support of my long-time friend, Senhora Maria Tereza Pimenta; she worked with me many times in expediting my research in the various national and private archives, and on several occasions she joined my wife and me in topographic research trips across Portugal. Her aid was valuable indeed, and her keen interest and sense of humor were deeply appreciated.

At the Arquivo Nacional da Torre do Tombo, I must recognize the extraordinary cooperation of the director, Dr. José Pereira da Costa, and his staff. My inordinate requests for manuscripts and photocopies were always honored promptly and professionally. The director of the Arquivo Historico Militar, Coronel Nuno Bessa de Almeida Frazão, and his attentive staff were highly effective and gracious in fulfilling my requests for documents and duplication. I am indebted to the director of the Biblioteca Nacional in Lisbon, particularly to Senhora Maria de Fatima Viega de Maçedo Carrilho of the Divisão de Reservados for her careful attention while I was working with the Almada e Lencastre papers. Dr. Isabel V. Sepeda was also most helpful in introducing me to this collection. I must also express my gratitude to the director of the Academia de Ciências for permission to use his vast archival collection. Regarding topographic research, I must recognize my debt to Senhor Eduardo Rodriguez, who accompanied me through the fortifications of Almeida on two occasions. Similarly, it is a pleasure to recall the aid of Sergeant Manuel Agustinho and his aide, Manuel Ramus Rodrigues, of the Guarda Fiscal who spent an afternoon reconnoitering the area surrounding Fort La Concepción.

In Spain, I owe an enormous debt of gratitude to the Uhagón-Foxá family—Dña. Margarita de Foxá Torroba and Lieutenant General D. Ricardo de Uhagón Ceballos, and their sons, D. Ricardo, D. José Enrique, and D. Santiago—owners of the monastery of La Caridad.

They welcomed us to the magnificent old monastery on three occasions and arranged for me to meet several Miróbrigians knowledgeable about the siege in 1810. We spent several evenings after dinner in the courtyard of the monastery discussing the siege; their enthusiastic encouragement was highly contagious and their hospitality overwhelming and sincerely appreciated. A special acknowledgment is due D. José Enrique and his gracious wife, Dña. Angelica Vivas de Uhagón, who spent several days with us, visiting sites relative to the siege from the ruins of the convent of San Francisco to the mills and fords along the Agueda. Their aid was invaluable. The information provided by Señor Leonardo Dorado Martinez, former mayor of Ciudad Rodrigo, was most useful and our tour through the town to the pertinent sites was enlightening. I am similarly indebted to Señor Bienvenido Calvarro Martin, who accompanied us to various sites outside of Ciudad Rodrigo that were vital for my understanding of the siege. I would also like to recognize the cordial reception by the Bishop of the diocese of Ciudad Rodrigo, His Excellency Demetrio Mansilla Reoyo; his permission to examine the cathedral's archives was most generous. While working at the Archivo Historico Nacional in Madrid, I found Señora Carmen Crespo very helpful in guiding me to the relevant documents concerning the siege of Ciudad Rodrigo and the war in the province of Salamanca.

I would like to thank the Keeper of the Public Record Office and the Trustees of the British Museum for their cooperation in facilitating my research in England. I am also indebted to the directors of the Royal United Service Institute for permission to utilize their manuscript collection in London.

At Florida State University, there are many to whom I owe a debt of gratitude. Dr. Werner Baum, dean of the College of Arts and Sciences, was supportive and provided financial support at a vital juncture in my research. Dr. Robert M. Johnson, dean for Graduate Studies and Research, also provided funds to continue research in France and England. At the Florida State University Foundation, I am indebted to the President's Club and the Committee on Small Grants, chaired by Professor Eugene Nichols; their support made additional research possible in Spain and Portugal. I am pleased to recognize the aid of the director of the Strozier Library, Mr. Charles Miller, and his highly competent staff, whose efforts to acquire, process, catalogue, and administer the French Revolution and Napoleon Collection have reduced my dependence on interlibrary loans to a minimum. I must acknowledge my debt to Mr. Joseph Evans of the Strozier Library who provided me with the aerial photograph of Almeida, thanks to his work with the U.S. Air Force in 1958. I would like to recognize the excellent work of Mr. Howard Ferstler, who transformed my slides into the photographs accompanying the text. I am equally indebted to my cartographer, Mr. Peter Krafft, who carefully prepared the detailed maps for the book.

I am pleased to thank the editor of *Military Affairs*, Dr. Robin Higham, for permission to borrow freely from my article published in December 1980. Similarly, I am indebted to the director of the University of Minnesota Press for authorization to reproduce several maps and photographs that appeared in my book on Pelet in 1973.

On a personal note, I am pleased to recall the aid of one of my former graduate students, the late William R. Johnston, with whom I spent many evenings discussing the battle of the Côa. The same is true of two of my other ex–graduate students: Dr. Francisco de la Fuente worked with me to unravel the complex negotiation process surrounding the capitulation of Almeida, and Dr. John Severn carefully read the galleys during his Christmas holiday. I recognize a particular debt to Miss Celeste Plaisance, whose extraordinary talents and efficiency with the word processor saved both time and funds and eliminated many of the usual frustrations in preparing this manuscript for publication. As always, I am indebted to my wife, Annabel, who accompanied me, step by step, across the areas of Spain and Portugal described in this book. From climbing under the barbed wire fence and scrambling up the breach at La Concepción to walking through the communication trench behind Grand Teso, she has always kept her sense of humor and put up with my often unreasonable requests in the completion of this study. Moreover, she has been involved in each phase of preparing this manuscript for publication. Finally, I must acknowledge my father, whose determination to survive a massive stroke, while I worked on this study in his hospital room, provided me with added incentive to bring this work to fruition as the "Twin Sieges."

Foreword

The 1984 International Congress on the Peninsular War, held at Ciudad Rodrigo and Almeida, became a catalyst that spawned a series of conferences devoted, at least in part, to the Iberian Peninsula during the Revolutionary Period (1789–1815). Consequently, there has been a renaissance in the study of Napoleonic literature in general and the Peninsular struggle in particular during the last decade.

Three years after meeting at Ciudad Rodrigo and Almeida, the University of Southampton and Florida State University sponsored The Wellington Congress: the Life and Times of the First Duke of Wellington. A significant number of presentations were devoted to the Peninsular War. Twelve papers were subsequently published in *Wellington Studies in the Military and Political Career of the First Duke of Wellington*, edited by Professor Norman Gash for Manchester University Press. Ten additional papers were published in a special issue of *The International History Review*, at Simon Fraser University.

In 1989 the third conference was organized by Florida State University with the support of the University of Southampton, the British Historical Society of Portugal, the Calouste Gulbenkian Foundation, the Historical Service of the Portuguese Army, the Portuguese Academy of History, and Manchester University. This meeting, the International Congress on the Iberian Peninsula (1780–1840), was attended by over 150 scholars from nine countries. Thirty of the congress papers were published by the British Historical Society of Portugal as *New Light on the Peninsular War; International Congress on the Iberian Peninsula: Select Papers, 1780–1840*, edited by Alice Berkeley.

The fourth in the series of congresses convened in the fall of 1989 at Florida State University in Tallahassee to commemorate the Bicentennial of the French Revolution and the Napoleonic period. A large number of papers presented on the Peninsular War were published in the *1989 Proceedings of the Consortium on Revolutionary Europe; Bicentennial of the French Revolution.*

The renaissance in Napoleonic literature is further exemplified by the republication of this volume as the Napoleonic Library's twenty-seventh title since 1985. Reprints of such works as the memoirs and journals of Marbot, Simmons, D'Urban, Blakeney, de Rocca, and Webber are invaluable for those interested in the field.

In the academic community there has been a flowering of research in the Napoleonic period. Coupled with this activity, several American universities, primarily in the southeast, organized the Consortium on Revolutionary Europe to concentrate on the Revolutionary Period (1750–1850). This organization celebrated its twenty-fourth anniversary in 1994; the number of presentations published by the Consortium is now approaching one thousand.

Historical associations and re-enactment societies devoted to the Napoleonic period have been organized throughout the world. In America the Napoleonic Society of America boasts a membership of almost 1500 and similar associations exist in England, France, and other European countries. Re-enactment societies of the Napoleonic period are scattered throughout Europe, from the Czech Republic to Germany, France, Belgium, Russia, and England.

Preface

IN THE SUMMER of 1984, the 174th anniversary of the sieges of
Almeida and Ciudad Rodrigo, an international congress was convened on the *Guerra de la Independencia* or *Guerra Peninsular* to
commemorate the twin sieges and the men who served in them. The
various sessions of the meeting were held in the castle, the town hall,
and the other public buildings of Ciudad Rodrigo, the great hall and
cloister of the monastery of La Caridad, and the military museum in
the demilune beside the bastion of São Pedro at Almeida—all of significance during the siege. Although the general theme of the conference was devoted to the Peninsular War, special emphasis was
concentrated on the sieges, the battle of the Côa, and other operations that took place during the summer of 1810. Consequently, the
completion and publication of this study were timed to coincide with
the meeting and to present, for the first time, a comprehensive yet
detailed account of the men who fought and died there.

Although the sieges of Almeida and Ciudad Rodrigo were only
two in a long series of events that led to the collapse of Napoleonic
Spain, they were symptomatic of the struggle that spread across Iberia. The results of the siege lulled Masséna and his army into a false
sense of security that was shattered on the rocks of Bussaco and
wrecked on the Lines of Torres Vedras. The twin sieges became a
watershed of resistance and a vital element in Wellington's strategy
for the defense of Portugal and the independence of Iberia. In Wellington's own words, "As long as we shall remain in a state of activity
in Portugal, the contest must continue in Spain." Ultimately, the war

in the Peninsula, described by Napoleon as his "bleeding sore," cost France 300,000 casualties and the myth of its invincibility. Napoleon sent his most distinguished generals into Iberia to command the most illustrious corps of the *Grande Armée*. They carried out complex operations, facing monumental problems without adequate resources or manpower. Yet, they achieved brilliant battlefield victories. Their successes, however, were illusionary, and the French armies claimed only the territory occupied by their forces. The men of the army endured unspeakable hardships stoically amid a long and bitter war with the Anglo-Portuguese and Spanish armies; they suffered the horrors of a brutal guerrilla war that undermined their strength and destroyed their morale; and they died needlessly fighting for a cause that had ceased to exist. Nevertheless, Napoleon refused to recognize the hopeless nature of the war that dragged on without end. The resulting consequences of the Iberian struggle became catastrophic for both France and Napoleon since they played a major role in the collapse of the First Empire and the end of French domination of Europe.

There has long been a strong regional fascination with the sieges of Almeida and Ciudad Rodrigo, but interest in them has been minimized by the dramatic events of some of the more familiar Peninsular sieges and battles. Indeed, the twin sieges have been superficially examined in the classic multivolume studies of the Peninsular War over the past two centuries as exemplified by Napier, Belmas, Gómez de Arteche y Moro, Luz Soriano, Oman, and Fortescue, but seldom have more than a few pages or a chapter at most been devoted to them. This work, therefore, is the first effort to present an extensive account and analysis of the sieges and the attending military operations.

This book would probably have been only another variation of the existing accounts of the twin sieges without the use of the private archives of the Masséna family and the materials recently catalogued in the Torre do Tombo. With access to the Archives of Masséna, it has been possible to reconstruct the daily operations of the French army against both fortresses while, at the same time, providing the reader with a refresher course in siege warfare. Perhaps even more significant is the presentation of details on the administrative operations of a siege army. Masséna's first aide-de-camp, Pelet, cogently pointed out the staggering difficulties faced by a besieging army in a desolate, exhausted, guerrilla-infested country, but even he failed to grasp the enormity of the problem. In the study of military operations, seldom do historians have an opportunity to consider the logistical problems involved in siege operations. Indeed, the 500 cartons of documents of the Armies of Portugal and Spain in the French archives clearly indicate this lack of documentation concerning logistical problems. As a result, the vast collections of letters by the quartermaster general, the *ordonnateurs*, and the paymasters preserved in the Archives de Masséna provide unique insights and details hitherto unavailable to scholars studying the Napoleonic War in general, and siege warfare in particular. As the documents poignantly indicate, the major enemies faced by the French army at Almeida and Ciudad Rodrigo included not only their fortifications and garrisons but also the mind-boggling logistical problems.

In completing a study of this nature it has been necessary to undertake extensive topographic research at and surrounding both Almeida and Ciudad Rodrigo. In a series of seven visits to the actual sites (which, for the most part, have changed surprisingly little in the ensuing years), it has been possible to comprehend the relationships among the various components of the sieges and the magnitude of the various problems faced by both the besiegers and the besieged. Descriptions of fortifications, buildings, geographic sites, etc., which seemed nebulous and unclear in an eyewitness account, became perfectly obvious in examining the actual locations; a maze of siegecraft terminology became intelligible and a *rideau* or defile became unambiguous. It is hoped that the photographs and maps accompanying the text will convey additional meaning to the events and sites described.

A glossary of technical military terms and illustrations of the most common siege components have been included for the reader's convenience. Current spelling of geographic names has been taken from the *Reportorio Toponimico de Portugal* published by the Cartographic Section of the Portuguese Army and the gazetteers published by the United States Board of Geographic Names. However, in certain instances, the 1810 spelling is retained, as San Felices el

Chico instead of Saelices el Chico, since all contemporary accounts used the former spelling. Similarly, variations in spelling and the use of diacritical marks in foreign works reflect the literary style used in the era in which they were written. For example, current spelling of Português and ciências are obvious derivations of Portuguez and sciências from the nineteenth century.

Chapter 1

The Spanish Quagmire

THE SIEGES of Ciudad Rodrigo and Almeida played a significant role in Napoleon's Peninsular War. Yet they have attracted little attention and been cast in the shadows of the more dramatic Iberian sieges such as Saragossa, Gerona, Badajoz, and San Sebastián. Nevertheless, the sieges of Ciudad Rodrigo and Almeida, carried on within striking distance of the Allied army, had a lasting impact upon the outcome of the war. These sieges did not inflict massive casualties upon the belligerents, but they took their toll in a commodity valuable to both the French and the Allies—time. For the Allies any time gained by the sieges would become one of their most valuable assets. On the contrary, any loss of time would doom French strategy in Spain and Portugal. Ultimately, the lengthy siege of Ciudad Rodrigo seriously undermined the French timetable for conquest, while the premature fall of Almeida threatened Allied strategy for the defense of Portugal. In consequence, the ramifications of these sieges became a watershed for future events in Iberia.

The history of both France and England has been inexorably intertwined with the fate of Iberia for eight centuries. Early in the thirteenth century the French engaged in a struggle with the Catalonians for control over Provence and Languedoc. Similarly, British bowmen fought alongside the Portuguese at Aljubarrota in 1385 to resist Castilian domination. The ensuing centuries were marked by a series of alliances and wars between the Iberian nations, Britain, and France. During the eighteenth century, France and Spain activated their "Family Compact" on numerous occasions against England and Por-

1

tugal. Likewise, when Portugal was threatened by Bourbon armies, the British reacted by landing troops to maintain their loyal ally. When war erupted during the Revolutionary period, it was not unnatural to find these four powers immersed in the struggle. Fearful of the ideology spread by revolutionary France, the Iberian nations joined England and the other continental powers in the First Coalition against France. However, in 1795 Spain withdrew from the war, and soon the Spanish king signed an alliance with France. Portugal, on the contrary, remained faithful to its British alliance and continued the war, at least nominally.

When Napoleon became First Consul, he resolved to intervene in the Peninsula and crush Portugal, Britain's most constant ally. In 1801, a French army supported by Spanish forces marched against Portugal in the War of Oranges. The Spanish invaded Portugal, and within eighteen days the Portuguese Prince Regent, Dom João, was forced to accept humiliating peace terms, which were ultimately included in the Treaty of Madrid, signed 29 September 1801. For the next six years France continued to consolidate its influence in Spain while Portugal struggled to maintain its precarious neutrality.

With the defeat of Russia at Friedland and the signing of the Treaty of Tilsit in July 1807, Napoleon turned to Iberia and, more particularly, Portugal. The Continental System had been implemented to drive British trade from the continent and undermine its ability to serve as the paymaster of Europe. Initially two nations—Portugal and Sweden—refused to adopt the Continental System. When Napoleon threatened war, the Prince Regent agreed to close his ports and sever all ties with England, but he would not arrest British nationals or seize their property. Napoleon, in the meantime, negotiated the Treaty of Fontainebleau with Spain for the destruction of Portugal.

Even before the treaty was signed, General Andoche Junot led a French army of some 25,000 men supported by Spanish troops across Spain into Portugal. He occupied the capital of Lisbon, but the Prince Regent and the royal family escaped capture by sailing to Brazil, accompanied by a British fleet. At the same time, Spanish armies occupied the Algarve in the south and Porto in the north. Junot consolidated French control in central Portugal while Napoleon sent another 100,000 veterans across the Pyrenees into northeastern Spain.

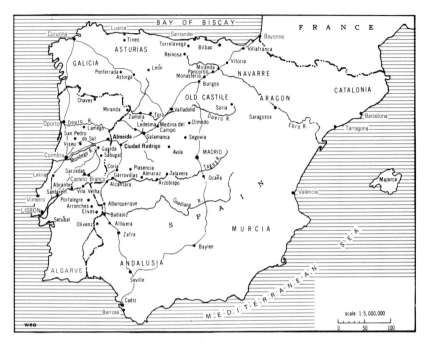

Map 1. Spain and Portugal at the time of the Peninsular War

Napoleon had reached his irrevocable decision to depose the ineffective and unreliable Bourbons. He induced Charles IV, king of Spain, and his heir, Ferdinand, to join him at Bayonne. There he forced them to renounce the Spanish throne in his favor. When he attempted to lure the other members of the royal family to Bayonne, the citizens of Madrid rose up in the famous revolt of "Dos de Mayo." Although the insurrection was brutally repressed, opposition was rekindled in Asturias, and the winds of revolt spread across Spain under the leadership of the clergy and nameless governmental officials.[1]

Soon after Napoleon learned of the Spanish insurrection, he instructed Junot to dispatch 4,000 men with sixteen cannon to occupy the Portuguese fortress of Almeida, closely observe the Spanish cities of Ciudad Rodrigo, Salamanca, and Valladolid, and open communications with Marshal Jean-Baptiste Bessières in Old Castile. On 24 May 1808, the first contingent of troops, under the command of the old veteran General Louis-Henri Loison, marched for Almeida. The day he reached the fortress, 5 June, Loison dispatched two officers to Ciudad Rodrigo to request passage and food for 12,000 troops. The governor, Brigadier General Luis Martínez de Ariza, was sympathetic to their request; but the citizens, informed of spreading opposition to the French domination, had already begun preparations to resist French occupation. The Junta of Defense had been organized and the convents, seminaries, and a church had been taken over for the planned defense force. All able-bodied men aged seventeen to forty had been called upon to serve. Six companies of urban militia, five battalions of *cazadores*, three batteries of artillery, one company of sappers, and a squadron of cavalry, totaling over 8,000 men, were quickly raised. Repairs were begun on the city walls, magazines were established, and shelters were designated in event of an attack. The irate citizens of Ciudad Rodrigo rallied the populace and drove out the French officers. The military authority of the governor was assumed by the Junta of Defense and Lieutenant Guerrero. In violent demonstrations on 10 June, Governor Ariza and several French sympathizers, termed "Afrancesados," paid for their sympathies with their lives.[2] Undiscouraged, Loison turned his attention to the Spanish fort of La Concepción, situated on the frontier between Almeida and Ciudad Rodrigo. On 12 June, a French column approached the fort, offering to relieve the garrison. The governor, apparently well aware of the events of the previous week at Ciudad Rodrigo, slipped out a postern gate the same night with the garrison and joined the defenders of Ciudad Rodrigo.

On 16 June, Loison received urgent instructions to march on Porto to suppress a Portuguese insurrection against the French commander. Leaving 1,800 troops at Almeida under General Hugues Charlot, Loison marched as far as Mezanfrio only to be turned back by Portuguese irregulars. Before reentering Almeida on 29 June, Loison received a pressing dispatch from Junot ordering his immediate return to Lisbon, which was threatened by insurrection. Loison strengthened the fortifications at Almeida. The northern bastions of La Concepción were blown up and its garrison and guns moved to Almeida. As soon as a garrison of 1,250 men had been organized to defend the fortress, Loison led his column of 2,450 men out the gate of São Francisco and down the dirt road toward Lisbon, 250 miles away. For the next three months the small French garrison at Almeida was isolated and abandoned to its fate. Observed and harassed by the militia of Guarda and citizens in the environs, the French foragers experienced difficulty replenishing their ever-diminishing magazines. To celebrate Napoleon's birthday on 15 August they carried out a successful sortie dispersing the militia, but their success was meaningless and they remained virtual prisoners at Almeida.[3]

Little information reached the garrison at Almeida until they were informed of the signing of the Convention of Sintra by Junot and the British general, Sir Arthur Wellesley. According to the treaty, the French army and its equipment would be evacuated from Portugal by the British navy as soon as possible. In October, British forces finally reached Almeida and evacuated the garrison to Porto, where British vessels waited to transport them to France. Portuguese and British troops occupied Almeida, and the fortress did not come under direct enemy attack for almost two years. Similarly, Ciudad Rodrigo was spared the effects of war until 1810.[4]

On 8 October 1808, General Sir John Moore temporarily stopped his ill-fated army at Almeida to consolidate his movements and discipline the officers of the British 6th Foot garrisoning the fortress. Ciudad Rodrigo was passed three days later as Moore's army advanced toward Valladolid to support a Spanish offensive. Two months later, when Moore's disintegrating army was pursued to La Coruña, both Almeida and Ciudad Rodrigo were spared the devastation and suffering accompanying the retreat.

In July 1809, Wellesley advanced up the Tagus River with his army to threaten Madrid, the capital of Napoleonic Spain. King Joseph ordered Marshal Nicolas Soult, commanding the 2d Corps, to collect his troops as well as Marshal Edouard Mortier's 5th Corps, and Marshal Michel Ney's 6th Corps; they were to march on Plasencia immediately to attack Wellesley or cut his communications with Portugal. By the time Soult reached Plasencia on 1 August, Wellesley had already fought the Battle of Talavera and was preparing to withdraw across the Tagus at Arzobispo and retreat down the Guadiana valley.

Soult prepared to follow the British into Portugal with his three

Figure 1. Marshal Michel Ney, Duc d'Elchingen, Prince de la
Moskowa, by Langlois

corps, but Napoleon rejected the plan. Nevertheless, Soult instructed Ney on 16 August to march from Salamanca to Ciudad Rodrigo to disperse the Spanish corps there and seize the town. Ney responded that such an operation appeared "very extraordinary." How could he "attack a town defended by at least 80 cannon" without food or a siege train? Despite Soult's agitation for immediate action, King Joseph detached the 5th and 6th Corps from his command. Soult appealed unsuccessfully to Marshal Jean-Baptiste Jourdan, King Joseph's chief military advisor, and finally to Napoleon, but he did not give up his project.[5] In considering Wellesley's foray into Spain, it is obvious that the campaign had a direct and disturbing effect upon the future of both Almeida and Ciudad Rodrigo. Two French corps, deployed in distant areas of Spain, had been repositioned and were now within two or three days' march of both fortresses.

In October 1809, Soult was named King Joseph's "major general" to replace Marshal Jourdan. Although the king was able to convince him of the necessity and convenience of invading and occupying Andalusia, Soult continued to press Ney to begin the siege of Ciudad Rodrigo as a prerequisite for the invasion of Portugal. Ney's 6th Corps, however, was in wretched condition. At the end of September, Ney departed for Paris by way of Madrid, leaving his senior divisional commander in charge of the 6th Corps. Before his return two months later his corps had been engaged in two major battles with the Spanish army commanded by the Duque del Parque. When Ney finally rejoined his troops at Salamanca on 16 December, he found the 6th Corps reduced to impotency with less than 11,000 men and 1,000 cavalry. Hence, the immediate future for Almeida and Ciudad Rodrigo seemed encouraging since the French were incapable of mounting an offensive against them.[6]

The officers and men of the 6th Corps ushered in the new year, 1810, with suffering and discontent. Operating in the exhausted province of Salamanca for almost five months, they seemed condemned to lack provisions. Yet Soult was still obsessed with the scheme of involving Ney's 6th Corps in an immediate attack on Ciudad Rodrigo, followed by the invasion of Portugal. With his newly acquired authority, Soult hoped to use the 6th Corps to seize the Spanish fortress of Ciudad Rodrigo, guarding the approaches to the

Portuguese mountains. With the fortress as a base of operations, Soult visualized the 6th Corps sweeping through Lower Beira and Estremadura to Lisbon. At the same time he would lead an army down the Tagus valley, closing a pincer on the Portuguese capital. Nevertheless, the impending campaign in Andalusia forced him to give up his scheme. Complaining to Marshal Alexandre Berthier in frustrated terms, Soult wrote: "All reports agree on the small number of troops at Ciudad Rodrigo, and no army is near enough to support them; hence, circumstances seem favorable to undertake the siege which, from all indications, should not last ten days after the trenches are opened. If the equipment were ready, I would not hesitate to send it to Salamanca, but we wait for the necessary wagon teams from France."[7] Ordering Ney to "maneuver in a manner to make himself master" of the province of Salamanca, Soult suggested that the Puerto de Baños and the approaches from Portugal in the vicinity of Ciudad Rodrigo be observed and threatened. Siege guns were to be collected at Burgos and a munitions depot was to be formed at Pamplona. On 3 January, however, Soult finally acknowledged the impracticability of his plan.[8] Ciudad Rodrigo might be vulnerable, but he was incapable of taking advantage of the situation.

Fifty-four miles to the northeast of Ciudad Rodrigo, across the gentle rolling plains of Old Castile, Ney's 6th Corps was billeted in the villages surrounding the town of Salamanca. Three infantry regiments and a battalion of cavalry were quartered in the scattered churches and convents of the city, while a similar unit was posted 12 miles to the south at Alba de Tormes. An advance guard, commanded by General Antoine-Louis Maucune, composed of the 6th Léger and 100 men of the 15th *Chasseurs à cheval*, held the hamlet of Vitigudino 26 miles northeast of Ciudad Rodrigo. Other units were posted along the communication route and in the villages surrounding Salamanca.

Through the bleak days of January these positions were maintained, but during the first week of February the lack of food became so critical that Ney was forced to disperse several battalions. The troops would have a better opportunity to gather food but, at the same time, they would be scattered over an area of 75 miles and therefore vulnerable to an attack by the Allied army, poised along the Portuguese frontier. The 6th Corps was weakened further since most of the artillery had been dismantled when the caissons were pressed into service hauling food for the troops.[9]

In Paris, meanwhile, the Emperor resolved to strengthen the position of his armies in the province of Salamanca and the other areas of northwestern Spain. A detachment of 12,000 men under the command of General Loison was ordered to march toward Benevente to cover Ney's northern flank. At the same time, elements of General Junot's future 8th Corps were ordered to concentrate in the vicinity of Burgos to support a possible siege of Ciudad Rodrigo.[10]

January of 1810 was a month of astonishing and decisive victory for Soult's French army in Andalusia. With the fall of Seville and other major cities in the south, King Joseph, convinced the Spanish could no longer resist French arms, instructed Soult to issue orders for an advance on Ciudad Rodrigo. Writing to Ney on 27 January, Soult intimated that the Marshal need only present himself in force before the fortress to reap the fruits of victory. Ney may have disagreed with Soult, but he began preparations immediately. Scattered elements of the 6th Corps began concentrating in the vicinity of Salamanca. On 8 February, arrangements were completed for troops at Valladolid to reinforce the Salamanca garrison, and two days later the corps was ready to march. After ten days' ration and 40 cartridges were distributed to each soldier, the columns of the 6th Corps passed through the west gate of Salamanca and marched across the old Roman bridge toward Ciudad Rodrigo. The advance guard of the army included the cavalry brigades of Generals Jean-Baptiste Lorcet and Philippe-Antoine Ornano, followed by the infantry divisions of Generals Jean-Gabriel Marchand and Julian-Augustin Mermet. The infantry columns were succeeded by a rear guard composed of the 39th Line. The reserve artillery and the baggage train marched along a parallel route with a cavalry escort. Crossing the plains of Old Castile, the advance guard reached the village of San Esteban, less than 20 miles from Ciudad Rodrigo, that evening while the infantry and baggage were scattered 18 miles to the rear.[11]

On 11 February, French cavalry columns passed through the defile a league east of Ciudad Rodrigo and poured onto the sprawling plain surrounding the fortress. Ornano's dragoons swept along the

Figure 2. Lieutenant General Don Andrés Pérez de Herrasti, Governor of Ciudad Rodrigo. Portrait in town hall at Ciudad Rodrigo

east bank of the Agueda River searching for Spanish troops reported to be operating between San Martín de Travejo and Robleda. Marchand's infantry trailed behind the advance guard to within a league of the fortress; at the same time, Mermet's columns turned north from Sancti Spiritus to observe a British reconnaissance force, alerted by the governor of Ciudad Rodrigo.[12]

The following morning Ney sent a summons to the governor of the fortress, Lieutenant General Don Andrés Pérez de Herrasti, announcing, "All the forts of Andalusia have opened their gates to His Catholic Majesty. . . . You are reasonable, M. le Governor, to realize that nothing can delay these results in the future. It is in this context that I beseech you to give me assurances in response to my letter." The fiery old Herrasti responded immediately with vigor and determination, "I have sworn to defend this place for the legitimate sovereign, Don Ferdinand VII, until the last drop of my blood; this I am determined to do along with the entire garrison and the inhabitants. This is the only proposition I am able to make to you."[13]

Herrasti's defiant response shattered all hope of occupying the fortress without a formal siege. Although disappointed, Ney spent the remainder of the day reconnoitering the town fortifications while his chief engineer, *Chef de bataillon* Couche, studied the terrain and sketched diagrams for siege operations. Simultaneously, the French occupied the top of Grand Teso of San Francisco, an elevation dominating the fortress, and unlimbered several pieces of artillery and howitzers. The Spanish artillery, commanded by Brigadier Don Francisco Ruiz Gómez, maintained sporadic fire against Marchand's men while the horsemen of guerrilla chieftain Don Julián Sánchez, "El Charro," bickered with a detachment of French cavalry. After nightfall, flashes of gunfire illuminated the top of Grand Teso as the French began to fire shells into the town. The artillery of Ciudad Rodrigo, supplemented by the muskets fired from the walls, responded at once against the French positions. After perhaps one hundred shells had been lobbed into the town, the French ceased fire and the Spanish soon followed suit. Flames leaped along the roofs of several buildings in Ciudad Rodrigo, but they were soon extinguished—the bombardment was over with little loss of life to either French or Spanish.[14]

At 9:30 the following morning, the French troops began to withdraw from Ciudad Rodrigo. Ney, realizing King Joseph's assurance of success was without foundation and that his meagre force was inadequate to invest the fortress, resolved to withdraw. Marchand's infantry retired toward San Felices el Chico followed by Mermet's division and only the 3d Hussars of Ornano's brigade remained before Ciudad Rodrigo until Herrasti dispatched a strong infantry column against them. Fortunately, Ney, still in the vicinity of the fortress to complete final observations, recognized their threatened position and sent his own escort galloping to their aid. The Spanish infantry were forced back to Ciudad Rodrigo and the hussars withdrew along the road to San Felices el Chico. The casualties in this operation were inconsequential: Herrasti admitted the loss of two dead and seven wounded, and the French did not acknowledge any casualties.[15] Nevertheless, a Spanish observer in the fortress wrote, "One cannot imagine the enemy's losses during the battle, but it was obviously considerable because of the many deep streams of blood scattered about that could not be hidden." As the last of the French cavalry passed beyond the defile east of the fortress, a member of the garrison is said to have shouted, "The junta and people have resolved to defend themselves until none remain, and if the idol of ambition is not yet sacrificed with the victims of Zaragoza and Gerona, let M. Ney return with more force—Ciudad Rodrigo will happily stop him."[16]

Retiring through San Felices de los Gallegos, Vitigudino, and Ledesma, the first contingents of Mermet's infantry reached Salamanca on 16 February; only Marchand's soldiers remained in an advanced position, echeloned between Vitigudino and Ledesma to observe the garrison at Ciudad Rodrigo. Although the French had gained new intelligence regarding the location, strength, and quality of the Allied army, it was obvious to Ney that his mission had been premature: not only had he failed to capture Ciudad Rodrigo, but he had exhausted great quantities of food and supplies, he had lost a considerable number of draft animals and wagons on a 150-mile march, he had depleted his reserve ration supply, and, of major significance, he had undermined the morale and discipline of his men. Exasperated by this exercise in futility and the relative isolation of his dwindling corps, Ney complained to Soult several times in the days following his return to Salamanca. The Allied army, according to recent reconnaissance reports, totaled 40,000 men and it was increasing with the arrival of each transport from England.[17]

Admittedly, Loison, in the vicinity of La Bañeza with his division, and Junot, concentrating his army corps near Valladolid, had been instructed by Napoleon "to march to the aid of the 6th Corps without orders if the English advanced on Salamanca." Ney, nevertheless, refused to rely upon their unpredictable support. Hoping to anticipate any enemy movement from Ciudad Rodrigo or the Portuguese frontier, Ney extended Marchand's regiments from Ledesma through Vitigudino to the village of Yecla on the bank of the Yeltes River, less than twenty miles from Ciudad Rodrigo and the Portuguese frontier.[18]

Soon after the return of the 6th Corps to Salamanca, a courier arrived from Paris with an Imperial Decree dated 8 February announcing a modification in the procurement of financial resources. Although the commissariat of the 6th Corps had relied upon substantial financial support from Paris, since the impoverished provinces surrounding Salamanca could not sustain a corps, the Emperor's new directive announced that the occupied provinces would have "to afford sufficient resources for the maintenance of their troops"; and the French commanders "must not rely on the French treasury, which is exhausted by the immense sums which it is constantly obliged to send out." The order seemed reasonable, but it could not be implemented effectively in Old Castile. Aware of the exhausted conditions of the four provinces under his jurisdiction, the dismayed Ney complained bitterly to Soult, "It is difficult to believe that these provinces, which have suffered so extensively, will be able to satisfy these heavy contributions. The troops are nine months in arrears to the sum of three million francs, and it can only be met by an extraordinary contribution of the villages, convents, and landowners."[19] Nevertheless, a commission was formed to collect additional revenue from the occupied provinces. A goal of 28 million *réaux* was established, but it seems doubtful the collection reached this total.

In Paris, meanwhile, the Emperor had been intently observing the progress of his armies in Spain. After the successful campaign against Austria in the fall of 1809, Napoleon had become more and more frustrated by the war in the Peninsula that raged on without predictable end. The peace of the Empire would be threatened constantly until the Portuguese and Spanish insurgents could be crushed and the English driven into the sea. The Emperor had sent several of his most illustrious marshals across the Bidassoa River, leading warseasoned veterans of Jena and Friedland, but each had failed to achieve the anticipated victories. Convinced a major effort was necessary to end the "bleeding ulcer" and guarantee the safety of his Empire, Napoleon resolved to take the road to Bayonne as so many thousand other Frenchmen had done during the past three years.

As early as 7 October 1809, Napoleon began making arrangements for his appearance in the Peninsula. "I propose," he wrote to Henri-Jacques Clarke, minister of war, "to assemble 80,000 infantry and 15,000 or 16,000 cavalry by the beginning of December, and to enter Spain with these reinforcements." He concluded this letter listing the specific regiments destined to form this army. On 23 November, Clarke was instructed to alert the Imperial Guard for service in Spain: "My intention is to march to Spain . . . toward the 15th of next January." Five days later the Emperor anxiously instructed Berthier to assume responsibility for the correspondence of the Army of Spain and undertake the duties of chief of staff. He wrote, "Send your baggage and that of your aides-de-camp to Bayonne. You will send me an account of . . . the execution of my dispositions for sending a reinforcement of 100,000 men to Spain, and of every detail relating to artillery." When Napoleon appeared before the Legislative Corps on 3 December, he confidently announced to the members, "When I show myself beyond the Pyrenees, the terrorized Leopard will seek the ocean in order to avoid shame, defeat, and death. The triumph of my armies will be the triumph of the spirit of good over that of evil. . . .I hope my friendship and protection will render peace and happiness to the people of Spain." [20]

Through December, Napoleon continued issuing orders for the formation and movement of additional units destined for Spain. In the midst of this military buildup, Napoleon became embroiled in the awkward and rather embarrassing divorce from Josephine. It was not until 11 January that couriers again began to ride south from Paris along the clogged roads with new instructions for the French commanders in Spain. On 20 January, the cavalry of the Guard was between Bordeaux and Bayonne, preparing to march southward to the Pyrenees. On 12 February, Napoleon issued detailed instructions for his arrival in Spain and the subsequent invasion of Portugal. Ney's 6th Corps was to be increased to 36,000 men. With the support of Junot's reinforced corps of 30,000 soldiers, Ney was instructed to occupy the passes from Portugal with strong patrols of cavalry immediately, "in order to learn what is going on, alarm the English, and prevent them from coming south." He was expected to spread the news in Portugal of the Emperor's arrival with 80,000 men, to occupy the summit of the pass which separates Salamanca from Ciudad Rodrigo, and to place strong detachments around the latter.[21]

Upon receipt of Napoleon's instructions, Ney began to redeploy his corps throughout the province. Marchand's first infantry brigade remained echeloned between Ledesma and Yecla, but reconnaissance columns were pushed west to the villages near the Douro and Agueda rivers; here they would be able to observe Ciudad Rodrigo and closely watch the movements of the Allied troops. A unit of 2,000 men of the 25th Léger and a dragoon brigade led by Adjutant Commander Rippert were ordered to occupy the intermediate positions between Salamanca and Ciudad Rodrigo—San Muñoz, Matilla, and Rollán—to contain the garrison of the fortress and form a rather contiguous front with Marchand's infantry at Yecla. Ney's position was strengthened further when Loison marched to Salamanca after having been relieved at La Bañeza by a division of Junot's corps.[22] Consequently, the 6th Corps now included some 30,000 troops to contain the Spanish at Ciudad Rodrigo and observe the Allied army nearby.

On 2 March, Ney finally received definite instructions concerning the future movements of his force. Announcing that a siege train of 50 pieces soon would be concentrated in the vicinity of Burgos for use against Ciudad Rodrigo, Soult observed, "The intention of His Catholic Majesty is that you prepare for the siege as soon as possible."[23] The exasperated Ney, regarding the order as highly premature, ignored it. There were too many insurmountable problems to undertake what promised to be a grueling campaign. The extraordinary contribution intended to pay the troops' arrears had failed to materialize, and the commissariat, with only twenty serviceable wagons,

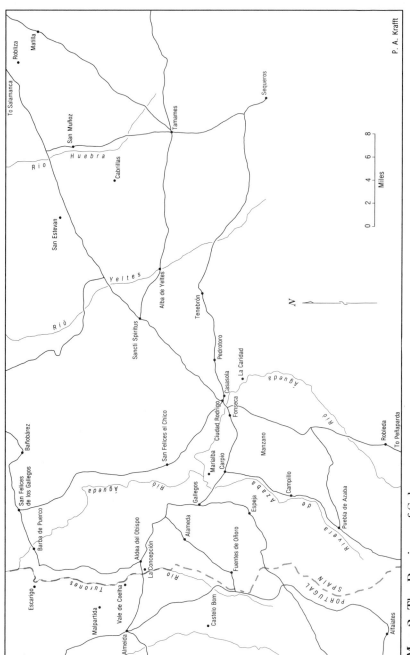

Map 2. The Province of Salamanca

was utterly incapable of transporting adequate food and supplies for the siege. At the same time, the fanaticism among the Spanish peasants increased in intensity, while the guerrillas extended their efforts against not only the French but also against the Spanish landowners, who were inclined to collaborate with the French. Food collection would have to be increased if Loison's division, recently attached to the 6th Corps, and the men of the siege train marching from France were to be fed. It was also imperative that reserve rations be gathered for a protracted siege against Ciudad Rodrigo. Infantry columns were sent into the provinces of Salamanca, Toro, León, and Zamora to requisition all available food. Such foraging into the countryside only excited the Spanish peasants to more violent reprisals against isolated Frenchmen who fell into their hands. "In Spain," remarked Ney's aide-de-camp, Captain Emmanuel-Frédéric Sprünglin, "we only found food by using bayonets." As March passed, the local guerrillas and brigands, supplemented by deserters from the impoverished Spanish armies, increased at an alarming rate. These partisans attacked not only small isolated French outposts but also the local villages, which did not support them with supplies and intelligence. Conditions became so acute that village registers were ordered kept by the local corregidors and alcaldes who were ordered to record the names of insurgents to be denied aid by the villagers. Since this procedure was unenforceable, few insurrectionaries were captured.[24]

Unfortunately for Ney, the arrival of Loison and his division in the province of Salamanca not only compounded logistical problems but also aggravated old personal antagonisms. When Loison served as one of Ney's divisional commanders during the 1805 campaign in the Tyrol, Ney had forced him to repay 290,000 francs illegally appropriated. Apparently relations between the two men remained strained for the next five years. On 11 March, this relationship deteriorated further when Junot accused Loison of taking 11 women from Benevente as hostages. Ney responded to Junot at once, indicating that complaints against Loison "are not astonishing to me. In a most severe manner I have ordered this general to return the women to their homes under safe escort."[25] In addition, Loison and his troops presented another grave problem for Ney. Composed of young conscripts, the men of his infantry brigades fell easy prey to the usual filth diseases contracted on campaign. By 20 March, only 9,000 men were under arms. Conditions became so crowded and unsanitary in the hospitals of Salamanca that a second infirmary was established in a local Jesuit school to shelter Loison's incapacitated soldiers.[26]

While Ney and his *état-major* struggled to find solutions to the perplexing difficulties faced by his troops, military operations continued against the Allies without interruption. Of all the positions along the Agueda River, the French and British were most frequently in conflict at the long bridge spanning the deep chasm below the village of Barba de Puerco 18 miles northwest of Ciudad Rodrigo. Most of Marchand's first infantry brigade commanded by Maucune occupied the village of San Felices de los Gallegos, less than four miles from the bridge, while Brigadier General Robert Craufurd's Light Division held Barba de Puerco on the heights overlooking the bridge. The first effective French probe occurred on 16 February when a column marched from San Felices de los Gallegos to the bridge, but the following morning the troops were withdrawn. Eleven days later another French column of 200 men crossed the bridge and climbed the road into Barba de Puerco, driving a patrol of the British 95th Rifles before them. The French pillaged several homes in the village and retired the next morning. On 1 March, Craufurd sent part of the 95th Rifles to Barba de Puerco, but the following day they were withdrawn mysteriously from the village. These continual changes at Barba de Puerco disturbed other British commanders in the vicinity. Colonel William Cox, governor of Almeida, less than 12 miles from the village, remarked to Major General George Lowry Cole, commanding a British infantry division at Guarda, "I know not what are the General's motives for this continual change; the poor inhabitants are the sufferers."[27]

Craufurd finally decided to post a strong picket at Barba de Puerco and the bridge on 8 March, but before he could do so Maucune's infantry were again on the move. Early on the morning of the 9th, Maucune's brigade, preceded by perhaps 150 cavalry, marched from San Felices de los Gallegos; before noon the bridge was firmly in their possession. Pushing through Barba de Puerco and the village of Villar de Ciervo, Maucune's 6th Léger and 69th Line almost cut off a detachment of the King's German Legion, driving them back toward

Figure 3. San Felices de los Gallegos

Fort La Concepción. Once the Allied positions had been reconnoitered, the French troops retired toward San Felices de los Gallegos carrying away everything they could find.[28] Two high-ranking British officers, Cox and Cole, were disturbed by Maucune's successful incursion across the Agueda, and they blamed Craufurd for withdrawing his pickets without authorization.[29] In consequence, Craufurd again occupied Barba de Puerco with four companies of the 95th Rifles on 13 March. The following day the entire Light Division was moved forward to support the 95th Rifles; the 1st Hussars of the King's German Legion were scattered along the left bank of the Agueda and an artillery brigade was concentrated at Fort La Concepción.

Before other French probes could be initiated against Barba de Puerco, Marchand's entire division was redeployed south of Salamanca, and the infantry brigades of Loison occupied Zamora and the advance posts on the east bank of the Agueda. Soon after Loison's redeployment, he was ordered to determine if the British units opposing him had been transferred to the Tagus and Guadiana rivers to obstruct French operations in the vicinity of Badajoz. Loison sent General Claude Ferey's brigade "to disperse the enemy's advance posts on the Agueda and push on as far as possible toward Almeida."[30]

Leaving San Felices de los Gallegos early on the morning of 19 March, Ferey's brigade, which included two battalions each of the 66th and 82d Line and the Hanoverian Legion, reached the eastern approach to the bridge before midnight. The French had chosen a good night for the attack; the moon was obscured most of the time by the rain clouds which drenched the soldiers, and the roaring waters pouring over the rocks in the chasm below the bridge muffled the movements of the advancing columns. According to Captain John Kincaid of the Rifles, "[Ferey,] at the head of 600 chosen grenadiers, burst forth so silently and suddenly, that, of our double sentry on the bridge, the one was taken and the other bayoneted without being able to fire off their pieces." Apparently Sergeant Betts's post, high among the rocks above the bridge, fired an alarm. With drums beating, the French 82d Line charged up the road from the bridge toward Barba de Puerco while the remainder of the British company on picket, commanded by Captain George Simmons, "had barely time to jump up and snatch their rifles when the enemy were among them." Ferey's soldiers continued to push Simmons's pickets up the road in hand-to-hand combat for fifteen minutes. As the fighting neared the village of Barba de Puerco at the crest of the hill, Lieutenant Colonel Sidney Beckwith aroused three companies of the 95th Rifles and rushed forward to support the faltering companies. The first lines of Ferey's column received a "thundering discharge," and confusion broke out in the ranks. Shattered and unable to continue, the French infantry retreated down the treacherous road and across the bridge where some 1,400 men of the 66th Line and Hanoverian Legion waited to support them.[31] The following morning Governor Cox traveled from Almeida to view the scene of the action; he recorded, "The bodies of two officers and seven men have been found dead, a sergeant and five men wounded have been taken prisoner, and three have been taken who were not wounded of the French." Another eyewitness counted one captain, Capdevielle, a subaltern, and 17 soldiers "stretched upon the rough ground." The British casualties included one officer dead and 17 soldiers dead or wounded; French casualties were placed at approximately 40.[32]

During the attack an incident occurred in the vicinity of Barba de Puerco that raised questions about the intentions and abilities of the Spanish. According to Cox a detachment of 50 Spanish soldiers nearby "behaved shamefully; they all ran away except the captain and four men without firing a shot, but as soon as the French retired they were all present to pillage the wounded, and would have gloriously put them to death if they had not been prevented by our soldiers."[33] Regardless of the validity of the incident, it reflects the ill will that existed between British and Spanish troops. Ferey's men had made a gallant but futile effort at Barba de Puerco, against the determined resistance of the 95th Rifles, but at least they learned that the British movements were only routine shifts in positions.[34] Thus ended the first series of encounters between these adversaries who were destined to meet each other on the field of battle countless times during the next three years.

On 24 March, Colonel Louis-Marie Laferrière, advancing south of San Felices el Chico, led a detachment of 150 men of the 3d Hussars and two infantry battalions toward Ciudad Rodrigo. Driving the Spanish pickets before them, the French column reached the plain surrounding the fortress. Once Laferrière was convinced the garrison had constructed no new defensive works, he retired with several prisoners. Upon their return to Salamanca his Spanish prisoners admitted that the town, which was garrisoned by 5,000 soldiers and 800 cannoneers from the local artillery school, was well supplied with rations, munitions, and over 100 pieces of ordnance.[35]

During the second week of March, the first caissons and guns of the great siege train rolled west from Valladolid. Since the train, supervised by General Charles-Etienne Ruty, included only 25 guns, Ney complained bitterly to Soult that "with so weak a force . . . it is impossible to undertake the siege of a fortress that contains at least seventy guns of all caliber."[36] Nevertheless, the wagons of the convoy rumbled past the great cathedrals of Salamanca during the first week of April to the artillery *parc* near the convent of San Francisco. Ruty, meanwhile, appealed to the men of the 6th Corps for some 400 volunteers to serve as an auxiliary unit for the train. The engineers, recently arrived from France, also faced serious problems; their equipment was stranded at the depot in Bayonne 300 miles away. For-

Figure 4. General Andoche Junot, Duc d'Abrantès,
by Mauduison

tunately, the paymaster of the 6th Corps was able to advance the engineers 150,000 francs for the purchase of new tools and 50,000 francs for rations. Anticipating shortages in the vicinity of Ciudad Rodrigo, they searched for siege materials, especially wood for the fabrication of gabions, fascines, and trestle bridges.[37]

As the siege train was collected at Salamanca, Soult anxiously awaited the investment of Ciudad Rodrigo. Ney, however, refused to be rushed into the operation. The trenches would not be opened before the fortress until a covering force was deployed to protect the investing operation. Detachments would have to be posted at San Felices de los Gallegos opposite the British position at Villar de Ciervo, at Carpio to guard the Portuguese frontier toward Guarda, at Fuente Guinaldo to seal the passes from the Sierra de Gata, and at the passes of Béjar and Baños to control the road from Plasencia to Estremadura. If these positions were not secured, the 6th Corps would be in an exposed and extremely dangerous position during the siege. With two of his divisions engaged in investment and support operations, Ney would have only one division to meet an attack if the Allies decided to cross into Spain. Ney, therefore, asked Soult to post units of Kellermann's division at Zamora and Toro while General Joseph-Léopold Hugo, governor of Avila, assumed responsibility for the Puerto de Baños. Similarly, two divisions of Junot's corps were to occupy Salamanca and Ledesma.[38] When Soult ignored the appeal, Ney wrote directly to Berthier in Paris, but without result.

During the last week of March, preparations for the siege of Ciudad Rodrigo suffered an inopportune setback when Junot was ordered to invest the town of Astorga. Most of the guns, destined for the siege of Ciudad Rodrigo, would be diverted to Astorga, and even more important, the 6th Corps would be without a covering force to protect its operations. When Ney learned of this change, he refused to advance against Ciudad Rodrigo and risk his men and the indispensable siege train. "It is impossible," wrote Ney, "that this double operation [sieges of Ciudad Rodrigo and Astorga] is in accord with the intentions of the Emperor." At the same time, he sent a persuasive letter to Junot suggesting that he ignore his orders and support the 6th Corps in the siege. Junot responded immediately, asking, "Is it wise to make a decision not indicated by the Emperor? Would he not have reason to reproach my conduct when he learned that the orders he had given me and expected, had not been carried out. And if he wanted my army corps for another operation, would I not be blamed for disobeying his orders?"[39] Junot's judgment was correct, but this did not remedy Ney's predicament. This incident served to emphasize the insurmountable problems plaguing Napoleon's commanders in Spain and Portugal. Since the strategy and movements of the French corps in the Peninsula were dependent upon specific instructions from the Emperor, the generals were forced to maintain a passive role for want of concrete directives from Paris, which were often intercepted or outdated before they arrived.

Ney would not advance against Ciudad Rodrigo until adequate support was available, so his men busied themselves searching the neighboring villages for supplies. Ovens were constructed at Salamanca, and soon a reserve magazine was established. As the collections continued, the men of the 6th Corps found themselves in active competition with Junot's troops; the Emperor had given the 8th Corps special permission to use the financial resources of León, Valladolid, and Old Castile. Nevertheless, Ney's men could not subsist by sharing the resources of these provinces. Ney appealed to Napoleon for permission to use the resources in the province of Avila, at that time under the jurisdiction of King Joseph. Napoleon not only agreed to Ney's request, but he also instructed the French governors at Burgos and Valladolid to send a combined total of 500,000 rations of biscuit to supplement the magazines of the 6th Corps. In the meantime, Ney anxiously requested Governor Hugo of Avila to aid his men in collecting supplies for the siege of Ciudad Rodrigo. The 11th Dragoons, commanded by Colonel Dejean, was ordered by Ney to enter the province to begin collecting foodstuffs and the equivalent of 150,000 francs. Correctly assuming that his position with King Joseph would be compromised, Hugo refused to permit the requisitions. Joseph was enraged by Ney's actions, and he demanded "justice" from his brother, the Emperor. Hugo threatened to use Joseph's newly formed Royal-Etranger Regiment to halt Dejean. All the villages and towns of Avila were instructed not to admit the dragoons, but Dejean was able to avoid an actual confrontation. Hugo finally agreed to countermand his orders. However, when the impulsive Ney learned of the controversy, he was unable to restrain himself and issued orders for the immediate invasion of Avila and expulsion of Hugo. After some reflection, Ney rescinded his order. To make the requisition more palatable Dejean was ordered to collect only food. At the same time, however, the 50th Line was dispatched into Avila to reinforce Dejean in case other disputes occurred.[40]

By the middle of April the perturbed Soult, unable to control his indignation over Ney's delays, denounced the Marshal for his refusal to invest Ciudad Rodrigo until the 8th Corps was available to support the siege. Suggesting the delay would "compromise the success of the campaign," Soult complained in a letter dated 14 April, "Today the siege train is completely united at Salamanca; everything is ready. Nothing more can stop you, not even the English army whose whole force is inferior to that of the 6th Corps." As an afterthought, Soult pointed out the Allies would not be anxious to advance against the French at Ciudad Rodrigo because Mortier's movements against the fortress of Badajoz in the south would act as a diversionary force in his favor. This seemed highly unlikely and Ney responded, "It will be impossible for me to approach Ciudad Rodrigo before the operation [of Astorga] is concluded."[41]

Ney's Corps had occupied the provinces of Salamanca, Toro, Zamora, and León for almost eight months; yet he controlled only the terrain actually occupied by his troops. In fact, French domination of these provinces was illusionary, and Ney could do very little to alter the situation. This dilemma, faced by the other French commanders in the Peninsula, was well dramatized by a letter to Soult from Ney: "Despite all the measures I have taken to destroy the bands of guerrillas, we have not yet succeeded. The brigands continue to torment us, intercepting our convoys and cutting off our isolated weak detachments. It is almost impossible to attack them for they are protected by the villages where they receive information, recruits, and horses." In addition to the guerrillas, Ney blamed much of the French ineffectiveness in the Peninsula directly on King Joseph and his ambitious schemes for Spain: "If the French had marched against the [British] instead of conquering Andalusia," Ney reasoned his cavalry would be available to hunt down the guerrillas. He concluded, "I wish the Emperor could come to Bayonne to regulate the principal operations and give each army corps positive instructions on the conduct to be followed. It seems to be the only way to avoid hereafter all the orders and counter orders that constantly arrive from the King's [Joseph] headquarters which are almost always as impractical as they are contrary to the interests of the Emperor."[42] This blunt letter may have lacked tact, but Ney's comments were valid.

In the meantime, Junot's corps brought the siege of Astorga to a rapid conclusion on 22 April, four days after the siege train reached the city. Two days after the surrender of the city, Ney learned of the withdrawal of Junot's corps from Astorga; he issued immediate instructions for the investment of Ciudad Rodrigo. The 66th and 82d Line, the Hanoverian Legion, and the 25th Dragoons of Ferey's brigade advanced to occupy a line between San Felices el Chico and Sancti Spiritus to blockade the fortress east of the Agueda River. Maucune occupied Tenebrón with the 69th Line and 15th Chasseurs à cheval despite the extensive flooding of the Agueda and its tributaries. This investing force was supported by General Edouard-François Simon's brigade between San Felices de los Gallegos, Toro, and Zamora. To maintain communications with Valladolid and the south, Mermet's division remained at Salamanca and Alba de Tormes with a detachment at the Puerto de Baños.[43]

It is curious that six weeks later, Ney was condemned by his superiors for his premature investment of Ciudad Rodrigo.[44] Indeed, the investment was premature, but the error was attributable directly to Soult. In a series of letters during February, March, and April, Soult had instructed Ney to invest Ciudad Rodrigo "as soon as possible" or "compromise the success of the campaign." Convinced of the premature nature of the investment, Ney procrastinated for almost three months. Twice during March, Ney refused to advance against the fortress, arguing that he lacked sufficient ordnance. When the siege train began to arrive, Ney complained about the lack of support from Junot's corps. It was only after two months of periodic harassment and the fall of Astorga that Ney agreed to invest Ciudad Rodrigo.[45] By the end of April, Astorga had capitulated and Ney had no alternative but to establish a partial blockade of Ciudad Rodrigo or be liable to charges of insubordination.

Thus, after some four months of inaction in the impoverished provinces of Old Castile, the 6th Corps was again ready to begin operations. Despite the numerous difficulties and hardships suffered by the officers and men of the 6th Corps, they were again anxious to take up the tools of war and follow their eagles on the campaign. In Paris, Napoleon was not unaware of the courage and determination of these veterans. In fact, on 17 April he had issued a decree designating the

6th Corps as the nucleus of a newly formed army destined to besiege Ciudad Rodrigo and Almeida, invade Portugal, and drive the English into the sea. He had little doubt that these men would continue to reap victory on the battlefields of Spain and Portugal as they had so many times before in Germany and Austria.

Chapter 2

Wellington's Peninsular Strategy:
The Role of Ciudad Rodrigo and Almeida

A s the French preparations for the siege of Ciudad Rodrigo were accelerated, the Allied commander, Sir Arthur Wellesley, now Viscount Wellington, struggled to prepare Portugal for an anticipated invasion. After his incursion into Spain had been thwarted at Talavera in the summer of 1809, Wellington became convinced that the success of British arms in the Peninsula depended upon his ability to mobilize and defend Portugal. Consequently, he began to formulate plans for the transformation of the country, but it was obvious that the success of his strategy hinged upon the resistance of the frontier fortresses of Almeida and Ciudad Rodrigo.

Among the numerous schemes proposed for the defense of Portugal the most extensive and time-consuming project was originally suggested by a Portuguese major, José Maria das Neves Costa. The major reconnoitered the mountainous terrain north of Lisbon between the Tagus River and the Atlantic Ocean at the end of 1808 to determine the feasibility of constructing fortifications to protect the capital. He sent maps and a memorandum to the Portuguese minister of war, Dom Miguel Pereira Forjaz, before June 1809 detailing his design. This information was forwarded in the fall to Wellington, who utilized the proposal as a basis for what became the renowned Lines of Torres Vedras. Accompanied by Lieutenant Colonel Richard Fletcher, commander of the Royal Engineers, Wellington carefully considered Neves Costa's plans in reconnoitering the area north of Lisbon. Wellington then issued his now famous memorandum of 20 October, establishing the parameters for one of the most important fortified lines ever constructed. The project would prove to be a monumental undertaking, requiring extraordinary financial resources, a vast reservoir of manpower, minute attention and direction, the utmost secrecy, and, even more important, adequate time to complete the work.

Initially, Wellington visualized a line of fortifications north of Lisbon, a fortified enclave on the Tagus below Lisbon for the evacuation of the army, and a few forward positions constructed on prominent topographic positions to delay the enemy advance. Workers recruited from the environs of Lisbon and several militia regiments were employed to begin work on the lines under the direction of Portuguese and British engineers. By the end of the summer 7,000 laborers had been conscripted from as far as 50 miles away to aid the militiamen and several regiments of *ordenanza* on the works. When the project was completed, three lines had been constructed across the Lisbon peninsula, a distance of 29 miles: they included 165 fortified redoubts armed with 628 guns and manned by 39,475 men. These self-sufficient fortifications varied in size, shape, and strength to conform to the terrain but they were all constructed according to a general format, which included banquettes, a five-foot parapet, and a ditch fifteen feet wide and ten feet deep surrounded by palisades. These fieldworks, some actually fortlets, were garrisoned with between 50 and 2,000 men. The adjoining terrain was utilized to enhance further these defenses. The roads approaching the lines were cut and barricaded, valleys were blocked with abatis, trenches were dug, hills were escarped and rock slopes blasted into perpendicular precipices, trees obstructing the line of fire were felled, bridges were mined, and rivers were dammed and flooded. To facilitate the rapid movement of troops and communications, lateral roads were constructed. The Royal Navy established and manned a telegraph system along and among the three lines for rapid communication. Navy gunboats were anchored in the Tagus to cover the flanks of the lines and support Allied troops in event of an enemy advance.

In addition to the Lines of Torres Vedras, Wellington and the Portuguese government made detailed plans for the mobilization of the provinces. The fortresses of Abrantes along the Tagus and Elvas opposite the Spanish fortress of Badajoz were reinforced with additional

Figure 5. Sir Arthur Wellesley, Duke of Wellington, by Thomas Lawrence

men, supplies, and equipment and their fortifications improved to withstand a major siege. Almeida, situated directly on Ney's line of march, received special attention. Several of Wellington's divisions were posted within marching distance of Almeida, and continuing efforts were made to improve fortress defenses.[1]

Arrangements were concluded for the destruction of all vital roads leading from Spain while the routes over which the Allied army was expected to pass were repaired and carefully fortified. The road up the Mondego valley from Ponte de Murcella through Celorico to Almeida and Ciudad Rodrigo was repaired and several defensive positions, especially at Murcella, were entrenched in anticipation of the French advance. Boats on the major rivers were registered and placed under the jurisdiction of local officials, and all the boat bridges on the Tagus, for a distance of 150 miles, were withdrawn. Orders were issued for the removal of "carts, mules, and other means of conveyance, and the provisions, of which the enemy might make use in the invasion of the country."[2]

To utilize Portuguese irregulars, ancient laws of the Kingdom were invoked to call up the *ordenanza*, similar to the French *levée en masse*. Drawn from the male population between the ages of sixteen and sixty, these irregular warriors promised to be extremely valuable to the Allied cause. The *capitãos mors* were instructed to organize 250-man companies of ordenanza "to do the enemy all the mischief in their power . . . by impeding his communications, by firing upon him from the mountains and strong passes with which the whole country abounds, and by annoying his foraging and other parties that he may send out."[3] On 1 March 1810, Lieutenant General Manuel Bacelar, the Portuguese governor of Beira, was cautioned to prepare for invasion. Arrangements were to be made for the destruction of the roads and bridges in the province; once this had been completed, detachments of ordenanza would be posted nearby to prevent the French from repairing them. In addition, the ordenanza were to guard the fords along the Côa River, less than two miles from Almeida. If the French did succeed in masking or capturing Almeida, all the bridges on the Mondego, Alva, Dão, Criz, and Zezere rivers were to be cut. Simultaneously, the inhabitants along the invasion route were to retire; those near the Mondego valley were to flee to the rugged Serra de

Alcoba, those close to the Zezere valley were to seek refuge in the villages along the river, and those in the vicinity of the Serra da Estrêla were to flee up into the mountain.[4] Wellington, pleased with this flurry of activity, was convinced Portugal could be defended if there was time to complete preparations for defense and mobilization. The people might become exasperated with his demands, but he was confident they would obey his orders.

During the first three months of 1810, Wellington closely watched efforts to organize and train the Portuguese army. This project was another in which time was a crucial factor. On 4 January he wrote an encouraging letter to Robert Jenkinson, Earl of Liverpool and secretary of war: "I have had opportunities of seeing fifteen regiments in the Portuguese service, and . . . the progress of all these troops in discipline is considerable. . . . I have no doubt but that the whole will prove a useful acquisition to the country." By the end of January the discipline in the army had improved substantially "and will soon, I hope," wrote Wellington, "be a valuable addition to our force." Nevertheless, he was forced to admit that "these troops are so sickly from the want of clothing and necessities not yet arrived from England . . . I have . . . given up all thoughts of moving at present." Despite the lack of funds the Portuguese army continued to grow in size; by the third week of February, Wellington estimated 20,000 men were ready for field operations in the regular regiments and over 29,000 militiamen were under arms.[5] Satisfied with the continual progress of Portuguese training, Wellington resolved to deploy them with regiments of his own brigades. On 22 February, instructions were issued for the incorporation of several Portuguese line regiments into the British divisions. The 11th and 23d Line were to be attached to Cole's Fourth Division quartered at Guarda and in daily contact with Almeida. The 9th and 21st Line were to be attached to Major General Thomas Picton's 3d Division posted at Pinhel, a two hour ride from Almeida. The Portuguese 1st and 2d *Caçadores* (light infantry) were to be attached to Craufurd's Light Division. Occupying the advanced posts of the army in the vicinity of Almeida and the Côa, this division was composed of several of the most renowned regiments in the British army, namely, the 43d Foot, the 52d Foot, and the 95th Rifles. With the movement of Portuguese infantry to the front, and more particularly

to the advanced posts of the army, Wellington reasoned they would
gain confidence and experience, and improve in morale, nourished
by the realization that they were defending Almeida and their national frontier.[6]

As each day passed, Wellington became more and more convinced that he would be able to defend Portugal: "If I can bring
30,000 effective British troops into the field, I will fight a good battle
for . . . Portugal." He promised, "If the Portuguese do their duty, I
shall have enough [troops] to maintain it; if they do not, nothing that
Great Britain can afford can save the country." But Wellington was
satisfied that a joint Anglo-Lusitanian force could defend the Kingdom of Portugal. As early as 14 November 1809, he confidently wrote
to Liverpool that the French would be unable to subdue Portugal with
"an army of 70,000, or even of 80,000 men, if they [did] not make
the attack for two or three months."[7]

Coupled with the problems associated with the reestablishment of
a viable Portuguese army, Wellington faced a staggering financial crisis. By the end of 1809, His Majesty's Government had agreed to provide £980,000 for the maintenance of 30,000 Portuguese troops for
service with Wellington's army; nevertheless, it was abundantly clear,
especially to the officials of the Portuguese Regency, that these funds
were seriously inadequate. The British appropriation did not fully
fund the 30,000 auxiliaries. Consequently, the Portuguese government had to provide £1 million to augment the appropriations for the
auxiliaries as well as fund some 74,000 militia and line troops, prepare the defenses of the country, and maintain civil and administrative functions of the country.[8] Wellington was deeply concerned about
the deteriorating financial situation in Portugal. "It will be impossible
to keep the Portuguese army together," he wrote, "if the Government
is not assisted with money to pay it regularly." He also complained of
the need for "money to pay the British troops with regularity. . . . The
constitution, and the whole system of discipline, efficiency, and
equipment of the British army, depend upon regular payments." Liverpool and the British Cabinet, keenly aware of the additional expenses
incurred by the Portuguese army, resolved to increase the Portuguese
grant to £120,000 a month for 30,000 Portuguese troops. Simultaneously, the subsidy for 36,000 British troops in Portugal and 7,000

men at Cadiz was increased to £180,000 per month. Thus the total cost of supporting 73,000 men in the Peninsula was £300,000 per month, a staggering figure, yet Liverpool optimistically observed, "There is no reason at present to suppose that His Majesty's Government may not be able to bear this amount provided it can really be limited to that amount, but it is not possible . . . that the whole or even considerable part of this sum can be provided in specie from England."[9]

Despite the large British subsidy, the great bulk of the war costs fell on the Portuguese. Under pressure from Wellington and his representative on the Regency Council, Sir Charles Stuart, the members of the council were induced to alter their tax structure by revising old taxes, creating new imposts, selling royal lands, establishing forced loans and a lottery, and modifying import duties. While attempting to mobilize Portugal by reorganizing, equipping, and training their army to carry on a war against a formidable enemy, Wellington was forced to the realization that the credit of the British government had "been stretched to the utmost." He cogently pointed out, "Many debts still remain due on account of Sir John Moore's army. The people of Portugal and Spain are tired out by requisitions not paid for . . . and nothing can now be procured without ready payment." Two months later Wellington reminded Liverpool, "The quantity of supplies drawn from Portugal for the use of the British and Portuguese armies has been so large, that it is most difficult now to procure any without payment."[10]

Wellington was also preoccupied with the safety of the British army, especially when he recalled Moore's fate during the disastrous retreat in 1809. He sent detailed letters to Liverpool, describing the minute precautions to be taken to evacuate the army if the need arose. Liverpool was apprehensive about his arrangements. Hoping to ease the secretary's anxiety, Wellington persuasively argued in a dispatch dated 1 March, "The British army ought to remain in the field in Portugal as long as may be practicable, and consistent with its safety. . . . I consider it highly desirable that we should maintain ourselves in Portugal as long as possible." He concluded, promising, "If you will let us have a large fleet of ships of war, and 45,000 disposable tons of transports, I shall try, and I think I shall bring them

[Allied army] all off."[11] This did not end the issue. Liverpool encountered increasing pressure from Parliament over the safety of Wellington's army; thus, he continued to press his commander: "I should apprise you, however, that a very considerable degree of alarm exists in this country respecting the safety of the British army in Portugal." He suggested it would be wiser to abandon Portugal "a little too soon than, by remaining in Portugal a little too long, exposing it to those risks from which no military operations can be wholly exempt." In the same letter, Liverpool questioned Wellington's judgment on evacuating the British army, if necessary, from Fort São Julião below Lisbon rather than from the formidable fortress at Peniche, forty miles north of the capital: "I am anxious, therefore, that you should seriously consider whether . . . it would not be more consistent with the principle of your instructions, viz., that the safety of the army is to be your first object, to look at Peniche as the place of embarkation rather than to St. Julian's."[12] Wellington was disturbed by Liverpool's wavering confidence and disgusted that his assurances would not satisfy the cabinet.

Despite the doubt and anxiety in London, Wellington's judgment was unshaken. "I believe," he wrote to Forjaz, "that if we are able to maintain ourselves in Portugal, the war will not end in the Peninsula." Alluding to the Lines of Torres Vedras under construction before Lisbon, he concluded, "If the enemy is not able to force us, when we have retreated to this position, he will be obliged to retreat . . . and he will be forced in any case to abandon all the Portuguese territory. If we are forced to abandon this position, we will always have the means to embark ourselves in the Tagus"—an unusually optimistic evaluation, at a time when the armies of Napoleon dominated Europe from the banks of the Tormes River at Salamanca to those of the Vistula flowing through Warsaw.[13] Yet he knew the Royal Navy was prepared to carry out whatever was necessary for the safety of his army. Wellington was determined to defend Portugal, but he completed detailed evacuation plans to satisfy the British government. It was also decided to evacuate the Portuguese army at the same time "because we may be very certain, that all that we leave behind will very soon be made French soldiers." Consequently, transport vessels totaling 49,000 ton and a fleet of men-of-war would be waiting to embark both armies as well as any citizens who felt their personal safety jeopardized.[14]

While the Allied army increased in size and discipline, debate raged in England regarding the safety of the army. Many reminded Liverpool that Moore, one of England's most illustrious heroes, who had fallen at La Coruña in 1809, believed Portugal was indefensible. "I have as much respect as any man can have for the opinion and judgment of Sir John Moore," Wellington admitted, "but he positively knew nothing of Portugal, and could know nothing of its existing state." Wellington recognized the vital significance of Portugal to the war effort as did few of his contemporaries: "As long as we shall remain in a state of activity in Portugal, the contest must continue in Spain." Convinced the French could not invade Portugal "without abandoning other objects, and exposing their whole fabric in Spain to great risk," Wellington promised, "all the preparations for embarking and carrying away the army, and everything belonging to it, are already made, and my intention is to embark it, as soon as I find that a military necessity exists for so doing." Nevertheless, unwilling to commit himself, he concluded, "I shall delay the embarkation as long as it is in my power, and shall do everything in my power to avert the necessity of embarking at all. If the enemy should invade this country with a force less than that which I should think so superior . . . I shall fight a battle to save the country . . . and if the result should not be successful . . . I shall still be able to retire and embark the army."[15]

To guarantee the swift evacuation of the Allied army in event of reversal, the government had already begun concentrating vessels in Lisbon harbor. By the end of January, 23,440 ton of transports, in addition to 7,000 ton en route from London, were anchored in the estuary of the Tagus, and six weeks later vessels representing 19,000 ton were en route from Gibraltar, Malta, and Cadiz, increasing the total to 49,000 ton. In addition, six men-of-war and a number of ordnance and cavalry vessels were preparing to sail for Lisbon.[16]

The baggage of many regiments had already been loaded aboard the transports in the Tagus in January and February to coincide with the arrival of reinforcements from England so inhabitants of the city would not be alarmed. By May each English vessel at Lisbon was well supplied with water and provisions and had been numbered and assigned regiments, ascribed specific berths, and provided with long-boats to transport the troops from the shore if evacuation became necessary.[17] As usual, the Royal Navy appeared ready for any eventuality; now circumstances would determine their use.

Despite Wellington's confidence in his army, dispositions, and strategy, he found himself continually pressed by the minister of war. Again and again he had explained in great detail his strategy for the defense of Portugal and the subsequent evacuation of the Kingdom. Liverpool, however, was not content, and he continued to question Wellington's judgment. In a dispatch dated 2 April to Liverpool, the harassed yet determined general struck back at his critics: "I am willing to be responsible for the evacuation of Portugal. . . . Depend upon it, whatever people may tell you, I am not so desirous as they imagine of fighting desperate battles; if I was, I might fight one any day I please." He wrote to Admiral George Berkeley a week later in a similar vein: "The Government are terribly afraid that I shall get them, and myself, into a scrape. But what can be expected from men who are beaten in the House of Commons three times a week? A great deal might be done now, if there existed in England less party, and more public sentiment, and if there was any Government." With the debate continuing in England, Wellington was perfectly aware of the personal risk involved in his unalterable position: "All I beg is," he wrote, "that if I am to be responsible, I may be left to the exercise of my own judgement; and I ask for the fair confidence of Government upon the measures which I am to adopt."[18]

It was not until the end of April that Wellington began to regain his confidence in the government. The king's private secretary, Colonel Herbert Taylor, wrote to Liverpool expressing George III's confidence in Wellington; he promised support "unfettered by any particular instructions which might embarrass him in the execution of his general plan of operations." At the same time, Liverpool finally acquiesced in Wellington's decision to embark at São Julião rather than Peniche.[19] Wellington's determination and perseverance had forced the government to accept his strategy. In event of disaster his career would come to an abrupt and inglorious end, but he was convinced he could rely on the Royal Navy to evacuate his army from the Peninsula.

A perplexing problem over which Wellington had little direct control threatened to upset his program of mobilization. Before Prince João and the Portuguese court fled into exile in 1807, he established a regency, the Governors of the Kingdom, to carry on the operations of government. Of the original five members, only two were still active by 1810. Consequently, Wellington sought to have the Prince Regent appoint men who were sympathetic to his views. Ultimately, he secured the appointment of Charles Stuart, the British ambassador, as a member of the Regency Council, but others with reservations about his defense policies also took seats on the Council.

There was also serious concern over the secretary of the regency, Forjaz, who also served as secretary of war and foreign affairs. Intelligent, effective, sincere, and constant in his support of the British alliance, Forjaz found himself under attack by two regents. Fed by the malicious gossip of the Marquez das Minas (de Sousa Lencastre e Noronha), the Patriarch (António de Castro) became extremely jealous of Forjaz's "exclusive management of the war and foreign department," and he labored to undermine Forjaz's position with the Prince Regent. Wellington and Stuart, "aware that the Patriarch and Forjaz hated each other," were constantly on guard to ensure Forjaz's position. "You may depend upon my cordial concurrence in any measures you may adopt for the support of Dom Miguel Forjaz," wrote Wellington; "I am quite convinced that he is the only man in Portugal fit for the situation which he fills."[20] This judgment proved valid for, through the discouraging months of 1810 prior to the sieges of Almeida and Ciudad Rodrigo, Forjaz determinedly supported Wellington while other Portuguese officials complained and sought to thwart or alter his strategy. From the extraordinary volume of correspondence to Beresford and Wellington, it is obvious that Forjaz was deeply committed to the British alliance as the best means of maintaining Portuguese independence. Although not concerned with overall strategy, Forjaz's contribution to the Allied effort was extraordinary; he was responsible, to a great extent, for maintaining a viable Portuguese army in the field. Indeed, the Allies owed a debt of gratitude to this man who has received so little notice from Portuguese as well as English and French historians.

During April, Wellington was confronted with another political issue when several members of an extremely influential Portuguese family began negotiations with Spain. Three individuals were involved in these discussions: the Principal Sousa, José António de Menezes e Sousa, recently appointed to the Regency Council; his brother, Conde de Linhares, Rodrigo de Sousa Coutinho, who served as prime minister in Rio de Janeiro; and a cousin, Pedro de Sousa Holstein, representing the Portuguese government in Spain. They hoped to regain control of the district of Olivença, taken from Portugal in the War of Oranges in 1801. In addition, these men sought to obtain Spanish recognition of the succession rights for the Prince Regent's wife, Princess Carlotta, sister of the imprisoned Spanish king, Ferdinand VII. In return the Portuguese would deploy their army to support the depleted Spanish forces in the war. Negotiations were carried on until Wellington put an end to their schemes. He condemned them vigorously: "The Spanish Government . . . wished to involve the Portuguese army, as well as the British army, more actively in its operations," but Wellington believed such a policy "would . . . put the French in possession of the Peninsula." When the Spanish officials intimated the Portuguese were shirking their duty in the common war against the French, Wellington stepped forward to defend them. He argued, "Portugal has done as much, and will do more, in the contest than any province in Spain of the same extent and population. It has defended itself; and with our assistance will continue to defend itself, unless attacked by very superior forces. . . . What province, of Spain," he asked, "with all the assistance of money from America, and of arms and clothing from England, has been able to send and maintain an army beyond its limits, or even to defend itself if attacked by 20,000 men?"[21]

Despite the many domestic, political, and logistical problems, Wellington's most immediate concern was related to the disposition of his army facing the French beyond Almeida. Based on his strategy this area was the most critical in the Peninsula. He would have to be in a position to move in strength to support the garrisons of Almeida and Ciudad Rodrigo in event of a French attack. Hence, the bulk of his army was posted there to support the fortresses as long as possible and assure adequate time for the mobilization of Portugal.

With an excellent network of spies, Wellington was well aware of most of the French movements in Spain, especially in the province of Salamanca, where Ney's corps was cantoned. Almeida served as the center of the Allied intelligence system in northwest Spain. The British governor of the fortress, William Cox, used his vantage point to dispatch agents into the French-occupied provinces to gather vital information. They often had less difficulty slipping through the French lines than crossing Spanish-controlled territory. From information collected by his agents, Wellington was convinced the French would attack Portugal through Almeida. Hence, his troops doubled their vigilance along the Côa and Agueda rivers while other units were alerted near Castelo Branco and behind the Zezere River.[22]

Although disturbed when Ney's French columns advanced to the walls of Ciudad Rodrigo during the second week of February, their subsequent withdrawal was viewed with satisfaction by the men of the Allied army. There was little movement by the three Allied divisions posted on the frontiers of Beira during the first two months of 1810, but the advanced pickets of both armies often skirmished with each other near Ciudad Rodrigo. The French were more aggressive, pushing reconnaissance columns down to the flooding Agueda River from Ledesma to Ciudad Rodrigo. In spite of these probes by the French, General Craufurd established only a corporal and four soldiers at Barba de Puerco with similar posts at Villar de Ciervo, Villar de Egua, and Aldea del Obispo, but they were of little use and actually in danger of being cut off. Wellington remained stationary, satisfied to be "able to assemble the army upon the Coa if it should be necessary . . . to prevent the execution of any design upon Ciudad Rodrigo." Nevertheless the movements of the French troops—Junot's corps in León, the withdrawal of Loison's division toward Salamanca, and the maneuvering of various brigades of Marchand's division at San Felices de los Gallegos and other villages along the Agueda—perplexed the British observers. Writing to General Cole of the Fourth Division, Cox complained, "The movements of the enemy are so various and so complicated, and one receives so many different accounts of them, that it is scarcely possible to make a tolerable guess as to their real design, or to calculate with any degree of accuracy their actual force."[23] Still Cox was convinced invasion would come and there was no doubt in his mind that it would be in the vicinity of Almeida.

Following the successful French incursions across the Agueda during the first ten days of March, Craufurd began to concentrate elements of the Light Division beyond the Côa. Pickets were established along the Côa from Castelo Rodrigo in the north to Alfaiates. Moreover, Wellington instructed Generals Cole and Picton to support Craufurd "without waiting for orders from me, if it should be necessary." The 1st Hussars of the King's German Legion, commanded by Captain George Krauchenberg, were called up from Guarda to occupy Castanheira, and Captain Aly's 4th Dragoons were extended toward Castelo Bom. Two companies of the 95th Rifles occupied the vital village of Barba de Puerco and the remaining companies were posted at La Bouza, Virmioso, and Escarigo; the 43d Foot and 52d Foot were deployed in various villages behind the 95th Rifles. The 3d Hussars swept the area between the Côa and Agueda rivers to the walls of Ciudad Rodrigo, and the horse artillery was collected at Fort La Concepción. On the night of 19 March, the advance posts of the Light Division demonstrated their vigilance and tenacity when attacked by a superior French force beyond the bridge near Barba de Puerco. Although the British pickets were withdrawn from Barba de Puerco three days after the action when the French received reinforcements, Wellington was confident that the French would be unable to penetrate his defenses. Writing to the influential military secretary at the Horse Guard, Lieutenant Colonel Henry Torrens, Wellington predicted, "The French threaten us on all points, and are most desirous to get rid of us. But they threaten upon too many points at a time to give me much uneasiness . . . and they shall not induce me to disconnect my army. I am in a situation in which no mischief can be done to the army. . . . I am prepared for all events; and if I am in a scrape . . . I'll get out of it."[24]

In December and January, Wellington had pressed the government for reinforcements to increase the complement of his army to 30,000 effectives. With such a force he promised to "fight a good battle for the possession of Portugal." Reinforcements began to pour into Portugal. Transports plying the Atlantic southward from Portsmouth

Figure 6. Brigadier General Robert Craufurd, from a drawing owned by R. Holden

and Guernsey landed thousands of men each month. By the middle of March, reinforcements for the British army had increased its complement to 29,502 rank and file, supplemented by 2,282 artillerymen. In addition, 2,400 men of the 1st Royals, 9th and 38th Foot, and various detachments belonging to regiments already deployed in Portugal, supplemented by 700 men of the 13th Light Dragoons, were disembarked in Lisbon before the end of March. Thus, Wellington's British army reached a total of 34,964 men. To guarantee a minimum force of at least 30,000 effectives in the field, the minister of war made arrangements for the transfer of an additional 8,070 men from the scattered British garrisons in the Mediterranean.[25] The newly organized and trained Portuguese regiments were beginning to join the British divisions near Almeida. The only difficulty seems to have occurred when Craufurd rejected the 1st and 2d Caçadores in favor of Colonel George Elder's 3d Caçadores, which held a respected reputation in the Portuguese army. Despite this minor discontent, and a slight decline in the field strength, Wellington was delighted with the 15 April returns of the army; there were 28,000 rank and file in the British army and the Portuguese army was estimated at 30,000 strong.[26]

In mid-April, information reached Allied headquarters that the Spanish town of Astorga had been invested, but not "vigorously attacked." Based on this and other French movements, Wellington was inclined to believe the French advance against Astorga was a diversion, but he relished each passing day that gave him more time. Thus, the days of April passed in relative peace, much to his satisfaction. Nevertheless, Craufurd, commanding the advance guard, continually pressed for an attack against the French. Other British commanders also visualized a British "dash" to Salamanca to seize and destroy Ney's magazines and siege train, but Wellington discouraged their proposals. Writing to Craufurd, he observed, "I do not know whether the state of tranquillity in which affairs have been for some time is advantageous to the French, but I know that it is highly so to us." Throughout Portugal his plans for mobilization were pressed forward. The British army was increasing in strength and confidence, and, he noted with pleasure, "The discipline and equipment of the Portuguese troops is improving daily. . . . The sick of this army are also coming out of hospital fast."[27]

On 25 April, French columns advanced to the walls of Ciudad Rodrigo to prepare for the investment of the town. Two days later Wellington learned of the advance and began to concentrate his army along the Portuguese frontier. British headquarters were advanced from Viseu to Celorico where the First Division was posted under the command of Lieutenant General Brent Spencer. Simultaneously, Major General John Slade collected his cavalry at Villa Velha and marched to Guarda. The divisions of Craufurd, Cole, and Picton were alerted for impending action, but Wellington, unaware of the fall of Astorga, could not convince himself that Ney was in earnest about an attack against Ciudad Rodrigo. It was only on 30 April that Wellington received accurate information describing the capitulation of Astorga's garrison eight days earlier. Although disheartened by the fall of Astorga, Wellington had decided "to attempt the relief of Ciudad Rodrigo if . . . expedient."[28]

Now the attention of the Allied and French armies focused on the old Spanish fortress of Ciudad Rodrigo. The French had established a partial blockade on the night of 25 April, and five days later the British army was concentrated in the vicinity of Almeida. If the French did intend to invest Ciudad Rodrigo, they would be forced to deploy an entire corps to cover siege operations and observe Wellington's threatening army. This was a brilliant maneuver, which complicated French tactics and caused considerable delay in siege operations. Not only would Ney's 6th Corps have to be supplied with provisions but now Junot's 8th Corps would also require similar support.

However, Wellington was apprehensive about the character and judgment of the governor of Ciudad Rodrigo, Andrés Pérez de Herrasti. Relations between Cox at Almeida and Herrasti were not cordial. Cox regarded him as ineffective, timorous, and unqualified to command the fortress that had become such an important element in Wellington's overall strategy. Soon after Herrasti assumed command of Ciudad Rodrigo, he and Cox had an unpleasant exchange of letters over a captured French officer, Lieutenant Vernon de Farincourt. In late November, Wellington wanted to send the prisoner to Soult's headquarters to arrange an exchange of prisoners. Cox sent him to Ciudad Rodrigo escorted by a Portuguese captain, Gill, to secure safe passage through Spanish territory. When they reached the fortress, Herrasti "very imprudently detain[ed] Farincourt . . . instead of sending him on to the Duque del Parque's headquarters." Despite the explanations of Gill and letters from both Cox and Marshal Beresford, the governor could not be persuaded to send the Frenchman on to

Spanish headquarters unless he saw his orders. In fact, Farincourt could not communicate with his escort and was "prevented from speaking to any body or even approaching the window of his lodging; this shows," wrote Cox, "a degree of ignorance and timidity scarcely credible." When del Parque reached Ciudad Rodrigo, he supported Herrasti's decision and returned the Frenchman and his escort to Cox. With the mission an obvious failure, Farincourt was finally sent to England, ending the two month controversy. Cox regarded Herrasti as the culprit in the incident. Cox's apprehension concerning Herrasti's attitude and abilities was further intensified by del Parque's indifferent attitude toward the governor and by Herrasti's efforts to minimize "the defeat and dispersion" of the Spanish army at Alba de Tormes to make it "appear less disgraceful."[29]

These incidents as well as Wellington's own experiences, especially during the Talavera campaign, contributed to his negative attitude toward Governor Herrasti. Writing to Bartholomew Frere, the British envoy attached to the Spanish Junta at Cadiz, Wellington complained, "I am afraid that the person charged with the defence of Ciudad Rodrigo is a very improper one, and not very likely to do his duty. As this place is a most important one, I shall be much obliged to you if you will make inquiry respecting this person's character, and urge that he may be relieved by one more deserving of confidence." In March, when French columns had advanced to the plains surrounding Ciudad Rodrigo, Wellington was amazed to learn the Spanish governor was unaware of their movements. Two days before Ciudad Rodrigo was actually invested, Wellington complained to Craufurd, "The Spaniards I believe think it necessary to our existence to assist and protect them; and I have more than once been obliged to remind different authorities . . . that their protection is their own concern." When Loison's division invested the fortress during the last week of April, Herrasti apparently appealed for British aid. Wellington, angered by what he regarded as incompetence and indolence, wrote to Cox, "If the force near Ciudad Rodrigo is only 4,000 men, and the Governor wishes to remove them, he is surely able to effect that operation himself. Why are the English to undertake it? If he is not able to effect that object, I am sure it will answer no purpose for us to relieve him, when he shall be more seriously pressed."[30] No doubt Wellington's opinion was influenced by Cox's attitude and his own relations with other Spanish generals, but he did Herrasti an injustice, as events were to prove.

Herrasti, on the contrary, appears to have had considerable confidence in the British commander in chief since Wellington's letters reflected a determination to support Ciudad Rodrigo. On 7 May, Wellington had written to the Spanish governor promising "I shall always be happy to have it in my power to render your Excellency and the city of Ciudad Rodrigo assistance; and the allied army under my command is at present in a situation from which it can move to the aid of Ciudad Rodrigo, if circumstances should permit me to do so." However, Wellington ended by cautioning that "the protection of that place is not the only object entrusted to me."[31]

The first four months of 1810 were full of problems and anxiety for Wellington, as they had been for Marshal Ney. Although confident of his army and strategy, there is little doubt of Wellington's crucial position. His plans for the defense of Portugal were a gamble, denounced in England as well as in Portugal. Outnumbered, with limited funds and supplies, facing an intelligent, able, and daring foe, Wellington remained steadfast in the face of staggering problems. With the support of the cabinet in London and the determination of the courageous but vastly outnumbered Portuguese people, the British general was unalterably committed to making his stand in Portugal or being driven into the sea.

Chapter 3

Masséna Assumes Command

A S THE STRUGGLE dragged on in the Peninsula without predictable end, Napoleon became increasingly exasperated. He had expected to take command of the armies himself and end the war with one great blow against Wellington's army and Portugal, but by March 1810 it was obvious he could not leave Paris for the most remote area in western Europe. A precarious peace was enforced throughout the continent, but the defeated powers east of the Rhine, as well as his erstwhile allies, were seething under the humiliations and exactions inflicted by France. Napoleon had been married by proxy to an eighteen-year-old Austrian archduchess, Marie-Louise, but this did not secure the goodwill of Europe. Therefore, Napoleon had no alternative but to remain in Paris, attentive to the fortunes of his vast Empire and those of his allied states. He would have to find a replacement—one who could breathe the air of victory into the French armies, represent the imperial standards, and complete the task of pacifying the Peninsula.

Napoleon had created eighteen marshals of the Empire by the beginning of 1810; he had observed each in his councils of war as well as on the field of battle. It should not have been difficult to choose one from among such an illustrious array of commanders. However, the Iberian campaign was vital. The future of the Peninsula and perhaps the Empire rested on the outcome of the expedition. A supreme effort was necessary to clot what Napoleon referred to as his "bleeding sore," and there appeared to be little doubt in his mind that Britain, supported by Portugal and Spain, was the source of that "sore." Al-

Figure 7. Marshal André Masséna, Duc de Rivoli, Prince d'Essling, by Louis Hersent

though Portugal's impact on the Continental System was minimal, it was the key to the Peninsula. Defiant and unconquered, the Lusitanians had already demonstrated their determination to transform Portugal into a sanctuary, a base of operations, and finally a battleground for the British army. Wellington was cognizant of the Kingdom's importance, and he continually reminded the government in London, "As long as we shall remain in a state of activity in Portugal, the contest must continue in Spain."[1] Moreover, the presence of the British was a continual threat to the French operations in Spain. Besides menacing isolated corps scattered throughout the Spanish provinces, Wellington and his army served as a source of moral, economic, political, and military strength to the Spanish people.

For two years the Spanish armies had continued the struggle with limited resources in each occupied province. Their field armies had been temporarily vanquished, only to reappear ready to contest further French expansion. The heroic resistance of their cities, as exemplified by the sieges of Saragossa and Gerona, had delayed French conquests and inflicted appalling losses on them. The irregular guerrilla armies had transformed the countryside into a violently hostile environment for the French. Several hundred thousand Frenchmen had been sent to pacify Iberia, but their control was limited primarily to the larger cities and the territory actually occupied by their troops. France could no longer sustain the extraordinary military and financial demands required by this struggle; yet who was to replace Napoleon and pacify the Peninsula? The Emperor sought a marshal who possessed qualities of leadership, initiative, decisiveness, a man with experience as an independent commander, capable of contesting the tactical and strategic ability of the victorious Viscount Wellington. For Napoleon there was only one man who fulfilled these requirements—his long time comrade in arms, André Masséna, Duc de Rivoli, Prince d'Essling.

Since 1794, Masséna and Napoleon had served together in various operations. During Napoleon's first Italian campaign, Masséna played a major tactical role in the destruction of five enemy armies and the invasion of Austria. While Napoleon was in Egypt in 1799, Masséna won the most brilliant victory of his career by turning back the Austro-Russian armies at Zurich, thus saving France from imminent invasion. The following year he was able to withstand a debilitating siege for 60 days. By forcing the Austrians to deploy vast forces against him at Genoa, Masséna made it possible for Napoleon to cross Great Saint Bernard Pass, surprise the main army, and defeat it at Marengo before reinforcements arrived. Again, during the War of the Third Coalition, he successfully engaged and contained a superior enemy army in Italy commanded by Archduke Charles while Napoleon advanced on Vienna. In 1809 his dogged determination and tactical ability led to the survival of his beleaguered corps at Aspern despite overwhelming odds. Two months later in the decisive battle at Wagram, Masséna insured victory by sustaining the left wing of the French army.[2]

Following the defeat of Austria and the Peace of Schönbrunn, Masséna returned to his estate at Rueil to recuperate from the rigors of the campaign. Suffering from a severe fall from his horse and chronic respiratory problems, he anticipated an extended furlough to regain his health and enjoy the fruits of his victories. Napoleon, however, had other plans for the "greatest name" of his military empire. Following the Emperor's religious marriage ceremony to Marie-Louise on 2 April 1810, he announced to Masséna, "I intend to give you an important command."[3] Speculation began at court immediately. Some saw Masséna commanding an observation corps in eastern Europe; others were convinced he would be appointed King Joseph's chief of staff in Madrid. There was little time for these rumors to circulate. On 16 April, Masséna received a rather surprising note from Henri Clarke, the minister of war, which announced, "His Majesty the Emperor has decided that the Prince d'Essling will command the Army of Portugal; he is invited to prepare his baggage to leave as soon as possible." The following day an Imperial Decree was published announcing the creation of the Army of Portugal, composed of the 2d, 6th, and 8th Corps of the Army of Spain.[4]

Masséna visited Berthier on 18 April to express his apprehension about assuming command of a new army since he had not yet recovered from the injuries suffered in the Austrian campaign. Moreover, he expressed serious reservations about the personal qualities and limitations of his subordinates, namely, Junot and Ney. No doubt Masséna hoped to appoint his own lieutenants; however, Junot was well qualified for the campaign since he had commanded the first invasion of Portugal in 1807 and was familiar with the country, the people, and the British army. Similarly, Ney had proven himself an excellent infantry general on the field of battle over a period of 15 years. In addition, he had spent two years in Spain and had the intense loyalty of the 6th Corps—nucleus of the Army of Portugal. Masséna's conversation with Berthier did not ease his anxieties. "The Emperor's orders are definite and they do not take personal considerations into account," cautioned Berthier.[5] Thus, Masséna left Berthier's house without the reassurance or sympathy he had sought. Berthier, however, was disturbed by Masséna's attitude; he confided his fears to the Emperor.

Although Masséna had already written a farewell letter to Napoleon before undertaking his mission, he was summoned to talk with Napoleon about his presentiments. Napoleon accused Masséna of isolating himself in a world of pessimism; he chided him for fabricating imaginary problems and he scoffed at his reasoning: "Are you more sick than at Wagram? Is it your rheumatism that torments you? The climate of Portugal is warmer and healthier than that of Italy, and it will put the agility of youth back into your legs." Aware of Masséna's concerns about inadequate provisions, the Emperor promised, "You will lack nothing in resources. . . . You will be absolute master, and you will make all your own preparations to open the campaign. Do not speak to me then of insufficient means." Sensing a weakening of Masséna's resistance, Napoleon sprang to the offensive: "Who will I send to Portugal to restore my affairs which have been compromised by incompetents? Am I able to leave Paris now? I can send you in my place, but you refuse me under imaginary pretext! You fear the insubordination of the generals under your command." The Emperor admitted that Ney and Junot were "impetuous and passionate" but these were not sufficient reasons to replace them; after all, each had commanded his troops victoriously for years. "Do you suppose they will disobey your orders with impunity and dare incur my disgrace?" When the one-sided interview ended, Napoleon encouraged Masséna to "leave then with confidence; all will go better than you think. With prudence and firmness, the obstacles you fear will pass away . . . and do not forget that you represent me."[6]

Before leaving Paris, Masséna received his instructions from Berthier. He was "to put himself in a position to hold in check 25,000 English commanded by General Wellington, and to follow the army to attack and destroy it." It is obvious that Napoleon did not expect the British army and 22,000 Portuguese "composed of poor troops" to thwart his plans. After capturing Ciudad Rodrigo, Masséna was expected to "constantly threaten to advance on Lisbon, and from there, force the English to cross to the left bank of the Tagus."[7] This was a simple matter, according to the Emperor, who set the month of May for the invasion of Portugal.

Accompanied by his seventeen-year-old son, Jacques-Prosper, his secretary, Vacherat, and a small entourage, Masséna left the comforts of Rueil before 5:00 on the morning of 26 April, boarded his calash, and set out on what proved to be his last campaign. As the carriages rolled south through Bois and Poitiers toward Bordeaux, Masséna's newly appointed first aide-de-camp, Chef de bataillon Jean-Jacques Pelet, joined his convoy. Meanwhile, Masséna had written to each of his three corps commanders on 21 April, "I am eager, to express my pleasure on having the opportunity to work closely with you. I have made arrangements to reach Valladolid as soon as possible where I will be able to express my delight in meeting a comrade who will contribute so much to achieving His Majesty's goals." Junot responded to his new superior in flattering terms, professing respect and devotion; nevertheless, he was perturbed since Napoleon, in a letter dated 30 October 1809, had promised him command of a 50,000-man army. Ney also viewed his subordinate position with disappointment; yet he wrote to Berthier, "Although it is difficult for me to be always in a subordinate position, I am at least obliged to recognize with satisfaction in these circumstances, that the abilities and experience of the Prince d'Essling justify the choice of the Emperor."[8] Ney, resigned to his fate, wrote to Masséna on 7 May, "I am pleased to recognize the excellence of the choice that His Majesty has made. . . . I hope that the circumstances will justify the confidence you have accorded me and that I will merit your friendship to which I attach the greatest importance."[9] General Reynier, commanding the 2d Corps, also sent a congratulatory note to his new commander, promising devotion and duty.

Figure 8. Chef de bataillon Jean-Jacques Pelet, by Clarabel B. Jett after a portrait at the Service historique de l'armée

Masséna's subordinates were well aware of his personal courage, his extraordinary composure under fire, his determination and resourcefulness, his ability as a tactician, and his charismatic influence over the rank and file of the army. Junot, as one of Napoleon's aides-de-camp, had had the opportunity to observe Masséna in the first Italian campaign of 1796; Ney had served as a divisional general when Masséna commanded the eastern frontier in 1799, and Reynier had commanded a division in Masséna's Calabrian campaign of 1806. Despite Masséna's impressive, indeed brilliant achievements, his generals were cognizant of his personal deficiencies. He was distrustful, calumnious, and dissolute. His amorous indiscretions were well known and often a source of embarrassment. Moreover, on three separate occasions he was denounced for financial misappropriation, reflecting both his avarice and his poor judgment in appointing corrupt subordinates.[10]

As Masséna was traveling south toward the Spanish frontier, French operations continued methodically in Old Castile. On the first of May, Ney appealed to Junot to redeploy his corps echeloned between Astorga and Valladolid so the 6th Corps might complete the blockade of Ciudad Rodrigo. Junot, unenthusiastic about the operation, declined to move his infantry until he received definite instructions from Paris. Recognizing he could do little about Junot's dilatory attitude, Ney wrote to Soult at Madrid announcing, "I will march with the hope that before the trenches are opened, the Duc d'Abrantès [Junot] will receive orders from Paris."[11] Accordingly, Ney began to redeploy his corps despite the torrential rains that had persisted since 26 April. General Mermet, charged with the immediate siege operations, began to draw his infantry brigades closer to the fortress during the first week of May. Maucune's brigade, supported by the 3d Hussars and three guns, occupied Pedrotoro, three miles east of Ciudad Rodrigo, with his left flank at the monastery of La Caridad; General Pierre-Louis Marcognet's infantry was echeloned behind Maucune near Tenebrón, and General Mathieu Delabassée's troops camped beyond the gorge at Sancti Spiritus, creating a wedge-shaped formation. To maintain communications with corps headquarters, General Louis-Joseph Cavrois's cavalry was extended eastward toward Salamanca. Supporting the investing brigades from the north, Loison's division was echeloned from Sancti Spiritus by way of San Felices el Chico to Ledesma; thus, only General Martial Bardet's brigade remained at Ney's headquarters in Salamanca.[12] The duty of this weak investing force was to repulse any sorties sent out by Governor Herrasti, cut communications with Wellington, and limit operations of the enterprising guerrilla chieftain, Julián Sánchez, who commanded a band of lancers at the fortress. The city was sealed off east of the Agueda River; nevertheless, Herrasti was able to maintain his communications with the British pickets a few miles away.

Anxious to avert a full-scale siege, Mermet sent a staff officer to the fortress on 12 May with a summons for the governor. If Herrasti agreed to capitulate, the French general pledged the garrison would be given the option of transferring their allegiance to King Joseph or returning to their homes under safe conduct. He also promised safety to the citizens of the city if the Spanish agreed to surrender, but added, "On the contrary, if you refuse all accommodation, His Excellency [Ney], whose arms have always been crowned with success . . . will act with all the force at his disposal, and in a few days he will reduce the fortress that you will be unable to defend and the garrison that you will be unable to save." He continued in a personal vein: "As far as I am concerned, I will regret having to shed innocent blood, and you . . . will have caused the loss of an important and unfortunate town." The Frenchman concluded warning Herrasti, "The critical moment has arrived and there is no other path for you to take. . . . A valiant man has more right to public esteem, when he complies with conditions compatible with honor and the necessity of circumstances than when, through willing stubbornness, he shows himself insensible to conciliation and the voice of reason." Once Herrasti realized the nature of this letter, he refused to read further. Turning to Mermet's officer, he firmly declared, "Since the answer I have given previously is final, it should be understood that no more representatives will be admitted in the future under a flag of truce. Now we have to talk only with guns." [13]

As the investing brigades consolidated their positions around Ciudad Rodrigo, Ney became more anxious about their safety. He was painfully aware that Craufurd's Light Division, supported by some 30,000 troops, was within six miles of his infantry divisions. He described his predicament to Soult on 10 May, "Half of my army corps is camped beneath the walls of Ciudad Rodrigo to open the trenches, and I only await the decision of the Duc d'Abrantès to furnish a garrison for Zamora, to relieve my communication posts, and to know that he intends to support me in case of necessity." [14] Later the same day Ney sent his first report to the newly appointed commander in chief of the army, André Masséna. After complaining of Junot's refusal to lend him desperately needed supply wagons, Ney observed that the commander of the 8th Corps had not "provided for the garrison of Zamora, Toro, and the line of communications from Salamanca." Assuming a rather familiar demeanor with Masséna, Ney announced, "I wish to chat with Your Highness at the same time on the entire operation, and particularly on Portugal. It seems to me a combined march [by the 6th and 8th Corps] on Viseu, headquarters of Lord Wellington, will decide the fate of the campaign." If 5,000 men and some field artillery engaged Ciudad Rodrigo while the remainder of the army attacked the Allied army, Ney assumed that Wellington would retreat and "we will then be able to continue the sieges of Ciudad Rodrigo and Almeida at our leisure, occupy essential points in Portugal, and disarm and pacify the countryside." The next day Ney wrote again: "All the intelligence seems to indicate that Lord Wellington will come to attack the corps besieging Ciudad Rodrigo before the fire commences." Consequently, he suggested, "I hope Your Highness considers the alternative of anticipating the English and advancing against them instead of awaiting them." [15] Masséna might well have wondered by what right his subordinate suggested such a bold course; even the Emperor had not taken the liberty of giving him tactical advice for the campaign. Ney's strategy seemed feasible, but Masséna had just arrived and wanted to assess the situation himself rather than rely upon the observations and advice of his subordinate.

In the meantime, Masséna had crossed the Bidassoa River into Spain. Although bands of guerrillas were active near the defiles of Salinas and Pancorbo, Masséna's convoy, escorted by two hundred horsemen, reached the great city of Burgos on the banks of the Arlanzón without incident on the night of 8 May. Masséna and his immediate entourage spent the night in the mansion of the local corregidor and the following morning, he visited the splendid cathedral dominating the city and the ancient ruins of El Cid's castle. Rising before dawn on 10 May, Masséna and his party pushed southwest toward Valladolid, a distance of 82 miles. [16]

While Masséna was completing the last segment of his trip, Junot had collected his divisional commanders and members of his personal staff at the sumptuous palace of Charles V in Valladolid to welcome their new chief. The night before Masséna's arrival, the Duchesse d'Abrantès, wife of General Junot, entertained these dignitaries along with Generals Reynier and Kellermann at her "elegant little court" at the palace.[17] Tension and anxiety were evident beneath the chattering conversation, but the final arrangements had been made for the arrival of Masséna. Junot and his wife assumed that the vast palace could easily accommodate Masséna's entire staff as well as their own; thus, plans were made to occupy the palace jointly.

The following morning one of Masséna's aides arrived at Valladolid announcing that the Prince would arrive later in the day. Anxious to impress his new commander, Junot collected a delegation of some two hundred officers and chasseurs to ride out and welcome Masséna and his staff. A league beyond the city they sighted an open carriage, trailed by a convoy of carriages and wagons, racing toward the city. After Junot formally greeted him, Masséna's calash was escorted to the palace through the streets of the city which were lined by troops in brilliant uniforms. Apparently some embarrassment occurred when Masséna alighted from his carriage. His young traveling companion, dressed in the guise of a cavalry officer with the Legion of Honor, was none other than his current mistress, Henriette Leberton. According to the malicious Baron Marbot, who served as one of Masséna's aides-de-camp, "When Junot rushed in accompanied by the Duchesse, he fell into Masséna's arms; then before all the staff he kissed the hand of Mme. X . . . and introduced his wife. Imagine the astonishment of the two ladies. They stood petrified and did not speak a single word! [Masséna] had the wit to restrain himself; but he was deeply hurt when the Duchesse d'Abrantès, pleading indisposition, left the dining room just as Junot was leading in Madame X." No doubt, the presence of Madame Leberton, compounded by the petty intrigues of Madame Junot, intensified already strained relations between Masséna and Junot. Although the duchesse continued to hold her "petite court" at the palace, she refused to associate with Masséna's companion. In fact she refused to invite the Prince to dine at her table and she would not accept invitations to grace his table.[18] This unfortunate situation would, as the days passed, become a source of continual friction between Masséna and his subordinates. Obviously Masséna was deeply hurt by the ostracism of his favorite,

Figure 9. Palace of Charles V at Valladolid

especially since it was carried on by one whose reputation was not beyond repute. Masséna was completely at the mercy of Madame Junot's vicious tongue; he could only ignore the gossip and isolate himself in the immense palace until his headquarters were advanced to Salamanca several weeks later.

Masséna spent the first days after his arrival at Valladolid recovering from the strain and fatigues of his long journey. On 12 May, he issued a proclamation announcing his satisfaction and honor at being given command of the Army of Portugal, yet he cautioned, "Soldiers, you know discipline and obedience are the first guarantees of victory. What obstacles can resist your valor when rigorous discipline prepares you for success. You will find always in my conduct and that of my comrades, your commanders, firmness in adversity. Your fatigue, your privation, and your danger will be common to us and you will justify the confidence the Emperor has in your devotion."[19] Three days after his proclamation had been read to the troops, the restless Masséna announced his intention to visit Ney at Salamanca. He had already received Ney's suggestions for future operations and now he wanted to discuss specific details with him. Accompanied by Junot, his artillery commander, General Jean-Baptiste Eblé, and his first aide-de-camp, Pelet, Masséna traveled to Salamanca. According to Pelet who rode in an open carriage with General Eblé, "Marshal Ney came to meet the Prince and the latter entered the Marshal's carriage. We found many troops outside Salamanca. The 50th and 59th Line were under arms. Both regiments looked like magnificent, truly elite units. . . . The entrance to Salamanca was also brilliant. The reputation of the Prince had overcome the pride and the apathy of the Castilians who gathered to see him." That night Masséna, Ney, and Junot discussed the forthcoming campaign and several times Ney raised his project of attacking Wellington, followed by the siege of Ciudad Rodrigo. Early the next morning they left Ney's headquarters for the return to Valladolid.[20] The impact of this meeting was obvious, for soon after returning to his quarters Masséna wrote to King Joseph, "I have decided on the siege of Ciudad Rodrigo." However, he also raised an alternative plan: "Perhaps I will decide to march with two corps united to fight the enemy; it will be the surest means to reduce the time in taking Ciudad Rodrigo and Almeida."[21]

Following his visit to Salamanca, Masséna carefully considered the strategy to be employed against the Allied army and Ciudad Rodrigo. On 20 May, Pelet drafted a six-point analysis of the various options, concluding, "I dare to believe that the English will attempt no important action against the siege," thereby negating the necessity of attacking Wellington.[22] However, Ney was anxious to move at once. Two days after the conference he wrote to Masséna announcing the arrival at Ciudad Rodrigo of supply and munitions convoys from Almeida. He pressed Masséna about his intentions either "to march to attack the British army [or] to besiege Ciudad Rodrigo." Ney waited impatiently for some response until the morning of 20 May and then wrote an impassioned and clearly insubordinate letter to Masséna: "I believe the trip Your Highness made to Salamanca was to determine plans for the military operations appropriate either to invade Portugal and force Wellington to battle, or to continue the siege of Ciudad Rodrigo." Since Masséna did not respond to Ney's letters, although, "the circumstances demand[ed] a prompt decision," Ney issued an ultimatum: "I beseech Your Highness to inform me of your decision, because if you do not, I will give orders . . . to return [the troops] to their old cantonments . . . until Your Highness has made a decision." This measure, according to Ney would "economize the food and disperse most of the soldiers, who, by remaining in poor weather, would soon be in the hospitals."[23]

Ney regretted his impetuous actions; a few hours after his letter had been sent, he received Masséna's decision. "The 8th Corps will be placed in a manner . . . to support the siege of Ciudad Rodrigo." At the same time, Junot was instructed to relieve Ney's troops at Ledesma, Zamora, Toro, and Salamanca, to maintain communications between Salamanca and Valladolid and, finally, to move the siege pieces from Astorga to join the siege train destined for Ciudad Rodrigo. To describe Masséna's reaction to this letter as one of shock would be an understatement. What right had Ney to threaten him with such an ultimatum? Was he not the commander in chief of the army? Masséna did not respond to the imprudent Ney until the following day: "Your [letter] has singularly astonished me. I cannot conceal from you that I am not accustomed to such a manner. I will always be pleased to welcome the advice of my comrades, when it is not dictated by sentiments other than the desire to cooperate for the good and the triumph of the arms of a sovereign whom we love equally. The 8th Corps will support you but they will only be able to concentrate in their new positions by the end of the month." [24]

Once Ney was assured the siege would soon begin, he worked frantically to complete arrangements for the investment. The village of Sancti Spiritus was transformed into a workshop for the engineers who labored to fabricate the various sections for two trestle bridges, and Pedrotoro was modified to serve as a depot for the siege train and its attendants. His men redoubled their efforts to collect food and supplies although they often found themselves in bitter competition with the men of the 8th Corps. When it became obvious that the Spanish villages were not meeting their quota of requisitions, hostages were taken from the families of the wealthy landowners. This punitive action proved to be counterproductive, and the villages resorted to money payments rather than providing their requisite in grain. Despite these efforts, Ney's aide-de-camp, Sprünglin, noted before the siege began, "The 6th Corps had ration enough for six weeks, of which a large portion was biscuit; the artillery train had 12 ton of barley for the draft animals; and the men of the cavalry had one month's provisions." [25] Indeed, a formidable reserve, if Sprünglin's accounts were correct, but it was certainly inadequate for the siege of Ciudad Rodrigo, not to mention the siege of Almeida. Nevertheless, Ney was anxious to begin siege operations as soon as possible, and he wrote confidently to Masséna, "If the British are strong enough to interrupt our work or offer battle . . . I will inform Your Highness in enough time so you can support me or come yourself to take command of the situation. All the gabions and fascines are ready (10,000 each); all the trench tools are in their place, and I only await your decision to commence the siege." Ney's analysis of the situation, however, was questioned by Pelet who recorded in his journal, "Preparations were still far from complete when the Marshal announced that we would be ready to start the siege on the earliest favorable occasion." [26]

May was a decisive month for Ciudad Rodrigo and the future course of events in the Peninsula. Napoleon had named a brilliant but aging field commander, created a new army, and completed his strategy for the siege of Ciudad Rodrigo, the destruction of the Allied army, the conquest of Portugal, and the termination of the Peninsular struggle. However, his optimistic evaluation of the project and self-deception regarding the obstacles faced by his Army of Portugal seriously undermined his timetable for the subjugation of the Peninsula. It was a time for innovative strategy, decisiveness, and overwhelming resources, but Masséna was encumbered by matériel restraints and a timeworn strategy that had already proved ineffective in Iberia.

Chapter 4

The Allied Army in Beira

WHILE THE month of May was one of frustration for the French commanders, especially Marshal Ney, it provided Wellington with a splendid opportunity to continue preparations for the defense of Portugal, uninterrupted by the threat of French attack. As each day passed the Allied army grew in discipline, experience, resources, and size. Although the pickets of the Light Division closely watched Ney's troops, posted around Ciudad Rodrigo, it was evident that both the French and British sought to avert a renewal of military action during the inclement weather. Reflecting this restrained atmosphere, Wellington wrote to Admiral Berkeley on 8 May, "The French are in the same positions. But I imagine that their inactivity is to be attributed to the rains, which have fallen very generally, and swelled the rivers and destroyed the roads in Castile." In a similar vein, Governor Cox, on the Portuguese frontier at Almeida, explained his lack of communication with Cole at Guarda, noting, "There has been nothing interesting to communicate. Since the advance of the enemy [in April] everything has remained pretty nearly in the same situation." [1]

The brigades of Maucune, Marcognet, and Delabassée remained stationary around Ciudad Rodrigo during the month of May, and the various elements of the Allied army retained the positions they had taken up at the end of April. Cole's Fourth Division was bivouacked at Guarda, Picton's Third Division remained at Pinhel, and Spencer's First Division was established at Celorico, headquarters of the British army.

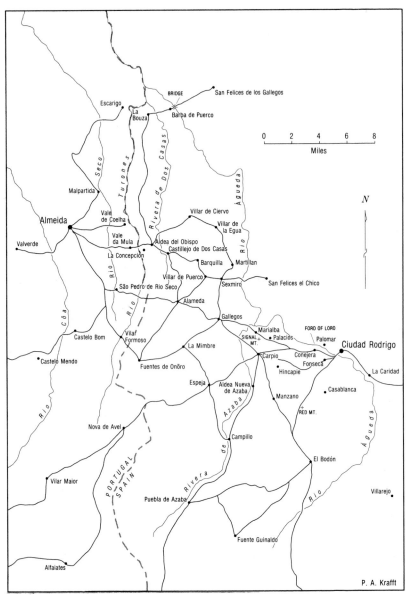

Map 3. Area between Ciudad Rodrigo and Almeida

Craufurd's Light Division, posted in the area between the Côa and Azaba rivers, occupied the villages surrounding Gallegos and Espeja, less than ten miles from Ciudad Rodrigo; their function was to encourage Spanish resistance at the fortress and sound the alarm if the French began to prepare for an attack. At the same time, the cavalry of the King's German Legion was posted along the lower Agueda in the villages of Barba de Puerco, Villar de Ciervo, and Villar de Egua. Always on the alert, they patrolled the left bank of the Agueda from Fuente Guinaldo on the south to its juncture with the Douro River on the north. Headquarters of the Portuguese army was established at Fornos de Algodres where Marshal William Carr Beresford began to concentrate the independent Portuguese brigades as they arrived from Coimbra. Only six miles apart, Wellington and Beresford maintained a highly efficient communication network with each other so that they might together respond promptly to any threat.[2]

Wellington was grateful for the continued inactivity of the French in Old Castile. However, his difficulties were not ended; he still faced innumerable domestic problems, the most significant of which were the mobilization of Portugal and the maintenance of his army on the distant frontiers of the Kingdom. During this somewhat unexpected lull in military operations, Wellington eagerly appealed to the Regency Council for direct support. With his army in eastern Beira concentrated for possible action to sustain Ciudad Rodrigo, Wellington found the British and Portuguese armies without adequate supplies. Each army had its own commissariat, resulting in duplication, competition, and general inefficiency. The British general complained about this situation but he was forced to admit, "Unfortunately . . . the orders of our own Government, and various other considerations,—some political, others military, and others financial,—do not allow of this amalgamation." He attempted to minimize "clashing" between the two competing commissariats by arranging a compromise. Therein the Portuguese would be permitted to draw upon the British magazines, but this did not solve the problem.[3]

Coupled with the inability of the Allied army to secure provisions in the exhausted province of Beira, the commissariats faced the insurmountable dilemma of procuring carriages, wagons, carts, and draft animals to transport food to the army. Wellington insisted that the Portuguese government exert its authority to force citizens to aid the Portuguese and British armies with provisions and transportation. He had earlier complained to the British ambassador, Stuart, in Lisbon, that well over 1 million rations belonging to the two armies were within 42 miles of the army and over 40,000 carts, with bullocks, were in the same area, "yet a sufficient number cannot be got for the public service upon this emergency, to move up the magazines to the army." If his troops could not be supplied in advance, Wellington threatened to "withdraw them from the country all together." Although the loyalty of the local magistrates and the peasants was not questioned, the British general pointed out that "the frontiers of the country are so seriously menaced, that something more than mere professions and goodwill are required on the part of the Magistrates and people; and either the Government must come forward and punish with vigor those who withhold the assistance they have . . . or my duty to the King will oblige me to withdraw his troops from the country." In consequence, Wellington issued a harsh decree to the Portuguese itemizing the various crimes of omission "of which the people [might] be guilty in respect to the transport of the army." If any citizens refused "to supply carts, boats, or beasts of burden when required," if they balked at removing "their articles or animals out of reach of the enemy," if they would not surrender their wagons to the local magistrate, or if they were reluctant to serve as teamsters for the army, they would be liable to the most stringent penalties of the law. This decree was not issued too soon, for the Portuguese army was in wretched condition. Its quartermaster general, Benjamin D'Urban, complained acrimoniously of the Portuguese government: "We are like to be starved. The Government . . . has again deceived Marshal Beresford as to Provisions. There are not above 5 days' consumption in hand and no hope of more when that's done. If there be no treachery in this, there is the most shameless imbecility, iniquity and sloth that has ever disgraced an Executive Government."[4]

Despite Wellington's complaints against the local magistrates, a large number of the village corregidors labored faithfully, under serious handicap, to provide the Allied army with needed supplies. In a letter to the government at Lisbon, the corregidor of Lamego, Luis António de Araujo Amorim, carefully and courageously documented his problems: "I have worked day and night, that the army may not want on account of my exertions. I have always taken the necessary steps for getting the number of carts that have been and are required of me as well as respecting supplies, and now I am at a loss as I have not the means of taking any further steps. I have found great difficulties in the compliance of my orders." He complained that the corregidor of Trancoso refused to send any wagons, claiming the British commissariat had requisitioned them. Moreover, when the peasants refused to surrender their carts, they were arrested by the troops employing the "greatest violence" against them. The situation became so acute that Cox wrote indignantly to the commander in chief of the Portuguese army denouncing the "unpleasant consequences" in establishing the "unnecessary system of vexation and terror [against] a willing and obedient people who, having already supplied all that their means afford, are urged by the strongest coercive measures, to comply with requisitions which must eventually force them to abandon their houses, and fly with their families from the horrors of starvation." In fact, he did not hesitate in denouncing a fellow officer, General Craufurd, for dragging the capitão mor of Castelo Bom from his home and imprisoning him at Gallegos, as well as inflicting corporal punishment upon a civil magistrate of the same district "because he did not furnish a quantity of corn, which . . . did not exist in the whole territory under his jurisdiction." Marshal Beresford forwarded Cox's letter to Wellington himself who responded accusing Cox of "illiberal" treatment of a fellow officer. "In our present situation," he lectured, "it is necessary that the people of Portugal should furnish the troops with carriages to move our magazines, or that they should feed the troops in the advanced stations, or the troops must be withdrawn." Cox reponded that his letter was "not intended to become a published document," and he substantiated his accusations with specific names and locations. Wellington agreed that British officers had no "power of confining and punishing a magistrate" and that he would "not permit such a practice."[5] This case is one of many that clearly illustrate that these logistical problems were as perplexing to the commander in chief of the army as to the citizens of the country.

To minimize these confrontations, Forjaz formed a special commission to accompany the Portuguese army; it would act "with powers to try offenses, or rather to apply the law in such cases as may happen . . . without the necessity of future appeal to the seat of Government." Thus, the acquisition of supplies could no longer be delayed by the tactic of bureaucratic litigation in Lisbon. Despite the operation of this special commission, Wellington was still appealing for transports two weeks later: "We are now in the greatest distress for carriages, and I have consequently no forage for the cavalry. I have forwarded many complaints to the Special Commission, but have not yet heard of the result." Irritated by what he regarded as incompetency, Wellington instructed Stuart, "Tell Dom Miguel Forjaz that, notwithstanding my good opinion and respect, and regard for the Government, I am determined to proclaim to the people of this country, and to the world, my reasons for withdrawing from my position in this country [because the government would not] exert themselves to enforce obedience from the magistrates and people of the country."[6]

According to Wellington, many of his problems centered around the operations of the *Junta de Viveres*, responsible for the procurement of food and supplies for the Portuguese army. He was convinced that the Junta, unwilling or unable to form a transportation network to supply the Portuguese army, requisitioned wagons and food from the local peasants without compensation. Charles Stuart complained bitterly of "the repeated irregularity . . . of the Junta de Viveres, whose bad arrangements press the hardest on the people." Wellington was less inhibited in his criticism: "I suspect that they are not honest; and I have never yet seen a statement from them which did not contain a direct falsehood or a subterfuge. It is really distressing, that in addition to other difficulties we should have to contend with and refute the false reports of their useless establishments, which the Government will support, notwithstanding every thing that has been urged against them."[7] Indeed, the British clamored against what they regarded as the ineffective operations of the Junta, but its failure was, in part, the result of British success in competing for the meagre resources in the province. One-third of the wagons procured by the British commissariat were turned over to the Portuguese forces, but this procedure hardly solved the critical logistical problems. Friction was also intensified by daily conflicts over provisions. For example, when the British drew upon a magazine near Almeida, the Portuguese complained that their resources were being indiscriminately exhausted by the British.[8]

"To keep up the spirits of the people, and insure a proper execution of their duty on the part of the magistrates," the Regency Council drew up an intemperate proclamation. Wellington and Stuart reacted to it immediately as a volatile problem; they felt the decree "was not at all calculated to produce the effect required." Stuart drew up another proclamation; it was modified by Wellington, impatient to have the decree published: "Let us have it out soon. I hope it will be of use to us." Nevertheless, the Regency Council altered the contents again. The exasperated Stuart complained bitterly, and Wellington insisted that the decree should be edited "without bombast, and ought, above all, to be short." For the next three weeks, while the Allied army concentrated along the frontier in a constant state of alert, Wellington was plagued by dissent and recrimination over the document. Finally, by 26 May, Forjaz was persuaded "to omit many very exceptional passages," but Stuart still complained, "There remains a degree of violence in the paper, more suited to the local and provincial governments of Spain than to the regular and legal authorities of this country." Several of the Portuguese officials were anxious to prevent alarm by deferring the publication of the proclamation but on 6 June the proclamation appeared in the *Gazeta de Lisboa*, followed by posting in each Portuguese village. Signed by João António Salter de Mendoça, the proclamation appealed to the Portuguese to demonstrate their patriotism by resisting the French. Lauding the newly reorganized Portuguese army "helped by the valorous and intrepid British battalions," the document called on all true Portuguese, regardless of their station in society, to "support together the social ties that contribute to the strength and virtue of the nation." For those who neglect their duty and "disobey the measure dictated for the security of the state; those who promote dissension spreading terror or false confidence . . . the law will avenge severely and their crimes will be repeated with infamy and abhorrence for posterity."[9]

Another continuing domestic crisis facing Wellington revolved around deteriorating economic conditions. His Majesty's government had not only promised to provide £180,000 a month for the maintenance of the British army in the Peninsula, but it had also made a solemn commitment to pay £120,000 for a 30,000 man Portuguese army. A large part of the promised subsidy was not forthcoming. By the first week of June, Wellington was predicting a deficit of £204,212 for a thirty day period in May and June. He wrote an ominous letter to Liverpool warning, "If circumstances do not permit the Government to make the remittances required regularly from England, it is my duty to inform your Lordship that it is impossible for the army to continue in this country. . . . Every day's experience proves that the army cannot be maintained in the Peninsula without money to pay for every thing that is received." Wellington was also alarmed about the condition of the Portuguese forces. "Deficiency in the funds to pay and support the Portuguese army . . . will be attended by the same bad consequences." As the days passed the need for additional funds became more acute, but no response was received from Liverpool. A week later, Wellington had reached a decision: if funds could not be sent, he would recommend the immediate withdrawal from the Peninsula. "If you cannot supply us with money, you ought to withdraw us. We are reduced to the greatest distress. Tomorrow is the day for paying the troops one month in arrears, and we have nothing to give them. . . . We owe the Portuguese Government a large sum: they are in the greatest distress, and we cannot relieve them." [10] A curious dilemma: with conflict imminent near Ciudad Rodrigo, Wellington had hoped for the unquestioned loyalty and commitment of his army while, in fact, it could hardly be fed or paid.

Liverpool did not respond to Wellington's plea for over a month: "So many serious considerations are involved in this question that much inquiry as well as deliberation has been necessary and I do not find myself yet prepared to enter at length into the subject." He did not render a definite answer to Wellington, but he ordered 210,000 Spanish dollars sent aboard the *Philomeb* with 450,000 more promised "in the course of a few days." Yet Liverpool could not promise a substantial increase in financial resources until August when "a considerable quantity of bullion [was] expected in this country from America." To alleviate the effect on the Portuguese economy, Liverpool readily agreed to give them wheat and flour in lieu of the arrears owed on the subsidy. Accordingly, Wellington was instructed to purchase with bills on England foodstuffs from any American vessel reaching a Portuguese harbor. Finally relief would be on the way. The Anglo-Portuguese army would have to wait for at least two months for the normal quota of supplies, but there was no longer the feeling of abandonment that had begun to develop in the administration of the army.[11]

Although Wellington's major concern was focused on his domestic problems, he had not forgotten the French army across the frontier. During the second week of May, he learned of the appointment of Marshal André Masséna to command the new army destined for the invasion of Portugal. None of the British generals had encountered Masséna on the field of battle, but they were not unfamiliar with his achievements, especially in Italy, and his reputation as a brilliant tactician. In a letter to his family, an English major attached to Beresford's headquarters described Masséna as "a very clever and enterprising officer. . . . He is one of B's best generals. I dare say he will shortly attempt something." The quartermaster general of the Portuguese army, D'Urban, characterized Masséna as "the best General France has; Bonaparte thinks the Defenders of Portugal of some consequence or he would not send him." Nothing definite of Masséna's arrival was learned until a young French lieutenant, dishonored in a duel with his captain, deserted to one of Craufurd's outposts on 18 May. He described in detail Masséna's arrival and his conference with Junot and Ney at Salamanca on 15 May; in addition, he informed the British that Masséna's army of 80,000 men, now titled the Army of Portugal, was ready to invade Portugal at the earliest moment.[12] Similarly, a number of deserters brought in reports that "they [French] really do not intend to undertake the siege of Ciudad Rodrigo; but that Masséna will advance on Portugal by the Agueda and Coa, supported by troops under Marshal Ney, which will at the same time make a flank movement by Alcanzas and Puebla de Sanabria."[13] These last rumors caused increased tension at Allied headquarters; if this was, in fact, Masséna's plan, Wellington might be driven back to Lisbon before the Lines of Torres Vedras had been completed.

With the continued rumors of impending invasion, Wellington resolved to refortify the impressive old Spanish fort of La Concepción,

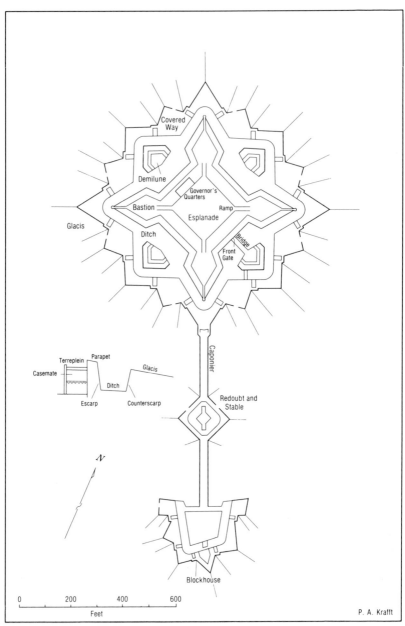

Map 4. Plan of Fort La Concepción (1810)

located on the main road, five miles east of Almeida. If the French were to seize this fort, they could saturate the countryside with patrols and push the Allied pickets behind the Portuguese frontier; they could also threaten Wellington's army if he attempted to relieve the garrison at Ciudad Rodrigo. Hence, plans were completed for the immediate repair of the fort, which had been partially destroyed by the French in 1808 when Loison evacuated the country.

The fort of La Concepción was one of the most perfectly conceived and constructed fortifications in the Peninsula. Struck by its beauty, symmetry, and design, a soldier of the 95th Rifles who served there described "its beautiful proportions, which had excited the admiration of so many beholders"; similarly, a British officer in the Portuguese service declared, "I never saw a more complete or perfect fortification with every part bombproof, even stabling for two hundred horses." Situated on the crest of a hill above and between the Spanish village of Aldea del Obispo and the Portuguese village of Vale da Mula, the fortress "was perfectly laid out, defiladed, and constructed. The skillful engineer in charge had calculated everything perfectly." This square bastioned fortress with demilunes raised before each curtain enabled the garrison to maintain a heavy crossfire on all fronts. The curtains were high and well constructed, with broad ramparts that formed the ceilings of the bombproof casemates. The vast esplanade, the magazines, and the living quarters for the garrison were brilliantly conceived. According to Masséna's aide-de-camp, Pelet, who was a student of military architecture, "The ramps, the traverses, the talus, the openings of the embrasures—everything down to the channel at the bottom of the moat—showed great care in construction. The good covered way also had a revetment wall; it surrounded the fort and glacis all the way down to the bottom of the two valleys in a well-defined slope." This masterpiece, built of large grayish-white granite blocks, was supplemented by a massive blockhouse constructed 400 yards to the southeast, overlooking the neighboring heights and deep valleys. The blockhouse, protected on all sides from enemy crossfire, was connected to the main fortress by a double caponier; midway, a triangular demilune had been constructed to house the cavalry and permit easy exit or entrance. Perhaps the most extraordinary aspect of this truly beautiful structure was the manner in which it blended into the topography. The terrain was escarped so effectively that an enemy approaching from any direction would be unable to see the fort until he was almost upon it.[14] Governor Cox of Almeida first attempted to enlist Spanish laborers to work on the fortifications, but he was soon forced to employ the Portuguese 9th Line for the task. Directed by Captain John Burgoyne of the British engineers, a nucleus of skilled Portuguese carpenters and stonemasons cleared away the debris in the ditches, erected palisades, repaired the breaches in the bastions, and, with the aid of the soldiers, repaired the bridges, covered way, drawbridge, and gates. Since the garrison of the fort might be forced to retire suddenly, orders were also issued to mine its formidable bastions; hence, it would be useless in French hands. Once the initial repairs had been completed, Cox ordered the 9th Line, supported by 120 artillerymen from Almeida, to garrison the fort. Four pieces of six, two howitzers, eight pieces of four, and four pieces of eight were dragged into La Concepción on 1 June along with 12,000 rations, 100,000 rounds of musket, and 100 shells for each artillery piece. In addition, four companies of the British 45th Foot were deployed at Vale da Mula and Aldea del Obispo, less than two miles from the fort, with orders to reinforce the garrison in event of an attack. Wellington was fortunate that the repairs at La Concepción had been started before the first of June because the French were again on the move. Ney's cavalry were on the banks of the Agueda by 30 May, and his entire corps had begun to concentrate in the vicinity of Ciudad Rodrigo.[15]

With the passage of May, Wellington, aware of the extraordinary progress his army had made during the past month, looked confidently to the summer campaign. He had not eliminated all the obstacles related to the frontier fortresses and the defense of Portugal, but his unshakable faith in his own ability and that of the army held out the hope of success. This optimism is evident in his letter to John Villiers on 5 June: "Massena is in my front, and is collecting all he can for an attack upon this country; but I do not think he will be able to make much progress till the French shall abandon their southern projects. They have been six weeks before Ciudad Rodrigo, and have

Figure 10. La Concepción: The front gate, curtain, and bridge from ditch

Figure 11. La Concepción: The esplanade, ramparts, ramp, and interior of front gate

Figure 12. La Concepción: The esplanade, rampart, casemates, and governor's quarters

Figure 13. La Concepción: The ditch, covered way, caponier, redoubt, and blockhouse from south curtain

Figure 14. La Concepción: The ramparts, parapet, and ramp

not yet passed the Agueda. . . . I hope," he wrote, "their progress will not turn out to be as sure as it has been slow."[16]

Wellington's determination to resist the French was underscored by the recent returns of his army. While the promised reinforcements were beginning to filter into Lisbon from Britain, Portuguese manpower had reached staggering proportions. By the first of May, a total of 51,280 troops of the line and 54,229 militiamen were under arms, seconded by 329,016 ordenanza mobilized for the defense of the Kingdom. "The Portuguese army are in a good state," Wellington declared. "We have arms for the militia, and upon the whole we have an enormous military establishment at our command. We only want money to put it in operation and to keep it up."[17]

Wellington was also encouraged by the activities at Ciudad Rodrigo. Although he had expressed serious reservations about the abilities and determination of the governor of the fortress, his attitude began to change as the month of May passed. He was obviously preoccupied with Ciudad Rodrigo; most of his correspondence referred to the fortress in some context since it was vital to his basic strategy for the defense of Portugal. Indeed, at times he considered the possibility of marching to relieve the fortress. After he learned of Herrasti's refusal to parley with General Mermet, despite the Frenchman's threats to put the entire garrison to the sword, the British general began to reassess his attitude toward the governor.[18]

When the junta and governor of Ciudad Rodrigo requested musket balls, Wellington acted immediately. Cox was instructed to draw on his massive magazine to send 100 rounds for each inhabitant and member of the garrison. Within five days Cox dispatched three wagons laden with 2,225 pounds of musket balls to Ciudad Rodrigo. Yet when the governor requested two mortars and several light guns, left the previous year by either the Duque del Parque or the Marquis de la Romana when their armies passed through Beira, Wellington rejected the appeal. He warned Cox, "If they are of very large size, and capable of throwing shells to a great distance, I should think it advisable not to send them, as they may eventually be used against yourself." Consequently, these mortars and field pieces were mounted and sent to arm La Concepción at the end of May.[19]

At the same time Wellington wrote a reassuring letter to Herrasti:

"The army under my command is also in readiness to move to your assistance, if I should find it practicable to afford it to you. I do not propose to move till . . . the enemy shall have brought forward the whole of his means, and that my movement may be of the utmost possible benefit to you. I assure you that I am sincerely interested in the fate of Ciudad Rodrigo, . . . your Excellency, the garrison, and inhabitants." However, he concluded cautiously, "I hope you will believe, that if I should not be able to attempt your relief, it will be owing to the superior strength of the enemy, and to the necessity of my attending to other important objects."[20]

By the end of May, the English and French were concluding their preparations for the summer campaign. Both had labored tirelessly to perfect their tactics and strategy and solve their logistical problems. Both had endeavored to instill their men with the ardor for victory and the justice of their cause; nevertheless, the Allies had achieved the decided advantage as a result of the French delays. Now the overture was drawing to a close; the first movement in the symphony of war would soon begin on an insignificant plain surrounding the poorly fortified town of Ciudad Rodrigo, which would gain immortality in the pages of Spanish history.

Chapter 5

The Investment of Ciudad Rodrigo

Dscalerise the eighteenth century immense changes took place in
the art of warfare, especially in tactics, strategy, and the imple-
ments of war. With the outbreak of the Revolutionary Wars and the
appearance of such strategists as Napoleon, Masséna, and Jomini,
the science of warfare was further transformed. However, in the area
of siege warfare there were few developments beyond the accomplish-
ments of Vauban, who developed and systemized techniques that remained in effect throughout the nineteenth century. Consequently,
without the introduction of innovative tactics, as exemplified by the
field armies of the Republic, the French siege armies were relegated
to the same time-tested Vauban tactics that were common knowledge
to all military men. Success, therefore, was a result of resources, determination, courage, and sacrifice.

Sieges were relatively routine operations throughout most of Europe, but in the Peninsula they assumed gigantic significance. Even
outdated or incomplete fortifications in Spain and Portugal became
formidable obstacles requiring full-scale attacks. This was true of
Ciudad Rodrigo where, according to Pelet, "the obstacles of the
countryside, the inclement weather, and lack of every necessity"
forced the French to secure hundreds of wagons and thousands of
draft animals to transport staggering quantities of provisions from
throughout Old Castile to the siege site.[1] Indeed, the logistical problems faced by Masséna's army were more imposing than the 120 guns
of Ciudad Rodrigo and its defiant garrison.

Weeks before Ney completed the concentration of his corps for the investment of Ciudad Rodrigo, convoys of wagons and mules had begun to transport munitions and siege supplies toward the fortress. As early as 18 May, Spanish spies reported the departure of thirty-four ammunition wagons laden with shells. However, it was not until 28 May that 43 siege pieces, collected at the convent of San Francisco in the suburbs of Salamanca, were mounted, harnessed, and readied for the march. Early that morning Ney's artillery commander, Ruty, ordered the convoy westward across the old Roman bridge spanning the Tormes River, accompanied by an escort of the Hanoverian Legion and 11th Dragoons. This first great convoy, drawn by some 900 horses, also included 54 wagons of timber for gun platforms and sandbags, two wagons of coal, 50 wagons of shot and shell, and 30 wagons of biscuit. Although there were three roads to Ciudad Rodrigo, two were impassable as a result of the incessant rains. The only practical route passed through Matilla, San Muñoz, Cabrillas, Alba de Yeltes, and Pedrotoro. Yet according to Pelet, the roads, "dissolved by the continuous rains, were in such a terrible state that the first convoy of artillery which left Salamanca . . . for San Muñoz" took six and one-half days to travel thirty-six miles. This arduous movement upset Ney's schedule drastically; he had expected the artillery to reach Pedrotoro, three miles from Ciudad Rodrigo, on 29 May, but the last pieces only reached San Muñoz on 3 June.[2]

A second great convoy of over 600 horses set out for San Muñoz on 30 May, dragging 100 wagons laden with projectiles, pontonier equipment, trench tools, sandbags, and wine and grain. With six draft animals drawing each wagon, the second convoy passed the artillery en route and reached San Muñoz in one day. Although the roads and bridges were being repaired, the route from San Muñoz to Cabrillas was a quagmire of mud that all but halted the heavy siege pieces. San Muñoz was designated as the midway depot and numerous outposts were scattered along the route to insure the safety of the convoy, but the guerrilla chieftain, Julián Sánchez, raided these posts with considerable success.[3]

On the morning of 29 May, Ney, accompanied by General Bardet's brigade, marched out of Salamanca and proceeded along the mud-clogged road toward San Muñoz. The following morning he pushed on to Ciudad Rodrigo to assume command of the investing

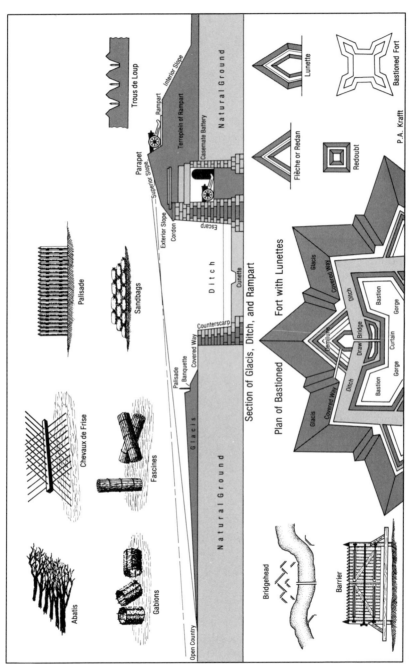

Figure 15. Fortress and siege defenses

force. He established his headquarters at the "immense" monastery of Nuestra Señora de la Caridad, situated three miles south of Ciudad Rodrigo, perhaps 100 yards from the Agueda River. The monks of the Premonstratensian Order had fled before Mermet established his divisional headquarters at the monastery. The vast accommodations of the fifteenth-century monastery made an excellent location for Ney's headquarters and an elegant setting for receptions and reviews. Ney's staff, as well as the état-major of the artillery and engineers, were housed in the various apartments and on the two floors of the cloister that opened out on the great courtyard with its sparkling fountain. The vast chapter halls and library were used by Ney and his staff to plan and discuss forthcoming siege operations; the great dining hall, the spacious kitchen, and the numerous storage facilities easily provided for their needs. There were several stables nearby, but the beautifully decorated monastery church was also used to house the horses. Beyond the church a number of ovens were constructed to bake bread and biscuit for the corps. Besides its utilitarian value, the structure was one of the most impressive monasteries in Old Castile. The cloister, with its unusually beautiful symmetry, its Romanesque architecture, its striking detail, its massive staircase, and its exquisite gardens, was dominated by the splendid dome and imposing façade of the church. The entire complex was surrounded by well-attended gardens, courtyards, and a high wall barring unwelcome visitors. This magnificent old monastery still stands majestically along the bank of the Agueda, its reddish-brown stone brilliantly reflecting the burning sun.[4]

It was late on 30 May when Ney reached La Caridad, but he soon left for Ciudad Rodrigo to examine its fortifications. Upon his return to the monastery he wrote to Masséna urging him to visit the siege site, hoping he would recognize the necessity of deploying the 8th Corps to support the 6th Corps. Early the following morning Ney left for Ciudad Rodrigo with Ruty, commander of the siege artillery, and Chef de bataillon Couche, in charge of the engineers of the 6th Corps, to reconnoiter the defenses of the fortress and decide upon the point of attack.[5]

The fortress of Ciudad Rodrigo had a long and illustrious history. Initially constructed on the ruins of the ancient Roman city of Mi-

Figure 16. Monastery of Nuestra Señora de la Caridad:
Panoramic view

róbriga, it was rebuilt and fortified in the twelfth century by Juan de
Cabrera for King Ferdinand II of León to guard the Portuguese fron-
tier 27 miles away. It represented the power and authority of the
Spanish monarchy in Old Castile. Although besieged and captured in
1706 during the War of Spanish Succession, the citizens of Ciudad
Rodrigo had demonstrated a strong loyalty to the Spanish monarchy
for six centuries and this was not to change in the Guerra de la
Independencia.

Strategically located, the fortress of Ciudad Rodrigo was a constant threat to isolated French units operating in the province of Salamanca; it was a temporary headquarters and refuge for the Spanish
army and the guerrilla bands posted along the Portuguese frontier, a
depot for military supplies, and the seat of the Revolutionary Junta of
Old Castile. As the last hope of Spanish resistance in Old Castile, the
fortress served as a psychological rallying point for the people in
northern Spain, a symbol epitomizing the strength and authority of
Ferdinand VII, and a possible base of operations for Wellington's
army during an attack on Salamanca, Valladolid, or even Madrid. On
the other hand, it was an obstacle to the French only because Napoleon had ordered Masséna to besiege and capture the fortress. His

Figure 17. Monastery of Nuestra Señora de la Caridad: Courtyard and church

army might have masked or bypassed it and advanced directly to confront the Allied army. If seized, the city could have been useful in serving the French as a staging area for the invasion of Portugal, a depot for troops and provisions, an outpost of French power in a sea of Spanish insurrection, and a vital link in the line of communications with Paris. It was not, however, a prerequisite for the invasion of Portugal.

The town, situated on a rocky but flat plateau dominating the fertile plain of Ciudad Rodrigo, was bound on the southeast by a steep precipice dropping down to the Agueda River 80 feet below the ramparts. The terrain on the east (right) bank of the river was cut by sandy, rather deep ravines separated by a few hillocks; beyond were steep rocky knolls forming a semicircle. On the west bank of the Agueda the gentle slope, culminating in the abrupt elevations of Manzano, was covered by woods extending to within 1,200 yards of the fortress.[6]

The defenses of Ciudad Rodrigo consisted of an ancient stone and red brick wall 29 feet in height, 30 feet thick, and almost a mile in circumference. Elliptical in shape, without major salients and inadequately flanked by square bastions, the base of this wall was formed by an earth rampart along three-fourths of its length; the remaining segment of the enceinte, protected by the perpendicular escarpment bordering the Agueda, was quite formidable and needed few additional defenses. Since the wall of the fortress had been breached in 1706, a modern wall or faussebraie had been erected four years later in front of the old one—except along the Agueda where it was unnecessary. Twelve feet in height and irregular in form, this faussebraie was augmented with redans and preceded by a dry moat 20 to 24 feet in width, perhaps ten feet deep, with a stone-covered scarp and counterscarp, culminating in an extremely steep glacis.

Along the northern flank of the faussebraie, five salients were constructed with an equal number of recesses; on the east were four poorly traced bastions with extremely small and unequal flanks. In fact, the only fortification outside but contiguous to the fortress was the demilune of San Andrés and its value was questionable. The curtains between each bastion of the faussebraie were within a few feet of

Figure 18. Monastery of Nuestra Señora de la Caridad: The church and facade

Figure 19. Monastery of Nuestra Señora de la Caridad: The cloister

Figure 20. Monastery of Nuestra Señora de la Caridad: The grand hall

Figure 21. Ciudad Rodrigo: Aerial view

the old enceinte, impeding communication with the fortress ramparts and hardly favorable for the defense of the city. This modern fausse-braie was erected primarily to shield the main wall from the enemy artillery on the plain below the fortress; however, the Spanish engineers had neglected to build it high enough to protect the old wall if long-range siege pieces were employed on the neighboring hills. Although Ciudad Rodrigo towered above the surrounding countryside for miles it was dominated by two hills northwest of the town—Grand Teso of San Francisco and Little Teso. These rocky elevations, rather elliptical in shape, were separated by the tributaries of the swiftly

Figure 22. Ciudad Rodrigo: The castle and Roman bridge over the Agueda River

running Rapeiro River. Since Grand Teso was 150 feet above the valley floor, 42 feet above the old city wall, 69 feet above the faussebraie, and only 600 yards from the fortress, the siege guns placed along its crest could easily strike both walls as well as the interior of Ciudad Rodrigo itself. Governor Herrasti was well aware of these weaknesses in its defenses, and he posted an infantry unit atop Grand Teso. However, when the French invested the fortress, Loison's men overran the Spanish post on Grand Teso and drove them back into the city.

Ciudad Rodrigo was surrounded by suburbs, gardens, and irregular terrain which served to obstruct its approaches. The suburb of San Francisco was located some 800 feet northeast of the city while that of Santa Marina, often called Puente, was situated to the southeast on what appeared to be an island formed in the Agueda and connected to the fortress by an ancient Roman bridge almost 400 feet in length. The Agueda River, flowing north from the Sierra de Gata along the southern wall of the city, became a serious obstacle to the French in the spring of 1810 because of its extensive flooding. In fact, the tributaries of the Agueda stretched across the plains surrounding Ciudad Rodrigo, saturating the area between the city and the French positions.

With the successes of the French armies throughout Spain during the first months of 1810, it was obvious to Governor Herrasti that the French would soon be threatening his fortress. After Ney had offered lenient terms for surrender during the second week of February, the governor had toiled determinedly to prepare the fortress for the anticipated attack. Brigadier Don Juan de Belestá of the Royal Engineers was charged with the task of repairing and perfecting the defenses of the city and suburbs, while Commandant General Don Francisco Ruiz Gómez began to train and organize his artillery brigades.[7]

Hoping to form a third line of defenses east of the fortress, the engineers entrenched the suburb of San Francisco, constructing earthen parapets six or seven feet high with salients formed by four redans; its flanks were covered by the fortified convents of San Francisco on the north and Santo Domingo to the south. The convent of Santa Clara, along the eastern perimeter of the suburb, was screened with a high breastwork, and the main road to Salamanca, which

Figure 23. Ciudad Rodrigo: The cathedral and cloister with evidence of damage sustained during the siege

passed nearby, was cut and barricaded. Palisades were raised from both the convent of Santo Domingo across the plain of Toledo to the newly constructed demilune of San Andrés, and from the convent of San Francisco to the northeast wall of the town. The convent of Trinidad, "within a pistol shot of the walls," was demolished since it obstructed the fortress fire; the debris from this structure was used to erect the demilune of San Andrés between the gates of Conde and San Pelayo. Northwest of the town the convent of Santa Cruz was prepared to resist an attack. The walls of this convent facing the fortress were destroyed since they afforded the advancing French protection, and the remainder of the cloister was fortified with an extensive network of barricades and redoubts. Finally, the moat and the many *trous de loup* below the walls of the city were cleared of debris and garbage to impede the enemy advance.

Simultaneously, a detachment of 300 garrison soldiers labored energetically to improve and augment the interior defenses of the fortress. Under the direction of a young engineer, Lieutenant Colonel Nicolás Berdejo, the parapets of the main wall and the faussebraie were reinforced. Bombproof ammunition depots were constructed on the ramparts for immediate use, and large subterranean vaults were excavated in the cathedral as well as beneath large private homes to store the massive quantities of powder. Broad terrepleins were constructed on the ramparts to aid the artillerymen. Heavy wooden bombproof shelters were fabricated for the garrison and citizens at several convenient locations, notably along the ramparts of the main wall bordering the Agueda. The old castle along the west wall of the city above the Agueda was repaired to serve as a citadel for a few hundred soldiers of the garrison, and the cathedral tower was transformed into a lookout post. The four gates of the city—Conde, San Pelayo, Colada, and San Jago (Santiago)—were strengthened and additional gun emplacements were constructed near the gate of Conde overlooking the suburb of San Francisco. To complete the internal defenses of the city, Herrasti's representative in Lisbon, Evaristo Pérez de Castro, appealed to the Portuguese government for fire-fighting equipment; it arrived 20 days before the fortress came under attack.[8]

The Spanish garrison, composed of both veterans and inexperienced recruits, included 857 volunteers from the infantry regiment of

Figure 24. Ciudad Rodrigo: The shell-pitted cathedral tower
and facade

Avila, 311 provisional infantry from Segovia, and 706 troops from Majorca; in addition 2,432 men, formed into three battalions and a civic guard, were recruited from the residents of Ciudad Rodrigo. With 310 officers, approximately 240 lancers of the guerrilla chieftain, Julián Sánchez, and 390 artillerymen, primarily from the local artillery school, the garrison of the fortress contained over 6,000 men.[9]

The armaments of Ciudad Rodrigo were formidable—100 cannon and 18 howitzers or mortars. Hoping to augment his artillery, Herrasti had appealed to Wellington on several occasions for both artillery and ammunition before his supplies were cut by the French. Specifically, the Spanish governor requested two large Spanish mortars left at Almeida in 1810 as well as several light pieces that had been destined for Fort La Concepción. Wellington refused, fearing they might be used against Almeida, but he was willing to send musket balls. Indeed, Herrasti had collected an extraordinary supply of munitions that would serve to harass the French mercilessly.

With funds from the Spanish Regency, Herrasti and the Revolutionary Junta purchased large quantities of food from the Portuguese while the governor-general of Old Castile, the Marquis de la Romana, sent vast consignments of flour meal. The town accumulated 247,000 rations of biscuit, a full magazine of vegetables, and extensive quantities of other foodstuffs to feed the garrison and the 10,000 inhabitants still in the city. In fact, by 15 April the alcalde, Manuel Huertas, and the captain general of the province, Don Juan de Vivares, were able to assure the city of a six months' supply of food.[10]

By the end of May, the people of Ciudad Rodrigo, encouraged by their governor, Bishop F. Benito, and the town clergy, were determined to resist the French.[11] Herrasti had indicated his intentions to the town junta as early as January 1810 when he wrote, "The Supreme Junta, the Council of War, and I have decided to defend this place to the death. Until now I have opposed the enemy, who attacked us with the most determined resistance and I am determined to continue. The strength of the fortress and the thickness of its walls are all prepared for the defense. Providence and fortune will serve us."[12] Hence, the Spanish were confident in their resolve to resist the French. The fortifications had been repaired and improved; the maga-

Figure 25. Ciudad Rodrigo: The rampart, parapet, and
gun embrasures

zines were overflowing with both munitions and food; the governor
and members of the town junta were men of ability and determination. The French, on the contrary, appeared disorganized and without
direction and, perhaps most important, Wellington's army hovered
along the frontier ready to march to the aid of the Spanish.

In reconnoitering the fortress on 31 May, Ney, Ruty, and Couche
quickly recognized the weaknesses of the fortifications at Ciudad
Rodrigo. They readily agreed that the northwestern wall, before the
King's Tower and the cathedral, was most vulnerable to an attack.
Ruty and Couche noted that this area was poorly escarped; it could be
attacked immediately without capturing the suburbs, offered the least
flanking fire, and, more important, was dominated by the heights of
Grand and Little Teso. Their reconnaissance report also included detailed information about the terrain, construction of the trenches, and
locations for the artillery. At 11 in the morning, as Ney and his staff

were riding around the fortress, the governor sent an infantry column out of the fortress to disrupt the work of the French and to gather intelligence. A counterattack was ordered and, despite a heavy fire from the walls of the fortress, the column was repulsed. Before returning to La Caridad, Ney made a partial tour of his units, which had drawn closer to the fortress.[13]

Ferey's brigade had reached the bank of the Agueda on the evening of 29 May, but the remainder of Loison's division did not arrive around Ciudad Rodrigo or begin to assume control of the left bank of the Agueda until 1 June. Ferey proceeded directly to the heights of Palomar overlooking the Agueda and began preparations for the construction of a trestle bridge opposite Cunejera near the recently discovered ford of Loro. Simultaneously, the engineers had their prefabricated trestles hauled to a site some three miles south of Ciudad Rodrigo, below the monastery of La Caridad; there on the first of June they began to erect a bridge. Despite the rising water and the threatening maneuvers of enemy patrols on the west bank of the Agueda, the basic span rose quickly above the water. Three hundred workers moved to the left bank of the Agueda to begin work on a bridgehead; they chopped into the rocky soil and threw up three redoubts to the left of the bridge. The cavalry established posts opposite the bridge as far south as the heights above Villaporilla, but they were constantly observed by the anxious British and Spanish horsemen. Although the bridge was completed within three days, several additional days were required to finish the irregular but formidable bridgehead which took the form of a demilune, protected from the rear by palisades; this bridgehead, built to accommodate 300 men, was supplemented by a battery of three guns established on the east bank of the river overlooking the 240-foot bridge and its defenses. Meanwhile, Ferey's men traced the bridge north of the fortress at the ford of Loro opposite the village of Cunejera on 2 June. The next morning, material for the trestles and the pontonier's equipment were hauled to the ford while a bridgehead was traced to house 600 men and a battery of four pieces.

The Allies sent reconnaissance columns daily to observe progress on the bridges and exchange fire with French dragoons on the west bank of the river, but the work progressed unhampered. Yet, the

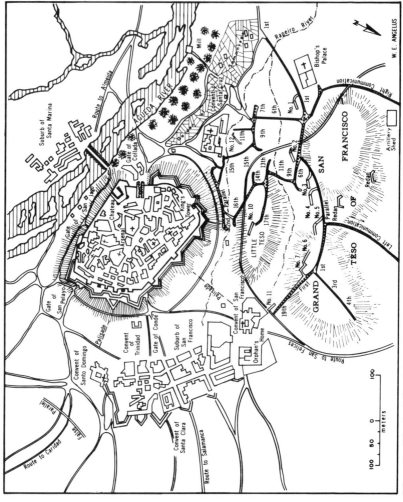

Map 5. Ciudad Rodrigo

French engineers experienced some anxious moments from the forces of nature and the ingenuity of the Spanish troops. The swift current of the swollen Agueda threatened to wash away the trestles as the British expected, and the Spanish troops of General Martín de la Carrera attempted to destroy the bridges by sending logs and trees down the swift-moving water; but most of the debris went aground along the winding banks of the Agueda before reaching the bridges.[14]

While the bridges and the necessary bridgeheads were being erected across the Agueda, French columns continued to concentrate in the vicinity of Ciudad Rodrigo. Simon's brigade of Loison's division camped immediately to the left of General Ferey while the 3d and 15th Chasseurs à cheval were posted nearby. Bardet's brigade of Mermet's division occupied the ravine to the right of Sancti Spiritus in the direction of Pedrotoro, and Delabassé's brigade of the same division occupied Sancti Spiritus. Marchand's first brigade commanded by Maucune camped with his right at Pedrotoro and his left in the direction of La Caridad; Marcognet's brigade moved to the height of the Cantarranas above the monastery. A brigade of cavalry, which included the 3d, 6th, 15th, and 25th Dragoons and a company of light artillery, was established at La Caridad under General Charles-Mathieu Gardanne, and finally the 10th and 11th Dragoons of General Jacques-Louis Milet's brigade occupied Tenebrón and Tamames to cover the siege parc.[15]

With Ney's troops concentrated near the fortress, French skirmishers began to advance toward the walls of the city before dawn on 1 June to establish a double cordon of posts within "half a shot of the wall." The Spanish governor, assuming the French object was Grand Teso, dispatched a column of about 300 infantry and 120 cavalry to contest the French advance. Loison reacted by sending a detachment of tirailleurs; supported by cavalry, they crossed the plain below the fortress and drove the Spanish back to the city walls. Later in the day, another Spanish column of some 300 horsemen and 1,000 infantry slipped out a city gate to obstruct French movements. Loison again took appropriate action, sending two infantry companies and one of grenadiers to support his tirailleurs. The Spanish were turned back and pursued to the fortress while the French retired behind their posts. At the same time, a French column of cavalry crossed the ford of Loro, under only two feet of water, and moved along the left bank of the Agueda toward Villaporilla chasing several enemy cavalry posts before them.[16]

Meanwhile, when Ney returned to La Caridad upon the completion of his reconnaissance, he wrote to Masséna who had just advanced his headquarters from Valladolid to Salamanca. Announcing the decision to attack the northwestern wall of the fortress, Ney detailed the deployment of his corps, the need for provisions, and the necessity of moving the 8th Corps to support the siege: "All is disposed to commence the siege of Ciudad Rodrigo. . . . I await Your Excellency with the greatest impatience."[17] Even before Ney's dispatch arrived at Salamanca, Masséna had left the city, accompanied by Junot, Eblé, and Pelet, to visit Ciudad Rodrigo. As soon as they reached La Caridad, Ney directed them to the banks of the Agueda, where some of Loison's men were laboring to complete a trestle bridge across the river. Returning to the monastery, Masséna and his officers were received in the spacious halls of the complex.

Early the next morning Masséna went on horseback to inspect the troops and reconnoiter the fortifications of the town. According to Pelet, "The divisions of Marchand and Mermet were superb, even in the midst of the mud. Each company of Maucune's brigade had set up great eagles [made] of grass in the front line of battle." After riding around the fortress, examining the walls and the entrenched suburbs, Masséna agreed upon the point designated for the attack. Masséna and Ney seated themselves in front of Loison's division to decide upon the dispositions for the attack. There was apparently some discussion about the engineer to be assigned the task of conducting the siege. Since General Joseph-Félix Lazowski, engineer commander for the entire army, had not arrived yet, Ney wanted his commanding engineer, Couche, to direct the siege; Junot and perhaps Masséna wanted Colonel Eleonor Dufriche de Valazé of the 8th Corps to conduct the work. Couche was given the assignment and, according to Pelet, "The artillerymen announced that within three hours the fire of the enemy would be silenced, that in a few days the fortress would be captured, and with the establishment of the first battery a breach would be opened in both walls." At the same time Ney complained to Masséna of "difficulties everywhere. . . . There was little agreement and even some bitterness between them."[18]

Following the reconnaissance of Ciudad Rodrigo, Masséna, Ney, and their staff returned to La Caridad. Ney again raised the proposal of an attack against the Allied army along the Portuguese frontier. Masséna responded with the arguments developed in Pelet's memorandum of 20 May, but Ney was not pleased. Indeed, such an attack might have resulted in failure; but if Masséna had exhibited the same daring he had as the victor of Zurich, he might have struck decisively. The risks were great, but the rewards of a decisive victory would have been monumental. If the Allied army had been crushed and driven into the sea, the conquest of Portugal could have been the mortal blow to organized resistance in the Peninsula. Nevertheless, Masséna's decision seemed final, and Ney accepted it, at least momentarily.

When he and his staff left La Caridad on 4 June for Salamanca, Masséna was deeply disturbed by the turn in events. Despite assurances that all was ready for the siege, his aide-de-camp recorded, "This army corps suffered to an exceptional degree . . . and from the very beginning water gushed out everywhere, even on the highest ground. Soldiers were in mud . . . and exposed to almost continual rain and extreme variations in heat and cold." Wine and brandy were unavailable and often the men were reduced to one-quarter rations per day. There were no ambulances; the troops lacked cartridges and it seemed "there were not enough for one battle, and yet there were people who talked only of attacking the English." [19]

Upon his return to Salamanca, Masséna wrote a melancholy letter to Berthier describing his distractions and concern over Ney's judgment. Convinced that Herrasti, with the aid of Wellington and the Spanish armies of La Romana and La Carrera nearby, would stubbornly defend the fortress, Masséna saw all his problems compounded. The continual rains were disabling, the roads impassable, and a piece of twenty-four with 12 horses could make only a two-hour march in one day: "The arrival of supplies proves most difficult because of the lack of transportation." The country surrounding Ciudad Rodrigo was exhausted for a distance of ninety miles. "It is the worst territory in Spain," he lamented. "We do not have food for our horses." He blamed part of this situation on Ney who had deployed two divisions around the fortress for over two months, exhausting the countryside. "I am obliged to say to you," he wrote, "that I believe the Marshal Duc d'Elchingen [Ney] is in too much of a hurry. It is necessary for us to be strong enough, and he is much offended that his corps has been placed entirely in the vicinity of Rodrigo." Masséna complained of sickness, the lack of shoes, the scarcity of lead and powder, the continual harassment of the guerrilla bands, the Spanish army threatening his rear, and the general demoralization of his troops. He concluded with an unsubstantiated attack on Ney: "I am anxious to unite and prepare everything to achieve His Majesty's intentions and to repair the damage caused by the Duc d'Elchingen in his haste to begin operations which should only be commenced when all the means are collected."[20] Nevertheless, Masséna refused to consider a withdrawal of the 6th Corps, fearing any retrograde movement might be interpreted by the enemy as a sign of weakness. Although Masséna was probably unaware of details concerning the delays in undertaking the siege, it is a fact that Ney successfully thwarted Soult's orders to invest Ciudad Rodrigo for almost three months.

Two days after Masséna left La Caridad for Salamanca, the brooding Ney resolved to take matters into his own hands. On 6 June, he sent a letter to Junot clearly proposing insubordination. Attacking Masséna's lack of activity and initiative, he suggested that the Prince feared his reputation might be compromised in a battle with the British army. "If we unite," he suggested, "we will be able to attack the English." He hoped this action would gain the country with one blow and have disastrous results in England. Specifically, Wellington might be disgraced, the Marquess Wellesley, Wellington's brother and British foreign minister, might be dismissed, and a general peace would be established in Europe. After complaining of what he regarded as Masséna's inflexible attitude toward the enemy and his callous treatment of the 6th Corps, Ney made a startling observation: "I believe you will agree to come to take part in the glory that awaits you in fighting the English or finding a glorious death in doing your duty. Not only will I leave you the choice of your position but I will share with you the troops I have at my disposal. . . . If the Emperor were with us for only a moment, I have the confidence to believe that His Majesty would support my opinion."[21] Realizing the serious implications of such an operation, Junot wisely refused to cooperate with Ney. This rash action might have cost Ney his command as well as his favor with the Emperor, had Masséna been aware of this letter.

While Masséna was caught up in his administrative duties and pressing logistical problems, Ney's troops were engaged in daily conflict with the troops of Wellington and Herrasti. In fact, soon after Masséna had left La Caridad on 4 June, a Spanish column of 80 horsemen rode out of Ciudad Rodrigo toward the village of Carpio. After reconnoitering the movements of French dragoons advancing in the direction of La Caridad, they retired without firing a shot. About 50 British cavalry advanced to observe the French activities after 4:00 P.M., and less than an hour later a sortie of 800 infantry, a limited detachment of cavalry, two howitzers, and a field piece advanced out the gate of Colada toward the Agueda where the mill of Barragan, several large farmhouses, and the vegetable gardens of Samaniego and Céspedes were located. Loison had posted a company of infantry in one of the farmhouses, and they "held well" against the Spanish attacks and artillery fire. He immediately sent five companies of grenadiers of the 66th and 32d Line and 150 cavalry of the 3d Hussars with one cannon to support them. Two infantry companies, covered by cavalry, moved forward in a skirmish line toward the houses and the little woods at the foot of the plain without firing a shot.[22]

Once the woods were reached, the charge was beat and they advanced with bayonets. The Spanish were dislodged from the houses, a small convent, and the gardens of Samaniego and Céspedes; the French pursued them toward the fortress glacis where skirmishing erupted. A large crowd of curious men, women, and children gathered on the glacis to watch the struggle; when the Spanish were driven back, the onlookers complicated a difficult situation by mixing with the Spanish troops as they struggled to enter the fortress through the gate of Colada. The Spanish in the covered way and on the ramparts opened a brisk musket fire on the French, forcing them back from the town walls. Once this sortie had been repulsed, Loison posted three reserve companies of grenadiers in the ravine between Grand Teso and an elevation toward the northern wall described by the engineers as the "*bonnet de prêtre*" because it was shaped like a priest's hat. Moreover, two companies of the 26th Line and 150 men of the 15th Chasseurs à cheval were strategically positioned near the gorge west of the Grand Teso to strengthen the French position. Consequently, if the Spanish threatened the French tirailleurs in the houses and in the woods below the fortress or along the Agueda, they would encounter serious difficulty. The same would be true if their sorties were attempted from the gate of Colada or the suburbs.[23]

Simultaneously, a detachment of Loison's tirailleurs commanded by an engineer officer set out to establish several positions atop Grand Teso. This was accomplished without difficulty and they began the construction of fieldworks immediately. Early the following morning, two positions had been entrenched but the last was not completed until the following night. Similarly, Simon's men, constructing entrenched posts to the south of Grand Teso, were delayed in completing these positions since they lacked the necessary tools.[24]

While some men of Ferey's brigade, posted behind Teso, maintained a sporadic fire on the fortress, other troops continued their work on the bridges spanning the Agueda. The bridge below La Caridad had been completed and 300 workers were now laboring to complete the bridgehead on the west bank of the Agueda. Work on the trestle bridge near the ford of Loro was progressing satisfactorily and a battery, composed of a piece of eight and a howitzer, was begun behind the bridge where two battalions of infantry were to be established. However, the enemy cavalry carefully reconnoitered and observed the work on both bridges, especially the span at the Loro ford.

At 5:00 P.M. on 4 June, the Spanish troops seriously threatened the pontoniers as the floor was being laid on the bridge near Loro. Loison sent a column of perhaps a hundred horsemen across the ford to attack the Spanish and force their withdrawal. With this successfully completed, they reconnoitered the British posts, exchanged carbine fire with a detachment of English cavalry, and turned back an Allied convoy destined for the fortress.

As this reconnaissance was being carried out, a detachment of Ferey's troops occupied the houses parallel to Grand Teso. That night the French engineers advanced their posts to within 400 yards of the fortress ramparts while officers Treussart, Vincent, Moulin, and Shaumara of the engineers led a detachment on the left bank of the Agueda; they seized the trenches and trous de loup beyond the suburb of Santa Marina but suffered 15 casualties. A Spanish sortie of 300 to 400 cavalry slipped out of the fortress to determine the French activities around the fortress, but they retired within an hour and a half; it was obvious to Herrasti that considerable damage had been done. The French had succeeded in repulsing his sorties; they had drawn their posts in closely around the fortress; they would soon have possession of the west bank of the Agueda; and, perhaps most important, they had occupied the vital position atop Grand Teso.[25]

In the meantime, Ney, anxious to determine the intentions of the Allies, ordered Loison to send three reconnaissance columns across the Agueda to probe the enemy posts and determine their strength. On the morning of 5 June, three columns crossed the Agueda and fanned out along the three major roads. One unit advanced almost two miles beyond Manzano driving 30 horsemen before them. The second column marched on Gallegos, dislodging some 60 British cavalry. Captain Krauchenberg of the King's German Legion gathered his hussars and the British 16th Light Cavalry to stem the French advance, but he was forced to fall back, covered by the Portuguese chasseurs.[26] The third reconnaissance, which included a brigade of dragoons, a battalion of *chasseurs de siège* composed of 300 sharpshooters from the 6th Corps and three pieces of artillery, marched toward Carpio. It encountered several isolated columns of enemy cavalry but succeeded in capturing a few Spanish prisoners for purposes of intelligence. During this reconnaissance the British moved forward with almost 400 cavalry along the left bank of the Agueda, extending their squadrons toward the mountains and a point opposite Loison's division. At the same time 300 Allied lancers appeared on a hillock to the west to observe the French column and assure themselves of the limited nature of the French probe. One hundred British cavalry also appeared at the ford of Loro to observe Ferey's men as they labored to complete the bridge, but fire from a piece of eight dispersed them.[27]

During the night of 5 June, a company of Loison's voltigeurs occupied the gardens below the fortress supported by a company of grenadiers, while Simon's troops, with the newly arrived trench tools, labored to complete the entrenchment atop the hill parallel to Grand Teso. Another detachment threw up a fortification in the gorge of Grand Teso to cover Loison's division in case of enemy attack.[28] The next morning, however, the Spanish assumed the offensive. At 6:00 A.M., Governor Herrasti, fearing that his resources would be cut off with the capture of the houses and the vegetable gardens of Samaniego and Céspedes, concerned with his loss of the mills of Barragan and Cañizos several days earlier, and anxious over the contracting French posts around the fortress which further isolated him from his Allies, resolved to strike back against the French. A force of between 500 and 600 Spanish infantry attacked the entrenchments to the left of Grand Teso. The French sentinels and advanced posts were surprised and overrun, but a reserve unit was rushed forward to repel the attack. The Spanish were driven back to the suburb of San Francisco with undetermined losses; the French suffered 11 casualties. Approximately three hours later another sortie, composed of perhaps 600 town militia dressed in their white capes and stockings, advanced along the Agueda to dislodge the French from the houses and vegetable gardens of Samaniego and Céspedes. The inexperienced Spanish troops fought with passion and determination, but the French were well prepared to receive them. Two companies of voltigeurs and a company of grenadiers, held in reserve in several of the farmhouses, waited quietly for them and fired point-blank into the Spanish columns, chasing them back to the glacis with perhaps 40 casualties.[29]

Preceded by a heavy cannonade, the third and most ambitious Spanish effort was made at noon with 2,500 or 3,000 infantry, supported by four guns in the faussebraie and several pieces of horse artillery; again they attacked the French posts in the houses and gardens below the fortress. Observing the Spanish advance, Loison ordered Ferey to rush three companies forward to support them while a fourth company occupied a strategically located farmhouse. Loison then instructed General Simon to advance through the gorge and up a hill parallel to Grand Teso with eight companies of elite infantry in order to carry out a flanking attack should the Spanish be successful in the gardens. A battalion of the 32d Léger was moved to the gorge on the right and behind Grand Teso, and the cavalry was mounted and ready to advance with artillery if necessary. There was a heavy exchange of musket fire, and the fortress guns thundered in unison with the field artillery supporting the flanks of the "intrepid" Spanish column. However, reinforced by the companies of Ferey's brigade arriving from all directions, the voltigeurs assumed the offensive and pushed the enemy troops back to the walls of the city with bayonets.

The Spanish appeared to want to defend the convent below the glacis of the fortress, apparently near the gate of Colada, but they were forced back into the city; yet their fire continued for three more hours. Finally, Loison was forced to recall his young troops, many of whom were seeing fire for the first time. The French sustained at least 10 dead and 40 wounded, many of them on the glacis of the fortress, and claimed that the Spanish had 100 wounded and 30 dead.

That evening Loison ordered Ferey to reentrench the large farmhouse near the Agueda, to open trenches to the left and right of this position in order to protect the troops from the fortress fire, and to establish a redoubt on its left; there two howitzers and two pieces of eight would be established to sustain the posts in the vegetable gardens and prevent the enemy from leaving the fortress without coming under French fire. In addition, this position would be fraised and palisaded with the trees from the nearby woods and sentinels would be posted in foxholes two and one-half or three feet deep.[30]

At dawn the following morning, 7 June, a reconnaissance column of 200 cavalry issued from the fortress toward the position occupied by Loison's entrenched voltigeurs and the foxhole sentinels. The French surprised the Spanish and forced them back in such confusion that they fired only one shot. As the day passed, French troops began to chop down many of the trees in the wooded areas bordering the two mansions at the foot of the glacis and along an avenue running to the mill opposite the farm on the Agueda. Although the houses in the gardens nearby were creneled and entrenched, the officers in charge occupied only a small convent and three houses to its rear and right. Dissatisfied, Loison ordered Ferey to occupy and entrench the houses situated in the general area of the garden and to extend his position to the Agueda to ensure his flanks.[31]

That same day, work was terminated on the bridge and bridgehead below La Caridad while efforts continued on the bridge at the ford of Loro. Six hundred workers were sent to work on the bridgehead on the west bank of the river, and as usual they were temporarily interrupted by a British reconnaissance column. Nearby, a convoy of 100 mules carrying grain slipped by the French positions and passed through the suburb of Santa Marina and across the Roman bridge into Ciudad Rodrigo. Loison was disturbed about the apparent success of the convoy, so the following day while the workers labored to complete the bridgehead on the rocky west bank of the Agueda, he sent a squadron of cavalry across the bridge at Loro to occupy the left bank and complete the investment of the city; yet, "it was impossible for the horses to leave the main roads for an instant without sinking up to their stomachs." [32]

As work continued before the fortress and along the Agueda, orders were issued for a detachment of dismounted dragoons to cross the Agueda on the evening of 8 June and reconnoiter the suburb of Santa Marina. The troops carefully noted the defense of the suburb, especially two fortified convents linked by an epaulement, but works to cover this position were unnecessary since it was completely dominated by the fortress guns. Spanish troops occupied this suburb only during the daylight hours, confident the French would not seize it.

With the French posts now in direct contact with the enemy pickets west of the Agueda, Ney ordered four squadrons of dragoons under Loison and Gardanne to reconnoiter the British position. A platoon of tirailleurs and a detachment of cavalry were sent to the heights above Carpio, but they were driven back by horsemen and infantry of the British Light Division. It was only with the support of Gardanne's four cavalry squadrons that Carpio was finally reconnoitered. The French pushed on to determine British strength at Gallegos but some 250 cavalry and infantry waited to repulse them. As the British approached, Loison's troops fell back on the Agueda. He posted vedettes along the west bank of the river while the squadrons of General Milet's cavalry were extended from the right of the Loro bridgehead to Fonseca to watch the British posts. The intelligence collected by Loison's reconnaissance columns seemed to confirm the statements made by recently captured enemy soldiers that the British "wish[ed] to limit themselves to the defense of Portugal." [33]

While efforts were being made to complete the investment of the fortress, acting Quartermaster General Michaux at Salamanca was busy wrestling with overwhelming logistical problems. As early as 19 May, Michaux had begun laboring to improve and regularize the commissariat of the army; he sought to collect sufficient food for the troops, establish hospitals, and secure the necessary vehicles for the wagon trains and the ambulance corps as well as trying to eliminate

the continual friction among the various brigade and divisional commanders. A continuing crisis revolved around the testy brigade commander, Eloi Taupin, who had earlier threatened to shoot anyone attempting to forage on the east bank of the Yeltes where his troops
were posted.[34] When units of the 8th Corps were moved forward into
the province of Salamanca, Taupin's troops seized the food magazines
at Zamora which had been gathered "with great difficulty" by Loison's
division. Ney complained to Masséna indicating that the siege of
Ciudad Rodrigo would have to be renounced immediately unless he
gave "the most stern orders that our magazine be respected." The
controversy dragged on several weeks with countercharges by Taupin
that Loison was collecting requisitions in money rather than provisions. Ultimately, Loison was able to write "in a victorious manner
[that] 'I hope M. Taupin will only be embarrassed by his report.'"[35]

Kellermann, governor of the provinces of Valladolid and Palencia, also caused considerable friction. He had been instructed to continue the collection of the requisitions in León, Palencia, and Valladolid to supply the 6th Corps even though the 8th Corps was moving
into the province of Salamanca, but he exhibited little interest or initiative in fulfilling these orders. Vast quantities of grain and barley
began to accumulate at the depots in Valladolid and Medina del
Campo, but General François-Etienne Kellermann refused to provide
transport or troops to escort the convoys; as a result, Michaux's magazines at Salamanca remained depleted. On 10 June, Masséna wrote
to Kellermann, "The needs of the army are such that it is urgent that
provisions collected . . . be sent on to Salamanca. All delays, all opposition on the part of the commanders and others of authority are to
cease at this instant because it can only result in exposing the army to
a shortage of subsistence. You will please . . . give the order to accelerate by all possible means the return to Salamanca of the forage
expeditions that have been directed to the different points of the provinces you command." Similarly, Michaux had to combat the policies
of Ney and Junot who issued extra rations of food and fodder to their
états-majors.[36]

Ney complained bitterly about the lack of supplies and Masséna
promised to "do all that is possible." Michaux was instructed to accelerate the shipment of supplies to the 6th Corps; he implemented

this order to the best of his ability. On 3 June, a vast convoy carrying food departed from Salamanca for Ney's headquarters, and the following day 50 pack mules left the magazines with flour for Ney. On 5 June, 40 caissons of flour and biscuit rolled out of the gates at Salamanca followed by 60 more wagons the next day. Ney now had five days' flour, biscuit, and meat and 21 days' rations of barley. Nevertheless, 70 more wagons, including 10 of rice, began the journey to La Caridad on 7 June. When the quartermaster general appointed by Napoleon, General Jean-François Lambert, arrived at headquarters, Masséna sought to continue the shipments without interruption. He wrote to Lambert, "Send another convoy of 60 wagons of food at dawn tomorrow." Accordingly sixty caissons left the morning of 8 June laden with biscuit, flour, and rice followed by yet another convoy carrying 100,000 rations of rice, vegetables, flour, and bread. At the same time, Masséna sent his chief of staff, Fririon, to personally inform Ney "of all my concern in sending subsistence." Five days later he again assured Ney, "The subsistence of your corps is always on my mind. I have ordered the quartermaster general to send you 8,000 rations of bread or biscuit every day." Orders were also issued for the construction of bake ovens at Pedrotoro and Alba de Yeltes and repairs made to those at Tamames in an effort to guarantee continued subsistence for the siege.[37]

Michaux also faced several serious problems concerning the collections of contributions and requisitions before Lambert's arrival. In an effort to secure additional financial resources, Michaux requested that troops be sent into the province of Avila to collect some 4,820,344 réaux that remained uncollected from the levy Ney had imposed in May. He was acutely aware that little money could be collected in the provinces of Salamanca, Zamora, and Toro, or the city of Peñaranda, which had already been exhausted by the continued French occupation. In addition, he recommended that Avila and Segovia, which are "rich and have conserved more resources than the others," be required to provide 32 ton of barley, 48 of grain, and five and one-half of beef for the army during the month of June. When the troops began to carry out these orders, King Joseph, who hoped to keep many of Avila's resources under his control, had his aide, Joseph Daultane, complain to Masséna. Daultane wrote, "Confidentially, if Michaux continues to operate the same system he did in Aragon under the orders of the Duc de Montebello . . . the province of Avila will soon be abandoned by its people and become a nest of insurrection." He concluded, "The province will not refuse to furnish all that is possible for the subsistence of the army, but the contributions of twelve réaux each day per man appears to be a little high." Michaux also considered increasing his financial resources at the expense of the 6th Corps by appropriating from their treasury the bars of gold ingots, valued at 390,000 francs. With these funds he hoped to purchase grain, barley, and meat, especially for the quartermaster general of the army and the magazines at Salamanca.[38]

Another basic concern of Michaux was the establishment of an effective hospital administration. He visited the hospitals of the army which he found "as good as possible" considering the circumstances. He began to transport between 50 and 60 sick to Valladolid daily aboard the empty caissons returning for more supplies. Hospitals were established at Salamanca as well as along the evacuation route at Medina del Campo and Cantalapiedra. Minimum food requirements were set; hospital storehouses were continually supplied; depots were established for convalescents; and the mode of evacuation was formalized. With the arrival of Lambert, six hospitals were established in various monasteries and public houses in Valladolid to accommodate 2,000 patients. At Salamanca three hospitals were expanded to accommodate 1,800; the facility at Zamora included 400 beds, Tordesilla's hospital had space for 500, and Toro could house 300 sick. Small hospitals were maintained by the health service at León, Benavente, Palencia, Astorga, and Rio Seco, where the troops of the 8th Corps were taken. Finally, an ambulance corps was established to facilitate the rapid movement of the sick and wounded; ambulance depots were established at Ledesma, Tamames, and other vital locations throughout the province.[39]

As the convoys of food and supplies were dragged along the mucky roads from Salamanca to La Caridad, the siege pieces, accompanied by limbers and caissons laden with artillery supplies, continued their laborious movement to San Muñoz. By 3 June, the third artillery convoy of 580 horses departed from its depot at Salamanca, hauling gun carriages, wood for platforms, projectiles, powder, grain, wine, and other provisions for the artillery. An enormous artillery train of 1,020 horses followed two days later; it reached San Muñoz with projectiles, tools, and various supplies as well as two pieces of twelve and a twelve-pound mortar. On 7 June a 580-horse convoy again left Salamanca with projectiles and powder, reaching San Muñoz the following day. Simultaneously, 14 wagons to which Ney "attached the greatest importance," departed San Muñoz for Ciudad Rodrigo, transporting the engineers' equipment. Nevertheless, many of the wagons and artillery supplies destined for the Army of Portugal were rerouted to Madrid or Cadiz so the transportation crisis continued. In fact, Lambert was forced to ask Masséna to order that all detached caissons and teams be returned to their battalions and to reprimand severely those, especially general officers, who used the "horses and caissons for their own personal service."[40]

In addition, Eblé, without funds to purchase the most vital necessities for the artillery, wrote to Masséna on 8 June requesting 10,000 francs. Masséna did not reply so he wrote again three days later asking for 5,000 francs "so the expenses of the artillery [would] not delay the works." Recognizing Eblé's legitimate requests as well as the financial problems faced by the army, Masséna wrote to Berthier in Paris the same day, "The service of the artillery and the engineers and the unexpected needs that redouble in the army at each instant demand that today I put at the disposition of the quartermaster general a sum of 68,000 francs of which 12,000 are destined for the artillery, 6,000 for the engineers, and 50,000 for the urgent expenses of all kinds." The following morning, he had 5,000 francs transferred to Eblé. At the same time in Paris, Clarke anticipated Masséna's problems: he authorized Eblé to draw upon the artillery stores at Bayonne and form intermediate depots at Burgos, Valladolid, and Salamanca.[41]

Coupled with these logistical problems, the roads were still in wretched condition. Masséna instructed Eblé to detach his artillerymen to work on the roads "without loss of time." However, the deplorable condition of the roads persisted as Ruty's letter of 8 June clearly demonstrated: "The roads are damaged by the continuous rains that we have experienced for two months, offering the greatest difficulty to the artillery wagons, and especially to the heavy caliber guns. The roads around Ciudad Rodrigo are actually impracticable for heavy artillery. The same circumstances prevent us from occupying the left bank of the Agueda in force."[42]

With preparation for the siege increasing in intensity, Ney became more apprehensive about his ability to carry on the siege without a strong force to support his operations. He had appealed several times for Junot's Corps to be deployed to support him but Masséna refused to commit the 8th Corps until "the roads [were] practical for the artillery to reach Ciudad Rodrigo and subsistence [was] assured." By 9 June, Masséna was convinced that the moment had arrived to begin siege operations; he ordered Junot to move his troops in support of Ney's corps. General Bertrand Clauzel's infantry division, supported by General Ann-François Trelliard's dragoons, was to occupy San Felices el Chico to observe Craufurd's Light Division along the Azaba River. General Jean-Baptiste Solignac's division was to echelon between Ledesma, Zamora, and Toro, seconded by the 4th Dragoons and a battery of light artillery. The regiments of General Joseph Lagrange's division were posted at Salamanca, Puerto de Baños, Tamames, and on the communication route as far as Cabrillas, while General Charles-Marie Escorches de Sainte-Croix's horsemen, with the exception of a regiment observing the Orbigo and the Tera, would concentrate in the vicinity of San Felices el Chico opposite the enemy.[43]

Before these orders could be implemented, a potential crisis developed that threatened Masséna's plans for the invasion of Portugal. On 8 June, an alarming dispatch from General Kellermann reached Salamanca describing an attack on the French garrison of Astorga and several neighboring towns by 5,000 Spanish and 7,000 British troops. Masséna issued immediate instructions for Junot to concentrate Solignac's troops at Zamora while Clauzel's entire division advanced to Ledesma, followed by Sainte-Croix's cavalry, in order to aid General Louis-François Lauberdière and his garrison of 800 men defending Astorga. General Nicolás O'Mahy's force of 5,000 men advanced to Astorga, but they failed to capture the city and retired before French reinforcements arrived. Similarly, the Spanish troops attacking León were repulsed by Chef de bataillon Graffenried and 350 men of the 3d Swiss battalion. Masséna was most apprehensive about these attacks because he feared they were only a diversion for a major attack to be carried out against the 6th Corps by Wellington.[44] Nevertheless, the attack proved to be ineffective and Masséna returned to his plans for the siege of Ciudad Rodrigo.

By mid-June conditions were improving for the French. Masséna wrote an encouraging letter to Junot: "The good weather continues. The roads are drying. M. le maréchal Duc d'Elchingen will be able to open the trenches before Ciudad Rodrigo on 15–16 June." In consequence, Junot was ordered to move his divisions to the positions designated in his instructions of 9 June, in order to cover the 6th Corps against an attack by the British.[45] Yet Masséna was deeply depressed.

Tension between Masséna and his subordinates continued to mount. His authority was flouted before the army corps. Often he would see posted orders of his corps commanders signed as the "General in chief" of the corps while, in fact, he alone held that rank. Similarly, his subordinates wrote directly to the Emperor describing his orders in minute detail. They attempted by subtle insinuations regarding Masséna's judgments to raise doubts in Napoleon's mind. Opposition from the military governors of the provinces under his jurisdiction limited his resources and caused him considerable anxiety. It was evident that Masséna's prediction to Napoleon concerning his subordinates was becoming a reality; in his letters to Berthier he indicated that he could no longer expect the loyal support of either Ney or Junot. This correspondence was read by both Berthier and Napoleon, but they refused to act. Persuaded that he was exaggerating the situation, they were convinced any dissension would fade in the face of the enemy.[46]

It was only on 12 June that Masséna received his first letter from Berthier regarding the Emperor's intentions for the Army of Portugal. Napoleon had learned from his usual source, the English newspapers, that Wellington's army included "only 23,000 English and German, and 22,000 Portuguese" troops. Thus, he calculated, "The Prince d'Essling with the 6th Corps and the remainder of the 8th Corps, making all together more than 50,000 men, ought to take Ciudad Rodrigo, and defeat the English if they advance." At the same time Berthier was instructed to write to the king of Spain that "as the English alone are to be feared, he should place General Reynier with the 2d Corps, under the orders of the Prince d'Essling, to march upon

Alcántara and maneuver on the right bank of the Tagus . . . so this will protect the Prince d'Essling and prevent the siege from being raised."[47] Masséna was depressed by Berthier's letter since it did not consider the perplexing logistical and strategical problems facing his army. Napoleon's instructions were simple but they were based on incomplete information and erroneous assumptions which had little relation to Masséna's predicament. Before the Prince recovered fully from the impact of the first letter, another dispatch, dated 29 May, arrived announcing the increase in Wellington's army to 49,000 men. At the same time the Emperor assumed complete control over the details of the campaign: "I do not choose to enter Lisbon at present, because I should not be able to feed the town and . . . the immense population. . . . The summer must be spent in taking Ciudad Rodrigo, and afterwards Almeida; . . . the campaign must be managed methodically and not by disconnected expeditions." Turning to the complement of the army, Napoleon ordered reorganization of various divisions in Junot's corps, detaching several regiments for service with other units in northern Spain. As a result, "the Prince d'Essling will thus have under his command seven infantry divisions, 54,000 strong, and 11,000 cavalry which make an army of from 65,000 to 70,000 men." In addition, Napoleon promised not only to cover Masséna's northern flank and rear with Kellermann's division but also to send a reserve of 20,000 men to Valladolid. The Emperor concluded reiterating his previous instructions: Masséna "is to besiege with them [6th and 8th Corps] first Ciudad Rodrigo and afterwards Almeida, and will thus prepare himself to march systematically on Portugal, which should not be entered until September, when the heat is over, and, above all, after the harvest."[48] Masséna was stunned and discouraged by this second dispatch. Not only would his freedom of command be drastically limited by Napoleon's orders from Paris, but his army would include only 68,000 men, less than half the number the Emperor had intended for the campaign. Napoleon had conveniently forgotten or ignored his promise to Masséna in Paris that he would lack nothing. Masséna could do little more than appeal for additional support and hope for the best. By this decision, however, Napoleon made one of the most drastic and far-reaching blunders of his career. He had underestimated the staggering problems facing Masséna while miscalculating the determination of Wellington's Anglo-Lusitanian army and the garrison at Ciudad Rodrigo to resist the French juggernaut. Moreover, while his strategy called for the sieges of Ciudad Rodrigo and Almeida, it conveniently coincided with Wellington's scheme for the mobilization of Portugal and continued resistance in the Peninsula.

In the Allied camp during the first two weeks of June, the bulk of Wellington's division retained the positions they had occupied in April. Only Craufurd's Light Division was constantly redeployed. With his headquarters at Gallegos, Craufurd's pickets patrolled the area between the Agueda and the Azaba rivers observing the French outposts on the opposite bank of the Agueda. Ney's cavalry was across the Agueda by 1 June and reconnaissance columns continued to probe Craufurd's pickets, but Wellington was unaware of their crossing until four days later. One British soldier recalled, "We were stationed so close to the outposts of the French, as to render it necessary for the soldiers to sleep fully accoutred, and the officers, consequently, with their clothes on, ready to get under arms in an instant; and we were, as a matter of course, always under arms one hour before break of day. In short, the French cavalry were eternally in motion, in large bodies, towards our chain of posts, and we as often under arms waiting for them." [49]

Besides the continual pressure of the French probes, the pleas of the Spanish Regency regarding Ciudad Rodrigo and the needs of his Portuguese allies, Wellington was plagued by schemes and proposals submitted by the impatient Craufurd, who was Ney's counterpart in the Allied camp; Craufurd wanted to drive in the French pickets, slip additional munitions into the fortress, and maneuver in force against Ney's corps. Indeed, Wellington was anxious about the concentration of the French army around Ciudad Rodrigo, but he was not willing to risk any movement until he was assured of Masséna's intentions. [50]

In a highly personal letter dated 11 June, Wellington wrote to his brother: "This *bicoque* has been in part invested for nearly two months; and a fortnight has elapsed since the guns moved from Salamanca; and the French are not yet in possession of the ground they must have for the siege. This is not the way in which they have conquered Europe!" He complained sarcastically, "Having obliged the

French to collect an army for this enterprise, that is, to make the attack of the worst fortified place in the world, I fear that I can do no more for it. I think that I might have delayed still longer the complete investment of the place . . . if the Government possessed any strength, or desired to have any thing done but what is *safe and cheap*. But, with an army considerably inferior in numbers . . . I think I ought not now to risk a general action in the plains to relieve the place." Yet he did leave his brother with some hope: "I do not yet give the matter up. The defence of a Spanish place must not be reckoned upon according to the ordinary rules. If they will defend themselves as others have, the French must feel the consequences of Massena having weakened every other point to collect this large army." If Masséna reduced his forces against Ciudad Rodrigo, Wellington promised, "I shall be at hand to assist and relieve them." [51]

Apparently Wellington, as Masséna, was subject to periods of depression. On 15 June, he wrote to Hill expressing his worst fears: "I do not feel very confident in the capacity or inclination of the people at Ciudad Rodrigo to hold out, not withstanding all their boasting; and when the enemy shall get possession of that place, he will have it in his power to choose his own point of attack." Simultaneously, he complained to Stuart, "The French have not yet fired a shot at the place, nor have they brought up the heavy ordnance; but the people begin to cry out. I fear, that after their boasting, they will not hold out." [52] Nevertheless, Wellington hoped for the best. If the people and garrison of Ciudad Rodrigo stubbornly resisted the anticipated attack and if the fortress of Almeida delayed the French advance, he hoped for three months, he was confident that Portugal would be saved and the struggle in the Peninsula would continue.

Chapter 6

Open Trenches at Ciudad Rodrigo

AS PREPARATIONS continued at the siege site, detailed plans were drawn up to open the trenches. General Ruty, accompanied by Couche, carefully examined the topography of Grand Teso to determine plans for tracing the trenches and artillery batteries. They surveyed the defenses of the city noting its weaknesses and strengths, especially in the area designated as the point of attack. The curtain of the northeast section of the wall, directly before the cathedral and the King's Tower, was again reaffirmed. Once a decision was made to excavate the first parallel on Grand Teso, it was agreed that the communication trenches would be dug from behind this height to permit the troops easy access to the parallel. The general format for the system of trenches and the locations of the batteries were also laid out. Both Ruty and Couche noted that the convent of Santa Cruz posed a distinct threat to the siege operations.[1] Accordingly, Ney wrote Loison, "We have carefully determined the area where the first parallel will be opened . . . and we realize that the convent to the right, Santa Cruz, now occupied by the enemy, will not impede our workers in achieving their goals but it disturbs them very much."[2] Hence, the convent would have to be seized by a coup de main immediately.

On the night of 9 June, Captain François led 100 chasseurs de siège against the convent. Supported by two companies of voltigeurs and one of grenadiers, François slipped from behind Grand Teso and advanced to the convent where they battered down the door with hatchets. The Spanish were initially surprised and 21 were bayoneted. During the affray François was stabbed and four others were wounded but the convent was seized. The following morning the fortress artillery opened up a heavy and accurate bombardment on the convent, forcing the French to retire with numerous casualties. The Spanish troops reoccupied the convent at once. It seemed clear to the French that Herrasti was determined to contest every French maneuver as the thundering fire from the fortress intimated. Deserters had already reported that each day the governor predicted the arrival of the British who were obliged to support them. Indeed, a crucifix had been placed in the water at the fortress as an appeal to God for rain, and many of the citizens and garrison were convinced the city could not fall.[3]

On the night of 13 June, final plans for the siege reached a feverish pitch as the engineers and sappers made plans to trace the first parallel and the communication trenches. Three hundred chasseurs de siège seized all the remaining Spanish posts to the right of the convent of San Francisco and below the fortress. They established entrenched posts less than 1,200 feet from the walls of the city to tighten the investment, while a double line of cavalry posts was established on the west bank of the Agueda to face both the fortress and the Spanish and British pickets. As soon as Junot's 8th Corps had moved into position to support the siege, Ney prepared to transfer a large infantry unit to the west bank of the river to guarantee the investment. This move did not intimidate the Spanish governor, who sent a column of about 160 cavalry out of the Colada gate and across the Roman bridge to attack Milet's cavalry on the left bank of the Agueda. After less than an hour of skirmishing, Sánchez's cavalry retired into the fortress.[4]

Simultaneously, French reconnaissance columns were increased to determine the exact location, strength, and intentions of the British and Spanish troops beyond the Agueda. Consequently, Ney wrote convincingly to Masséna, "All the particular reports, as well as the spies, seem to confirm that the English will only leave their cantonment when our fire commences. . . . We are assured that Lord Wellington is not disposed to risk a battle with us. All the transports are ready to receive the British army; they are on the road to Lisbon and Oporto and they are already evacuating the sick and the heavy baggage to England."[5]

Despite Ney's impatience, his corps was not yet ready to undertake the siege. General Joseph-Félix Lazowski, assigned by Napoleon to command the engineers of the army, was still at Bayonne trying to secure tools and caissons for the engineers. He had requested a parc of 6,000 tools, 20 caissons, and 120 mules, but with "no funds nor means [at his] disposition" he was ignored by everyone. A small engineer convoy of fourteen caissons laden with equipment did leave Salamanca on 8 June, but Couche was forced to collect all the shovels and picks from the 6th and 8th Corps for use in the trenches. Lazowski had complained to Berthier on 19 June and he included a letter from Masséna, indicating, "The army of Portugal is entirely without caissons and the necessary tools for the engineer service"; he pleaded that they be provided "as promptly as possible." Indeed, 32 caissons carrying 8,000 to 10,000 tools had been sent from Bayonne to Saragossa and a second convoy of 10,000 tools moved to Madrid, but the needs of the Army of Portugal were apparently ignored. Yet, it was satisfying to know the last of the siege pieces was now en route from San Muñoz to Pedrotoro accompanied by the caissons loaded with projectiles and powder. To accommodate these vast quantities of supplies, the engineers threw up a vast storage shed behind Grand Teso under the watchful eye of Ruty.[6]

With siege preparations well advanced, Ney resolved to open the trenches on the night of 15 June. This schedule was announced to Masséna several days earlier but he was deeply involved in logistical and administrative matters, especially the assimilation of Lagrange's regiments into the various divisions of the Army of Portugal.[7] Hence, Masséna was unable to witness the initial trenchwork. In his place he sent General Eblé to observe and assist in the siege operations and to send daily reports on the progress of the siege.[8]

Meanwhile, as French siege preparations were drawing to a close, Ney's headquarters issued detailed instructions early on 14 June for opening the trenches before Ciudad Rodrigo. His divisional commanders, Marchand, Mermet, and Loison, were to organize and provide the necessary manpower for the siege operations. Each division would contribute proportionally to the 2,300 trench workers. Six detachments of 300 or 400 men each were assigned various tasks in the operation, and a seventh unit was to be held in reserve behind Teso. After exchanging their muskets for picks, shovels, and fascines at the engineer's depot behind Grand Teso, the workers waited for dusk; joined by their guards, they marched to their designated areas. They had been instructed by the engineers and sappers, assigned to each detachment, to advance quietly to their positions and lie on their stomachs three feet apart in a line just behind the proposed trench, already traced, and await their officer's orders.[9]

Nine companies of grenadiers, under the command of Chef de bataillon Delomme, were organized to protect the trench workers. They would advance with the workers and then proceed some 50 paces beyond the trenches and lie on their stomachs. Several sentinels and posts would be established in front of them to sound the alarm if the fortress garrison attempted a sortie against the trench workers. In addition to the workers' guards, five companies of infantry commanded by Colonel Fririon were collected and posted behind the trenches to protect them. Three battalions were situated on the crest of Grand Teso just behind the trenches; the others were posted on the flanks.[10]

With all the arrangements successfully completed shortly after dusk, the trench workers waited anxiously for orders to begin digging. Yet, they remained quietly on their stomachs atop the cold damp soil until after the guns of the fortress had begun firing on the false attacks ordered by Ney. One French unit attacked the suburb of Santa Marina on the island and along the west bank of the Agueda below the fortress; a parallel was begun to the east of the fortress beyond the convent of Santo Domingo. With the attention of the garrison concentrated on these attacks, especially at Santa Marina, orders were given at 10:00 P.M. to begin digging. The officers, aware they would be held personally responsible by Ney for any failure, encouraged and pushed their workers as firmly as possible. The laborers continued their work uninterrupted until 3:30 A.M., excavating the parallel to a width of four and one-half feet and a depth of two and one-half feet. In all, 1,400 feet of parallel had been opened up less than 1,500 feet from the fortress, and the communication trenches had been partially completed before the Spanish realized Ney's deception.

The garrison immediately unleashed a heavy bombardment on the parallel, but the French workers were already crouched in the trenches digging below the ground surface. At dawn the workers retired from the trenches and marched back to the depot behind Grand Teso; the guards before the parallel withdrew to the trench to continue digging until the day shift of trench workers arrived to begin work. The guards then retired to their quarters only to reassume their duties again that night. The trench guards behind the parallel were replaced at noon and thereafter in 12-hour shifts just as were the workers' guards and the workers themselves. The casualties suffered by Ney's men during these crucial, dangerous, and highly detailed operations were remarkably light; initially Ney acknowledged 10 dead and 70 wounded, but after careful examination of the regimental rosters he modified the losses to include 18 dead and 49 wounded.[11]

The Spanish, on the contrary, were alarmed by the French success, especially along the left bank of the Agueda. Herrasti sent a column to thwart the French attack on Santa Marina, but it was repulsed and driven back across the old Roman bridge and into the city by Loison's light cavalry. Nevertheless, according to deserters, both the governor and the bishop of the diocese continued to encourage the citizens to resist the French. It had been announced that the French artillery had been stuck along the muddy Spanish roads and would never arrive; they were also told that if the French did bombard the city, the citizens and garrison need only resist for eight days since Ney did not have sufficient munitions or food. So the Spanish were determined to resist each French maneuver, confident the city could survive.[12]

On 16 June, the Spanish bombarded the trenches all day long; yet the first parallel and communications trenches were enlarged and improved but with serious complications. As the workers labored to deepen the trenches, water gushed into the parallel; the heavy spring rains had saturated the ground, forming underground springs. To the right, the water ran into the trench for 300 feet, rendering it "absolutely impracticable." Two gutters were constructed to drain the water from the communications trench on the right, and a large terra cotta aqueduct was fabricated at the center of the parallel to carry water into the garden by the bishop's palace; however, these efforts were inadequate, and the water continued to rise, forcing the troops to withdraw from the right side of the trenches. Those on the left continued to dig; the width of the trench was increased to eight feet, and work was begun on the banquettes where the soldiers would stand to fire on the fortress.[13]

At four o'clock the following morning, 17 June, Herrasti sent a sortie against the French. Thirty infantry supported by 200 soldiers from the convent of San Francisco advanced against the left flank of the trenches to reconnoiter or, if possible, attack the trench workers. Although the guards attacked the Spanish troops driving them back toward the convent, it was obvious that a flanking trench would have to be excavated to repulse further attacks from that direction. Accordingly, the next two nights were devoted to digging the flanking trench while other detachments totaling 600 men extended and improved the parallel. Three hundred and sixty feet of trench were excavated to complete the flanking trench; the banquettes were completed along the entire parallel, which was enlarged to ten feet in width and four feet in depth. The engineers sought to drain some of the water from the trenches; with the formation of slit drains through the parapets, the water began to recede in the trenches, but the men still had to work in mud up to their knees while the laborers on the extreme right were not yet able to return to the trenches.[14]

By the evening of 19 June, seven pieces of twelve had reached Pedrotoro after a three-day trip from San Muñoz, and they were soon followed by pieces of sixteen. However, the pieces of twenty-four remained at the depot because of the muddy roads in the vicinity of Alba de Yeltes. The road by way of Sancti Spiritus was reconnoitered. Soon a decision was made to detour the heavy artillery along this road, but the problem was hardly solved since forty caissons were stuck in the quagmire between Alba de Yeltes and Pedrotoro. Eblé had already requested troops from both the 6th and 8th Corps to improve the roads for the passage of the heavy artillery and caissons, but his appeals had been ignored. In the meantime, as the siege train was moving lubriciously toward Ciudad Rodrigo, Eblé and Ruty supervised the construction of six gun batteries—one before the bishop's palace and five on the heights of Grand Teso. With a total of 18 howitzers, 10 mortars, and 28 siege guns strategically placed to take advantage of Grand Teso's elevation, the guns of each battery could strike both the main wall and the faussebraie without risking an overcharge.[15]

As the siege preparations continued uninterrupted, Ney still nursed illusions of a possible attack on the British. His cavalry had been in constant contact with their British counterparts for many weeks. On 19 June, Ney posted the 76th Line on the road to Espeja supported by Milet's dragoons on its left while a battalion of the 15th Léger occupied a position before Fonseca on the route to Carpio to observe the British posts. Craufurd, commanding the British advance guard, countered with a reconnaissance along the rideau of Carpio and he doubled his vedettes and posts. La Carrera then sent 50 or 60 of the Queen's Dragoons and some lancers behind the 76th Line on the road to Puebla de Azaba, but they were drawn off by Milet's horsemen. On 21 June, the 76th Line set out on the road to Carpio where they observed a reconnaissance column of about 100 Portuguese horsemen and some infantry, but there was no skirmishing. At 10:00 A.M. an Allied column of 800 cavalry and 600 infantry supported by two cannon moved on the French posts along the Carpio road near the Agueda. Hearing the gunfire, Loison immediately ordered up two battalions of infantry and four squadrons of cavalry to support his posts. Two battalions of the 15th Léger skirted the west bank of the Agueda and moved into the farm and a part of the woods to the right of a French cavalry post. The 3d Hussars were ordered to march directly on Marialba, the 15th Chasseurs à cheval were to advance on Carpio, and the 15th and 25th Dragoons commanded by Gardanne and Cavrois were to move between these two cavalry units as a reserve.[16]

General Ferey pursued the Allied column and seized Carpio with two companies of the 15th Léger, supported by two platoons of dragoons and the 15th Chasseurs à cheval. After some exchange of musket and pistol fire, the British infantry and cavalry withdrew from the village. The French seized and burned the guardhouse in the village but not before the British had set their signal fires. In less than an hour, troops from the various Allied posts in the vicinity had gathered in the ravine between Carpio and Marialba to launch a counterattack. With some 1,500 horses and between 6,000 and 7,000 infantry, supported by six pieces of light artillery and two field pieces placed behind an epaulement between Carpio and Marialba, they advanced in line against the French. At the same time another detachment estimated at 32 platoons of British infantry and four squadrons of cavalry appeared on the road from Espeja, escorting a supply convoy. When they sighted what appeared to be a major confrontation with the French, they moved rapidly to support the Allied columns. After a cursory examination of the enemy's position and strength, Loison ordered his men to withdraw behind their posts along the west bank of the Agueda. Describing this reconnaissance, Loison wrote to Ney, "The result of all these maneuvers [indicates] that the enemy prepares to attempt some operations against the troops placed on the left bank of the Agueda." He suggested that the French occupy the heights of Marialba and Carpio to control the narrow defile through which the enemy would have to pass in order to attack the French positions. Then, if the Allies did advance, they could be delayed until Clauzel's division united with the 15th and 25th Dragoons or until the French troops could withdraw to the bridgehead at the Loro bridge.[17]

Based upon these reconnaissance reports and the continuing enemy pressure, Ney again turned to his favorite project—an attack on the British. Pointing out that circumstances "were very favorable" for an attack on the enemy, he noted, "The army of Lord Wellington is not camped in line; it is in column echeloned from Carpio to beyond Fort La Concepcion. General Craufurd will evidently be compromised if we march on him with the dispatch and the resolution of which the army is capable; this maneuver would have the most favorable results, or at least, cause the English army to withdraw far from here, and permit us to become masters of Ciudad Rodrigo, eliminating any obstacles for us to fear henceforth." He continued, "I believe that the fortress will be in our power in eight days if it is not aided by the British."[18] Although Ney was determined to attack the enemy, Masséna had already sent his chief of staff and first aide-de-camp to convince him that such a movement was inappropriate. "The Marshal

Figure 26. San Felices el Chico

listened to all this reasoning with patience but was not convinced," recalled Pelet.[19]

In addition to his continual agitation for an offensive, Ney still complained about the serious lack of food and its related problems. When Masséna moved the 8th Corps forward to support the siege, Clauzel's division was sent to San Felices el Chico and Loison's division was ordered to draw closer to the siege. However, Loison bitterly opposed this change complaining, "I have lost all the organizations that I have formed with great difficulty such as the ambulance and the magazines, the ovens, the army stores, and finally all the resources or means which make it possible for my corps to subsist." The quartermaster general could not provide adequate supplies and Loison had only two days' rations on hand, so he appealed to Ney to have Clauzel's troops sent to San Felices de los Gallegos. Ney took up this argument when writing Masséna on 19 June. The Prince was sympathetic, but it was obvious Clauzel's entire division could not be accommodated at San Felices de los Gallegos; some of his units would have to remain at San Felices el Chico until ovens and other accommodations could be constructed at San Felices de los Gallegos. This response seemed ludicrous to Loison; several times he had unsuccessfully requested workers to construct ovens for his division. With only one uncompleted oven available, Loison found it "impossible to continue the distribution of rations to the soldiers." Moreover, he was forced to deny subsistence to the colonel of the Hanoverian Legion, declaring that no more than four or five pounds of meat existed in his division.[20] This scarcity was even evident at Masséna's headquarters, and the distribution of food became a point of contention. When General Sainte-Croix captured some 400 head of cattle during a reconnaissance, they were given to the 8th Corps. Masséna was forced to intervene; he declared the distribution "null and void" and instructed Lambert to send half of the cattle to the 6th Corps.[21]

There was no question that inadequate supplies were a serious problem, especially for the troops of the 6th Corps actually engaged in the siege; they had little time to forage even if food could be found in the exhausted countryside because of constant threats of attack from the enemy in the fortress or across the Agueda. When Pelet visited the 6th Corps before Ciudad Rodrigo, he recorded, "We slept with General Marchand's division. The conversation there was only about the lack of food. The shortage was so severe that we could not obtain bread, forage, or lodging for our escort of five dragoons. According to several of the officers, abandoning the siege was the only way to relieve this misery."[22] However, aid was on the way. On 18 June, 23 caissons left Salamanca with 35 ton of flour for Mermet's division; 22 mules and 60 donkeys carried over 16 ton of flour and a ton of salt to Marchand's division followed by four caissons laden with hospital supplies. The following day 60 head of cattle, almost eight ton of meal carried by 30 mules, and additional foodstuffs piled atop four requisition wagons left for Ney's headquarters. On 20 June, 25 more caissons departed Salamanca for the 6th Corps; 20 wagons carried flour and five were laden with shoes for the infantry.[23]

As the great bulk of Ney's corps became committed to the siege, he appealed to Masséna for the 8th Corps to cover his operations. The Prince was in full accord and wrote to Junot, "If [Ney] is attacked, at first notice you will unite your corps at San Felices el Chico or San Felices el Grande [de los Gallegos] following the movements of the enemy. . . . It is wise that you place yourself in the center of your troops in order to execute, if needed, the orders that I will give you." He cautioned, "If Ney informs you that the enemy is marching on him, you are to unite your corps and maneuver according to circumstances without awaiting my orders."[24]

With the necessary arrangements completed to support and sustain the siege, Ney's operations were pushed ahead vigorously. On 20 June, the sixth night of open trenches, the sappers opened two approaches, often referred to as zigzags, *boyaux*, or *cheminements*, in front of the parallel; these approaches were trenches constructed in zigzag fashion toward the point of attack. The approach on the right was excavated 90 feet to the right of the communication trench for a distance of 672 feet; at right angles with the wall of the convent of Santa Cruz, it reached a point 480 feet from the convent. The approach to the left was advanced 360 feet to the left of the tower at the convent of San Francisco; both approaches were at least three feet deep and four feet in width. The French artillery was arriving to protect the trench workers but in the meantime the chasseurs de siège were posted in foxholes large enough for three men, 100 paces before the workers; they were to pick off the enemy artillerymen who were detected on the fortress ramparts.[25]

The following night a gang of workers executed a return of 360 feet on the approach to the right while others labored to widen it to nine feet, construct banquettes, and heighten the parapets to protect the trench workers. A line of skirmishers was moved into advance positions, perhaps 150 feet from the walls of the convent of Santa Cruz, but the effective fire of the fortress and the convent exacted a high casualty rate. At the same time the engineers and artillerymen began the construction of six batteries; five batteries were soon well advanced but the emplacement on the extreme left progressed slowly as a result of the rocky soil. Through the evening and night of 22 June, Couche's sappers labored to perfect the approaches while the parapets were completed along the entire development of the first parallel. Work continued on the batteries and the communication trenches from the first parallel to the gun emplacements; the embrasures were traced and some of the guns were partially armed as Ruty and Eblé anxiously prepared for the initial bombardment.[26]

While the French continued work before the fortress, Herrasti encouraged his artillerymen whose accuracy took a terrible toll of Frenchmen. Some casualties were sustained by the garrison troops but they were inconsequential in comparison with the French losses. However, the time was soon approaching when the French artillery would be armed, bombardment of the city would begin, and the Spanish monopoly of firepower would be challenged. According to a deserter, Herrasti toured the ramparts on 20 June, praising his troops and announcing the arrival of letters from the governor of Almeida and General La Carrera; he indicated that 40,000 British and Portuguese troops would march to their aid. Nevertheless, he realized that Julián Sánchez and his corps of lancers would soon be blockaded in the fortress unless they broke out. Accordingly, at 2:00 A.M. on 23 June, Sánchez slipped out of the city with approximately 100 men along the road to Fuente Guinaldo. Sánchez surprised the French post, killing three and wounding 15, but he lost four dead and 20 wounded in the daring escape. With French confidence shaken in its cordon of posts around the fortress, Herrasti resolved to redouble his efforts against the enemy. He had several cannon moved into the

Figure 27. Ciudad Rodrigo: The monument to Don Julián Sánchez, "El Charro," on city wall

faussebraie; a new mortar battery was organized and it fired rapidly with considerable effect, claiming eight dead and twenty wounded within twenty-four hours.[27]

By the afternoon of 23 June, it had become obvious to Ney and his staff that the convent of Santa Cruz would have to be seized since it threatened the approach on the right and caused many casualties among the workers. Consequently, Ney issued orders for Mermet and Marchand to make flanking attacks on the right and left of the convent of San Francisco to serve as a diversion. Simultaneously, Loison would organize and carry out an assault on the convent of Santa Cruz. After dusk 300 men were concentrated at the front of the approach, commonly referred to as the *tête de sape*, for the attack. One hundred fifty chasseurs de siège and 20 sappers under the command of Captain Meltzen, moving from south to north, were to attack the rear gate of the convent wall, while a second column under Captain François, advancing in the same direction, would attack the front gate. A third force of three companies of grenadiers of the 82d Line would attack the convent, moving from the north, under the direction of Chef de bataillon Rocherond.[28]

At midnight, after the moon had been obscured by clouds, the columns moved across the open ground toward the convent. Meltzen's sappers blew in the barricaded gate near the chapel and entered the courtyard of the convent complex. François's column successfully broke through the front gate and joined Meltzen's men. The Spanish garrison of the convent, composed of the third battalion of the Avila Regiment commanded by Don Antonio Rodríguez Camarga, retired to the main building of the complex after stubborn resistance. With a small contingent of perhaps 15 men, François pursued the Spanish troops to the cloister and Meltzen's sappers blew open the door. François led his troops into the building just as Captains Ildefonso Preita and Angel Castellanos withdrew their defenders, perhaps 100 men of the Avila Regiment, to the upper floors of the structure. As they retreated up the staircase, the stair treads were taken up to delay the French pursuit. François tried to lead his men up the dismantled staircase "with saber in one hand and a torch in the other," but he was shot dead and his men driven back. Hoping to rally the French, Meltzen then attempted to climb the stairs only to be hit twice; he fell, mortally wounded. The French fell back but the brutal gunfire continued for over two and one-half hours.[29]

While the fighting continued around the cloister, Captain Clemins-Louis Treussart, with a small detachment of 25 men, successfully detonated 100 pounds of powder against the convent wall, opening a gaping hole opposite the French trenches; the French would now have easy access to the convent in any subsequent attack. Treussart gathered the disorganized troops of François and Meltzen, ignited the chapel and several other buildings in the complex, and retired to the

French trenches under the murderous fire of the Spanish riflemen in the upper windows of the cloister. The other attack planned for the 82d Line failed to materialize effectively due to Rocherond's incompetence, and his troops returned to the trenches without engaging the Spanish. This misguided attack inflated the French casualty rate to 15 dead and 53 wounded. The Spanish sustained some losses, but Herrasti was elated with the success of Camarga's regiment. Not only were the determined attacks on the convent of Santa Cruz repulsed, but the diversionary attacks of Mermet and Marchand were turned back. That night the governor wrote in his journal, "The night was full of glory for us, and they paid dearly for the single barbaric satisfaction they gained" in burning some buildings at the convent of Santa Cruz.[30]

While Loison's attacks were carried out against Santa Cruz, the sappers continued the approaches; the one to the right was excavated 360 feet, parallel to the convent of Santa Cruz, and the approach on the left was extended 300 feet toward Little Teso. The workers in the approach near the convent were forced to retire when the fires from the burning buildings illuminated their movements and made them excellent targets for the Spanish marksmen on the city ramparts. Work was also continued on the batteries; the parapets were completed and the construction of about fifteen platforms was well under way. By dawn Batteries Nos. 1, 2, and 4 had been completed, the first two armed and the other in the final stages of construction. During the day one approach was improved; the one on the right was expanded in width to six feet and sunk to a depth two and one-half feet, but the approach on the left was not occupied by the workers because of the heavy fire from the convent of Santa Cruz, still partially occupied by the Avila Regiment.[31]

Meanwhile back at headquarters in Salamanca, Masséna encouraged his quartermaster general, Lambert, to accelerate the collection of food and to speed the convoy on the journey to the siege site. With the successful collection of foodstuff in the districts and provinces of Palencia, Valladolid, Avila, Zamora, Segovia, Arévalo, Toro, Salamanca, Peñaranda, and Medina del Campo, 100 ton of wheat, 92 ton of barley and rye, 200 gallons of wine, 1,300 head of cattle, and

1,500 head of sheep had been collected within an eleven-day period ending on 19 June, thus assuring the troops of a basic food supply during a critical stage in the siege operations. However, less food would be gathered in the future by the troops of the 6th and 8th Corps because those troops assigned to forage duty would be recalled before the artillery opened fire on the fortress. Consequently, all available vehicles of every description were pressed into service. As soon as teams could be secured, the convoys fanned out along the road from Salamanca hauling food to the various divisions of the 6th and 8th Corps.[32]

With the actual bombardment drawing near, Lambert made a special effort to move as large a quantity of foodstuff as possible. On 20 June, he sent 20 ton of wheat, 4,272 rations of biscuit, and 2,700 pairs of shoes to Ney's headquarters at La Caridad. The following day 30 requisition wagons, carrying 25 ton of flour, and 50 mules laden with wheat set out for Mermet's division at Sancti Spiritus while 18 caissons moved toward San Felices el Chico loaded with 9,752 rations of biscuit for the troops of Clauzel and Loison. On 22 June, 40 mules dragged 10 ton of wheat to Sancti Spiritus and a convoy of three wagons followed by a long line of mules carried six ton of grain to San Muñoz. To support Junot's 8th Corps, Lambert dispatched convoys of 30 caissons and 14 requisition wagons to his headquarters carrying 17,500 rations of biscuit, 35 ton of grain, and 150 head of cattle. At the same time, 20,000 rations of biscuit were sent on to Loison and Clauzel at San Felices el Chico; 74 mules were driven toward Mermet's headquarters at Sancti Spiritus with an additional eight ton of wheat while 100 rations of bread were shipped to Matilla. On 24 June, another scheduled convoy destined for the 6th Corps left Salamanca with 50,000 rations of rice and all the grain that could be carried in the caissons of the 4th Equipment Battalion, 30 pack mules, and the requisition wagons of the artillery parc.[33]

With the basic administrative work completed at Salamanca, Masséna resolved to vacate his headquarters at the University of Salamanca on 24 June and move to La Caridad to assume a more active role in the siege. However, Lambert was instructed to remain at Salamanca where the army's main depots were located; he was to continue the steady stream of supplies to the army and to solve the nagging logistical problems that persisted. On 25 June, a number of convoys left Salamanca for the 6th and 8th Corps. One column of 27 caissons carrying 12,378 rations of biscuit, three ton of salt, two ton of barley, 800 rations of white bread, and almost 18 ton of coarse grain, trailed by four wagons of brandy and 100 head of beef, advanced toward the 6th Corps. A second wagon train of seven caissons moved to San Muñoz with 6,222 rations of biscuit, and a third column of 36 mules carrying grain, rice, and barley followed by a wagon of wine traveled to the 8th Corps. Lambert anticipated additional requisitions would soon be collected and made available for the army; nevertheless, he appealed to officials in Paris for permission to have 353,844 rations of biscuit transferred from the depot in Bayonne to the magazines in Valladolid for use by the Army of Portugal. By 26 June, his request had been approved and forwarded to Berthier for final action.[34]

Despite Lambert's success in collecting and distributing these vast quantities of food, he still faced serious problems. The 68,000 francs advanced to him by Masséna on 10 June for Eblé, Couche, and the most pressing needs of the army had been exhausted within two weeks, and another 50,000 francs were necessary to meet the needs of the army. Wagons and caissons were again detained at their destination rather than immediately returned for continued use. Moreover, a strong case had to be made in order to retain the armed escorts so vital for the protection of the convoys. Supplies for the hospitals, especially at Valladolid, caused Lambert considerable grief and forced him to appeal to Kellermann for support "in the moment of crisis." The cost and maintenance of the system of posts along the communication routes were also a constant concern to Lambert, but they were ultimately maintained by funds from the army treasury.[35]

When Masséna left Salamanca on 24 June, he left many of his logistical problems behind but encountered new tactical difficulties that taxed his patience and abilities. He was concerned about the ambiguous role of the British army, writing to Berthier on the day before he left, "We could hope to be masters of this place soon if it were abandoned to its own forces; but the movements made by the English army appear to announce its intentions to defend it or delay its reduction."[36] Upon Masséna's arrival at the site of the siege operations, he transferred his residence to the monastery of La Caridad and Ney shifted his headquarters to one of the engineer's sheds behind Grand Teso. Now the full power of the besieging army was to be unleashed against Ciudad Rodrigo.

Chapter 7

The Bombardment and Supporting Operations at Ciudad Rodrigo

ALTHOUGH Masséna was establishing his état-major comfortably in the spacious quarters at La Caridad and Ney had taken up quarters three miles away behind Grand Teso, a serious controversy erupted between the two marshals. According to Pelet, 27 June had been designated as the date to commence fire on the fortress and not earlier than the 26th. Despite this decision, Ney resolved to begin the bombardment early on the morning of the 25th; apparently he hoped the fortress would fall at once and he would be given credit for the victory while Masséna was far away. Unknown to Ney, Masséna had already arrived at La Caridad. Consequently, when Ney issued orders to commence fire the following morning, Eblé informed the Prince immediately. Masséna was furious and sent Pelet and Fririon to Ney's headquarters without delay. Pelet recalled, "We had hardly arrived when the Prince himself came, complaining about the haste and the disastrous effects it might have." After a heated conversation which created new animosity and distrust between Masséna and Ney, it was agreed that the bombardment would begin early the next morning. [1]

At 3:00 A.M. on 25 June, Ruty alerted his artillerymen, and an hour later orders were given to commence firing on the fortress. According to an eyewitness, "At dawn every battery opened fire at the same time with all 46 of their guns. At first the city appeared disconcerted. Initially, it replied with rather sporadic and uncertain fire; later there was a more intensive fire from a number of guns which were superior to ours and of a larger caliber. Soon guns were firing vigorously from both sides and the noise was terrible." [2] The howitzers, although heavily bombarded by the Spanish, fired over 600 shells the first day scoring a direct hit on a powder magazine, dismounting a large gun, and overthrowing a segment of the rampart. The mortars ignited a number of fires in the suburbs and inside the fortress, causing havoc among the inhabitants, killing 150 and wounding 500. The Spanish responded effectively, and before the day had ended they had silenced every gun in Battery No. 6. Another Spanish shell ignited an expense magazine between Batteries Nos. 5 and 6, exploding 900 pounds of powder, ruining the epaulement, and putting a temporary halt to several guns. These explosions claimed the lives of 12 cannoneers and wounded 42. At the same time, the trench workers and their guard suffered inordinate losses as the musket fire from the convent of Santa Cruz, supplemented by the heavy bombardment from the fortress, resulted in 21 dead and 162 wounded.[3]

While the French were commencing their bombardment of the city, the terrain beyond the Agueda was firmly secured. Gardanne led the cavalry of Lorcet and Cavrois across the Agueda, driving the British pickets beyond the Azaba River. Gardanne's brigade camped on the west bank of the Agueda to the left of the 15th Léger, where an artillery battery was established. Lorcet's brigade moved forward to the heights of Marialba and Cavrois's brigade drove in the Allied posts with little opposition, occupying a position on the ridge of Carpio. Two cavalry squadrons were posted to observe the approaches and ravine of the Azaba; two other squadrons took up positions at Fonseca supported on the left by Milet's cavalry. Loison ordered Ferey to move a battalion of infantry up on the wooded heights dominating Marialba to support Gardanne, with units extending back to the Agueda so the Allies could not turn the right flank of the French posts. Craufurd, in response, withdrew his troops behind the Azaba but retained his positions at Espeja, Vilar Formoso, and Gallegos.[4]

On the eleventh night of open trench, 25 June, the sappers continued work perfecting the approach on the left while a second return was excavated on the approach to the right in order to open a trench toward the wall of Santa Cruz. At 11:00 P.M., 300 grenadiers attacked the convent, which had been pounded by artillery. The troops entered without difficulty thanks to the two breaches blown in the wall by the sappers. The convent was seized with little opposition and the

Figure 28. General Jean-Baptiste Eblé

Spanish retired to the fortress. Three gaping breaches were made in the convent wall to permit easy access in case of a counterattack, and 150 men were left in the garden and a barricaded building while the upper floors of the convent were burned. With the convent of Santa Cruz firmly in the hands of the French, Ney found his men within 360 feet of the fortress glacis and in possession of the ground necessary to protect their approach to the right. While the attack was carried out, Ruty's artillerymen, supplemented by 300 trench workers, labored feverishly to repair the damage of the preceding day. There was little fire from the fortress to obstruct their efforts because the Spanish were working to clear away the debris, repair their battered fortifications, and prepare their batteries for another day's fire. At four o'clock the following morning the artillery fire commenced. Battery No. 6, on the extreme right, ignited a Spanish magazine; howitzers and mortars dropped incendiary shells into the town causing numerous fires and exploding two powder magazines. The main batteries continued to pound the revetment, the parapet of the enlarged salient, and the curtain wall as far as the King's Tower in front of the cathedral. In response, the Spanish maintained a continual and accurate fire on the French positions, exacting heavy casualties.[5]

When Masséna visited the siege site to examine the trench work and the artillery operations during the first day of the bombardment, he was obviously dissatisfied with the efforts of Ruty and Couche. He issued instructions to utilize pieces of sixteen and twenty-four to blast a breach in the fortress wall, to draw artillerymen from the 6th and 8th Corps, to limit the use of projectiles, and to send all available caissons to Salamanca for additional powder and shells. At the same time he wrote to General Eblé, "You will order General Ruty to do nothing in the future except what you order, based upon my instructions. You will write a report to me each night on what has passed in the day and one in the morning on what has occurred in the night." He cautioned Eblé, "Everything demands that this siege be conducted with the greatest vigor. It is important to the health of the army that it be ended as soon as possible. Do not neglect the art of siege warfare so the fortress of Rodrigo falls. I will only leave the bivouac when it is in our power." So Masséna had a hut thrown up near the hamlet of Casasola by Grand Teso to insure the prompt fulfillment of his orders.[6]

Masséna was greeted by other disappointing news. While he was reconnoitering siege deployments, Julián Sánchez attacked a detachment of foragers from Mermet's division less than three miles from Trelliard's quarters. Although the French had only three dead and 15 wounded while the Spanish suffered four dead and about 20 wounded, they were forced to acknowledge that the Spanish guerrillas were still able to carry out their raids with relative impunity in the midst of the French army.[7]

As the approach to the left crept slowly toward the fortress, the workers came under the murderous fusillade of the Spanish garrison in the convent and suburb of San Francisco. Ney decided to attack it; on the evening of 26 June, Captain Martin, with a force gathered from the trench workers, marched against the convent supported by 20 sappers carrying powder and the necessary excavating tools. They soon came under such devastating fire from the convent and the fortress that the men were forced back immediately in disorder, leaving Captain Jean-Pierre Cathala of the sappers at the convent gate; he waited until dawn and slipped back to the French lines. This abortive attack cost the French 25 casualties and undermined the morale of the men in the trenches. While the attack was mounted against San Francisco, the second return of the approach to the right was advanced 360 feet and a third return of 360 feet was opened in the direction of the northern salient of the town. At the same time Captain Treussart traced a flying sap in spite of the heavy fire of musket and grape from the fortress. On the approach to the left, a third return was excavated toward the graveyard of Calvary on Little Teso. The French howitzer batteries continued their fire throughout the night; within twenty-four hours they had fired over 1,200 shells, exploding one powder magazine and turning isolated areas of the town into holocausts.[8]

At daybreak on 27 June, the French guns redoubled their activity. Although the mortars and howitzers had fired all night at the rate of 60 to 70 shells, Eblé and his staff soon saw the added effect of all 46 guns in operation. With the change in composition of the batteries, as Masséna had ordered, the batteries bombarded the breach and faussebraie with considerable success; several Spanish guns were overthrown in duels with their French counterparts and fires burned uncontrollably throughout the city. The fortress cannoneers also inflicted serious damage on the French; two pieces of twelve were dismounted and a piece of sixteen was blown up, causing ten casualties. The trench work progressed more slowly during the night. By dawn the third return of the approach on the right had been excavated to the wall below the convent of Santa Cruz and a fourth return of ninety feet had been dug, but the workers were forced to evacuate the trench temporarily when the enemy turned several pieces on them. On the left the third return of the approach was begun with a flying sap of 460 feet.[9]

The mortars and howitzers continued to bombard the city and suburbs throughout the night. The following morning, 28 June, the main or breach batteries, Nos. 4 and 5, again opened fire on the breach, the adjoining wall, and faussebraie while the other batteries fired on the various defenses and interior of the city. A powder magazine was exploded before noon, igniting an expense magazine of shells; the Spanish continued firing but at a noticeably reduced rate. By 2:00 P.M. the breach seemed to be complete; the faussebraie and a segment of the main wall appeared to be in ruin. Ruty surveyed the breach and announced to Ney that it was practicable. Apparently there was some disagreement since the counterscarp remained intact, but Ruty's judgment prevailed.[10]

Accordingly, Ney sent an aide-de-camp, Captain Esmenard, to the fortress under a flag of truce to deliver a summons to Herrasti. Ney announced in his letter: "His Highness, the Prince d'Essling, . . . has ordered me to make this last summons. I am pleased to render justice to your fine defense and to the courage that the troops of your garrison have shown but these efforts, always recognized by the French army, will destroy you if you continue your defense much longer." He cautioned, "Although with regret, the Prince d'Essling will be forced to treat you with all the rigor that the laws of war authorize. If you hoped to be aided by the English, you are deceived. How could you fail to realize that if this had been their intention, under no condition would they have permitted Ciudad Rodrigo to be reduced to such a deplorable condition? Your situation can only grow worse. You have to choose between honorable capitulation and the terrible vengeance of a victorious army."[11]

The governor of the city presented the details of Ney's summons to the town junta; it was rejected after lengthy deliberations. When Esmenard returned to the French camp, he carried a letter from Herrasti who announced: "After forty-nine years in the service, I know the laws of war and my military duty. The fortress of Ciudad Rodrigo is not in a state to capitulate and no breach is formed that makes it necessary. In consequence, I can only invite your Excellency to continue your operations against the fortress. I will know myself . . . when the circumstances are such as to request capitulation after taking care to protect my honor which is more dear to me than life itself."[12] Ney was disappointed by Herrasti's decision and he immediately ordered the bombardment to commence again. Before Esmenard returned to Ney's headquarters, Spanish officers plied him with misinformation about the low morale of the garrison, the "perfidy of the English," and the fact that the fortress could resist no more than "four or five days."[13] This intelligence was sent on to Masséna and soon became common knowledge throughout the army. When the fortress did not fall five days later, the effect of this Spanish propaganda on French morale became devastating.

The French artillery was firing by 6:00 P.M. and the trench work was begun again, but Ney was disturbed and possibly embarrassed by the premature summons. Ruty justified his recommendation by reminding Ney that several Spanish soldiers had climbed down to the bottom of the breach from the fortress walls and reascended a few minutes later proving the breach was practicable; however, this was hardly convincing since the counterscarp was still undamaged. Ney and the French were also galled by what they regarded as Spanish violation of the two-hour truce; during the lull in the fighting, the garrison constructed a parapet of sandbags across the ridge of the breach, cleared the debris from the bottom of the ditch, and repaired the gun emplacements along the northern wall.[14]

While the hopes of Ney and the 6th Corps had been dashed by the defiant letter of Herrasti, the governor drew new confidence from the French summons. He recorded in his journal, "Marshal Ney, infu-

riated at seeing his proposals rejected and the terrorism with which
he threatened us scorned, . . . ordered all his guns to open fire
again." The Spanish responded with all their artillery along the northern wall as mortar and howitzer shells showered the town. Shots from
the heavy French siege pieces struck the tower of the cathedral and
houses were burning throughout the town, but organized bands of
citizens methodically went about their assigned duties, combating the
fires, supplying munitions to the ramparts, and aiding the wounded.
Herrasti recalled that two blind beggars and many women and children were carrying ammunition and water to the soldiers on the ramparts throughout the siege: "Excited by examples of their parents and
by the patriotic spirit exhibited by the garrison and inhabitants of the
town and further encouraged by the sight of the danger, [the children]
demonstrated a most ardent zeal for the public cause and the fact that
noble and valiant Castilian blood ran through their veins." [15]

That night Herrasti, fearing an attack on the suburbs, especially
in the area around the convent of San Francisco, dispatched a column
of 300 infantry and 50 horsemen to establish themselves before the
walls of the convent. However, the French were probably too disheartened with the rejection of their summons to undertake such an
attack; in addition, soon after the French had resumed fire on the fortress, the Spanish scored a direct hit on a piece of sixteen and disabled a piece of twelve. Eblé's mortars and howitzers continued to
bombard the town throughout the night but the Spanish demonstrated
distinct superiority in firepower. The sappers had again begun to dig
their approaches toward the northeastern wall of the fortress. The
fourth return of the approach on the right was pushed 300 feet. Before the excavation was two feet deep the Spanish unleashed a staggering bombardment on the front of the sap with five cannon at approximately 4:00 A.M. that overthrew 30 gabions and drove the
workers out of the trench for five hours, causing 14 casualties. The
approach to the left, partially obscured from the Spanish on the ramparts, was continued without interruption, until it reached a point
480 feet from the crest of the glacis. [16]

The following morning, 29 June, the breach batteries recommenced fire on the breach, repaired by the garrison during the truce,
and before noon it was again in ruin. Nevertheless, the assault could

not be ordered because the counterscarp was still intact. It could only be destroyed when the suburbs and convent of San Francisco were in French hands. To accomplish this dangerous task, orders had already been issued the previous day for the construction of Battery No. 7, composed of three pieces of twelve, located to the left of Battery No. 6; this battery was to bombard San Francisco and its suburbs into submission. In addition, Ruty ordered the construction of two additional mortar and howitzer batteries, designated as Nos. 8 and 9, to bombard the suburbs and convent of San Francisco; the former would be located in the front of a cemetery and the latter at a site opposite the point of attack.[17] Nevertheless, the French faced serious problems since the fronts of the approaches were still 480 feet from the crest of the glacis. According to an eyewitness, "There was noticeable deliberation and hesitation in the operation. The trenches were making little progress. The approaches were sometimes poorly laid out. A few of them were enfiladed, especially on 29 June. The fire of the enemy regained its superiority; our guns fired little."[18] As a result a piece of twenty-four and one of twelve were disabled by the Spanish guns and the casualties totaled 21 that day.

Later that day, another controversy erupted between Masséna and Ney over a report submitted by Ruty and Couche. They had written to Ney noting the lack of progress in the siege operations and cautioning that the supply of projectiles for the pieces of sixteen and twenty-four was dangerously low. With less than 600 rounds remaining for these guns, they suggested the gunfire be carefully restricted and guns of smaller caliber be employed. "The only measure to take," they wrote, "in order to assure the success of the siege is to conserve the supply of large caliber projectiles exclusively for the period when we shall attack the breach with the certitude of establishing ourselves there immediately." Perhaps the most disconcerting aspect of the letter was the statement that they would not be able to crown the glacis "before eight or ten days." Ney forwarded this letter to Masséna with the comment that he "had initiated the project that they had recommended." Without doubt, he must have been appalled by their suggestions. It was only three weeks since he had reconnoitered the fortress with Masséna; and the artillery commanders had promised them "that within three hours the fire of the enemy would be silenced, that in a few days the fortress would be captured, and that with the establishment of the first battery a breach would be opened in both walls."[19]

Masséna was furious with this report. According to his aide-de-camp, "Apparently it was an attempt to blame the error of rushing the siege operations on the Prince, who had ordered the batteries to fire." Masséna and his staff "thought this report was made to justify the delays and relieve him [Ney] of the responsibility for erroneous decisions." There was no doubt that munitions were disappearing, food was being consumed, the soldiers were suffering, casualties were mounting, and "poor use of the remaining munitions could reduce [the French] either to a bloody but fruitless attack on a partially completed breach or to the disgrace of raising the siege."[20] Masséna recalled the boasts made by Ruty and Couche when he had reconnoitered the fortress with Ney earlier in the month, as well as Ruty's letter of 8 June, which promised, "On arriving at about 300 feet from the glacis, the sappers will have nothing or almost nothing to fear from the walls [and as soon as the trenches are opened] the siege will not drag on long if it is sufficiently covered by an observation corps."[21] Yet such predictions were unfulfilled as the Spanish garrison continued their determined defense. Fearing a protracted siege and enormous losses in manpower and resources, Masséna resolved to initiate major changes in the siege operations.

Masséna impatiently convened a meeting of Ney, his divisional generals, and the commanding artillery and engineer officers to express his concerns and announce his decisions concerning siege operations. Since General Lazowski had not yet reached the army, Masséna ordered Colonel Valazé to assume direction of the siege replacing Couche while General Eblé, superseding Ruty, undertook the specific task of supervising the batteries in order to reduce their fire without suspending it. With these arrangements completed, Masséna returned to La Caridad and Valazé entered the trenches to carefully analyze current and anticipated progress of the siege work. These modifications in the siege operations aggravated the already strained relationship between Masséna and Ney. Ney regarded the replacement of his officers, Ruty and Couche, as unwarranted meddling while Masséna viewed the changes as absolutely necessary.[22] As Pelet recalled, "Henceforth it became necessary to entreat the Prince to maintain as much moderation as firmness in his relations with the Marshal, for under the circumstances he truly had reason to complain about him. Disagreement was apparent on every occasion."[23]

While controversy raged at Masséna's headquarters, the sappers and engineers continued their labors the night of 29 June, the fifteenth night of open trenches. The two approaches were extended in the hope that they would soon reach terrain suitable for the excavation of the second parallel. On the right, the approach was perfected and a flying sap was begun in a slight ravine which could be used as a basis for the second parallel; by pushing the sap in two directions, the sappers by morning had excavated 420 feet of trench. On the left a fifth return of 240 feet was completed and a sixth begun in the approach along the flank of Little Teso toward the area designated for the second parallel. During the night the artillerymen repaired the damaged batteries. Battery No. 8 was completed and armed with two six-pound mortars; they began firing at 8:00 A.M. and by noon several fires had been ignited in the suburbs of San Francisco. However, Battery No. 9, which was to include two howitzers manned by the artillerymen of Marchand's division, had not yet been completed. The mortars and howitzers continued to drop shells on the town all day while again the artillerymen labored to alter the composition of their batteries. The "breach batteries" fired little and the other artillery pieces were limited to 50 rounds per day. The Spanish responded with a heavy bombardment blowing up a powder magazine of Battery No. 3. The night of 30 June, the sappers continued their work extending the second parallel; they opened a flying sap on the right, running from this parallel toward the breach. Again the enemy guns rained death and destruction on the trenches throughout the night as incendiary bombs illuminated the sky and silhouetted the laborers; there were 43 casualties. On the approach to the left a seventh return was excavated in order to reach the second parallel while a communication trench was begun toward a hill where the new breach battery was to be established. The engineers, working for several days on Battery No. 7, finally completed and armed the three pieces of twelve before dawn. However, within an hour after the battery had begun to bombard the suburbs of San Francisco, a shell from the fortress ignited its magazine, silencing all three guns and destroying its epaulement.[24]

The following morning, 1 July, Masséna called a meeting attended by Ney, Junot, Eblé, and Ruty to discuss problems relative to the siege. Valazé, who had spent the previous day examining the siege works, attended the meeting to make proposals for the successful conclusion of the operation. Although he did not approve of all the projects that had been previously undertaken, Valazé indicated that it would be possible to utilize the work as the basis for his operations. It was obvious to him that to destroy the counterscarp, the suburbs of San Francisco would have to be captured, the trenches would have to be pushed to the crest of the glacis, and a gallery would have to be sunk to the counterscarp to blow it up. Regarding artillery operations, Valazé pointed out that the artillerymen would have to establish a breach battery on Little Teso at a distance of about 480 feet from the breach to destroy any subsequent repairs made on it by the garrison; he also suggested that two enfilading batteries be constructed for use against the artillery along the northern wall, contiguous to the breach. Much to Masséna's dismay, Valazé concluded his recommendations by declaring that eight days would be required to raise the new breach battery on Little Teso and reach a position where the sappers could successfully blow up the counterscarp.[25]

In opposition to Valazé's proposals, Ruty pointed out the advantages of erecting the "breach battery" at the edge of the glacis, but Valazé countered by describing the insurmountable problems of such a plan.[26] After considerable discussion, Masséna decided to adopt Valazé's plan and push the siege operations with the utmost dispatch. The heavy artillery would be employed as necessary in order to end the siege as fast as possible. There is no doubt that Masséna had been deceived by the continual stream of Spanish deserters who reported stories of suffering and despair; now with grueling siege work before him, it seemed he would have to tax his resources to the utmost to subdue the stubborn garrison and its governor. Exasperated, Masséna complained to Berthier, "I expected that the actual breach on which we have fired until now, and which is well advanced, would force them to capitulate without the need of making other works but it is necessary . . . to crown the counterscarp and pound a breach 120 or 150 feet in the fortress; then we will make a practicable breach to deliver the assault." He warned, "I will make another summons and if they refuse a capitulation, I will take it by force and put the garrison to the sword without sparing the inhabitants who are the most stubborn." He acknowledged, "A great deal of misinformation exists in the fortress. The garrison would not delay in surrendering; but a mob of priests and other people of their kind, who have taken refuge in the town, oppose it."[27] Masséna, also disturbed about the collection and distribution of supplies from Salamanca, complained to Berthier, "We experience many difficulties concerning subsistence, especially on account of the lack of transports. There are neither horses nor wagons in the countryside; we bring everything here by our own means and three days are required for the convoy to arrive from Salamanca."[28]

Despite these anxieties, Lambert continued to gather and dispatch massive quantities of food and supplies to the army, but it was no longer a daily occurrence. No convoy left on 25 June but at ten o'clock the following evening four columns left Salamanca. One column of 40 caissons carried 33,181 rations of biscuit, 373 gallons of brandy in four hogshead caissons, and almost seven ton of grain followed by 100 head of cattle to Masséna's headquarters at La Caridad. The second column, composed of six requisition wagons, left for San Muñoz with 4,000 rations of biscuit and five ton of grain while the third column started out for Matilla carrying 2,000 rations of bread, 52 gallons of wine, 640 pounds of barley, and 222 pounds of rice for the ambulance corps, aboard four requisition wagons. The last wagon train of 11 caissons and 40 pack mules advanced to San Felices el Chico with 20 ton of flour, three of barley, and 203 gallons of brandy in two great casks aboard two requisition wagons. The following night another convoy of 27 caissons left for Mermet's headquarters at Sancti Spiritus with 18,000 rations of biscuit, 18 ton of flour, and three ton of salt. The next convoy did not set out until the night of 29 June when 23 caissons departed from Salamanca for San Felices el Chico with 27 ton of flour followed by two caissons laden with almost a ton of barley and a special wagon of food for Junot's personal use. However, despite the dedicated efforts of the quartermaster corps, driven unmercifully by Lambert, the massive shipments of supplies fell short, and by 1 July it was reported that men of the 6th Corps were already reduced to half-rations.[29]

During the last half of June, Wellington and the Allied army carefully observed the progress of the siege and the Spanish defense with some skepticism, but as days passed they developed a feeling of respect and admiration for the Spaniards. Wellington was inclined to believe that the fortress would capitulate when the French concentrated their efforts against it.[30] Just before the trenches were opened, Herrasti sent several letters to both Wellington and Governor Cox of Almeida about the lack of supplies. Cox wrote to Beresford that the Spaniard's letters "do not give a very pleasing picture of the state of the garrison; their flour is out. . . . They are also in want of meat and firewood." Wellington assured the governor that he was aware of his situation and referred to their earlier correspondence on this subject. "I have made every effort," Wellington wrote, "to have a diversion created in favor of Ciudad Rodrigo with some success; and I will not fail to do every thing in my power to assist the place, but I refer you to my former communications." The same day he skeptically wrote to Craufurd, "I fear there is much more food than the garrison and inhabitants can consume. They had provisions for forty days for the whole population when invested. . . . Under these circumstances, and at this period of the operations, I do not think it would be proper to make an attempt to give them relief." To discourage Craufurd's continual agitation for a movement in favor of the fortress, Wellington admitted, "It would be much more justifiable to incur a risk to make the attempt, after the garrison shall have shown their determination to resist, by standing a serious attack," concluding, "The more probable event, [is] that the place will be lost, and that we shall not be able to make any attempt to relieve it."[31]

In addition to the agitation generated by his general officers, Wellington was also pressured by the Spanish government to move in favor of the fortress. The Spanish government at Cadiz appealed to the British minister plenipotentiary in Cadiz, Henry Wellesley, younger brother of Wellington, to make some diversion in support of the city. Sir Arthur wrote to his brother, "Tell the Regency that I have not lost sight of Ciudad Rodrigo, and that I shall do every thing in my power to relieve the place." However, he pointed out that the French had 50,000 men to oppose his 33,000 troops of whom 14,000 or 15,000 were Portuguese or Spanish troops of "doubtful description."

In addition, he noted that such a move would force him to leave the defensive mountains to cross the plains and two rivers to raise the siege. He asked, "Is it right, under these circumstances, to risk a general action to relieve or to raise the siege of Ciudad Rodrigo? I should think not." Concluding, he suggested: "If they hold out like men they are worth saving, and I will incur a risk to save them." At the same time he wrote to Lord Liverpool that unless the French reduced their forces before the fortress, "I apprehend that any attempt which I should make to relieve the place, or to raise the siege, would fail, and might be attended by fatal consequences to the general cause." In any case, Wellington was not optimistic about Spanish resistance. Each time their guns fell silent, Wellington assumed that the fortress had surrendered; however, this was not the case. He admitted bewilderment about the "very extravagant notion of the strength of Ciudad Rodrigo" held by the French who believed it would "hold out for twenty days after they shall have opened a breach," but they were, in fact, more sanguine in their judgment than the British general.[32]

Interrelated with the effectiveness of the Spanish defense of Ciudad Rodrigo was the Allies' reaction to the probes of the French reconnaissance columns and the ultimate safety of the Light Division once the fortress had been captured. The French had increased their patrols on the west side of the Agueda when the trenches were open on 15 June. The reconnaissance reports were carefully coordinated with the interrogation reports of deserters and spies so that the exact location and strength of Craufurd's positions were well known to the French; more general information was also available concerning the location, strength, and movements of the entire Allied army and its subsidiary units. In addition to the daily French patrols, Craufurd's pickets were often overwhelmed and driven back by vast reconnaissance columns of infantry and cavalry moving along the roads to Gallegos, Carpio, Marialba, and Espeja. Usually skirmishing resulted in minimal losses. However, on occasion, the potential for battle became a reality. When the 76th Line was threatened by a strong Allied force near Carpio on 21 June, Loison sent four regiments of cavalry and two battalions of infantry to support them. The British retired until Craufurd responded with massive reinforcements, forcing the French to retreat precipitately toward the banks of the Agueda.[33]

As the French reconnaissances continued, Wellington corresponded with Craufurd almost daily suggesting various alternatives he might consider in withdrawing before overwhelming forces. On 22 June, he issued a "memorandum" of movement outlining Craufurd's line of retreat "in case of the surrender of Ciudad Rodrigo, which I consider not an improbable event." Aware of his general's impetuous nature, he cautioned Craufurd as well as the Spanish general, La Carrera, not to "risk an attack by a superior force" but to return toward La Concepción. Apparently Craufurd was unclear on the specific circumstances regarding his withdrawal, so Wellington wrote on 24 June differentiating between a retreat in the face of an enemy attack and a withdrawal following the surrender of Ciudad Rodrigo. Wellington spelled out his strategy: "My object is to be able to continue in our present situation as long as possible, both to encourage a continued resistance at Ciudad Rodrigo, and to be able to relieve the place, if it should be advisable to attempt it."[34]

Despite his instructions to Craufurd, Wellington decided to visit Almeida and the forward posts of the Light Division. He arrived at Almeida along the Portuguese frontier at 2:00 P.M. on 25 June to converse with Cox about the defenses of the fortress. Early the next morning he toured the positions of Craufurd's Light Division to determine if the troops were capable of resistance and organized withdrawal. Upon his return to Almeida he wrote to Craufurd suggesting several modifications to cover his troops if an immediate withdrawal became necessary. However, even before the letter was delivered, Ney had ordered three cavalry brigades to push Craufurd's troops back beyond the Azaba. Supported by infantry and artillery, the French advanced to the heights above Marialba and Carpio and took up positions on the Azaba opposite Craufurd's posts at Gallegos, Espeja, and Vilar Formoso.[35]

Although the French only claimed two enemy horses killed and one taken in their advance to the Azaba, Wellington was not satisfied with Craufurd's advance posts. He suggested modifications in Craufurd's deployment on 26 June, and two days later he wrote, "Your situation gives me a great deal of uneasiness." If the French should attack at dawn, "you would find it very difficult to withdraw your corps." It was important for Craufurd to hold his positions as long as feasible, "but we must not risk such a loss as your corps would be." He suggested that Craufurd should post his division in the woods between Gallegos and Alameda with a battalion of infantry, a detachment of cavalry, and three guns established in Gallegos; moreover, pickets were to be posted on the heights above the village so the Light Division would be ready for any eventuality. Rather than ask Craufurd to "turn this disposition over in [his] mind" as he had two days earlier, Wellington concluded, "I beg you to make your arrangements accordingly for to-morrow morning." [36] Consequently, the Light Division was withdrawn toward Almeida with the bulk of the division in the woods behind Alameda and its pickets at Gallegos.

Despite the French occupation of the terrain between the Agueda and Azaba rivers and the contracting lines around Ciudad Rodrigo, Wellington was still able to communicate with the fortress. Spanish messengers slipped through the French lines with letters from Herrasti. When Sánchez had escaped from the fortress with his lancers on 22 June, he brought detailed information about each phase of the siege. Two days later another messenger made his way from the fortress to Wellington's camp with new information and appeals for aid. Wellington was gratified and encouraged by this information while still admitting to Liverpool, "It would be impossible to relieve, much less raise the siege of Ciudad Rodrigo, without fighting a general action, with forces which . . . are infinitely superior in number to any that I have it in my power to bring against them." Wellington was a realist, but it did not stop him from encouraging "the Governor to persevere in its defence." As he had repeatedly written the governor, aid would ultimately "depend upon a larger view of the interests of the allies in the contest than the mere preservation . . . of that place." But his letters do indicate a marked shift in attitude toward the Spanish garrison and its governor. He confided to his brother Henry, "I only lament that it is impossible for me to relieve the brave garrison of Ciudad Rodrigo. . . . The garrison still keep up a vigorous fire. The town was in flames in two places the day before yesterday, when I was at our advanced posts, which are in sight of it." [37]

As the bombardment continued and the month drew to a close, Wellington became anxious about French maneuvers on the west bank of the Agueda. The 14th Light Dragoons were ordered up to Vale da Mula on 29 June to maintain communications between Almeida and La Concepción. Craufurd was still proposing complex and inoperable modifications in response to Wellington's instructions for the advance posts. Wellington pointed out weaknesses in his suggestions and repeated his warning that he should remain vigilant.[38] The following day Wellington had cause for alarm. Large units of French infantry and cavalry supported by artillery were marching to the left bank of the Agueda. The reports of several Spanish deserters who had come into the French camp during the day revealed that Herrasti had issued instructions for the garrison to break out of the fortress, cross the Roman bridge to the west bank of the Agueda, and reach the safety of the Allied army. Consequently, Marcognet's brigade and artillery moved across the Agueda opposite the fortress; a second brigade took up a position at La Caridad with a battalion on the left bank of the river to link up with Marcognet's forces. Marchand was ordered to march at the sound of the first shot to cut off the Spanish escape route; Montbrun was alerted to move with his infantry and cavalry at the first sign of enemy movement; Taupin, on the road from San Felices el Chico to Ciudad Rodrigo, was cautioned to prepare for any eventuality; finally, all troops on the west bank of the Agueda were to remain under arms all night. Although unaware of the French motives, Wellington ordered an infantry battalion to Castinheira to survey Castelo Bom and Castelo Mendo; supported by Royal Dragoons near Sabugal, they were to form a link with a brigade of Cole's Fourth Division in the south. Meanwhile, La Romana had arrived with a detachment of men from Badajoz to reinforce the Allied army.[39]

Herrasti continued to send multiple messengers to the British forces across the Agueda almost daily, informing them of the conditions within the fortress and appealing for support. However, as the weeks passed, Herrasti became more frustrated and perplexed by Wellington's attitude. He recalled, "Each day that passes since the enemy bombardment of the fortress began, while the glory of our defense grew and inflamed us with the determination to continue, the hopes we placed in the aid of the English diminished since there was no signal or evidence whatsoever that they would make a movement to give us [aid]." The garrison often mistook a returning French reconnaissance column as troops in flight, pursued by the British, but this never proved to be the case. On the night of 30 June, a priest of the cathedral, Don Sebastián Gallardo, offered to take a message through the French lines; he was sent to apprise the British general at Gallegos of the conditions in the fortress and to induce him to march and raise the siege. As he attempted to pass through the French lines, a post of the 10th Dragoons captured the priest with the message. He was tried before a military court as a spy and sentenced to be executed, but Masséna intervened on his behalf in return for information. The priest explained the nature of his mission and his goal of lighting the signal fires to inform the garrison of British plans. Hoping to deceive Herrasti, Masséna ordered the priest to be escorted to the heights of Manzano so he could set the required number of fires signifying that Wellington would not march to aid the town.[40]

The life of Father Gallardo had been preserved, but his very presence at the French headquarters was the cause of deep and bitter recrimination. The compassionate Pelet wrote, "I found much devotion and patriotism in his actions. Everyone did not think the same, and his presence excited more anger than I would ever have been able to imagine. Initially, it was necessary to defend him from insults; we placed him with the sentries at the Prince's quarters, giving him protection rather than guards." With the sympathetic aid of both Masséna and Pelet, the priest remained in the French camp. The Prince hoped to send him back into the city with a more lenient offer of capitulation, but Gallardo "refused absolutely, saying he would be hanged there because he had not been hanged by us." A dramatic sketch of Gallardo is left by Pelet: "I can still see him with his African complexion, his haggard and silent face, his fixed and firm eyes, wearing the black jacket of a peasant and a large hat for protection against the rays of the burning sun. Beside him were some scraps of food for which he was obliged to me. Seated on the corner of a rock among his enemies, he watched the ruin of his country. This climate, these bare rocks, this arid country, this black face full of religiosity and fierceness, brought back recollections of captive Israelites after the destruction of Jerusalem. The man had shown great character when he responded to the first insults of the soldiers with some kind of disdainful 'Well, shoot me'."[41] Although the priest ultimately fled to the hills with Pelet's acquiescence,[42] he was induced to write to his nephew, Agapito Gallardo, chaplain of the third battalion of Volunteers, describing the rage of Masséna and his troops at the prolonged resistance of the town. Despite the specter of an assault on the town and the threat that the citizens would be put to the sword, Herrasti and the junta encouraged the garrison and habitants to have confidence in the future. Nevertheless, the governor could not resist writing in his journal, "We all recognize very clearly that we have no hope; because in twelve days of continual and terrible fire that makes known the condition of the fortress to our allies, nothing indicates a movement in our favor . . . but we resolve to gloriously finish our defense until the last extreme, continuing our efforts and constantly repelling the enemy with the greatest firmness."[43]

In the French camp all was not well as the month of July began. Dissension was apparent among the various generals charged with the siege operations. Friction between Ney and Masséna had now become public knowledge. Frustration was obvious on all sides. The troops had to be encouraged to rush the siege to its ultimate conclusion before the army suffered irreparable damage. New orders had been issued to improve the mode of operations before the walls of the city. Realizing that the trenches, absolutely necessary in order to reach the counterscarp, could not be advanced until the convent and suburb of San Francisco were captured, Valazé asked Ney to issue orders for the capture of San Francisco as soon as it became expedient.

On the afternoon of 1 July, Ney ordered General Simon to organize the attack on the suburb of San Francisco; at the same time Battery No. 6 with its two howitzers and four pieces of twelve began to bombard the suburb. At 9:00 P.M., 600 infantry and 150 workers were concentrated at the base of Teso for the attack and Simon organized them into three columns, the first commanded by Chef de bataillon Spring with 200 men from the Légion du Midi, the second 200 directed by Captain Wasse, and the third 200 under Captains Martin and Duplan; this force, augmented by 150 trench workers equipped with trench tools and explosives, was led by officer Moulin of the sappers. By 9:15 P.M., as the moon passed behind dark clouds, Simon sent forward a small detachment of volunteers armed only with sabers; they silently cut the throats of three sentinels.[44] The first column, closely following, surprised another Spanish post before they had time to fire a shot; some of the enemy were killed while others fled to the hospice and guardhouse only to be pursued and bayoneted. As soon as these first entrenchments were seized, Simon ordered the first column to charge the covered way extending from the convent to the town. Despite the heavy fire and stubborn resistance of the defenders, their position was turned and seized by the French. After reaching the esplanade and fountain near the convent church of San Francisco, Simon's troops occupied the building despite the harassing fire from the fortress. The third column, also successful in overcoming enemy resistance, took up positions to the left of the convent, in the hospice, and on the ground floor of the convent. However, the second column encountered unexpected and determined resistance in its efforts to reach the convent. The troops advanced to the breach in the convent garden wall below Little Teso under a heavy fusillade from the Spanish in the covered way. Wasse's men crossed the breach and, after securing it with a company to cover their rear, advanced toward a gate that promised access to the suburb, only to find themselves in a stable without egress to the suburb. They ran to the right, along the wall to the end of the convent, on a cart path leading to the esplanade. Finally, they discovered a passage leading up a staircase into the convent, where they joined Simon and the other columns of the attacking force.[45]

After securing the convent, Simon quickly reconnoitered the convent buildings by torchlight. He then ordered Moulin to put his trench workers to the task of digging interior communication trenches and sealing all gates and outlets facing the town. At the same time a company of carabineers of the Légion du Midi probed the suburb "cautiously and without engaging in anything." Advancing under the heavy fire of the fortress they discovered that the suburb had been abandoned, the provisions carried off, and the animals killed. Although his assignment was successfully completed, Simon's men had "not fire[d] a shot during the expedition." He posted 200 infantry and 150 workers in the convent, burned the hospice and guardhouse which might be used in a counterattack, and retired to the French camp at 2:00 A.M., well pleased with his efforts and the fact that only two of his men had been wounded.[46]

While Simon was leading the successful attack on the convent of San Francisco, Valazé methodically directed the trench work on the night of 1 July. The second parallel was continued and extended to the left to force the Spanish cannoneers to divide their fire along the entire length of the excavation, thereby reducing casualties among the workers. The approach on the left was continued along the lower slope of Little Teso toward the second parallel, and a new communication trench was begun behind Little Teso for the establishment of the new breach battery. The sappers were so close to the fortress that the musketry and cannon fire claimed 71 of them. Meanwhile, the artillerymen repaired and prepared Battery No. 7 to commence firing the following morning.

At dawn on 2 July, the French batteries resumed their bombardment of the fortress and suburbs, exploding several magazines. The fire continued unabated throughout the day, and at sunset the trench workers resumed work on the second parallel which was completed that night. Fifty gabions were thrown up along the approach extending toward the breach. On the left, about 100 gabions were set up in a double line before the approach to protect the workers from the deadly fortress fire as they dug toward the second parallel. Work on the communication trench to the proposed breach battery on Little Teso was completed; the artillerymen traced and began the construction of the battery which would house eight pieces of twenty-four. However, the rocky soil forced them to haul several hundred bags of earth to the site for the erection of parapets; these efforts were relatively ineffective and the French suffered 38 casualties during the night. Battery No. 12, designated as an enfilading battery, was traced north of the convent of Santa Cruz by Eblé's men after dark, and a second enfilading battery, No. 11, was begun near the recently captured convent of San Francisco. At the same time, Batteries Nos. 7 and 8, constructed to bombard the suburb of San Francisco, were dismantled to arm the new batteries.[47]

The same night Ney, encouraged by the successful attack on the convent of San Francisco, ordered another foray against the suburb. Accordingly, Simon ordered Chef de bataillon Bertrand Constantin to lead a column of 300 infantry and 240 trench workers against the suburb of San Francisco. At the usual time, 9:00 P.M., Constantin and an engineer, Lieutenant Dussard, led their column toward the suburb to the left of the convent of San Francisco; they entered the suburb without difficulty and seized the convent of Santa Clara. The Spanish opposed this attack with heavy grape fire from the fortress walls, but the French ensconced themselves in the convent and opened up a communication trench through the various houses and behind the walls of the buildings to the French lines as the pickets advanced onto the plain of Toledo east of the city.[48]

After 1 July, the French began to build up their forces beyond the Agueda. Ferey's infantry and Gardanne's cavalry were joined by additional cavalry and infantry from Junot's 8th Corps. General Jean-François Menard's infantry brigade, supported by three pieces of Gardanne's artillery, took up a position on the road running from the ford of Loro to within a half mile of the tiny hamlet of Palacios, where Junot had established his headquarters and posted Gardanne's 15th and 25th Dragoons. Taupin's brigade was positioned to the south, with his right on Signal Height and his left in the direction of Carpio where a force composed of the 3d Hussars, 15th Chasseurs of Lorcet, three pieces of light artillery, and two companies of Trelliard's 66th Line had been established. Sainte-Croix's 1st Dragoons occupied the area to the left of Marialba while one company of grenadiers and two of voltigeurs were posted along the road running to the four-arched bridge over the Azaba. The British had barricaded the west end of the span with wagons, but the French infantry and cavalry advanced their posts to the head of the Azaba, forcing the enemy's posts to disperse. Ferey established his headquarters nearby at Hincapie with the bulk of the 66th Line and four field pieces. Immediately to the east, Fonseca was occupied by Cavrois and Montbrun with the 10th Dragoons. The 76th Line was stationed at the foot of Red Mountain on the route from Ciudad Rodrigo to Fuente Guinaldo, less than two miles from the latter; behind it Milet posted squadrons of the 3d and 16th Dragoons. The 15th Léger was established on a rideau to the right of Fonseca, and the position from the Red Mountain to the infantry brigade situated across the Agueda above La Caridad was manned by the 39th Line, a battalion of the 69th Line, and the 11th Dragoons. As a result, this extensive French deployment between the Azaba and the Agueda, supervised by Junot, could be expected to halt all but a massive attack by the Allies.[49]

It was clear from the deployment of Ferey's brigade and part of Junot's 8th Corps, that the French wanted to discourage any Allied advance and assure the isolation of Ciudad Rodrigo. Even with a surprise attack by the bulk of Wellington's army, the French forces on the west bank of the Agueda would be able to contest any advance until Masséna could rush reinforcements to support them. If the British general had not already decided against an attempt to relieve the fortress, the skillful French deployment would probably have had the same effect.

Despite the strength of the French position behind the Azaba, Masséna was still anxious about Wellington's intentions. As a result, he ordered Junot to send out two strong reconnaissance columns on 3 July "in order to have news of the enemy . . . because it is necessary to know what the enemy does." Consequently, Trelliard sent a reconnaissance column of 100 cavalry to Villarejo and Montiago, where it encountered 50 enemy horsemen who retired without exchanging fire. The second reconnaissance force of 150 light cavalry proceeded south through Manzano, Casablanca, and Campillo de Azaba to El Bodón but saw only a few stragglers. Of these reconnaissances, Ney wrote that they "had seen nothing that indicated the least movement on the part of the enemy."[50]

Even before these reconnaissances had been completed, Masséna prepared to send out another probe of the British posts. At 7:30 P.M. on 3 July, he wrote to Junot, "Send . . . General Sainte-Croix or such others as you judge advisable with 600 or 800 cavalry and artillery, if you believe necessary, with orders to overthrow all the principal English posts in order to know the exact location of the British army and the line they hold." Before dawn on 4 July, Sainte-Croix, accompanied by Junot, advanced from Marialba toward Gallegos with five battalions of infantry and six squadrons of dragoons, supported by light artillery.[51] After crossing the Azaba River, the advance guard composed of 200 horsemen drove the British pickets back and pursued them for two miles. A captain of the 16th Light Dragoons recalled, "I mounted my men as they came upon us at a gallop, and I

Figure 29. Bridge over the Azaba River between Marialba and Gallegos

had some difficulty in getting all away." The British troops at Gallegos, composed of two squadrons of the 16th Light Dragoons, one
squadron of the 1st Hussars, and two guns under Lieutenant Colonel
von Arentschild, turned out and checked the French dragoons until the
main column came up. Once Sainte-Croix had collected his forces on
the heights above Gallegos, Colonel Grandseigne drew up the 1st
Provisional Dragoons and a platoon of the 3d Hussars and charged
into the barricaded village. Captain Krauchenberg led his squadron
at a gallop, supported by the 16th Light Dragoons, to within fifteen
paces of the French to contest their advance. Some horsemen, led by
Cornet Cordemann, dismounted and attempted to hold a small bridge
in the town. Soon the British cavalry, supported by two guns of Lieutenant Alexander Macdonald in the churchyard, withdrew from the
village "in very good order," and took up a position along a brook and
ravine beyond Gallegos.[52]

As Sainte-Croix's main force advanced toward the stream, another column attempted to outflank and cut off the British by seizing
the stone bridge a mile beyond Gallegos on the road to Alameda. The
British cavalry raced across the bridge and regrouped. As soon as the
leading French column, somewhat disorganized by the hasty pursuit,
crossed the bridge, Krauchenberg with 30 men of the 1st Hussars of
the King's German Legion charged. Although Captain Bellis with his
entire squadron of the 16th Light Dragoons refused to support him,
the German captain drove the French back across the bridge with the
loss of two officers and several men. Craufurd, on the scene, ordered
Macdonald to concentrate the fire of his horse artillery on the bridge,
but Sainte-Croix's cavalry carried it while other French columns maneuvered to outflank the British. Krauchenberg finally withdrew with
his hussars and joined the 16th Light Dragoons at a gallop, "with the
French dragoons close at our heels" for half a mile.[53]

Before Alameda the French came into contact with Craufurd's infantry. The 43d and 52d Foot were halted on the road, and the 95th
Rifles were formed in line with the Portuguese 3d Caçadores on the
left. The British and German horsemen were formed in a line with the
infantry and several pieces of artillery were deployed. The French
dragoons advanced on the Caçadores but were driven back. Soon
Craufurd withdrew his infantry across the Dos Casas River while his

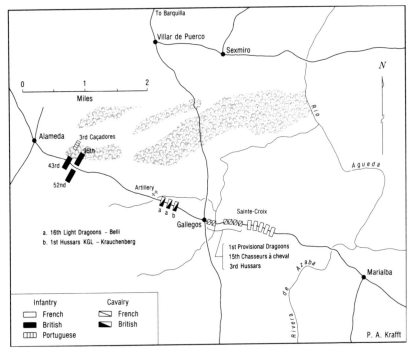

To Barquilla

Villar de Puerco

Sexmiro

N

0   1   2
Miles

Alameda   3rd Caçadores
                95th
        43rd
        52nd
                Artillery
                    a a b
                            Gallegos
a. 16th Light Dragoons - Belli
b. 1st Hussars KGL – Krauchenberg

Sainte-Croix

Río Águeda

1st Provisional Dragoons
15th Chasseurs à cheval
3rd Hussars

Azaba

Marialba

Infantry		Cavalry	
▭	French	◁	French
▰	British	◀	British
▥	Portuguese		

River de

P. A. Krafft

Map 6. Action at Gallegos, 4 July 1810

cavalry held before Alameda until they were about to be outflanked; the horsemen then retired through the village toward the Dos Casas, pursued by the French dragoons. Macdonald again opened fire on the French to protect the British withdrawal, and soon the entire division was behind the Dos Casas. Pickets were posted along the west bank of the river; Craufurd withdrew his infantry in the direction of La Concepción and took up a position straddling the village of Vale da Mula.[54] Junot carefully observed the British movements and reconnoitered the fortress of La Concepción before withdrawing his troops. An outpost was left at Gallegos with vedettes deployed in the direction of Alameda, but the remainder of Junot's force retired behind the Azaba. As a result of the reconnaissance, which cost twenty wounded and four dead, he wrote to Masséna "that the British army has withdrawn to the Portuguese frontier to defend the approaches, that La Romana is announced to be in the country with a corps of 8,000 men, that La Carrera is attached to the English with 6,000 [and] that the partisans, Don Julián and Mera, are flanking the right wing of the enemy army toward Fuente Guinaldo."[55]

As Junot was accompanying the main reconnaissance column against Craufurd's Light Division, Trelliard advanced on his flank into the woods to the south, but no enemy troops were encountered. Similarly, General Montbrun left Fonseca with cavalry, 800 infantry from Ferey's brigade, and several pieces of light artillery to survey the Spanish positions at Espeja and drive them toward Alameda. However, the Spanish posts were withdrawn on their approach, and when the French cavalry reached Espeja it was learned that La Carrera had retreated in the direction of Alameda. The positions of the enemy were now clearly determined and carefully observed, but Masséna wanted to see their deployments for himself. Therefore, with a small group of aides including Pelet, he visited Junot's headquarters at Palacios and the advance positions from Marialba to the Azaba, where he could examine the terrain occupied by the enemy's advance guard. After observing some of Craufurd's old posts, Masséna returned to Junot's headquarters for lunch "where the commanders had long dissertations on theology, literature, and politics."[56]

While these reconnaissances were carried out against the Allies, the siege operations continued uninterrupted. On the night of 3 July, the trench workers concentrated their efforts around the second parallel. The approaches were extended in the direction of the second parallel; from there an approach was pushed toward the breach. On the right, the sappers set up about 30 gabions facing the breach and 15 more on the first return. In the morning Captain Treussart, realizing that the Spanish defenders would be unable to see his men working in the advancing trench because of the pitch of the glacis and a depression in the terrain, ordered his men not to use the telltale gabion so that they could continue their work undetected. The men worked feverishly to push forward a flying sap from the second parallel to crown the glacis and reach within eighteen feet of the counterscarp. The Spanish lookouts on the cathedral tower finally detected the progress made by the French sappers and alerted the defenders on the fortress ramparts. The Spaniards responded with a heavy barrage of hand grenades and grapeshot, but the damage had been done. The sappers

Figure 30. Village of Gallegos

Figure 31. Bridge at Gallegos

threw up about 50 gabions filled with sacks of earth to absorb the impact of the shells and protect themselves from their furious enemy. Ney, delighted with Treussart's ingenuity and prudence, commended him highly to Masséna. At the same time, the sappers labored to the left of the first parallel to excavate a communication trench to the convent of San Francisco where the new enfilading battery, No. 11, was being constructed for four massive pieces of twenty-four. The garrison's incendiary bombs exposed the workers to a rain of grape, forcing them to retire and seek shelter from 5:00 to 6:30 P.M. The artillerymen, laboring to burrow into the rock of Little Teso where the breach battery, No. 10, was to be established, suffered from a devastating shower of grape. Finally, the French were forced to move three pieces of twenty-four into the enlarged Battery No. 5 in order to bombard the Spanish pieces firing on the Little Teso and the towers near the breach.[57]

On the night of 4 July, the sappers, under the direction of Lieutenants Moulin and Libel, crowned the salient of the counterscarp to the left of the breach while other workers labored to crown a second salient to the right. The approach on the left was finally pushed to the second parallel and deepened to ten feet to permit the safe passage of artillery wagons and equipment. At the same time, Simon advanced through the suburb of San Francisco to the convent of Santo Domingo, which had been reoccupied by the Spanish. The convent was seized with little difficulty and few casualties; Simon posted a company of elite there to ensure effective control of the entire suburb. All night the mortars and howitzers lobbed shells into the town. The following morning instructions were issued by Eblé for each battery to fire 15 shots during the day, except Battery No. 5 which was to fire 20 shots at the chateau tower and on the guns in the faussebraie. Throughout the day the artillerymen began to change and modify the armaments of the various batteries. The ricochet battery, No. 11, near the convent of San Francisco, was partially armed but the workers, engaged in the completion of the breach battery, suffered incessant bombardment from the garrison. The Spanish guns in the faussebraie were silenced but the garrison continued to rain havoc and destruction on Battery No. 11 and the breach battery. That night the mortars continued to fire, but three or four French batteries were inactive.[58]

In addition to the daily setbacks in the siege operations, mounting problems were encountered in the procurement and distribution of food and supplies. There was little indication of approaching disaster when Lambert wrote to Masséna on 29 June that Napoleon had issued orders for the shipment of 30,000 pairs of shoes from Paris to Bayonne and Salamanca and the release of available uniforms at Bayonne for use by the Army of Portugal. Moreover, the following day he enthusiastically indicated that 738 ton of grain, rice, and biscuit was being sent from Valladolid while 240 ton of food was being readied for shipment to Salamanca from Palencia. Two hundred thousand rations of biscuit and 40 ton of grain had been gathered in Segovia to be sent on as soon as the necessary wagons were available, and General Séras, operating in northern León and Old Castile, was instructed to collect and ship between 245 and 280 ton of flour to the army depot at Salamanca. Consequently, Lambert authorized the use of all private and commercial wagons within the area occupied by the army, but this did not solve the wagon shortage. Nevertheless, Lambert felt justified in concluding his letter with an optimistic air: "If we add to these supplies, the rations of Toro, Zamora, and León, everything leads us to believe that the critical situation that Your Excellency described will soon cease." [59]

On 1 July, Lambert resolved to send several huge casks of "good quality brandy" to the men of the 6th and 8th Corps, followed later in the day by 22 caissons laden with 38 ton of flour for Junot's headquarters at San Felices el Chico. The following morning 40 requisition wagons left Salamanca for Loison's division with 35 ton of flour followed by 37 pack mules carrying six ton of flour and three of rice. Thirty-nine more pack mules started for Junot's corps the same day with rice and grain, and there was a promise of another shipment of "good quality brandy." Lambert was satisfied that he had done everything within his power to ensure adequate supplies for the army; he described in detail the care he had taken in the organization, protection, verification, delivery, distribution, and retrieval of the wagons and animals. Nevertheless, the transportation problems were becoming more acute. On that day more food should have been sent to the 6th Corps but only 47 of the 100 wagons promised by Ney had been returned to Salamanca to pick up additional supplies, seven of those in disrepair.[60]

While Lambert's attention was directed toward the organization of convoys for the coming day, he received a stern letter from Masséna at Ciudad Rodrigo complaining that his reassuring letter of 30 June had not "extracted us from the difficult position in which we find ourselves regarding subsistence. The soldiers are on half ration. . . . The 6th Corps has received nothing and the convoys to the 8th Corps are insignificant. Make your disposition . . . so that the subsistence may be promptly expedited in sufficient quantities to us; see that all the caissons are loaded, half with flour and half with biscuit, and that requisition wagons leaving Salamanca go as far as Cabrillas or at least to San Muñoz with their loads."[61]

On 3 July, a convoy of 66 caissons, 12 requisition wagons, and 14 pack mules left the depot at Salamanca for Ney's headquarters carrying 41,920 rations of biscuit, 360 rations of white bread, and 62 ton of flour; a small train of donkeys followed the route to San Muñoz with three ton of flour. Lambert also promised to send another convoy the next day with "all the transport that can be collected" and he appealed to General Fririon at La Caridad to see that the commissioner of war, Montemuy, had all the caissons, wagons, and mules unloaded and returned immediately. Later that day he received a welcome letter from Masséna concurring with his requests of 24 June and 2 July that 50,000 francs be placed at his disposition for the unexpected expenses of the army.[62]

The next morning, 4 July, 13 caissons set out for the 6th Corps with 4,403 rations of biscuit and 14 ton of flour, followed by 120 head of cattle from Matilla. Within hours of this departure another wagon train left for the 8th Corps with seven caissons laden with almost 12 ton of flour, 38 mules carrying nine ton of flour, and five caissons loaded with 115,984 rations of rice. Nevertheless, during the day Lambert received a disconcerting letter from Masséna regarding his activities at Salamanca. He complained that opinions expressed in Lambert's letter were "neither too prompt nor too effective." Indeed, on 3 July, the 6th Corps had only received half of what had been expected and Masséna noted, "The 6th Corps has received nothing for today. I dare not appear before the troops as long as their complaints are legitimate and passionate. Send food by all the transports that you are able to collect." He concluded encouraging him to solve the logistical problems so the conduct of the administration would not be "a cause of embarrassment for us."[63]

Since a convoy was not scheduled to leave the depot at Salamanca on 5 July, Masséna apparently became more anxious about the needs of the army. He received another in a series of letters from Lambert regarding the cost and maintenance of the post stations on the route of communication. However, his correspondence from Ney had an ominous ring: "I have the honor to make known to you that the Second Division of the 6th Corps received only 2,400 rations of bread the day before yesterday, the 3d; yesterday I have made a distribution of rice for the men [and] one ounce of season rations; today it has absolutely nothing."[64]

With the increasing pressure on Lambert, he labored frantically to organize another convoy at once. Finally, on the night of 6 July, a convoy of 12 wagons laden with 36 ton of flour and 13 ton of biscuit left for the 6th Corps while 19 wagons headed for San Felices el Chico carrying 28 ton of flour and one of white flour. This was followed by 128 gallons of brandy in two cask wagons. Within 12 hours, another convoy was en route to the 6th Corps with 16 caissons and 25 mules laden with flour, biscuit, barley, salt, and brandy, and 24 caissons of flour and biscuit headed for the 8th Corps.[65] So with the final grueling days of the siege facing the troops of the 6th Corps, Lambert was able to accelerate his massive shipments of food to the various units of the army and insure them of at least a minimal diet.

Meanwhile, the work before the fortress pressed ahead relentlessly. On the twenty-first night of open trenches, 5 July, the sappers working on the approach to the right under Captain Cathala and Lieutenant Dussard threw up 40 gabions to crown the salient of the counterscarp before the breach and 30 more just below it. Each of the gabions was overthrown several times and set afire by enemy shells but they were replaced each time; there was a continual hail of grape, hand grenades, and shells, but the trench workers continued their task. During the day another critical excavation was carried on by Treussart in a most perilous segment of the trench where it was necessary to use sacks of earth since it was impossible to dig through hard rocky terrain. In the center of the parallel the communication trenches were widened to ten feet to permit the movement of infantry columns and artillery, and the communication trench on the left was united to the second parallel. Simultaneously, a detachment of laborers working in the suburbs opened a communication trench of 600 feet; extending from the convent of Santo Domingo to the ravine of Carazo, it joined Marchand's posts on the west bank of the Agueda. Supported by strategically placed barricades, the French trenches now formed a complete barrier and communication line around the fortress from the banks of the Rapeiro on the north to the waters of the Agueda on the south. The artillerymen completed the embrasures and platforms of Battery No. 11, which was armed with four pieces of twelve, so it could begin firing the next morning. Battery No. 9 was dismantled, the armaments of several batteries were modified, and the work on the breach battery was pushed ahead slowly under the constant fire of the fortress.[66]

On 6 July, the twenty-second night of open trenches, the junction of the approach on the left with the second parallel was perfected. The approach on the right from the first parallel was abandoned as a result of the fire from the new enfilading battery below the walls of Santa Cruz which created a constant danger for the workers. The approach before and to the right of the second parallel crowned the counterscarp between the two salients of the faussebraie, directly before the breach; as a result the sappers began the construction of a covered gallery or tunnel to blow up the counterscarp. Four gallery frames were erected for a distance of 12 feet. At the same time 40 gabions were thrown up to extend the trench which crowned the counterscarp. The workers in these areas of the trench suffered continually from the hand grenades thrown by the garrison but "our sappers nimbly picked up [the grenades] with their shovels and there was not as much damage done as we feared."[67] The enfilading battery, No. 11, near the convent of San Francisco, commenced firing on the area contiguous to the breach early in the morning, but its effects were less than had been anticipated. Indeed, a party of defenders in the faussebraie were forced to withdraw and several guns on the ramparts were dismounted, but it seemed obvious that the artillerymen were unskilled in their use of ricochet fire. To maximize the firepower in the vicinity of the breach, General Eblé ordered numerous alterations in the composition of the batteries. Several batteries were partially dismantled and seven mortars were moved to the new enfilading battery, No. 12, near Santa Cruz, but there were serious problems with the breach battery.[68] The Spanish continued their incessant bombardment "from every side with bombs, grenades, and muskets" overthrowing fifty feet of revetment and "its firing was delayed for twenty-four hours";[69] nevertheless, the artillerymen and engineers continued their work day and night because this battery was the key to the capture of the fortress.

As Pelet inspected the guns he "found most of the batteries under repair. Each one had several pieces or platforms out of service." Throughout 7 July, several batteries were silent or fired sporadically. The recently completed enfilading battery, No. 11, threw 150 ricochet shells into the fortress wall and faussebraie. Work on the other enfilading battery near Santa Cruz, No. 12, was completed, and the following morning its guns began firing.[70]

That night, 7 July, the French sappers completed their excavations in the suburbs and the communication trenches. At the same time the two approaches, below the crowned counterscarp, were pushed forward with renewed activity. Six more gallery frames were constructed in the mine gallery along the stone wall of the counterscarp for a distance of 30 feet. However, losses were heavy, five dead and twenty-eight wounded, since the defenders on the fortress walls could easily throw hand grenades into the trenches below them.[71]

On the morning of 8 July, Herrasti sent a sortie of 200 men to the west bank of the Agueda because of a severe water shortage. A post of the 76th Line was surprised and driven back with the loss of one officer and ten enlisted men. Encouraged by their success the Spanish sent a second sortie to recapture the convent of Santo Domingo on the southern flank of the suburb of San Francisco. They succeeded in breaking into a wood yard and seizing some tools, but before the Spaniards were able to penetrate the convent defenses, a sergeant of the sappers alerted the skeleton garrison. Supported by a company of voltigeurs from the 27th Line, they were able to repel the attackers and force them back to the glacis of the fortress, but not without the loss of 11 dead and three wounded.[72]

Eblé, meanwhile, sensing that the time for maximum effort had arrived, ordered the batteries to increase their fire accordingly. The mortars and howitzers maintained a steady bombardment while the new enfilading batteries increased their fire dramatically; Battery No. 11 fired 232 twelve-pound ricochet shells while No. 12 threw 250 shells on the enemy mortars. The breach battery, No. 10, still under heavy fire from the fortress, was partially armed; three pieces of twenty-four were rolled into position and the five other guns were dragged through the trenches toward the battery. The howitzers and mortars in Batteries Nos. 3, 4 and 6 continued to drop shells into the town throughout the day.[73]

On the night of 8 July, the twenty-fourth night of open trenches, the sappers reached the counterscarp; they commenced the construction of the top of the "T" shaped tunnel at the end of the mine gallery along the masonry wall of the counterscarp where the mines were to be placed. Captain Cathala, satisfied that the gallery extended three feet below the bottom of the ditch, chopped a hole through the three feet thick counterscarp. Simultaneously, the engineers joined and enlarged the two approaches that crowned the counterscarp to accommodate assault troops when the decision was made to attack. The dangerous trench work claimed 42 French casualties during the 24 hour period.[74]

The artillerymen on Little Teso armed the breach battery, No. 10, after midnight, and at 4:00 A.M. on 9 July it opened fire on the breach. The results of eight pieces of twenty-four pounding the breach at almost point-blank range were devastating. The other guns joined in the fire, and Eblé's artillerymen now demonstrated a marked superiority over their Spanish counterparts. An eyewitness recorded in his journal, "Enormous pieces of masonry were carried away, the buttresses caved in, and sod started falling down." The artillerymen of the other batteries joined in the bombardment firing on the breach and exchanging fire with the enemy guns. The fire of the ricochet battery near San Francisco was "poor and sporadic, but the mortars were frequent and effective. The fortress appeared to suffer greatly." By concentrating their fire, the Spanish artillerymen were able to silence three pieces of the breach battery, but the remaining five continued to bombard the breach. In all, 1,689 shells and 420 bombs were hurled against the fortress that day.[75]

As night fell on 9 July, the Spanish sappers entered the ditch and the faussebraie to clear away the debris and scrape the breach while the engineers threw up a parapet on the ridge of the breach as they had done each night for the preceding 13 days.[76] Accordingly, the French moved up three grenade mortars to the trench crowning the counterscarp to bombard the Spanish workers in the breach. The fortress guns fired on the French mortars but Eblé did not withdraw them until morning. Meanwhile, final preparations were completed to blow up the counterscarp. Valazé directed the packing of the mine chamber with 800 pounds of explosives. Cathala and a band of sappers planted the bags of powder along the stone wall of the counterscarp and Captain Joseph Coffinal ignited the mine at 2:30 A.M. The counterscarp exploded with an extraordinary blast leaving a breach 25 feet wide after the clouds of debris had settled. The charges had been carefully measured and placed in such a manner that the rubble from the detonation formed a ramp across the ditch about eight feet in breadth, thereby permitting the assault columns convenient and relatively safe access to the foot of the breach. The French suffered substantial losses, including Valazé who was grievously wounded in the head and chest, and more than 40 Spanish workers laboring in the breach and ditch were killed when the mine exploded.[77]

Thus ended the preparatory work for the assault. The initial bombardment had been disappointing, and fifteen valuable days had been consumed in pounding a practicable breach in the walls of the fortress. Supporting operations, however, had been more successful. The advance guard of the Allied armies had been driven back, almost to the Portuguese frontier, eliminating any threat to the besieging forces. The Spanish garrison, in the meantime, remained firm in its determination to resist to the last extreme, aware that its fate had been sealed by Wellington's decision to abandon them.

Chapter 8

The Assault and Capitulation of Ciudad Rodrigo

L ONG BEFORE dawn on 10 July, the French camp was alive with activity. The day for which they had labored had finally arrived. Eblé issued precise orders to each battery commander. The 17 guns and eight howitzers in Batteries Nos. 3, 4, 5, and 6 were to fire on the breach, the adjoining salients and curtains, and the Spanish gun emplacements along the northern wall of the city at the rate of eight shots per piece each hour. The breach battery would fire eight salvos from its eight pieces of twenty-four each hour directly at the breach, the wall, and the faussebraie adjoining the breach. The enfilading batteries would continue to fire on the northern wall of the fortress and the enemy mortars.[1] At 4:00 A.M. all 46 guns unleashed a concentrated barrage against the northern wall of the city, more particularly on the breach which had been partially entrenched the previous night. The Spanish had erected a palisade as well as a new parapet on the crest of the breach, but they were destroyed by noon and the walls around the breach were in ruin. "Bombs were falling down with great rapidity and excellent marksmanship. On every side arose thick clouds of dust and smoke, pierced by the flames of the fires," Pelet recalled. "The wreckage of buildings and walls was tumbling down with great noise, and several of the small magazines exploded periodically with tremendous detonations. The city seemed to be overwhelmed with so much firing." The French guns "were firing perfectly," and a cannon was hauled up near the breach to fire hollow shells against the breach to reduce the pitch of the ramp for the assault troops. Nevertheless, the Spanish defenders continued to fire

173

undauntedly against the French; yet, with each passing hour their efforts diminished in intensity until 4:00 P.M., when the guns fell silent.[2]

Earlier that morning Ney had begun making arrangements to take the fortress by assault. Loison, as senior divisional commander, was assigned the responsibility for directing the attack on the fortress. Two columns were concentrated in the approaches before the second parallel to reduce their exposure to the enemy guns. The first column, under the command of Major Delomme of the 6th Léger, was composed of three companies of grenadiers drawn from the infantry divisions of the 6th Corps; it was to be preceded by an advance guard that included 50 sappers, a battalion of the chasseurs de siège, and 100 trench workers under the command of Ney's aide-de-camp, Sprünglin. When the signal for the assault was given, Delomme was expected to cross the faussebraie, climb to the top of the ramparts; 25 men would move to both right and left to seize the flanking parapets bordering the enemy traverse. Once this was accomplished and the enemy dislodged from the traverse, the column was to occupy the houses adjoining the breach and entrench themselves while the engineers, 50 sappers, and 100 trench workers enlarged the breach, destroyed the traverse, and seized nearby houses.

The second column, composed of six companies of voltigeurs and commanded by Chef de bataillon Dutoyat of the 69th Line, was to follow the movements of the first column. After climbing up the breach, Dutoyat was ordered to leave two companies on the breach in reserve while the four remaining companies moved along the town ramparts to the gate of Conde, spiking any guns taken; they were expected to blow up the gate with petards and facilitate the entrance of a battalion of the guard posted in the suburb of San Francisco. These troops would rush through the gate and occupy a position along the ramparts adjacent to and in the demilune of San Andrés. Mermet's infantry division would follow quickly and deploy for battle with its right at the demilune and its left at the gate of San Pelayo, where Marchand would be waiting to enter the town with his division. If successful, he would deploy his division on the ramparts with his right joining Mermet and his left linked with Loison's division. The latter would enter by the gate of Conde and move toward the old castle situated along the wall facing the Agueda. Some of his troops would invest the building while a detachment proceeded to the gate of Colada and threw it open to the troops in the trenches on the right.[3]

If the French columns were unable to overthrow the traverse in the breach, contingency plans were made for the attacking column to dig into the breach itself and spike the enemy guns while awaiting reinforcements. Ruty was to establish a six-pound mortar on the breach to sustain the troops entering the town. The trench guards, commanded by Colonel Fririon of the 6th Léger, were to be under arms with instructions to move in support of the attacking columns if they encountered difficulty in passing through the breach. It was also agreed that the signal for the assault would be given by raising a red flag on the breach battery atop Little Teso. Since Ney would need all his infantry divisions for the assault, he requested that Masséna replace his troops on the west bank of the Agueda with Junot's infantry; hence, they could rejoin their regiment and be deployed before 3:00 P.M. for the assault. Finally, Ney concluded his *Dispositions* with the rather unnerving announcement, "The ambulances will be in a queue from the trench to the communication trenches on the right."[4]

Meanwhile, in the days just preceding the assault, a volatile and highly emotional issue arose at French headquarters: "Everywhere there was talk of assault, of vengeance by the sword, of examples to be made." The soldiers conducting the siege "demanded the fortress as a prize to compensate for their hard work, tedious hardships, and great privations." Unfortunately, many officers sanctioned this talk by their silence.[5] Masséna himself had expressed a rather stern view regarding the garrison and inhabitants of the city in his recent letters to Berthier since they had categorically rejected each of his summonses. On 6 July, he had written, "I will pound the breach again in order to render it more practicable and take the town by assault. I believe they will not listen to talk of capitulation. They are fanatics directed by a gang of priests who have closed themselves up on the fortress and it is impossible to make them listen to reason." Two days later Masséna threatened, "All the dispositions are taken so that the breach will be made practicable in a short time. If the insurgents do not wish to listen to reason, I will mount the assault. What is most extraordinary is that the governor and the garrison would like to surrender and that it is only the junta and the priests who do not." Early on the morning of 10 July, Masséna again wrote to Berthier, "I have made all my dispositions in order to deliver the assault this evening unless a capitulation makes us master of this fortress."[6]

Nevertheless, those close to Masséna knew that he wished to avoid an assault; he assured them "that the fortress would be saved from such fury." Aware of Joseph Bonaparte's interest in the city as king of Spain, Masséna reassured him on 8 July, "Be completely assured that I will neglect nothing to bring about a capitulation that alone can preserve them [people] and the town from the destruction that the laws of war will authorize if the place is seized by an assault. I will summon them again and I hope as much as I desire that the results of the summons will place the principles of humanity and harmony together with our desires."[7] Nevertheless, according to Pelet, "All the army talked only about burning the whole city and massacring the entire garrison." By noon it was obvious a few more hours of bombardment would render the breach practicable for an assault. "Everybody seemed to be revolted at the proposition of a new summons. Everything was ready for the assault and everyone wanted the violence and fury [of a storming]," recalled Pelet. "The Prince grasped the horror of sacking the city and decided to do everything in his power to prevent it. . . . The Prince ordered that the city should be summoned at four o'clock for the third time, and if it had not lowered its flag after a quarter of an hour, then the signal for the assault would be given." When the governor of the fortress did not respond to this last summons, Masséna sent Pelet to the partially destroyed tower of the convent of San Francisco to determine if the Spanish had fortified the breach to resist an assault. Pelet recalled, "The tower shook under my step. I did not see any traverse . . . and only slight indication of a weak palisade on the crest of the breach." Couche, Constantin, and Sprünglin, who later took part in the assault, joined Pelet in the old tower. They thought they saw epaulements and barricades on the reverse of the breach so there was no agreement regarding the condition of the breach.[8]

While the assault troops began to concentrate in the trenches before the breach and the regimental bands played lively martial airs, Ney appealed for three volunteers to make one last reconnaissance of the breach to determine how effectively it had been fortified by the garrison. He told them, "You will be killed, but you will die as honorable men." From 100 volunteers who stepped forward, Ney chose a corporal of the 50th Line, Thirion; a carabineer of the 6th Léger, Bombois; and a chasseur of the 6th Léger, Billeret. They moved to the front of the trenches and scurried toward the breach. Masséna ordered Pelet to accompany them to the foot of the breach along with Couche and Ruty. Pelet wrote in his journal, "Those three grenadiers were superb, marching like heroes, and proudly announcing to everybody that they were going to open the path to glory. They were electrifying, and they electrified me. I could feel that I too was a grenadier and a volunteer, marching at their front." Arriving at the counterscarp, the three men ran quietly up through the two breaches. At the crest of the breach of the main wall, they fired their muskets into the town, waved their shakos, and shouted, "Vive l'Empereur!" several times. To the surprise of the troops, waiting in the trenches for orders to attack, the Spanish did not return the fire; the French officers called them back several times and finally ordered them to descend from the breach and return to the French lines. Pelet recalled, "Thirion was the most excited; coming down, he offered me some brandy to drink. I drank—it was from a brave man." This feat also electrified the troops who watched from the trenches and Ney was hard pressed to restrain the assault columns. Finally, he gave the signal for the red flag to be raised and the French infantry scrambled out of their trenches and began to scale the breach at about 5:30 P.M.[9]

Chaos reigned throughout the fortress. According to Herrasti, most of the buildings had been ruined or reduced to ashes. Not one house remained intact and several roads were obliterated by debris. The two walls and the base of the fortifications had been ruined from the front of Sancti Spiritu to the gate of Conde, and the breach in this particular area was wide enough to "accommodate 60 men abreast." It was no longer possible to post infantry or artillery near the breach to defend its approaches, and after 9 July it was utterly impossible to station anyone there without having them wounded instantly. The garrison had sustained a siege of 72 days, open trenches for 35 days, bombardment for 16 days, and an open breach for 13 days. By 10 July, well aware of the deteriorating situation, Herrasti wrote, "Our fire and resistance was exhausted, we no longer had any hope of aid, and the enemy had reduced the breach to a state so the assault could be delivered." The garrison had suffered 1,400 casualties, the inhabitants and garrison were liable to be put to the sword when the fortress succumbed, and the British army had withdrawn further from the fortress and taken up positions between La Concepción and Almeida. Convinced that he had fulfilled his military duty and satisfied his honor, Herrasti realized that "to die killing [or] to delay for a few hours the inevitable surrender" was useless. He recalled, "I yielded to the voice of reason and, after consulting with the junta, the military commanders, and the civil and religious authorities, united in an extraordinary session during the day, I, myself, regretfully decided to capitulate." [10]

The French had already crossed the ditch and were ascending the breach when Herrasti ordered the white flag to be raised on the breach; he sent a plenipotentiary immediately to request an interview with Ney in order to announce his willingness to surrender. The negotiator presented Ney with a letter from Herrasti announcing, "In consequence of what I have said to Your Excellency in my last correspondence, and after having fulfilled, as I intended, all my duties as military governor, I am ready to capitulate, and I beseech Your Excellency to designate a person with whom I can treat and the place where I can meet him." [11]

General Simon was sent to Herrasti to inform him that Ney awaited him in person at the foot of the breach. Accompanied by several aides, Herrasti in civilian garb descended the breach where Ney dismounted and greeted him with consideration. [12] The Marshal introduced several of his generals and congratulated the Spaniard on "the prudence and intelligence that [he] had had in asking for [surrender] at the precise moment in which the laws of war were still applicable, after having done everything in [his] power to fulfill the military duty of such a glorious defense." [13] He offered generous terms based upon the rights the garrison had earned in its courageous defense. Citizens and property were to be protected, officers would be permitted to retain their swords, baggage, and horses, and the sick would be transported to France with the able-bodied prisoners with the promise that they would be well treated. Ney completed his conversation with Herrasti, offering his hand to seal the conditions of the capitulation. The old governor climbed back up the breach and prepared to transfer command of the fortress to Adjutant Commander Rippert, who had been designated to assume control of the town. During these proceedings, both the French and Spanish soldiers climbed to the tops of their parapets to watch events unfold.[14]

The French troops occupied the gates of the fortress at once while Loison marched his troops through the breach and established them on the adjoining ramparts. Guards were posted at the batteries, magazines, arsenals, the gates, and the city treasury to insure against any disorder. After Simon, commanding the 82d Line, had collected the arms of the garrison and deposited them in the town arsenal, the Spanish troops were marched to the barracks and confined there until they could be sent to France as prisoners of war.[15]

Initially the French officers were able to maintain good discipline over their troops by organizing patrols; by dusk large numbers had entered the city through the breach and gates to complicate the situation. Upon instructions from Masséna, Pelet entered the fortress: "We did not have time to take all the necessary measures to maintain order in the midst of so much confusion." So much attention had been devoted to planning the assault that little thought was given to the establishment of order in the occupied town. Some of the Spanish garrison, released from their barracks, joined the French soldiers who were looting the stores and houses. At first some of the French guards engaged in these excesses and some of the junior officers "did not blush in carrying off shameful plunder with their own hands." Pelet recounted in his journal, "I realized there was no way of imposing any restraint except with saber thrusts. . . . I struck right and left at the pillagers, no matter who they were. My eyes were impervious to distinctions of rank, and if I recognized anybody, I only hit harder." Pelet and those accompanying him lodged complaints with the post commanders, who recalled their men and sent out patrols to halt the pillaging: "If the disorder did not stop completely, at least word spread that it was not allowed or tolerated."[16] Finally, to mollify the men in the ranks, Masséna ordered Ney to arrest all members of the junta, company commanders, and other "conspicuous persons" who exercised an influence in encouraging resistance during the siege. They were imprisoned until they could be sent off to Burgos.[17]

The next morning Masséna entered the fortress and walked along the ramparts with his staff. Herrasti, his artillery commander, and two engineers were presented to him and they discussed the rigors of the siege. The governor wrote in his journal, "The horrible spectacle that the fortress presented the day of the surrender was the greatest eulogy to its defense; in the midst of its ruins it is hardly possible to distinguish the buildings and to pass through the streets obstructed by ruins. It is only necessary to see the place in order to know how great the resistance has been." According to Herrasti, the Prince turned to him and said, "This picture indicates enough the brave defense that you have made; but you were too obstinate."[18] Similarly one of Masséna's staff wrote, "Everything adjoining [the breach] had been crushed, pounded, and destroyed. The ruins and devastation extended to the middle of the city. At every step one could see collapsed or burned houses." The 16 days of bombardment and 13 days of an open breach had taken their toll, but there were some French officers who felt that the Spanish defense could have been prolonged if the breach had been defended, the streets barricaded, and the houses fortified.[19]

Nevertheless, Herrasti and his garrison succumbed after a remarkable defense. Considering the circumstances, Herrasti later pointed out to the Spanish secretary of war: "The wall of the fortress is restricted, its fortifications weak and irregular, its location is dominated and its approaches are obstructed by suburbs, walks lined with trees, vegetable gardens, and rough terrain that facilitates approaches to within pistol shot of the wall on several points. The town does not have one bomb proof building, the same for powder storage. It is without magazines, without hospitals, [and] without supplies to shelter it. No cross fire defended the approaches. Finally, it did not have the support on which it counted and had been promised."[20]

In all, 28,286 shells and 11,859 bombs had been fired into the city during the siege, killing or maiming at least 1,800 Spanish soldiers and civilians.[21] "All the commanders, officers, troops, and individuals of other classes who have taken part in the defense of Ciudad

Rodrigo," wrote Herrasti, "have covered themselves with glory and have acquired the rights to the recognition of the country." Nevertheless, the governor could not forgive the British for what he regarded as their abandonment: "The valor, the fortitude, and the sacrifices of the garrison and the inhabitants deserved a better fate. They have had the misfortune of not being supported by the armies of our allies. After having defended themselves for such a long siege with firmness and vigor, they have been forced to surrender without receiving any succor." With the occupation of the city by the French, the citizens, excluding those arrested in compliance with Masséna's order, were free to go about their business. The soldiers, now prisoners of war, were marched off toward France in three columns of 1,200 men on three successive days.[22]

With the occupation of Ciudad Rodrigo, the French took possession of 118 pieces of artillery, almost a million cartridges, 73 ton of powder, 290 serviceable caissons and wagons, 7,225 small arms, and 87,008 projectiles of all calibers. However, the magazines of the fortress were a sharp disappointment to Ney since the "few days' food" would hardly fill the depleted stores of the 6th Corps. Simon took possession of the Spanish magazines and found 50 ton of wheat, seven ton of grain, 11 ton of rice, seven ton of vegetables, almost six of dried codfish, 11 ton of salted meat, 100,000 rations of biscuit, approximately 200 gallons of brandy, and 12 head of cattle.[23] There was no barley or straw for the animals, so intensive foraging was continued. As a result Ney wrote to Masséna, "You will recognize, without doubt, as I, the absolute necessity to order that the magazines of Salamanca continue to feed my troops until we are able to determine the state of resources of the country which have not yet been explored."[24]

As the siege came to a close, Lambert continued collecting provisions for the army. With requisitions reaching Salamanca from the surrounding provinces, Lambert began to send enormous quantities of foodstuffs to the army. On the morning of 8 July, 18 caissons and 10 requisition wagons loaded with 1,800 rations of coarse and white bread, 15,000 rations of biscuit, and 19 ton of flour set out for the 6th Corps. A column of 27 caissons loaded with 7,972 rations of biscuit, four ton of grain, three of rice, and three of biscuit also left Salamanca for Junot's corps. As soon as these convoys had left the depot, Lambert and his staff began to organize a vast new train for Loison's division. Early the following morning, it left with 26 ton of flour, almost 18 ton of biscuit, and five of salt aboard 35 caissons. A food convoy of 24 caissons and 86 mules followed soon thereafter with 26 ton of flour and 13 ton of biscuit for the 8th Corps. At dawn on 10 July, as the siege artillery was opening fire on the fortress for the last day, Lambert was dispatching 50 caissons laden with 26 ton of flour and nine of biscuit for Loison's division. So despite Ney's fears, his corps would be sustained by the magazines at Salamanca until satisfactory new arrangements could be completed.[25]

In addition to the food captured in the town, Masséna hoped to gather specie and other precious objects. A search was made of the public, private, and religious buildings. Thirty thousand réaux from the town treasury and some 285 pounds of silver plate from the churches were added to the military chests of the Army of Portugal, but little was found in the private residences. Masséna, realizing these funds would not permit him to rebuild and revitalize the town, imposed a contribution of 500,000 francs upon the town. At the same time work was begun for the construction of four new bake ovens since only one in the fortress was operable. There were five mills in the city; after minor repairs four were capable of grinding over 33 ton of flour per day. The hospital was in wretched condition and the pharmacy had been destroyed so French engineers were assigned the task of restoring the most basic facilities in the town. Masons, carpenters, and glaziers were also sent from the army to repair the house which was to serve as Masséna's headquarters. As early as 11 July, workers had begun to repair the walls of the city and fill in the trenches. Eblé was instructed to "put the fortress in a state of defense" and to begin organizing a new siege parc of 70 or 80 pieces with the necessary munitions and accoutrements for the siege of Almeida.[26] Henceforth, Ciudad Rodrigo would be a general depot for the Army of Portugal and headquarters for Masséna.

The capture of Ciudad Rodrigo was not accomplished without considerable loss by the 6th Corps. Fourteen officers and 168 enlisted men were killed and 34 officers and 1,009 men wounded. Artillery casualties were disproportionately high: six officers and 34 men killed and nine officers and 233 wounded. In addition, two heavy cannon, one howitzer, and two mortars were *hors de service*, but these losses did not dampen Masséna's enthusiasm.[27] He was gratified with the results of the siege, especially since the operations had been carried out in the desolate and exhausted plains of Old Castile with a large Allied army less than twenty-five miles away. In a letter to Berthier dated 12 July, Masséna described the efforts of his lieutenants in glowing terms. Of Ney he wrote, "His military talents and experiences are sufficiently known, that it will suffice to say that he has done all that can be expected of a great captain." "The Duc d'Abrantès," wrote Masséna, "has made excellent arrangements in order to observe and contain the army of Lord Wellington." Masséna concluded his letter praising Eblé, Valazé, and even Ruty and Couche who had caused him considerable discomfort during the siege.[28] However, he did not acknowledge the valuable services performed by Quartermaster General Lambert, who overcame a series of major problems and was able to provide enough food and supplies to feed and clothe 50,000 men each day. Lambert had suffered the wrath of Masséna and the criticism of the corps and divisional commanders but he surmounted each obstacle with considerable success and determination. In addition to his complex duties as quartermaster general, involving all the financial transactions of the army, Lambert also effectively supervised those branches of the service dealing with the logistical requirements of the army.

The capitulation of Ciudad Rodrigo had an adverse effect upon the commander in chief of the Allied army. "In this part of the country," wrote Pelet, "the great majority damned the British for supporting the disorder and doing nothing to protect them. The inhabitants of Ciudad Rodrigo cursed them more violently, especially when they broke their word of honor and betrayed the confraternity of arms which had been sworn."[29] Similarly, Ney recalled how the Spanish "complained of the perfidy of the English, who, after promising to aid them, prolonged their defense, and finally abandoned them. The indignation is such that many officers and soldiers requested to join the service in order to march against them."[30]

When General La Carrera, commanding a Spanish contingent in the advance guard of the Allied army, learned of the surrender of the fortress, he retired to Estremadura to join La Romana who had with-drawn earlier in the month. Some officers in the British army ques-tioned Wellington's decision to abandon the fortress. Even before the town was invested the governor of Almeida observed to Beresford, "I don't think the French ought to be allowed to take Ciudad Rodrigo, but if it falls, this place is likely to have the same fate." A young engineer at La Concepción, Captain John Burgoyne, wrote of Ciudad Rodrigo, "Why it is thus deserted to its fate, after solemn promises being given to relieve it, appears extraordinary. . . . If we are not able to attempt some effort in favour of this devoted place now, I fear we cannot expect much success in operations, when all the arrange-ments and combinations of the enemy are made." An English officer serving as quartermaster general in the Portuguese army, Benjamin D'Urban, complained that the British "had made no effort to save or to succour him [Herrasti]. . . . I think the time may soon come when our eyes will be opened to the policy of having done something for Ciudad Rodrigo." Conversely, other officers such as Charles Napier recognized the role of the fortress in Wellington's plan for the defense of Portugal: "I see no reason to find fault with Lord Wellington's con-duct now in not succouring Ciudad Rodrigo!" Napier regarded the siege as "little more than a battle-trap for his lordship, which he has not been caught in."[31]

Wellington's decision not to attempt a military operation to re-lieve or raise the siege of Ciudad Rodrigo proved to be both correct and necessary if the British army were to survive in the Peninsula. No doubt such an effort would have had a positive psychological effect on the garrison and the Spanish forces opposing Napoleonic domination in Spain, but the results of any successful movement against the French would have been only temporary. On the other hand, if the Allies had suffered a reverse, Wellington would not have been able to implement his plan for the defense of Portugal. The Spanish were bit-ter about their abandonment after a long and grueling siege, believing their sacrifices had been for naught. Wellington was well aware of this attitude as his letter to Liverpool clearly indicated: "The fall of Ciudad Rodrigo was felt as a great misfortune by the people of Cas-tille in general; and they are not satisfied with the British nation, as an effort was not made to raise the siege of the place. This dissatisfac-

tion," he admitted, "combined with the effect . . . produced by the
improved conduct of the French officers toward them, has probably
been the cause of their discontinuing all correspondence with us." In
fact, the Spanish ceased providing intelligence and even refused "to
forward the communications of those employed to acquire it."[32] However, Herrasti grasped the true significance of his defense: "Although
we did not succeed in holding the fortress because this was impossible without aid, we did succeed in the principal objective in the interest of the national cause, by engaging the considerable forces of
the enemy for such a long time, so they could not work elsewhere with
decided advantage in such circumstances. We gave all of Portugal
time to prepare for the invasion with which it was next threatened, to
remove the subsistence from necessary points, and to arrange all
of the means that later caused the destruction and collapse of the
French."[33]

In immediate terms, the French victory at Ciudad Rodrigo was
particularly important, not only because of the courageous defense by
the Spanish garrison but also because of the apparent inactivity of the
Anglo-Portuguese army within the proximity of the fortress. Without
utilizing the 2d Corps of his army, Masséna had contained Wellington
and conducted a successful siege against a determined enemy. Yet
this operation had been costly in manpower, resources, and morale;
the soldiers felt their sacrifices had been unappreciated when the
fruits of their labor had been denied them. Moreover, friction in the
army between Masséna and several of his commanders, especially
Ney, began to undermine the spirit of cooperation that was so necessary if the Army of Portugal was to be successful. Finally, as a result
of Napoleon's decision to besiege Ciudad Rodrigo rather than mask
the fortress and march directly against the Allied army, Wellington
was given almost three additional months in which to mobilize his
forces and perfect his strategy.

Chapter 9

The Action at Villar de Puerco and the Fall of Fort La Concepción

AFTER THE surrender of Ciudad Rodrigo, French reconnaissance activity intensified in the area between the fortress and the Portuguese frontier. Although their primary goal was to observe and report any changes along the line of Allied outposts, these columns also sought food and supplies in the abandoned villages through which they passed. Most of the incursions were uneventful; but on the morning of 11 July, a minor but noteworthy engagement took place between one of General Roch Godart's columns and a formidable segment of the Light Division commanded personally by Robert Craufurd.

Following the practice of the previous three or four nights, General Godert issued orders for a column, commanded by Colonel Armand, to proceed toward the Dos Casas River and reconnoiter the area adjoining the village of Barquilla. Accordingly, at 2:30 A.M. several infantry and cavalry detachments advanced in this general direction. One small unit of 30 cavalrymen, followed at some distance by 300 infantry of the third battalion of the 22d Line commanded by Captain Gouache, marched directly on Villar de Puerco. Further to the rear, Colonel Armand followed on the same road with three battalions of voltigeurs.[1]

In the meantime, General Craufurd, irritated by these continual incursions, resolved to ambush one of the French columns and discourage future activity in his sector. At midnight Craufurd collected a large segment of this Light Division, namely two battalions of the 1st Hussars of the King's German Legion, two squadrons of the 16th Light Dragoons, and three squadrons of the 14th Light Dragoons.

Supported by five companies of the 95th Rifles, two companies of the 52d Foot, and the Portuguese 3d Caçadores, he proceeded quietly toward the Dos Casas River and crossed before 2:00 A.M. Having ordered no speaking or smoking, Craufurd cautiously led his troops to within a mile of Villar de Puerco, where he posted five squadrons of cavalry in a wooded ravine to await the turn of events. Another squadron of the 1st Hussars under Captain Gruben was concealed in some farm buildings between Barquilla and Villar de Ciervo to cut off any French retreat; several detachments of the 14th Light Dragoons were posted at various points in the area of the anticipated attack. Companies of the 95th Rifles were marched to a cornfield behind a slight ridge overlooking Villar de Puerco and ordered to lie down while other companies of the regiment were established on the heights near Barquilla, supported by a detachment of the 14th Light Dragoons. Three companies of the 43d Foot were posted some distance behind the woods already occupied by Craufurd's cavalry force, the 3d Caçadores were concentrated at a ford on the Dos Casas, and Ross's horse artillery remained at Castillejo de Dos Casas, approximately three miles away. Craufurd's deployment seemed to be designed for any contingency and promised success at dawn if the French advanced to Villar de Puerco and Barquilla again.[2]

The French dragoons entered Villar de Puerco, still followed at some distance by Gouache's infantry. Just as the horsemen were leaving the village on the road to Barquilla, General Craufurd came forward alone to reconnoiter the village personally. In the dawn light, at about four o'clock, he immediately sighted the French cavalry on the Barquilla road. Returning quickly to his cavalry, Craufurd resolved to attack immediately, without calling up infantry or artillery, because the French force seemed so small. Turning to Krauchenberg, Craufurd ordered him to charge the French horsemen with his 1st Hussars, supported by Captain Ashworth's squadron of the 16th Light Dragoons. Following Craufurd's orders to proceed on the most direct road to Villar de Puerco, the men encountered serious obstacles in passing near the village; the cavalry were forced to string out and slip through a narrow defile flanked by a stone wall. Once beyond this gorge, Krauchenberg tried to form his men for an attack while one of Craufurd's aides-de-camp, Lieutenant Colonel James Shaw-Kennedy, and

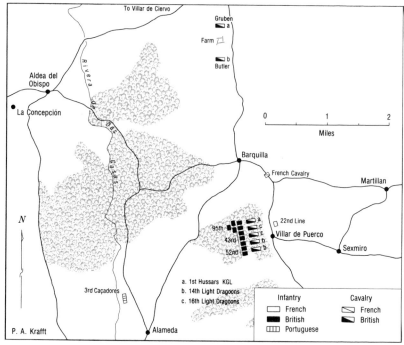

Map 7. Action at Villar de Puerco, 11 July 1810

Brigade Major William Campbell rode ahead to determine the location of the enemy horsemen. They galloped ahead to see French dragoons in the distance but pulled up short on seeing Gouache's infantry; his column had just left Villar de Puerco and was still partially concealed by the high-standing corn. They returned to Krauchenberg at once; with this information he decided to attack the French infantry although it was hardly visible among the cornstalks and he had the sun in his eyes. As Krauchenberg ordered the charge, a staff officer ordered Ashworth to form his squadron of dragoons in line with the hussars rather than behind them; as a result, when the attack was pressed forward, Ashworth's horsemen were extended too far to the right and hardly came in contact with the French square.[3]

While the Allied cavalry slipped through the defile and started to gallop down on the French infantry, Gouache, seconded by his old sergeant, Patois, "quickly formed" his grenadiers into a square by half section on a slight rise amid the cornstalks. "Without confusion," they waited to receive the shock of the 1st Hussars led by Krauchenberg, sword in hand. When they were within thirty paces of the square, Gouache ordered his men to fire by file. Almost a dozen men and as many horses went down in the dust and smoke in front of the square. The remainder of Krauchenberg's squadron and Ashworth's dragoons veered to the right and went off in pursuit of the French horsemen near Barquilla. A second squadron of the 16th Light Dragoons, commanded by Captain Bellis, following closely behind the first attack, experienced considerable difficulty in threading the defile. As a result, their attack, delivered with little order or purpose, was forced to the right of the square; its momentum carried it in the direction of Barquilla and the French cavalry. The disarray of this attack proved fortunate for Gouache's grenadiers, who were in the process of reloading their weapons after the first attack. By the time they had their muskets primed, the exasperated Craufurd had called up Lieutenant Colonel Talbot, dressed in nankeen pantaloons; he was ordered to attack with Captain Thomas Brotherton's squadron of the 14th Light Dragoons. Talbot led his cavalry down the road, through the defile, and charged the square, although he could hardly see the Frenchmen amid the dust and smoke.[4]

Gouache's grenadiers waited on the ground, crouched behind the bodies of the dead or dying enemies and their horses, until Talbot's men were almost upon them. They stood up and fired a volley; according to Captain Charles Cocks, who took part in the attack, "It is impossible to do justice to the intrepidity of this body of men. They stood the second charge as well as the first, knocked down some by a running fire, and bayoneted others." Eighteen men were either shot or pulled from their horses; those who reached the square were met with bayonet, and as many as twelve French bayonets were thrust deep into the horses' chests. Talbot himself was shot eight times and bayoneted; he fell dead "at the feet of our grenadiers," wrote Armand. In fact, Talbot's horse actually broke into the second rank of the square, but the French held firm. Talbot's quartermaster, McCormick, also fell mortally wounded. William Campbell had his horse shot from under him; unwounded, he crawled to his feet and "slowly stalked away," thanks to Gouache who prevented his men from firing. Similarly, Brotherton went down within a yard of the square with his slain horse on top of him. "Such was the steadiness of the men composing it [square] that not an individual left the ranks to kill or capture" him although Brotherton "lay completely at their mercy."[5]

The remnants of Talbot's cavalry withdrew in echelon by platoon while Craufurd prepared to attack again. Lieutenant Colonel Arentschildt, commanding another squadron of the 14th Light Dragoons, was ordered to attack the French square while three companies of the 43d Foot were called up from the rear. Meanwhile, several companies of the 95th Rifles lying in a cornfield behind the ridge were ordered "with scarce a pause between to 'fall in', 'double', and 'extend'." They ran through the field and up a rise, where they beheld the village of Villar de Puerco and saw Talbot's repulse by the French square. They were too far away to have any immediate effect on the outcome of the struggle.[6]

As Arentschildt prepared to advance against the French square, he noticed several cavalry detachments, which he assumed to be French, advancing on the battlefield; one trotted down the road from Barquilla, a second on the road from Valdespino, and a third by the route from Gallegos. He galloped to intercept them only to learn that they were Gruben's 1st Hussars, Butler's 14th Light Dragoons, and one of the cavalry units that had taken part in the pursuit of the French horsemen. By the time the error was discovered, Gouache's troops were cautiously retiring to Sexmiro while Colonel Armand was rushing three battalions of voltigeurs to support him. Craufurd realized any additional attack on Gouache's infantry would be useless. He ordered his men to begin the grim task of gathering their dead and wounded. Over 30 cavalrymen had been killed or severely wounded and as many as 30 horses were lost on the field of battle.[7] On the French side, the 31 horsemen who had preceded the infantry were overwhelmed and forced to lay down their arms; Gouache's extraordinary defense, without the loss of one man, against a vastly superior force captured the acclaim of both French and British, earning him a promotion and his sergeant the Legion of Honor.

Indeed, both Masséna and Wellington praised the courage and discipline of Captain Gouache and his grenadiers, but there were many in the British army who sought a scapegoat for their failure.

According to the commander of the Allied cavalry, General Stapleton Cotton, "Groundless, malicious reports circulated of the misconduct of the 16th Dragoons in the affair of the 11th at Villa [sic] de Puerco." An inquiry was suggested by several ranking officers, but Wellington intervened to stifle the controversy. Regarding the appearance of several Allied cavalry units when Arentschildt prepared to charge the square, Wellington observed, "The 16th had nothing to do with this mistake. . . . The French infantry appear to have behaved remarkably well, and probably were so posted that no efforts of cavalry could have forced them. It would really not be fair to the 16th, to have any inquiry into their conduct in the affair." A week later he wrote to Craufurd, "I have been much annoyed by the foolish conversations and reports and private letters, about the 16th light dragoons. . . . They appear in this affair to have conducted themselves with the spirit and alacrity of soldiers. They failed in intelligence, and coolness, and order, which can be acquired only by experience." However, Wellington expressed bewilderment to Craufurd: "I can only say that I have never seen an attack by our troops in which similar, if not greater, accidents and mistakes have not occurred, and in which orders have not been given, for which no authority had proceeded from the Commander, and in which there were not corresponding accidents and failures."[8]

Similarly amazed by the results of the action, Charles Vane, adjutant general of the army, observed, "That six hundred British dragoons should have been baffled by two hundred French infantry, was a circumstance for which no one appeared able to account." Craufurd himself was dismayed by this action and wrote to his wife lamenting the results, which were "attended with some mortifying circumstances." Nevertheless, many officers in the Light Division and throughout the army were more vocal in their criticism and placed the responsibility for the defeat directly on Craufurd. George Simmons of the 95th Rifles typified their attitude in his journal: "Our *wise* General had the 14th, 16th, and German Hussars all to assist, also Horse Artillery and seven companies of infantry, but let this small party of Frenchmen slip through our fingers so shamefully." An officer of the 16th Dragoons complained, "Never was a business so badly managed," and Wellington, in a confidential letter to his brother William Wellesley-

Pole, questioned Craufurd's actions at Villar de Puerco but refrained from criticizing him in public. If he had done so, it might have averted Craufurd's decision to engage the French on the Côa River less than two weeks later. In any case, the momentary concerns and complaints about the action at Villar de Puerco were soon forgotten with the continual French forays beyond the Dos Casas River.[9]

To maintain pressure on the Allied army and contain their movements, Masséna, on 12 July, ordered Ney to move the 6th Corps up to the right bank of the Azaba. Ney was to extend his right flank to Marialba and his left to Aldea Nueva de Azaba with strong detachments extending as far as Espeja and Gallegos. Masséna observed, "I believe it is useful to recommend that your reconnaissances go as far as possible on your front and left in order to observe the enemy and gain accurate news of his movements." The following morning Loison moved Simon's brigade forward to Marialba and Palacios. Ferey's brigade was advanced to Carpio with reconnaissance columns pushing down the road two miles beyond Gallegos. Supported by Trelliard's cavalry, Loison's deployment stretched from below Sexmiro on the north in a circular line through Espeja, and from Aldea Nueva de Azaba to Carpio in the south. In the process of occupying these positions, Loison and his staff became alarmed by the shocking inaccuracies of the Lopez map on which they were relying "since its locations of villages and other positions do not exist in reality. Gallegos is represented to be to the north of Espeja and it is to the east. Fuentes de Oñoro, represented at right angles with Gallegos and Espeja, is located in almost a straight line toward the northeast of these two villages."[10] Little could be done to correct this without a detailed survey of the terrain by Pelet and the other topographic engineers of Masséna's staff, but limited time made this impossible.

In addition to determining the exact locations and movements of the Allied army, Loison was instructed to establish his division firmly in order "to halt an enemy advance on Ciudad Rodrigo long enough behind the Azaba so that the divisions of Marchand and Mermet, as well as the dragoon reserve under the orders of General Montbrun, will be able to take part in the action if it becomes general." Loison carefully deployed his infantry and cavalry to fulfill the specific requirements prescribed by Ney and Masséna. The 15th Léger was

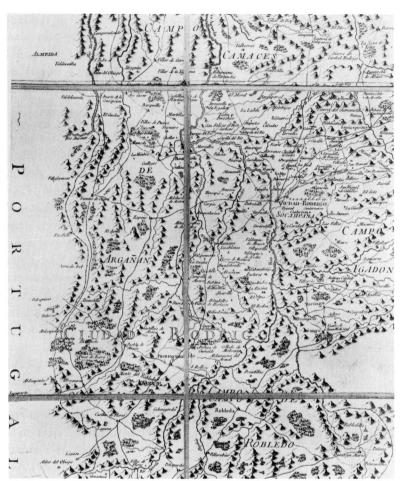

Map 8. Lopez map: Area between Ciudad Rodrigo and Almeida

posted to the left of Gallegos; a detachment of chasseurs de siège was
in the woods before the village; the 3d Hussars held a position behind
it; and a company of voltigeurs was lodged in the two churches on the
main street. The 32d Line, linked on the right to the 15th Léger, occupied a position in front and to the left of Trelliard's headquarters in
Carpio; the 25th Dragoons was posted to the south, in the direction of
Espeja. A second line of positions included the Hanoverian Legion at

the bridge on the Azaba and posts on the heights of Sexmiro, the 26th
Line at Marialba, the Légion du Midi at Palacios with the artillery
parc, the 15th Dragoons to the right of Carpio, and the 66th and 82d
Line at Hincapie. Patrols were pushed out from the French lines
while some entrenchments were constructed at appropriate positions.
Ney's aide-de-camp, Sprünglin, and a detachment of the chasseurs
de siège were assigned to man the signal fires along the outposts to
warn if the Allies were initiating a "grande maneuver." [11]

To support Loison's deployment, Ney ordered Mermet to establish
posts on the left bank of the Agueda near the bridgehead and ford of
Loro. Intermediate posts were to be maintained all the way to Palacios. If Loison were attacked, Mermet's division was to take up a
position on the heights behind Palacios without awaiting new orders.
Similarly, Marchand was ordered to secure the fortress of Ciudad
Rodrigo and the adjoining area, especially the monastery of La Caridad. Accordingly, the 6th Léger occupied the suburb of Santa Marina on the island in the Agueda and established posts from Manzano
to Fuente Guinaldo; the 69th Line was posted at La Caridad and the
bridge above it; and Marcognet's brigade garrisoned Ciudad Rodrigo
where the artillery parc of the 6th Corps was established. The cavalry
detached from Loison's division was posted at several villages including Tamames, Alba de Yeltes, and Cabrillas. The artillery company
attached to the 6th Corps was established near the 69th Line at La
Caridad. Finally, supply depots were organized for Loison's division
at Ciudad Rodrigo and the divisions of Marchand and Mermet at La
Caridad. [12]

To support the new deployments of Ney's Corps, Masséna instructed Junot to move his corps forward to discourage any attack by
Wellington. Solignac's division occupied a position between Vitigudino and Ledesma with an intermediate site at the bridge of Yecla.
The left of Clauzel's division was established at San Felices el Chico
and the right at San Felices de los Gallegos to form a junction with
Loison's troops at Marialba. As a result, Masséna's army was effectively deployed to protect Ciudad Rodrigo and to resist any advance
by Wellington's army. [13]

Even before Loison had completed his deployments on 14 July,
new orders arrived from Ney instructing him to undertake a recon-

naissance operation early the following morning. Therefore, at 4:00 A.M. on 15 July, Loison, accompanied by Generals Ferey and Trelliard, led the 25th Dragoons through Aldea Nueva de Azaba to Espeja; he was to determine the efficacy of the positions held by his regiments among Fuentes de Oñoro, Espeja, and Gallegos. At Fuentes de Oñoro his dragoons encountered and chased an English post of about 40 horsemen. Proceeding northward to La Mimbre, Trelliard found another English cavalry post, but it was so effectively covered by a deep and impenetrable ravine that he retired to Gallegos. Simultaneously, Simon, leading a reconnaissance on La Concepción, passed through Sexmiro, Martillan, Villar de Puerco, and Barquilla and reached a point less than two miles from the fort. According to some Spanish peasants nothing had been done to repair the breaches made in two bastions of La Concepción in 1808 when the French evacuated the fort; this rumor gave rise to speculation and hope that the fort would be undefended. Moreover, intelligence indicated that the British had withdrawn from Alameda, Espeja, and Fuentes de Oñoro; except for a few occasional patrols, the main line of Wellington's army had been withdrawn to Guarda on the south, Almeida in the center with an advance guard at Vale de Mula, and Pinhel on the north.[14]

During Loison's visit to Gallegos, two British plenipotentiaries, Major Charles Napier and Captain Cotton, arrived at the village posts to announce the safe arrival of money and letters sent for the officers captured at Barquilla on 11 July; they also carried a letter of greeting from Craufurd to Masséna. The men were blindfolded and taken to Loison's quarters, where they entered into a discussion on the capture of Ciudad Rodrigo and the Spanish complaints of British abandonment. According to Loison, one Englishman observed that the British army was careful in committing itself to a foreign cause, especially since such action against superior forces would risk the fate of Portugal. Loison, described by Napier as "a savage-looking fellow, yet . . . very civil," proposed a wager of 500 louis d'or that Wellington would not fight to save Almeida. As Napier prepared to leave, he asked Loison to "assure [Ney] of his gratitude for the kind treatment that he received from him when he was made prisoner at La Coruña." The Englishmen were returned to the French outposts without blindfolds "but made to gallop at full speed."[15] So passed a common occurrence between the two warring armies. This information was sent on to Ney, and the facade of humanitarianism obscured the brutality of the struggle.

On 17 July, a column of the 3d Hussars and 50 carabineers advanced through Alameda. They sighted an enemy post of 40 men nearby and shortly thereafter two squadrons of Allied cavalry were seen, but no skirmishing took place. The same day two columns of the 25th Dragoons advanced to the Portuguese frontier; one column encountered 50 British cavalry at Fuentes de Oñoro and the second, marching to the left of Espeja toward Nova de Avel, sighted 30 Allied cavalry, but no actual contact was made between these forces. Nevertheless, it was learned that Craufurd had established posts at Vilar Formoso and São Pedro do Rio Seco, and the advance guard of the army held Vale da Mula.[16]

On the morning of 19 July, reconnaissance missions were carried out all along the French line. One column was sent to Barquilla to seize a British post of some 20 men, but a French soldier alerted the post and then deserted. Alameda was again reconnoitered, and 30 enemy cavalry were observed in a ravine beyond the village. Another column of 50 dragoons advanced at 4:00 A.M. to Fuentes de Oñoro, which was temporarily held by 60 English cavalry. The horsemen withdrew after one man and three horses were wounded; the French also suffered one casualty in the affray. Finally, a column marched on Puebla de Azaba, but there was no trace of the enemy.[17]

On the morning of 20 July, new reconnaissance columns were sent out but no enemy patrols were sighted; however, it was reported that peasants had circulated rumors that the English were making a retrograde movement. In fact, all the reconnaissance reports, as well as the intelligence collected by French agents, confirmed the information sent by General Reynier posted near the Tagus that the English were making such a movement. In consequence, Masséna ordered Ney to "direct a strong reconnaissance on Almeida without engaging in a general affair. Take 5,000 or 6,000 men, the cavalry you believe necessary, and send it very near Almeida." Masséna reasoned, "Perhaps in seeing you arrive leading these columns, they will believe that the entire army is marching and will decide to surrender the place to you."[18]

Ney transmitted Masséna's order to Loison the same day, and that night 3,000 infantry from the brigades of Simon and Ferey were collected at Gallegos along with Trelliard's cavalry and a detachment of light artillery for the mission. The remaining infantry regiments and artillery of the division were deployed: the artillery was moved to the heights overlooking the bridge at Marialba; four companies of the Hanoverian Legion and Simon's remaining infantry were posted between Gallegos and Villar de Puerco; and Ferey's troops held a line from Gallegos to Alameda. After all the preparatory arrangements had been completed, Loison left camp at 2:00 A.M. with almost 5,000 men, marching toward La Concepción. Passing through Villar de Puerco, they reached Castillejo de Dos Casas where posts of the British 14th Light Dragoons had been established. Trelliard was ordered to sweep both flanks of the village as the chasseurs de siège, supported by 1,500 of Simon's infantry, marched directly on Aldea del Obispo where the Allied posts prepared to regroup. Meanwhile the 25th Dragoons, 1,500 infantry of Ferey's brigade, and the light artillery halted on the heights behind Castillejo de Dos Casas to support the advance. "These different movements," according to Loison, "were executed with precision and General Trelliard overthrew the English cavalry who sought to defend the plateau on which La Concepción was located." Loison was warned by several peasants that La Concepción, garrisoned by two battalions of Portuguese infantry, had been mined and would be abandoned and blown up when the French attacked. Therefore, before 5:00 A.M. he pushed forward as rapidly as possible through Aldea del Obispo and Castillejo de Dos Casas and across the Dos Casas River.[19]

Although the walls and profile of La Concepción were hardly discernible because of its well-formed glacis, Loison's cavalry and infantry raced up the hill toward the fortress. No doubt Loison hoped his advance guard would force the garrison to abandon the fort, which he knew from personal experience was formidable indeed. While La Concepción was being repaired, Wellington reversed himself several times on his strategy for the fort. On 28 May, he had ordered its commanding officer, "Defend the place to the last extremity, and you may be certain that you will be relieved."[20] Five days later, he modified his plans so that La Concepción could be evacuated and blown up.

Figure 32. Church at Castillejo de Dos Casas

Thus, while Captain Burgoyne directed the repair of the fort, he also supervised the sinking of mine shafts in the two undamaged bastions. In mid-June, Wellington again revised his scheme for La Concepción, writing to Craufurd, "I have occupied Concepcion with a view to be enabled to relieve Ciudad Rodrigo, and to cover your retreat upon Almeida, if you should be obliged to withdraw. . . . From the enemy's strength in our front, of which we have now a positive knowledge, it is almost certain that if you are obliged to withdraw from your position at Gallegos, it will be useless to hold Concepcion." Three days later he again wrote to Craufurd with precise instructions: "Craufurd will keep his advanced guard in front of Almeida, till threatened by an attack by a superior force, and when he retires from Fort Concepcion, he will blow up that fort."[21]

Consequently, while the breaches were being repaired and parapets erected on the damaged bastions, barrels of powder were stacked in the casemates of the curtain adjoining the mined bastions. Almost six ton of powder were piled in barrels in each of the four demilunes, two ton of powder in 60 barrels were arranged in the central arch of the redoubt, and three ton of powder in ninety barrels were placed in two casemates of the blockhouse. "Accidents frequently happen in the galleries," wrote Burgoyne, "from the inexperience of the people employed, who are not miners; the loose earth often falls in such quantities as takes a considerable time to clear the old place, sometimes a whole day." Moreover, the ruins of a previous building on the site delayed the construction of the mine shafts. Nevertheless, when Wellington arrived on 26 June to examine the progress of the workmen, Burgoyne was preparing to load and prime several mines. By 4 July "everything was prepared at the fort for evacuation," according to Burgoyne. The Portuguese 9th Line, a Portuguese artillery battery of six pounders, and four companies of the 45th Foot were withdrawn from La Concepción and ordered to rejoin Picton's division near Pinhel. A week later three companies of Portuguese caçadores on picket duty at the fort were replaced with ten horsemen of the 14th Light Dragoons to guard the gate and protect the mines. In addition, two companies of the 95th Rifles served alternately at La Concepción until the morning of 21 July when the French advanced on the fortress.[22]

As Loison's 25th Dragoons and 3d Hussars, followed by infantry, advanced rapidly up the hill toward the plateau of La Concepción after crossing the Dos Casas, the British cavalry retired before them. Captain Brotherton of the 14th Light Dragoons sent a well-mounted officer named Wainman to inform Burgoyne at La Concepción "that we were being driven back most rapidly, and that we had no time to lose." The mines were fired at 4:45 A.M. They exploded with a deafening roar hurling debris up on all sides; several men and horses of the 14th Light Dragoons, still on the plateau near the fortress, were killed during the explosion. Although Burgoyne, seeing one side of the fortress blown up and having reports of the destruction of the other side, expressed satisfaction with the results of the detonations, Loison claimed the speed of his maneuver had forced the British to evacuate the fort before all the mines had been properly set; three remained intact.[23]

In compliance with Ney's orders, Loison, now in possession of La Concepción and the plateau, ordered his troops down the gentle slope toward the Turones River and Vale da Mula, less than a mile away and certainly visible to the naked eye. The 95th Rifles, supported by what the French claimed to be 600 cavalry on the road to Almeida, attempted to hold the west bank of the Turones and halt the French advance, but they were dislodged and driven back through Vale da

Mula. Trelliard, with the 3d Hussars, swept both flanks of the village as the chasseurs de siège, supported by Simon's infantry, advanced up from the river and down the main street, driving the British 14th Light Dragoons before them. Craufurd, hoping to contest Loison's advance, ordered up several companies of the 95th Rifles at Junça, but it soon became obvious that the French had already overrun the village.[24]

At the same time several units of the British cavalry advanced along the road from São Pedro do Rio Seco and on the road from Vale de Coelha, a move which seemed to threaten the French flanks. Loison immediately ordered the 15th Dragoons, supported by infantry, to advance along the road toward São Pedro do Rio Seco and Junça. The 3d Hussars were ordered to a position between Vale de Coelha and Almeida, supported by the 15th Chasseurs à cheval and infantry. Realizing Loison's deployment would ultimately cut off their retreat, the troops of the Light Division retired toward Almeida. As the British withdrawal continued, it seemed as though they were preparing for a counterattack against the 15th Chasseurs à cheval to facilitate the retreat of one of their cavalry units imprudently engaged on the French flank. Trelliard called up a detachment of the 3d Hussars and the 15th Dragoons to thwart the British attack. Consequently, the 14th Light Dragoons recommenced their withdrawal toward the Ribeira das Alvercas, leaving some infantry to be sabered. Meanwhile, Craufurd concentrated the 16th Light Dragoons, a squadron of the 1st Hussars, and Ross's horse artillery in three columns, supported by infantry, in a ravine between Almeida and Vale da Mula. He advanced "rather audaciously" until Trelliard deployed his cavalry to prevent any counterattack. Leaving his pickets along the Alvercas, Craufurd withdrew his troops to the glacis of the fortress of Almeida. The French, meanwhile, withdrew from the Alvercas to the ravine between the river and Vale da Mula, terminating the action at approximately 10:00 A.M.[25]

The French retired to Vale da Mula and the Turones River, where they were deployed according to Ney's orders. The chasseurs de siège, the 15th Léger, the 3d Hussars, and the 15th Chasseurs à cheval held Vale da Mula during the day, but at night they withdrew across the Turones. The chasseurs de siège occupied La Concepción, supported by the 3d Hussars on the plateau. The 15th Léger and a detachment of hussars encamped at Aldea del Obispo, and the 15th Chasseurs à cheval, supported by three pieces of artillery, were posted in the area surrounding Castillejo de Dos Casas, which was held by the Légion du Midi. The remainder of Simon's brigade and the 15th Dragoons, along with three pieces of light artillery, were withdrawn to Barquilla; the remainder of Ferey's brigade and the 25th Dragoons retired to Villar de Puerco with posts at Alameda to maintain contact with General Mermet's division. Similarly, each of these units established intermediate posts with their adjoining forces.[26]

Thus, as 21 July drew to a close, Loison had fulfilled Ney's orders in each respect. His troops had marched through six miles of darkness, to Castillejo de Dos Casas, where they encountered the first of the enemy posts; driving the British troops through several villages, they captured the formidable fort of La Concepción, then crossed five rivers and succeeded in overthrowing every obstacle until they reached a point within four miles of Almeida. Nevertheless, Wellington seemed unimpressed; his letter to Charles Stuart insisted, "There is nothing new here. The enemy have made no movement of importance within these few days, excepting a strong reconnaissance on the 21st, which induced General Craufurd to blow up La Concepción, and to collect his advanced guard near Almeida." Perhaps if Wellington had had the time to consider carefully the implications of the French advance and the extent and strength of Loison's "strong reconnaissance," which was, in fact, a drive of thirteen miles and an advance of the French lines of seven miles, he might have made more stringent arrangements to reinforce, or preferably withdraw, the Light Division behind the Côa River. Craufurd seemed even less concerned than his commander in chief, although his pickets sent constant reports describing the concentration of enemy troops opposite his posts.[27] Two days later the Light Division would pay dearly in blood for this neglect.

Chapter 10

The Battle on the Côa

THE FRENCH continued their reconnaissances of the Allied posts despite the heavy contact on 21 July. The next day Loison's patrols moved down to Vale da Mula, surveying the Allied defenses, but there was little activity along the line. At 4:00 A.M. on 23 July, a French reconnaissance column moved beyond Vale da Mula where they encountered some 300 cavalrymen of the Light Division behind either the Rio Seco or the Alvercas, but there was no skirmishing. Information from a spy who obtained news from Padre Luis at Almeida prompted Loison to write to Ney, "The current rumor is that Almeida would have opened its gates if the reconnaissance of the 21st had been a direct attack on the place." Similarly, gossip mentioned a letter from the governor of Almeida, William Cox, to Wellington, cautioning that if the army did not march to support Almeida, "it would open its gates without firing a shot." This information was supplemented by the report of one of Masséna's aides-de-camp who described the success of Loison's advance on La Concepción. In consequence, Masséna wrote to Ney on 22 July, "My aide-de-camp arrived describing the success of your reconnaissance. No doubt, if you press near the English, they will abandon Almeida or blow it up as La Concepción. Therefore, I desire that you support General Loison with other troops in order to push the enemy firmly on Almeida. I have no doubt that we will have a propitious success."[1]

Ney responded immediately, "I have put the troops in movement to invest Almeida and learn if the English wish to defend this fortress." He also requested that Junot support his operation by sending

a column through San Felices de los Gallegos to protect his northern
flank while a unit of the 2d Corps advanced in the direction of Guarda
to support his southern flank. Loison, meanwhile, preparing for the
advance, noted the lack of activity along the enemy line. Simultaneously, the British were also encouraged by the inaction of the French
posts on 23 July. Craufurd's aide-de-camp, Shaw-Kennedy, recalled,
"Everything remained quiet at the out-posts this morning."[2]

Craufurd's regiments were deployed eastward, beyond the glacis
of Almeida, with their northern flank resting near an old stone windmill tower. These positions were taken despite Wellington's admoni-
tion to Craufurd. As the siege of Ciudad Rodrigo was drawing to a
close, Wellington had written to Craufurd, "In case the enemy should
(*threaten to*) attack General Craufurd with a superior force, I wish
him to retire upon Almeida, and eventually, should he find it necessary, across the Coa, holding the high grounds on the left of the river."
After the surrender of Ciudad Rodrigo, Wellington again wrote to
Craufurd clarifying and reiterating his instructions, "I do not wish to
risk any thing beyond the Coa, and indeed . . . I do not see why you
should remain any longer at such a distance in front of Almeida. It is
desirable that the communication with Almeida should be kept open
as long as possible . . . and therefore I would not wish you to fall
back beyond that place, unless it should be necessary." Craufurd,
however, retained his position before Almeida until the pressure of
the French reconnaissance columns made retreat necessary. Wellington, guarding against overreaction, had written to Craufurd on 16 July,
"It is desirable that we should hold the other side of the Coa a little
longer, and I think that our doing so is facilitated by our keeping La
Concepcion. At the same time I do not want to risk any thing in order
to remain at the other side of the river, or to retain that fort. . . . I beg
you, therefore, not to have any scruples about doing it too soon."
Once La Concepción had been seized by Loison on 21 July, Wellington became both concerned and agitated about Craufurd's vulnerable position and wrote, "I have ordered two battalions to support your
flanks; but I am not desirous of engaging an affair beyond the Coa.
Under these circumstances, if you are not covered from the sun where
you are, would it not be better that you should come to this side with
your infantry at least?"[3] Nevertheless, the stubborn Craufurd re-

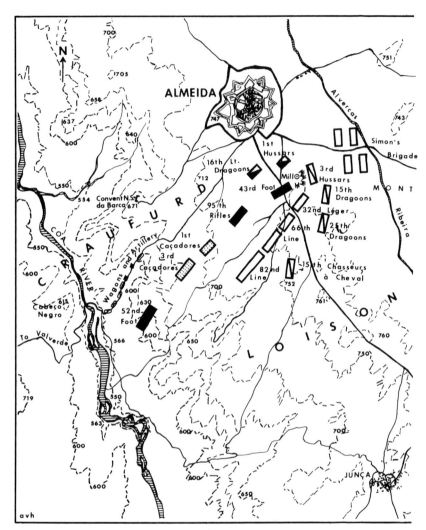

Map 9. Battle on the Côa, 24 July 1810

tained his precarious position beyond the Côa; on his front was an ever increasing enemy army and to his rear a steep and rocky road running almost two miles through uneven crevices to the gorge on the Côa—crossed by one narrow bridge that spelled the difference between capture and safety.

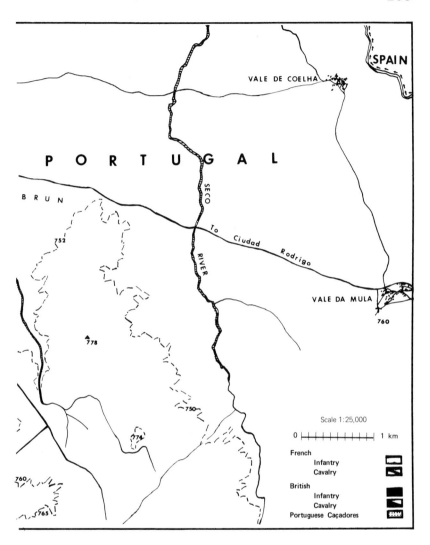

The atmospheric conditions on the night of 23 July were unusual, producing an extraordinarily violent storm that left a distinct impression on all those present. One of the officers of the 95th Rifles recalled, "We experienced a storm that for violence, while it lasted, exceeded anything I had ever before beheld. The lightning, thunder, wind, and rain were absolutely awful." Another officer of the same regiment reflected, "The thunder and lightning of that night was the most tremendously grand I ever beheld either before or since. . . . I sat upon a stone like a drowned rat, looking at the heavens." The French soldiers were equally affected by the "extremely heavy" storm that thundered across the heavens before dawn as they prepared for the attack. It was indeed appropriate for this most violent of storms to be followed the next morning by one of the most violent and bitterly fought battles of the Peninsular War.[4]

At one o'clock on the morning of 24 July, the various regiments of Loison's division marched to a staging area in the valley of the Dos Casas below La Concepción. Despite the memorable storm, the soldiers picked their way slowly along the muddy roads, aided by the lightning. After some five hours the water-soaked men had reached their destination; there they were organized into attack columns. At 6:00 A.M. orders were issued for the advance, and General Auguste Lamotte led the 3d Hussars and the 15th Chasseurs à cheval forward, followed by the chasseurs de siège, the 15th and 25th Dragoons, and the two infantry brigades of Loison's division, marching in two great columns. To support the attack the other infantry divisions of Ney's corps and the 10th Dragoons were deployed. The French infantry, preceded and followed by cavalry, crossed the plateau of La Concepción and began the descent down the slope toward the Turones River. Once this rivulet had been crossed, squadrons of the 3d Hussars, commanded by Colonel Laferrière, swept around the flanks of the village of Vale da Mula while others advanced through the village supporting the chasseurs de siège; they drove in the outposts of the 95th Rifles, which fell back immediately along the road toward Almeida, covered by the 14th Light Dragoons and the 1st Hussars of the King's German Legion. As the gunfire reverberated across the plain, the startled infantry of the Light Division, some cleaning their weapons after the terrible weather of the preceding night, sprang into action.[5]

The 3d Hussars and the chasseurs de siège pushed down the road from Vale da Mula driving the pickets and horsemen before them. When Laferrière neared the streamlet of Alvercas, he found a company of the 95th Rifles and two pieces of horse artillery, commanded by Captain Keith Stewart, formed along its west bank. They were

overrun immediately, but, once beyond the Alvercas, General Montbrun momentarily delayed the advance until his four cavalry regiments, the horse artillery, and the infantry brigades of Ferey and Simon could be brought forward and deployed for the attack. Stewart's
company fell back quickly toward the old stone windmill, located less
than 900 yards from Almeida, which had been fortified with two cannons, manned by a half company of the 52d Foot under Lieutenant
Henry Dawson, and supported by two pieces of Ross's horse artillery.
During this retreat, Lieutenant J.G. McCollough and perhaps twelve
of his men were overtaken and captured; the other men of Stewart's
company, in danger of being cut off, fled from Montbrun's advancing
cavalry. To distract the French, Captain O'Hare was ordered forward
to support Stewart's men with a company of the 95th Rifles. His men
raced forward to an old wall of fieldstone to await the French. Nevertheless, the situation was becoming critical. Observing the French
advance, an officer of the 95th Rifles recorded, "The whole plain in
our front was covered with horse and foot advancing towards us. The
enemy's infantry formed line and, with an innumerable multitude of
skirmishers, attacked us fiercely . . . with drums beating, frequently
the drummers leading, often in front of the line, French officers like
montebanks running forward and placing their hats upon their
swords."[6]

The 95th Rifles opened a "very heavy fire" on Ferey's infantry as
they neared the wall. There seemed to be some hesitation in the
movements of the chasseurs de siège as they approached the wall and
the British behind it, so Ferey ordered Chef de bataillon Alban Martinel to charge the 95th Rifles with his voltigeurs of the 32d Léger,
supported by the 4th battalion of the 66th Line under Captain Pelat.
The French advanced rapidly in "close column" without firing a shot
as Montbrun's artillery fire plowed into the wall. The voltigeurs
hurdled the wall with mounted bayonets and engaged in close combat
with the waiting British riflemen. "The movement was executed with
as much intrepidity as precision," recorded Loison, "and the enemy,
startled by such a sharp attack, found his only escape in immediate
flight." As O'Hare's company retreated toward the 43d Foot and deployed 100 yards to the rear to take advantage of the terrain, the Portuguese artillerymen on the ramparts of Almeida, mistaking the rifle-

men's green uniforms for the French, concentrated their fire on them, claiming more casualties. O'Hare withdrew his company in two sections to cover his retreat, but the section led by Lieutenant Johnson was outflanked by Colonel Laferrière's 3d Hussars who swept around their left flank. Despite the concentrated fire of Johnson's riflemen at almost point-blank range, the French hussars, apparently taken by some Englishmen for the 1st Hussars of the King's German Legion, galloped into the 95th Rifles where "our men were trampled down and sabred, on every side." As the 15th and 25th Dragoons of Montbrun maneuvered to support the 3d Hussars, contingents of the 43d Foot led by Captain Wells's company advanced to support O'Hare's 95th Rifles but not before 11 men were killed and 45 taken prisoner. In fact, only one officer and 11 men of this company escaped the onslaught of the French cavalry. Meanwhile, the 15th Chasseurs à cheval, led by Chef de bataillon Valmabelle, galloped down the road from Vale da Mula to Junça to attack and turn the right wing of Craufurd's line held by the 52d Foot. Preceded by a swarm of skirmishers, Ferey's infantry formed into four columns to continue their rapid advance while Simon's infantry brigade swung north and moved directly to invest Almeida.[7]

In the ensuing two hours, during which the French attack was developing and long lines of French infantry and cavalry were deploying, Craufurd, who "might have retired across the Coa twice over," was busy organizing his defenses to resist the French attack. Instead of grasping the magnitude of the French attack and following Wellington's instructions "not to engage in any affair on the other side of the Coa," Craufurd resolved to maintain the Light Division, which included some 2,000 British and 1,219 Portuguese soldiers, an artillery battery of six pieces, and perhaps 800 cavalry against Ney's available force of some 20,000 men. Fortunately for Craufurd, only one of Loison's brigades (3,773 infantry) and 2,297 of Montbrun's cavalry were employed in the attack. Following current British tactics, Craufurd posted his regiments in irregular lines in order to capitalize on the terrain surrounding Almeida. The 43d Foot held a line extending from the windmill on the north to the 95th Rifles deployed behind some field walls directly to the south. The 1st and 3d Portuguese Caçadores held the center of the line, and the 52d Foot oc-

cupied the southern flank bordering the rugged and steep ravines that
extended down to the gorge of the Côa—swollen by the raging water
from the deluge the previous night.[8]

It is inconceivable that Craufurd expected to maintain the Light
Division, scattered along a line almost two miles long, with his limited manpower against the formidable French attack. His left was
quickly turned near the windmill, and his right was seriously threatened by the 15th Chasseurs à cheval in the direction of Junça. Ferey's
infantry, the chasseurs de siège, the 32d Léger, and the 66th and 82d
Line, advanced rapidly in four columns on Craufurd's position despite gunfire from Almeida exploding around them and the withering
fire of the Light Division thinning their ranks. It soon became obvious
that Ney had achieved his goal "to cut the enemy off from the fortress
and maneuver simultaneously to cut their retreat on the Coa"; he expressed surprise at Craufurd's rash deployment. "Craufurd, after concentrating his entire division under the cannons of the fortress, probably believed that we would take a position without daring to attack him
in this favourable position."[9]

With the advancing French infantry, the sweeping movements of
their cavalry, and the lively fire of their horse artillery, Craufurd's
position quickly became untenable. He sent Major Charles Napier
to instruct Colonel Sidney Beckwith of the 52d Foot, Major Charles
McLeod of the 43d, and Lieutenant Colonel Robert Barclay of the
95th Rifles to hold their positions in the rocks and behind the field
walls until Ross's horse artillery and the supply wagons could be
withdrawn down the narrow rocky road, which threaded its way between the stone walls and defiles to the gorge of the Côa. The 1st
Caçadores, commanded by Lieutenant Colonel Jorge d'Avillez Zu-
zarte, and the 3d Caçadores, under Colonel George Elder and António Correia Leitão, held their positions in the center of Craufurd's
lines, although not under major attack by the enemy, until ordered to
fall back by Colonel Beckwith. The 1st Caçadores, despite the efforts
of d'Avillez, retired across the rugged terrain and broken defiles and
"fell back upon the bridge at an accelerated pace."[10] When they
neared the ridge of the hill overlooking the gorge, they sighted the
bridge over the Côa, clogged with retreating artillery, baggage, and
cavalry. Apparently a wagon, after descending the long, very steep

Figure 33. Bridge on the Côa River

hill to the Côa, failed to negotiate the sharp curve where the road turned parallel to the river, thereby causing the delay. While some companies of the 1st Caçadores took up positions on the hill above the river to cover the approaches to the bridge, other companies rushed down to the bridge and began to crowd onto the structure since they had not been instructed to remain on the right bank of the river. Nevertheless, the appearance of the 1st Caçadores pushing through the cavalry and artillery on the bridge created an "unfortunate impression," which was corrected following an official inquiry.[11]

As Ferey's attacks increased in intensity, it became obvious that the 43d and 52d Foot, the 95th Rifles, and the 3d Caçadores would be outflanked and cut off from the bridge on the Côa if they did not retreat immediately. Belatedly, Craufurd ordered most of his infantry to withdraw, echeloned from the left, through the vineyards and across the irregular terrain while the 52d Foot was instructed to hold the extreme right as long as possible "in order to prevent the enemy approaching the bridge, by a road coming from Junça." However, his regiments were "hotly engaged and could no longer keep their ground, lest the enemy should turn their flanks and reach the bridge before them." Charles Napier of Craufurd's staff recalled, "The fire was hot and the ground very difficult for us," so the Allied infantry broke and retreated down through the tortuous rock and vineyards,

Figure 34. Côa River above the bridge

over field walls, "owing to the murderous position which kept us in fear of being cut off from the bridge." [12]

As the French infantry pursued Craufurd's retreating infantry, the chain of command broke down; "part of the troops were advanced, others drawn back," and each regimental or company commander assumed command of his own force and attempted to extricate his men from their critical position. Each unit fought desperately for its own escape, joining and cooperating with other fleeing companies, ignoring regimental organization, while Craufurd seemed overwhelmed by the impending catastrophe. A half battalion of the 43d Foot, seeking cover or hoping to execute a delaying action, took refuge in the ruins of an old building with stone walls some ten feet high. With limited egress and Ferey's men advancing steadily all around them, the men of the 43d dislodged some stones and with "a powerful effort burst the inclosure." Each tree, wall, or boulder became a refuge for the fleeing Allied infantrymen, but Sprünglin's chasseurs de siège and Martinel's 32d Léger, supported by Colonel Béchaud's 66th Line and Chef de bataillon Rocherond's 82d Line, overwhelmed all opposition as they charged down the hill toward the Côa. Even the less heavily mounted

15th Chasseurs à cheval took part in the pursuit, riding in among the stone walls to capture or saber Craufurd's retreating men.[13] "The French troops attacked vigorously and in the best order; the enemy opposed them with stubborn resistance," wrote Ney. "The enemy defended his terrain well and fired swiftly with musket and field artillery, but he was chased successively from his posts by an intrepid charge."[14]

By the time the 95th Rifles and the left wing of the 43d Foot under Captain Chris Patrickson, now intermixed, and part of Elder's 3d Caçadores reached the hill overlooking the bridge on the Côa, a large part of the Light Division had already crossed the river and were busy taking positions on the hills immediately above the Côa. The 43d Foot, on the left of the line, arrived above the bridge first, and Craufurd ordered a number of companies to hold there while the remainder of the regiment filed across the bridge. When several companies of the 95th Rifles, followed by the 3d Caçadores who performed "exactly the same as the British troops,"[15] reached the hill, they were instructed to form to the right of the 43d Foot.

The French infantry, supported by light artillery and a few persistent chasseurs, closed in on the rocky hillocks above the Côa bridge. Craufurd, assuming his entire division had crossed the Côa, ordered his rear guard to fall back to the river and cross the bridge. Ferey's infantry quickly seized these hills and opened fire on the bridge while their light artillery was unlimbered and commenced fire. At this crucial juncture it was learned that several companies of the 52d Foot, on the extreme right toward Junça, had apparently withdrawn so deliberately that they were now in danger of being cut off from the bridge and captured. Charles Napier galloped off to the 52d Foot to order their immediate withdrawal. Brigade Major Rowan with a detachment of the 43d Foot, as well as some companies of the 95th Rifles and 3d Caçadores, tried to recapture the hills immediately above the bridge; Beckwith, also aware of the importance of these positions if the 52d were to be saved, on his own authority ordered the 95th Rifles to reoccupy the hills just abandoned. Simultaneously, Major McLeod also grasped the desperate situation of the 52d Foot; he "immediately turned his horse round, called to the troops to follow, and taking off his cap, rode with a shout towards the enemy." He took a wing of the 43d Foot forward; they "ran up the hill, exposed to a desperate fire, as the enemy had a strong wall to fire over." Ferey's men, "astonished at this unexpected movement, stopped short"; they were forced back from the stone wall until the 52d Foot could withdraw and slip across the Côa. Once this precarious operation had been completed, the rear guard began its final retreat. The 43d Foot, 95th Rifles, and the Caçadores pulled back, followed by three companies of the 43d Foot under Captains Dalyel, Lloyd, and William Napier.[16]

On the bridge over the Côa two disabled artillery tumbrels slowed the passage of the rear guard and might have been captured by the advancing French; but an artillery officer appealed to the riflemen who then "lined the battlements of the bridge keeping up a constant fire whilst he got his horses harnessed and got clear off." With the Light Division across the Côa, both George and William Napier posted their companies of the 52d and 43d Foot, respectively, among the boulders along the river to watch the fords and turn back any daring Frenchmen while most of the 95th Rifles and Caçadores lodged themselves among the rocks of Cabeço Negro which formed an amphitheater dominating the bridge. The French "opened a biting fire, which was returned as bitterly," and the artillery on both sides of the Côa echoed down the valley amidst the din of musket and rifle fire, the beat of the drummers, and the shouts of the men.[17]

When the French reached the banks of the Côa, the last remnants of Craufurd's rear guard had just passed the bridge. Loison ordered Ferey to cross the bridge and pursue the enemy. Two companies of the 66th Line led by Captain Bonamaison and a company of elite under Captain Ninon approached the bridge at double-quick time with a drummer and at least one officer leading the column. The French were almost across the bridge before the British and Portuguese could gauge their range. Initially the approaches to the bridge had been left unprotected by Craufurd, but William Napier halted two companies of the 43d Foot near the end of the bridge. Captain Alister Cameron of the 95th Rifles also posted a company in the ruins of an old house near the bridge approach. Thus, when Ferey's infantry raced across the bridge, the concentrated fire of the 43d Foot, the Caçadores behind the stone wall and on the heights above the bridge, and all the infantry scattered among the crevices of Cabeço Negro above the river had a devastating effect on the French. Apparently Ninon and four of his elite succeeded in crossing the bridge; they lodged themselves below the structure or along the base of Cabeço Negro, but the remainder of the 66th and 82d Lines were cut down, line by line, as they ran cheering across the bridge. The attack continued until the wounded and dying "rose nearly even with the parapets [of the bridge], and the living mass behind melted away rather than gave back."[18]

With the repulse of the first attack, Ney intervened personally, ordering his aide-de-camp, Sprünglin, to storm the bridge with some 300 men. Between two and three o'clock two battalions of the 66th Line charged across the bridge in a column to shouts of "Vive l'Empereur!" Sprünglin saw a dozen of his men brave the fire of Craufurd's riflemen and reach the other side of the bridge only to be forced to seek refuge in the boulders below the bridge to escape the withering fire of the Light Division. According to an officer of the 95th Rifles, "The bridge was literally piled with their dead and they made breastworks of the bodies."[19]

Although Sprünglin claimed his losses were 90 dead and 147 wounded on this misdirected attack, Ferey's entire brigade had 80 dead and 272 wounded. It has also been incorrectly assumed that Sprünglin, nominal commander of the chasseurs de siège, led them in this attack; however, the chasseurs suffered no mortality the day of the battle while the 66th Line had 68 killed and 140 wounded, proving conclusively that they took part in both attacks on the bridge.[20] A third assault was made, but it was delivered with less enthusiasm and also beaten back. In his report to Ney, Loison explained his failure: "the vigorous resistance of the enemy, his superiority of numbers, and the advantage of his position did not permit our brave men to make themselves master of [the bridge]." Some of Ferey's men also sought to cross the river by a ford above the bridge, but the raging waters were too deep and swift and any Frenchman who approached the ford was shot by British sharpshooters.[21]

Following the assaults on the bridge the troops of both armies continued their heavy fusillade until approximately 4:00 P.M., when another torrential rain drenched the exhausted soldiers and ended one of the most vigorously fought battles of the Peninsular War. A

French officer with a white handkerchief approached the bridge and asked for permission to carry off the dead and wounded. As soon as this request had been granted by Major Stuart of the 95th Rifles, a party of unarmed Frenchmen came onto the bridge and began to administer to the wounded and dying, carrying them back to the right bank of the Côa. The British wounded, meanwhile, were taken up the steep mud road to the top of the hill overlooking the river where a chapel had been transformed into a temporary hospital. Their wounds were dressed "with greatest dispatch," and they were sent on to Pinhel via Valverde, either walking or in bullock wagons.[22]

A sergeant of the 74th Foot, Robert Grant, at Pinhel described the distressing scene:

> About 1½ hour after the action, all that was wounded and some not quite dead was brought in here. There the numbers at upwards of 500 wounded. They were the most shocking spectacle ever I beheld—many without arms, hands, legs, and wounded in the head, body, and every other part. They were the most piercing syte I ever saw—colonels, officers, and privatemen. . . . They are all carried on carts and conveyed from the field with all possible haste. The cries of them would pierce the heart of a slave. There was upwards of 47 officers, in all 24 of whom was killed on the spot. The rest I saw carried in here in a shocking state. [The following morning Grant went to an unroofed convent where the wounded had been laid] and there I beheld a sad scene— officers and men lying in their wet and bloody clothes. Clothed the same way as they were carried from the field and the ground on which they were lying without straw or any covering whatever, many of them dead of their wounds and lying almost naked. . . . Even when they were coming in, in numbers notwithstanding the loss on our side being very great, yet General Craufurd swears he will never give up when he has a British soldier left. . . . Heaven only knows the issue of this dreadful carnage. I send this by express. The moment I have time I will acquaint you of the events of the dreadful day.[23]

Both armies retained their position until late into the night. At eleven o'clock that evening the Light Division withdrew up the winding road to the hills overlooking the Côa and then followed the narrow route due west over the crest of a plateau toward Valverde. At 4:00 A.M., Loison moved two infantry companies across the bridge on the Côa and up the road to the ridge of hills above the river valley to observe the roads to Valverde and Guarda. The rain had stopped early in the morning, and after daybreak parties of Loison's men picked through the bodies littering the bridge searching for wounded. Even before the casualty list had been completed, it was obvious that Ferey's brigade had carried the brunt of the attack and suffered proportionally. His losses totaled 80 dead and 272 wounded; the 66th Line, leading the attack, had suffered drastically. Simon's brigade, disengaged from the main action in order to swing northwest and invest Almeida, had five men wounded. Montbrun's cavalry were not so fortunate; 53 men and 90 horses were lost in the attack. As a result Ney, who reported losses of approximately 50 men at two o'clock on the afternoon of the battle, was forced to revise his casualty list upwards, to between 400 and 500 men, by the end of the battle.[24]

The British losses in the battle were also considerable. According to two detailed letters from Loison to Ney, parties of French infantry had begun to bury the enemy dead even before dusk on the day of the battle. The bodies of 80 men of the Light Division were buried or, if the terrain was too rocky, thrown directly into the Côa from the right bank. The following morning, 25 July, 40 bodies were heaved into the river from the left bank; 57 were buried where they had fallen on the heights of Cabeço Negro that evening while 24 enemy bodies were laid to rest in a vineyard behind Ferey's position. On 26 July the remains of approximately 100 more enemy were interred, the majority wearing the green uniforms of light infantry interspersed with cavalrymen; they were buried in a ravine approximately 825 yards from the fortress. Based on the actual number of bodies interred or thrown into the Côa, Loison placed the dead at 301, the wounded at 500, and those captured at about 100 men; he also mentioned the capture of two guns at the windmill. The Allies, on the contrary, acknowledged 36 dead, 273 wounded, and 83 missing as well as the loss of the two guns, one Spanish and the other Portuguese.[25]

The casualty list of the participants has been the object of passionate partisanship over the past hundred years. In fact, two distinguished historians, Sir Charles Oman and Sir John Fortescue, have attacked Masséna's honesty and integrity in reporting his losses to Paris. In analyzing French claims of Allied losses, Oman declared that Masséna's report of Allied losses was "a work of fancy" and the information "an invention of Masséna's own." He declared that Masséna reduced French losses from 500 to 300, increased the number of prisoners taken from 100 to 400, and "added foolish gossip" about the loss of "sixty officers, of whom they buried twenty-four on the battlefield, about 400 dead and 700 wounded." Furthermore, Oman claimed that Ney had provided accurate information in his report "which Masséna deliberately cut down" or altered. Unfortunately, Oman condemned Masséna after examining what he regarded as a "doctored" draft of Masséna's dispatch at the Archives de la Guerre in Paris which was reproduced in *Le Moniteur*; he observed, "We actually catch him in the act of falsifying returns." Similarly, Fortescue acknowledged the veracity of Ney's report to Masséna, charging, "Massena thereupon garbled the report, multiplying the British prisoners taken by four, adding to this the capture of a colour, and reducing the French casualties from five hundred to three hundred. To this he appended some inventions, purporting to be taken from intercepted dispatches, which stated the British losses at sixty officers and eleven hundred killed and wounded." It is a pity that both Oman and Fortescue, rather than examining Loison's actual report at the Archives de la Guerre or Masséna's letter registry, assumed the worst and defamed Masséna's character for generations to come. In each instance they would have found that Masséna repeated the exact figures provided by Loison and Ney. In his report to Berthier, Masséna announced the capture of 100 prisoners; he placed the French losses at 400 to 500, as indicated in the actual reports of Ney and Loison, and the "foolish gossip" referred to by Oman was, in fact, actual quotes contained in two captured letters, written by British soldiers. Regarding the casualty figures of the battle published in the government newspaper, Le Moniteur, and denounced by Oman, it is obvious that the figures in Masséna's written and published reports were altered *in Paris* for national consumption and can in no way be attributed to him. Moreover, Masséna's claim of a captured flag was based directly on a letter from Ney, who wrote, "I also send to Your Excellency an English flag that was taken in pursuit of the fugitives on the 24th by M. Domel, drummer of the 25th Léger. General Mermet has failed to apprise me of this fact until now; I have only received this report now." [26]

In the midst of the battle, after Craufurd had transferred his headquarters to the left bank of the Côa, a curious incident occurred before his disbelieving staff. Lieutenant General Thomas Picton, in command of the Third Division of the Allied army at Pinhel, perhaps ten miles away, rode up to the hills overlooking the Côa. When Craufurd was informed of his approach, he went forward to meet him. According to William Campbell of Craufurd's staff, "Slight was the converse, short the interview, for upon Craufurd's asking inquiringly, whether General Picton did not consider it advisable to move out something from Pinhel in demonstration of support, or to cover the light division? in terms not bland, the general made it understood that 'he should do no such thing.'" Before returning to his division Picton rode further to the front "to take a peep at the bridge." Craufurd was obviously stunned by Picton's action; especially since Wellington had issued orders four months earlier to insure the safety of the Light Division. As early as 8 March 1810, Wellington wrote to Craufurd reassuring him, "I intend that the divisions of General Cole and General Picton should support you on the Coa, without waiting for orders from me, if it should be necessary; and they shall be directed accordingly." The last week of May, a memorandum was sent to Picton, Cole, and Craufurd instructing Picton to "observe the ford of Porto de Vide, as well as the bridge over the Coa, under Pinhel." Again, on 2 July, a memorandum was issued to the concerned commanders asking them "to communicate with each other." In consequence, Picton wrote to Craufurd two days later about establishing a post of dragoons at Valverde so "I may be enabled to co-operate with them [Light Division]." [27] When the Light Division was fighting for its life on the banks of the Côa, however, that promised aid was not forthcoming.

In the battle on the Côa the commanders in chief of both armies had issued strict orders to their subordinates to avoid any serious en-

gagement. Wellington had continually cautioned Craufurd and ordered him to retire behind the Côa and certainly not to engage in any
action on the east bank of the Côa. In his private correspondence
with William Wellesley-Pole, Wellington complained bitterly, "I had
positively desired him not to engage in any affair on the other side of
the Coa; and as soon as La Concepcion was blown up on the 21st, I
had expressed my wish that he should withdraw his infantry to the left
of the river; and I repeated my injunction that he should not engage in
an affair on the right of the river." Anticipating his brother's reaction,
"You will say, if this be the case, why not accuse Craufurd? I answer,
because, if I am to be hanged for it, I cannot accuse a man who I
believe has meant well, and whose error is one of judgment, and not
of intention." Similarly, many of the troops in Craufurd's command
were disturbed by his ill-conceived decision to fight on the Côa.
Charles Napier wrote, "It was a fierce and obstinate battle for the existence with the light division, and only Moore's regiments could . . .
have extricated themselves from the danger into which they were so
recklessly cast; yet it was their first battle, and Craufurd's demon of
folly was strong that day: their matchless discipline was their protection . . . and nothing but the excellence of his men and officers saved
the division." [28]

The battle on the Côa also became a topic of discussion among
the highest officials of the British army and government. The military
secretary at the Horse Guards, Lieutenant Colonel Henry Torrens,
wrote to Lieutenant Colonel James Bathurst, Wellington's military
secretary, upon learning of the battle, "I fully agree with you that
Craufurd ought not to waste lives we can ill spare in a petite guerre
which can have no effect, one way or other, in the ultimate success of
your operations. . . . I shall only add that it appears to me to have
been *badly executed* and *ill told*." He admitted to Colonel Gordon, "I
think our friend Craufurd made a bungling business of it." As more
details of the battle reached England, Torrens wrote to Wellington's
brother, "Lord W is between ourselves much dissatisfied with Craufurd, who, let his talents be what they may, certainly does not possess
either temper or genius to conduct the details of an outpost." In response to Bathurst's letter of 25 July, Torrens condemned Craufurd,
declaring, "The conduct of your commander of the advance guard ap-

pears to be founded in more ignorance and incapacity than I could possibly have supposed any officer capable of who lived the last experience of military operations in the field. I confess I am distressed and disappointed upon the occasion, as I had a very favourable opinion of Craufurd's talents." He observed, "But he appears to me to allow the violence of his passions and the impetuosity of his disposition to overthrow the exercise of his judgment upon occasions where discretion is no less essential than firmness to the efficient performance of the duties of a partizan. This subject is much talked of and I fear Craufurd's reputation as a general has received a shock which it will be difficult for him to recover." Similarly, Lord Liverpool, secretary for war and the colonies, reflecting the king's concerns, wrote, "His Majesty . . . laments the loss of those brave men who have fallen in the affair of the 24th." [29]

Masséna, meanwhile, had been strongly opposed to any major engagement with the Allied army. Although he had ordered Ney to push a large force on Almeida, invest the fortress, and summon the governor, he apparently became apprehensive, fearing Ney might become engaged in a general action. When his artillery commander, Eblé, informed him on 23 July that Ney had abruptly left Ciudad Rodrigo at midday to join the 6th Corps, Masséna sent an ordnance officer, Pierron, with instructions for Ney "not to undertake anything important before his arrival, which would be very soon." Soon thereafter, Masséna sent his trusted first aide-de-camp, Pelet, with instructions to join the 6th Corps and await his arrival. Pelet left Masséna's headquarters on the night of 24 July amidst the "extremely heavy" rain. After wandering aimlessly in the woods of Matilla in the downpour and darkness for several hours, he finally reached Ciudad Rodrigo early the next morning only to learn that a battle had taken place on 24 July, that the 6th Corps had occupied the east bank of the Côa, and that Almeida had been invested. According to Eblé, Ney had declared "that he was going to besiege and take the fortress and at the same time defeat the enemy." When Masséna arrived at Ciudad Rodrigo later in the day, "he was very angry," but his staff officers dissuaded him from going directly to Ney's headquarters. Instead he sent Pelet and his chief of staff, Fririon, to talk with Ney. When they reached Ney's quarters at Aldea del Obispo early on the morning of

26 July, Ney was still in bed. Fririon queried him politely, but Ney felt this form of questioning implied criticism of his action so he declared "that he had followed his orders but that nobody appreciated what he was doing for the others, that the enemy had resisted him, [and] that he had fought an excellent combat." Pelet expressed Masséna's concerns "by saying that after finding forty thousand enemy before him, . . . he had, without warning the Prince, advanced with his whole corps instead of making a simple reconnaissance." Pelet explained, "It was not surprising that the Prince had been worried about an unexpected movement."[30]

Apparently Masséna was placated by his staff officers upon their return from Ney's headquarters. With conciliatory words they described "his moderation, his willingness to take orders." However, that evening a letter arrived from Junot that enraged Masséna and his staff. Without consulting the Prince, Ney had written to Junot on 24 July inviting him to move a segment of his corps to Castelo Rodrigo "in order to menace the left of the enemy and oblige him to retire on Viseu." Junot, on the contrary, ignored the request and informed Masséna of Ney's proposal, pointing out, "In these circumstances, as in all other, I only desire to support the goals of Your Excellency's operations." Junot concluded his dispatch requesting "the honor of [conducting] the siege of Almeida." Masséna could hardly restrain himself. Ney's intentions were contrary to the discipline and good of the service. According to Pelet, Masséna "wanted to use his personal authority to humble this haughty spirit." A reconnaissance of Almeida was to be the pretext for Masséna's visit to Ney at Aldea del Obispo. After lunch and a reconnaissance of the fortress, Masséna spent the night at Ney's headquarters. The next morning Ney met with Masséna and his staff. The Prince announced that Junot's 8th Corps would conduct the siege, despite its limited strength, by transferring troops of the 6th Corps to him. "After much discussion the Prince quoted the letter written to the Duc; he showed it with some ill humor and sternly reproached the Marshal," Pelet recalled. Ney "contained himself; he spoke highly of the British army and exaggerated the difficulties of the siege, the danger of employing weak forces beyond the Côa, and the difficulties of crossing it. . . . At last he got his way and convinced the Prince, who had intended all along to give him the siege but wanted to make him believe he might not obtain it" because of the disobedience on 24 July and his efforts to draw Junot into his operation.[31]

In addition to the losses, both in manpower and matériel, the friction created between the commanders and their subordinates, especially Masséna and Ney, and the lost opportunities in the final outcome of the battle left the combatants exhausted and disillusioned. The French had mauled the Light Division badly and driven it back across the Côa with considerable loss, but Craufurd's unit had not been destroyed as an effective fighting force. The French troops had effectively demonstrated their courage and determination as "the finest infantry in the world." They had reaffirmed their confidence in their arms and commanders and handled their enemy brutally in the first major engagement of the campaign. According to Loison, "A very important advantage resulted from this success [and] it is that the combat of the 24th will prove to the English that [they have] no position that our infantry can not seize, and to our soldiers that the English army is no more difficult to conquer than the Spanish and the Portuguese." The Light Division, deployed in their characteristic line to maximize firepower against the French columns, experienced little success in repulsing Loison. The French had successfully occupied several thousand acres of farmland covered with maturing grain and captured many wagons laden with wheat that the Allies had been unable to withdraw or destroy because of Ney's rapid advance. Nevertheless, the disappointed French commanders had hoped for a decisive victory culminating in the destruction or capture of the Light Division. In a letter to Masséna, Montbrun apologized, "I regret that the overwhelming topographic difficulties that we encountered deprived us of the results that would have demonstrated to His Majesty how much his cavalry, by their conduct, merited his favor."[32] Indeed, if Marshal Ney had been familiar with the terrain between Almeida and the Côa, he would certainly have realized the critical nature of Craufurd's predicament and acted accordingly, but fortune served British arms well that day.

Meanwhile, the Allies had little to applaud. Despite their fortuitous escape from Ney's corps under the most trying circumstances, many had been killed or wounded and their confidence in their commanders had been shaken. Their pride had been bruised, their communications had been cut with Almeida, now surrounded by French troops, and their enthusiasm for the forthcoming campaign had suffered a serious blow. Yet they had demonstrated their courage and poise against a formidable foe commanded by highly competent officers. Even in defeat they reflected glory on their founder, Sir John Moore, and from that day forward they would never again suffer such a defeat at the hands of the French. Indeed, Liverpool, after expressing satisfaction at "the brilliant gallantry" displayed by the English troops, announced, "The King has been gratified in observing that the courage and discipline of the troops in this contest with very superior numbers, not only enabled them to frustrate every effort of the enemy to cut off the Light Division, but ultimately to repel successfully and repeatedly the desperate attempts of the enemy, to force the bridge over the Coa."[33] Writing to defend his action to the public in England, Craufurd exaggerated his enemy's strength and heaped praise on the stand of his Light Division: "A corps of 4,000 men remained, during a whole day, in presence of an army of 24,000 men; it performed, in the presence of so superior a force, one of the most difficult operations of war, namely, a retreat from a very broken and extensive position, over one narrow defile. . . . We did not lose a gun, a trophy, or a single article of field-equipage." Although Craufurd placed Loison's forces at 24,000 men, the French attack involved only Ferey's infantry of 3,773 men and four regiments of Montbrun's cavalry totaling 2,279 horsemen.[34] Nevertheless, his forces, outnumbered two to one, did succeed in extricating themselves from a hazardous position. Also of prime importance to the British was the recognition that the recently trained Portuguese troops possessed the qualities of first-rate soldiers. Elder's caçadores, in the midst of the fighting throughout the day, performed as bravely and effectively as the British regiments of the Light Division. The importance of this information was noted with satisfaction in the highest levels of the British army as well as by the king who commended "the steadiness of the 3d regiment of Portuguese chasseurs."[35]

Thus ended the savagely fought battle on the Côa in which the troops of each army discharged their duty in the best military tradition. This bitter episode between the sieges of Ciudad Rodrigo and Almeida became characteristic of the ensuing campaign and reflected the fierce determination of the soldiers and officers to overcome their opponents. It provided little comfort for either Masséna or Wellington, and it ultimately had a significant psychological effect upon the garrison defending Almeida.

Chapter 11

The War of Logistics

TWO DAYS after the fall of Ciudad Rodrigo, Masséna returned to Salamanca. During the next month he strained to solve the complex logistical problems, complicated by corruption and malfeasance, while his quartermaster general, Lambert, struggled in a morass of conflict and chaos to carry out his orders. In many ways this period between the fall of Ciudad Rodrigo and the siege of Almeida had a more serious impact upon the army than either siege. "There was . . . a morale sickness," according to Pelet, because "the soldiers were already wearied by the attacks against Ciudad Rodrigo; they had become apathetic as a result of the delays in the works of the last siege, the inclement weather, the lack of food, and finally of having been denied the prize" of the final assault against the city. Opposition toward Masséna's campaign strategy became more serious among the officers, who were unaware of his specific orders from Paris. Indeed, it was a period of frustration and embarrassment for Masséna, his officers, and his soldiers at a time when they had expected few difficulties.

During the siege of Ciudad Rodrigo, Lambert and his predecessor, Michaux, had overcome a multitude of logistical problems in order to feed and supply Masséna's army. When they captured the town's magazine and observed the maturing grain in the countryside, they assumed that their supply difficulties had come to an end. As time passed it became increasingly clear that their problems had just begun. On the day the town capitulated, Lambert intuitively cautioned Masséna, "You know the efforts that I have made since my arrival to coordinate all the elements of the army service and the ad-

225

ministration of the provinces under your command; my task was not light or easy." Two days later when it was realized that the captured magazine could not even sustain the 6th Corps, much less the 8th Corps, and that the maturing crops were hardly ready for harvest, Lambert's comments seemed prophetic indeed. Some of Ney's troops had been on half ration since 7 July. Two days after the town fell, Ney requested that Masséna continue supplying his troops from the magazine at Salamanca until they could procure food from the occupied countryside.[1]

Junot and his *ordonnateur*, Michaux, were equally vocal in their complaints about supplies. No food had reached the 8th Corps between 11 and 14 July and the First Division, commanded by General Clauzel, was suffering acutely. Michaux accused Masséna's ordonnateur at Ciudad Rodrigo, Clapier, of rerouting a supply train destined for Clauzel's headquarters; hence the 24 requisition wagons and 14 caissons laden with 14 ton of grain and 22,038 rations were diverted to Ciudad Rodrigo. Michaux complained bitterly to Junot, Lambert, and even Clapier. He accused the ordonnateur of permitting Clauzel's troops to starve while he favored the needs of the 6th Corps; his claims were substantiated by comparing the number of rations allotted to the 6th and 8th Corps between 1 and 14 July. The 6th Corps had received 332,242 rations while the 8th Corps had received 155,577—a difference of 176,665 rations. He also complained of the transfer of administrative officers from the 8th Corps. Regarding transportation, Michaux asked Junot, "How will I be able to transfer the food and even the sick? You know that the country we occupy is stripped entirely of oxen, mules, and wagons." He pointed out that Masséna had told him to expect nothing from the magazines at Salamanca and to fabricate 200,000 rations of biscuit—an impossible order! He concluded, "Where will I find grain in a country that is unable to meet the daily needs of the 8th Corps?" He questioned Lambert, "How will the First Division and artillery exist if no subsistence is sent here," and he threatened to resign if Lambert were not "more favorable toward the position of the 8th Corps."[2]

Lambert responded sympathetically the next day to Michaux, promising to do everything possible for the 8th Corps. Following Masséna's instructions, he ordered Michaux to form a reserve magazine of 200,000 rations utilizing "all the resources of the province of Zamora"; 24 caissons, as well as available farm wagons, would be put at his disposal, but all convoys from Salamanca would cease; finally he authorized the collection of 22,820 gallons of wine, of which one-third was to be distributed to the 8th Corps and two-thirds to the hospitals. Meanwhile, Junot wrote directly to the Prince on 17 July: "[It is] indispensable that the entire province of Zamora as well as other areas be made available, and that the regiments detached from the 8th Corps be returned so that they can be employed to forage." Despite Lambert's support, Masséna seems to have reversed himself in a letter the same day: "It is not possible to give you the entire province of Zamora to feed your corps; our position demands massive provisions for Ciudad Rodrigo—general depot of the army." The 47th and 70th Lines would be returned to the 8th Corps, but he suggested that Michaux redouble his efforts to collect food in the area occupied by the 8th Corps. Junot was shocked and dismayed when he learned of Masséna's decision. He wrote again describing the suffering of Clauzel's division which lacked 4,000 rations each day. Unable to relieve the suffering of his men, Junot apparently sanctioned the unauthorized seizure of a convoy carrying 16 ton of wheat and 75 head of cattle en route from Benevente to Salamanca.[3]

On 20 July, Ney again complained, "The situation of the troops of the 6th Corps becomes worse each day because of the lack of food. Absolutely nothing exists in the magazine; for several days the soldiers have been reduced to half rations." He noted that while his troops were repairing the breach at Ciudad Rodrigo and filling in the trenches and battery positions below the city, they had been "insufficiently nourished"; during the hot weather many became sick and had to be sent to the hospitals. The food shipments from Salamanca were described by Ney as "hardly sufficient to serve a division." The Prince responded promising the arrival of "considerable wheat"; in fact, two convoys were en route and the second was laden with 99 ton of corn, flour, and barley.[4]

Pressure on Lambert from Masséna and the corps commanders was the result of various circumstances. Although the provinces of Palencia, Valladolid, and Avila had fulfilled Lambert's appeals for requisitions, Salamanca and Zamora were deficient, and the provinces of Toro, León, and Segovia had contributed nothing to the magazines at Salamanca. The army was utilizing 45,606 rations of biscuit each day, 1,368,207 per month. Consequently, Lambert requested and received permission to employ troops for the collection of requisitions throughout the provinces under Masséna's control.[5] The major reason for the lack of provisions, however, can be traced directly to the belligerent attitude of the governor of the Sixth Military District of Spain, General Kellermann.

As early as 10 July, Lambert cautioned Masséna, "It is urgent to put an end to these particular acts [that compromise] the security and needs of the army." Two days later Lambert's anger exploded when he accused those responsible for the interruption of supplies sent to Salamanca from Valladolid. He appealed forcefully to Masséna who alone was "able to put an end to what occurred at Medina del Campo," where Major D'Hebert la Tour, commissioner of war, was in command. Instead of sending the wagons to the army depot at Salamanca, he ordered the wagons unloaded and returned to Valladolid. Provisions from Valladolid, Palencia, Penafiel, Segovia, and the other areas began to accumulate until 240 ton of corn, wheat, flour, and barley had been discharged at Medina del Campo by the major who exercised exclusive power directly from Kellermann. Complaining acrimoniously of the deterioration and destruction of the supplies at Medina del Campo while the men of the army suffered serious deprivations, Lambert asked Masséna to write directly to Major D'Hebert la Tour and instruct him to send all provisions at Medina del Campo to Salamanca immediately. He also requested that a daily report of the provisions at Medina del Campo be forwarded to him along with bills of lading for the supplies that would be sent on to Salamanca the following day. This information concerning the major did not surprise Masséna since his chief of staff, Fririon, had complained to Kellermann about the interruption of supplies during the first week of July. Kellermann responded on the twelfth of the month, "I have a commissioner at Medina who has an inclination to be independent." According to the general, he administered the district of Medina "as if it were a divided state, separated from my government." Yet, he pleaded ignorance and promised "to reprimand this conduct." He also mentioned

that the 600 ton of supplies had been sent to Salamanca in the previous fifteen days.[6]

On 13 July, Lambert pleaded with Kellermann not only to send
all available wagons with the biscuit and rice from Valladolid but also
to continue fabricating 20,000–30,000 rations each day. "I beseech
you," he wrote, "to give your cooperation for this disposition which is
no less pressing and important than when our object was to aid the
army during the siege." However, to ensure the shipment of food from
Medina del Campo, Lambert sent an inspector, M. Cautair, to the
town with letters for Major D'Hebert la Tour. The inspector spoke
with the major and M. Dubuisson, who vociferously disagreed with
each other about the shipment. He was stunned to learn that although
the major wanted to send all of the supplies at Medina del Campo to
Salamanca, "he receives daily orders from General Kellermann, who
proscribes that all the provisions sent from Valladolid and other
points be discharged [there] and the wagons returned." While Cautair
was at Medina del Campo, a convoy of about 30 wagons arrived with
grain piled to the top of the side boards. Despite his "urgent en-
treaties" the wagons were unloaded again and returned to Valladolid.
Upon his pleading it was agreed that 400 asses loaded with barley
would go to Salamanca. Accordingly, Cautair wrote directly to the *ordonnateur général* at Valladolid requesting his intervention; the wagons should continue to Salamanca "without being obliged to discharge their cargoes at Medina as they have done until now." He also
complained that the food was being indiscriminately dumped since
storage sacks were not available.[7]

When Lambert learned of events at Medina del Campo, he wrote
immediately to Masséna: "The orders of General Kellermann paralyze
the transportation and will make us short of everything. I am not
afraid to accuse him; he is destroying all administration by his
unprecedented and culpable resistance. Some provisions exist in
abundance at Medina while we starve." Masséna was dumbfounded
by Kellermann's attitude and insubordination. A staff officer was sent
to Valladolid to instruct Kellermann to send all the provisions that had
been collected in the Sixth Military District to Salamanca. Once the
wagons had been discharged at Salamanca, they would return to Val-

ladolid conveying the sick from the regimental hospitals. Simultaneously, Masséna wrote to D'Hebert la Tour informing him that he would countenance no delays in the shipment of supplies at Medina del Campo. To pacify the enraged Lambert, Masséna wrote convincingly to him; he implied that Kellermann was doing his utmost to supply the magazine at Salamanca, and he cautioned Lambert to have the wagons discharged at Salamanca or Kellermann's efforts to supply the army would be paralyzed. He noted that the general would employ 24 wagons and teamsters solely for the purpose of transporting 120,000–150,000 rations from Medina del Campo to Salamanca each week; thus it seemed the entire magazine could be moved to Salamanca in 15 days.[8]

In a conciliatory vein, Masséna wrote to Kellermann announcing his decision to transfer the army magazines to Ciudad Rodrigo: "I am making plans to march on Almeida. In consequence, I must concentrate most of the resources and subsistence in the fortress." Kellermann would be expected to furnish wagons for the transfer. "I give you my word," promised Masséna, "that they [wagons] will go no further [than Salamanca]." As soon as the sick were boarded, the wagons would be returned to Kellermann at Valladolid or elsewhere in the area under his jurisdiction. He instructed the general to "enjoin the major at Medina del Campo to create no obstacle for the arrival of the provisions. . . . You know better than anyone the importance of the march of the Army of Portugal. Food is necessary in order to continue military operations. . . . Do all that I would do in a similar situation and imagine yourself as commander in chief of the army."[9]

Masséna now assumed that his logistical problems had been solved, but the next day Lambert was again complaining about the ineffective transportation system of the army: "You alone are able to persuade General Kellermann" to halt his obstructionist tactics. The exasperated Masséna wrote a menacing letter to Kellermann: "The unloading at Medina del Campo of provisions that come from Valladolid and the other parts of your district creates a great embarrassment at this moment and becomes a subject of anxiety in my operations." Again he repeated his promise: "I have given you the assurance that the wagons sent to Salamanca will not go beyond there." To demonstrate this fact he ordered 3,000 sacks fabricated for

759 ton of grain so there would be no need to retain the wagons at Salamanca. "You know that the commissariat is the most essential [unit] in the army," and he warned of the "terrible consequences" for those who thwarted his plans for the campaign. Masséna concluded his letter poignantly: "Acknowledge the reception of my letter and inform me of what you have done for its prompt execution." [10]

Kellermann responded upon receipt of this letter, declaring that a list of difficulties was not necessary to encourage his zeal for "the service of His Majesty and the glory of Your Highness," but he admitted, "My zeal and good intentions are not enough." He promised to send 360 ton of corn and barley to Salamanca that day, followed by two other shipments of comparable size as soon as possible. Consequently, he ordered the requisition of all wagons within the district of Medina to transport food from Medina del Campo to Salamanca; he was reluctant to utilize his wagons to carry the sick back to the hospitals of Valladolid, suggesting that some of them be sent to Avila, Segovia, Arevalla, or even Aranda. [11]

Two days later Kellermann announced that he had collected the "transportation from the districts of Medina and Olmedo in order to transfer the magazine from Medina to Salamanca." However, he requested additional escort troops to repel the numerous and often successful attacks by the guerrilla bands. Meanwhile, Masséna accepted Kellermann's explanation for the delays at Medina del Campo but reiterated his order to secure adequate transportation. He also felt the need to repeat his promise that the wagons would be "regularly returned" after reaching Salamanca, and he assured the general that he would "never forget [his] support." He was less placatory about transporting the sick to Valladolid: "We absolutely lack transportation to send them elsewhere." [12]

Lambert seconded Masséna's conciliatory efforts in an encouraging letter to Kellermann; in effect, he apologized for one officer who had sent twelve wagons beyond Salamanca and another who was dilatory in unloading the vehicles there. On occasion, Lambert even ordered the return of wagons without the sick "despite the congestion in our hospitals" so that there would be no delay. At the same time, Kellermann promised "extraordinary effort . . . to move the greatest possible quantity [of provisions]." All the wagons at Tordesillas, Medina del Campo, Olmedo, and Valladolid, including those employed in the harvest, were requisitioned to haul supplies to Salamanca. Although Kellermann placed an embargo on all wheat magazines within his jurisdiction, he was apparently disappointed by his efforts to collect grain and requisition wagons; only 1,000 farm wagons were made available to the army. He declared, however, "I give orders that all the wagons are to be discharged at Salamanca and that the officer in charge of the escort only turn them over to the proper troops."[13]

It is noteworthy that few convoys arrived at Salamanca during the controversy between Lambert and Kellermann, but just before 20 July the wagons began to arrive with increasing regularity. Every day between 21 and 27 July a convoy left Salamanca for Ciudad Rodrigo. A total of 123 caissons and wagons reached the depot with 92 ton of flour, 89,291 rations of biscuit, and 1,173 sickles, followed by herds of cattle and sheep. During the last four days of July, convoys, which included at least 74 wagons and caissons and 188 mules, left Salamanca with over 38,000 rations and 132 ton of flour or grain for Ciudad Rodrigo. Meanwhile, as food filtered into the army depot from most of the provinces of the Sixth Military District, General Jean-Marie Dorsenne at Burgos announced the "absolute impossibility" of fulfilling Masséna's request for 800 ton of barley and 320 ton of wheat since he was feeding 3,000 horses, forming a magazine of a million rations under Napoleon's direct orders, and could not devote two months to fulfill the request.[14]

On 26 July, Masséna transferred his headquarters to Ciudad Rodrigo to have more immediate control over siege preparations for Almeida. He was not impressed with the arrival of grain shipments which appeared meager in comparison to the needs of the army. He had many questions: Why were Lambert's wagons not put to better use? What was the fate of the 40 ton of vegetables sent from Burgos and stranded at Villodrigo? How could the abuses be halted at the depot? Why were the bakers of the 8th Corps at Salamanca not sent to work at Ciudad Rodrigo? How could they halt the illegal seizure of animals from convoys by French troops? He declared to Lambert, "Your convoys are not significant enough; reinforce them; our position demands it. Divide your transports in three columns and see that one departs for Salamanca each day."[15] Masséna, aware that the flour mills surrounding Salamanca were grinding 25 ton of flour and baking 50,000 rations every 24 hours, decided to concentrate operations so the biscuit could be fabricated at Ciudad Rodrigo. He had already advanced special funds to the sappers at Ciudad Rodrigo to repair and reactivate the 16 ovens in the city, and two hydrological engineers had been sent to advise on repairs and the best means of operations. All of the usable ovens and mills within 12 miles of the city were operating at full capacity. In addition, a commission, composed of engineers, food suppliers, and a local citizen named by the civil governor, Señor Casa Seca, was sent out on 28 July by Clapier to reconnoiter, locate, and put into operation the ovens and mills within a reasonable distance of the route from Ciudad Rodrigo to Almeida.[16]

Within two days the commission reported on its survey. Most of the villages had ovens capable of producing 40 to 50 rations each day, but the larger ones like Gallegos had 15 ovens capable of baking 110 to 150 rations per day and five or six ovens capable of baking 500 rations a day. The 6th Corps had built five ovens at both Aldea del Obispo and La Concepción, and 30 operable mills were designated for use by the army; it was also agreed that the large church at Gallegos would be transformed into an advance magazine. Based on this promising report, Masséna wrote to Lambert at Salamanca indicating sufficient ovens were now available in the vicinity of Ciudad Rodrigo. Henceforth, grain and wheat could be sent to Ciudad Rodrigo rather than delayed until it could be baked at Salamanca. Yet, Masséna's first aide-de-camp recalled that after the grain was harvested, "the troops could not find any method to have bread made from the grain." As a result, when the commissariat had no means to distribute the flour, the soldiers were forced to purchase bread from the sutlers. Large magazines were organized at the convents of San Augustin and Tercera Orden de San Francisco and at the cathedral. The spacious monastery of La Caridad, which had been utilized to store grain, was transformed into a hospital for some 600 convalescing soldiers on 6 August. With facilities capable of producing 40,000 rations per day in the vicinity of Ciudad Rodrigo, Masséna ordered many of the regimental bakers, especially those of the 8th Corps, supposedly at Salamanca, as well as Spanish bakers, to reinforce the brigade of bakers already at the town. He also asked the town junta to provide 430 ton of wheat from the town magazine.[17]

On the first of August, 500 sheep and 100 head of cattle left Salamanca for Ciudad Rodrigo. The following day only 25 caissons were available to carry 43 ton of flour, so 200 mules were employed to transport grain. Simultaneously, another convoy left Toro with 35 ton of grain, 30 ton of flour, and 36 ton of barley.[18] Yet this had little impact upon Ney, who sent Masséna an urgent dispatch requesting bread from the magazine at Ciudad Rodrigo; he claimed that the 6th Corps had no operable ovens. The Prince was dismayed by the request: "I assure you that I am really surprised in your requesting me to send bread from here, after the assurance that you have given me that your corps would be fed in the area it occupied." Apprehensive about using rations intended for the invasion of Portugal and hoping that Ney would only need rations for five or six days, he agreed to send 8,000 rations a day to the 6th Corps from Ciudad Rodrigo. When he requested wagons to retrieve the rations, Ney responded that only 10 were available and they could hardly haul enough provisions since two days were necessary to make one delivery to the 6th Corps; consequently, food would only arrive every other day. Seeing the ordonnateur at Ciudad Rodrigo, Clapier, as the culprit in this matter, Ney denounced him bitterly and complained of the transfer of the commissariat and bakers of the 6th Corps to Ciudad Rodrigo and other areas. Supplies had not reached the corps in ten days and the men, on half ration, held out little hope that food would be forthcoming from Ciudad Rodrigo. Disorders broke out and the exasperated Ney appealed to Masséna for the return of his staff and bakers. He remarked sarcastically, "It is not with promises that armies are nourished," but adequate provisions did not reach the 6th Corps until the men harvested the grain fields in the vicinity of Almeida. It is curious that despite this shortage of wagons, the ever resourceful Loison succeeded in forming his own private parc by hiring Spanish wagonmasters and requisitioning wagons for the use of his division. On this occasion, however, Loison's 47 wagons were already committed to the harvest and transporting sick to the hospitals.[19]

Meanwhile, the wagons continued to roll westward across the Castilian plain toward Ciudad Rodrigo. On the morning of 3 August, 19 wagons filled with 31 ton of flour and 70 sickles left Salamanca, and another convoy with 19 ton of barley and three ton of grain for the artillerymen left for San Muñoz. On 4 August, 24 caissons with 40 ton of grain, 111 sickles, 1,000 pair of shoes, 156 head of cattle, and 656 sheep set out from Salamanca trailed by 300 mules carrying 17 ton of barley. Twenty-three wagons were scheduled to leave for Ciudad Rodrigo the following day, reflecting the growing cooperation between the various units of the army.[20]

On 6 August, Masséna received a very disturbing document, issued by Kellermann as an Order of the Day on 26 July. After the general was notified in a letter from Berthier that Zamora and León had been placed under his jurisdiction, he wrote to Masséna promising to "fulfill [his] intentions and augment the Army of Portugal." Despite these protestations of loyalty and support, Kellermann apparently decided to assert his independence. Based upon Napoleon's decision to place Zamora and León under his jurisdiction, he assumed that his powers would be comparable to those exercised by the other governors of the military districts of Spain. Consequently, he issued his infamous "Order of the Day" on 26 July, which only reached Masséna eleven days later. In this insubordinate order he declared, "In the future, the civil, military, and administrative authorities should not comply with any requisitions for food or powder which do not originate from [the general]." From these orders he temporarily excluded the Army of Portugal.[21] Masséna was dumbfounded when he saw Kellermann's order; it was a direct threat to his authority and the fate of his army. He responded immediately: "It is not without surprise that I received your Order of the Day of the 26th. I am obliged to remind you of your assignment. . . . As commander in chief of the Army of Portugal, I have supreme command of northern Spain and your government is included within it." Reiterating his "singular surprise," he demanded that the order be rescinded at once and cautioned, "I forbid you to touch the treasury. . . . You will conform to the contents of my letter and be more cautious in the future in your Orders of the Day." Kellermann expressed pain at the displeasure he had caused

Masséna with protestations of innocence. "Far from having claimed to be independent," he maintained that the order was based on his efforts to fulfill Masséna's needs.[22]

The day after Masséna had reprimanded Kellermann, 7 August, he was forced to write another firm letter to the general. He had just learned that despite the pleas of the *inspecteur des services*, Cautair, to continue the convoy to Salamanca on 1 August, the officer in charge of the wagons unloaded 160 wagons of biscuit at Medina del Campo "in accordance with the orders of General Kellermann." His patience exhausted, the Prince angrily dictated a letter to Berthier describing the general's flagrant insubordination. He denounced Kellermann for his questionable administration of finances and the "extraordinary contribution," for his attempt to usurp Masséna's authority, and for his insubordinate orders to discharge the cargoes of his wagons repeatedly at Medina del Campo "although he [knows] we have no means to re-trieve these supplies." He concluded, "I ask Your Highness to remind General Kellermann to improve his behavior and curtail the limits of his prerogatives. We experience enough actual difficulties in the col-lection of requisitions and in securing transportation" without the hin-drances of French officers. After completing this letter Masséna de-cided not to send it. Convinced that he could deal with Kellermann's unethical behavior by himself, he was also anxious to avoid the em-barrassment of accusing another marshal's son.[23]

Consequently, on 8 August, Masséna wrote to Kellermann again, insisting that the wagons continue on to Salamanca. At the same time Lambert was carrying on his own painful correspondence with the general. He reproached Kellermann for his "unmerited criticism" and complained of the condition in which the rations were arriving. "In the last convoy of biscuits," he noted, "sixty ton were opened at both ends [and] have all the appearance of being pillaged by the en-emy." Kellermann accepted the inevitable, at least temporarily, and ordered the wagons to continue on to Salamanca. By mid-August the transportation system between Valladolid and Salamanca was finally regularized. Kellermann did not learn from this embarrassing experi-ence. After the fall of Almeida, Masséna ordered the wagons to trans-port the supplies to Ciudad Rodrigo. Kellermann responded by issuing orders for the cargoes to be dumped by the side of the road after leaving Salamanca. This action forced Masséna to denounce the general to Berthier and Napoleon for gross insubordination but this opposition continued intermittently until the Army of Portugal crossed the frontier on 15 September and invaded Portugal. Kellermann was not the only provisional governor to suffer Masséna's wrath. General Jean-Victor Rouyer, governor of Zamora, had been instructed to collect 7,460,144 réaux still owed by the provinces of Toro and Zamora. Apparently he made few efforts to collect this contribution, especially in Toro, so Masséna ordered him to relinquish his command to General Jean-Baptiste Jeanin and report at Salamanca with his baggage. At first he refused to resign, claiming he held his command by authority of King Joseph. Ultimately, Masséna was forced to write to Joseph to secure his removal.[24]

Despite the continuing controversy between Masséna and Kellermann, supply convoys continued to ply the road westward toward Ciudad Rodrigo. On 7 August, five wagons loaded with 10,800 rations, a column of mules carrying 10 ton of barley, and a shipment of 40 ton of grain left Salamanca for Ciudad Rodrigo, while a ton of grain was dispatched to San Muñoz. At the same time convoys from all over northern Spain wound their way toward Salamanca. One hundred fifty wagons of grain were en route from Palencia; 40 wagons laden with 24 ton of rice advanced from Burgos and Victoria; 19 ton of barley, 50 head of cattle, and 200 head of sheep moved from Avila; and 21 ton of grain, three ton of oats, one ton of wheat, and 33 ton of corn left Medina del Campo. On 8 August another convoy of 15 caissons with 21 ton of grain, 132 sickles, and 1,400 pairs of shoes crossed the Roman bridge and left Salamanca.[25]

With massive quantities of supplies streaming into Ciudad Rodrigo, Masséna became convinced that Lambert could control the administrative branch of the army more effectively from Ciudad Rodrigo. Twice in a letter dated 8 August he declared, "Your presence is absolutely necessary here." Nevertheless, Lambert remained at Salamanca for another week, working furiously to complete his massive requisition effort. As Masséna prepared his departure for La Concepción to take personal charge of the siege of Almeida, he wrote to his quartermaster general, "You will definitely establish your administration at Ciudad Rodrigo and send Clapier to Salamanca as your replacement."[26]

In addition to the convoys concentrating at Salamanca for the trek to Ciudad Rodrigo, Lambert organized a small ambulance division for the army. With eight wagons, almost 5,000 feet of linen dressing, and 3,000 bandages, he hoped it would be used sparingly. Another task assigned to him by Masséna was the creation of a reserve column of 600 to 800 pack mules, drawn from throughout the 11 provinces, before 12 August. Lambert labored frantically to complete the train, but it had to be completed by his successor, Clapier.[27]

On 9 August, 22 ton of barley was loaded on pack mules to follow 23 caissons carrying grain and two ton of rice. That evening a second column left Salamanca with 33 ton of grain and 2,000 pairs of shoes aboard 29 caissons and eight ton of oats and barley on the backs of mules. The next day 23 ton of flour and four of oats left Salamanca on pack mules, following a long column of 42 caissons of flour and three caissons of rice. In announcing this shipment, Lambert also informed Masséna that Kellermann had again undermined the efforts of the commissariat by discharging 88 ton of wheat at Medina del Campo. On 11 August, 25 caissons hauled 41 ton of grain and pack mules carried 34 ton of flour; 17 more caissons carried 28 ton of flour and two wagons were laden with three ton of rice.[28]

With the initial preparations for the siege of Almeida drawing to a close, the magazines at Ciudad Rodrigo were increasing each day and the shipping center of Salamanca had 120 ton of grain, 116 of wheat, 18 of rice, 26 of barley, seven of rye, five of oats, 256,037 rations of biscuit, 137 head of cattle, and 902 head of sheep awaiting transportation to Ciudad Rodrigo. Extraordinary efforts were made to send a massive convoy on 12 August to demonstrate the commitment of the commissariat to the army that was about to open the trenches before Almeida. Consequently, 18 caissons loaded with grain, four with rice, and three with 12 ton of biscuit, followed by 30 extended wagons and some mules carrying oats and barley crossed the Tormes River and proceeded to Ciudad Rodrigo.[29] Although there were still interruptions in the arrival of provisions it is obvious that Masséna and his quartermaster general had been remarkably successful in securing adequate supplies to sustain the army during the siege.

Coupled with the pressing supply problem, Masséna faced the dilemma of securing adequate funding for the army. There were numerous items necessary for the subsistence and operations of the army that could not be acquired through requisitions; therefore, payment in currency was a necessity. Since February 1810, 17 million réaux in "extraordinary contributions" had been levied on the provinces of Salamanca, Toro, Zamora, and Avila by Ney but only nine million had been collected. Later Junot levied a total of 11 million réaux on the areas he occupied, namely, León, Burgos, Valladolid, and Palencia, but only six million had been accumulated. Consequently, 21,922,647 réaux were outstanding. To meet the needs of the army Masséna ordered Lambert to complete the collection of these contributions. According to Kellermann, the collection of these contributions was fulfilled in the provinces of Valladolid and Palencia in four days, but there were abuses in the use of the funds. As a result, Masséna wrote to Kellermann on 25 July warning him that all of the funds collected were to be reported promptly to the paymaster general of the army, Maury; none of the contributions could be utilized for his own troops.[30]

Another financial irregularity that again involved Kellermann apparently came to light inadvertently when officers escorting the prisoners of Ciudad Rodrigo to Valladolid complained of rumors that Spanish prisoners were securing their freedom. This soon mushroomed as others, including provincial governors, informed Masséna of the illegal traffic in prisoners. He learned that Spanish officers were buying their freedom with payments of gold to highly placed French officers, including Kellermann's own chief of staff and the senior health officers. Masséna demanded that this reprehensible traffic be halted immediately. Simultaneously, Kellermann had written to Masséna on the matter, suggesting that if Spanish prisoners were permitted to purchase their freedom after swearing allegiance to King Joseph Bonaparte, the extra funds could be utilized by the hospitals at Valladolid. Masséna was stunned! He replied indignantly, "The proposal in your letter seems so odious that I cannot consider it. I order that all the prisoners without distinction of rank, grade, or wealth be sent to France." It clearly was not in the interest of the Emperor or the French army to accept financial remuneration for such infamous conduct. Masséna insisted that a report and list of all prisoners be sent on to Burgos. He asked, "How could you believe that men who buy their freedom with money would ever be faithful to His Catholic Majesty?" and concluded with the damning statement "Such traffic should be repugnant to a soldier."[31]

Kellermann expressed astonishment that Masséna would have believed such a rumor; only his "respect and old attachment" would permit him to overlook the charge. He responded upon receipt of Masséna's letter, "You have been poorly informed on what has occurred at Valladolid on the subject of the prisoners of war. I am confident no one secured his liberty for money and that traffic of this kind has never existed, at least not with the concurrence of the chief in charge of the depot." He admitted that some Spaniards had come to him offering to take an oath to King Joseph and to "prove their sentiments by contributing to the public needs." Kellermann claimed that since that subject was "too delicate," he referred the decision to Masséna; the prisoners were retained at the depot to await his response. Regarding those who pleaded sickness, Kellermann claimed that a certificate from a health officer was required before he could grant permission for any infirm prisoner to return to his home. Nevertheless, Lagrange at Salamanca confirmed the charges mentioning a transaction in which 34 officers, prisoners from Ciudad Rodrigo, had been returned to their homes under the pretext of sickness in return for "a rather considerable sum in gold." He also reported it was common knowledge that for as little as 3,000 to 4,000 réaux in gold a prisoner could guarantee his freedom. If an authorized furlough could not be procured, the prisoners were permitted to "escape." Based on an impeccable source in Salamanca, Ney also reported that about forty Spanish prisoners from Ciudad Rodrigo had purchased their freedom for as much as 24,000 réaux each in gold, and he suggested several ways to ferret out the guilty French officers and end this abomination.[32]

Besides the "extraordinary contribution" and the usual forced contributions and requisitions, Masséna's quartermaster general turned to the Spanish treasury for supplemental funds, especially when they fell within the proscribed categories established in the *Budget de l'administration de la guerre*. Within a five-week period he utilized these funds to meet the requirements of the artillery and sappers seven times for a total of 112,000 francs. Funds were also transferred from the Spanish treasury to purchase additional wagons, animals, and transportation equipment.[33]

Masséna's administrators experienced considerable success in collecting funds between 21 June and 9 August. In fact, 429,362 francs were collected in five provinces to augment 593,936 francs already accumulated in the army chests. As a result, Lambert had wanted to pay the troops their salary for May and June, totaling well over five million francs; this proved impossible so only the Irish and Prussian troops in the 8th Corps were paid to halt their inordinate desertions to the Allies.[34]

In addition to the "extraordinary contribution," the requisitions, and the credits advanced by the Spanish treasury, Masséna ordered Clapier to levy an "extraordinary contribution" of 500,000 francs on the town of Ciudad Rodrigo in order to repair the damage to the city, the walls, and other vital structures. There was continual discussion about the amount of the contribution because Ney had levied a 120,000 franc contribution, followed by an additional 16,000 francs, for the construction of field forges for each of the eight dragoon regiments of the Second Division. This contribution was collected methodically, with the encouragement of the Spanish civil governor, Señor Casa Seca, a supporter of King Joseph and prefect of Salamanca. French courts were organized to inquire into the payment of the contribution, and the homes of many prominent citizens as well as the monasteries and convents were searched for precious metals and currency. Two commissioners of war, Achille Dequise and Victor Fay, held hearings, drew up detailed inventories of the property, and imposed heavy contributions.[35]

Perhaps the most curious case that ultimately came to Masséna's attention was concerned with Pedro Domingo Solis, the abbot of the Premonstratensian monastery of La Caridad, Norman de Castro, the second procurer, and Joaquin Guzman, a monk and close associate of the abbot. Before the French army reached La Caridad the abbot fled with the monastery's treasury, apparently hoping to hide and protect it at the hamlet of Gata, where he took up residence. After Ney learned of the flight of the abbot, he imprisoned Castro and Guzman at Ciudad Rodrigo. When they were later interrogated by the gendarmes, they declared that Solis had escaped to Gata with the wealth of the monastery several months earlier. On 17 July, Ney sent a column of the 76th Line and cavalry to Gata to arrest the abbot and retrieve the treasury. The column arrived and quickly located the abbot. Solis indicated that he had already sent the priest of Bodón with a letter to Ney announcing his intention to turn the treasury over to the legal authorities of "His Catholic Majesty or else His Majesty, the Emperor Napoleon."

The officer of the column, suspicious that the latter had written and predated his letter after the arrival of the troops, seized the treasury and arrested Solis. He was returned to Ciudad Rodrigo and imprisoned until the commander of the army gendarmerie, Colonel Pavetti, interrogated him and sent for confirmation of the letter that was written to Ney. The abbot drew up a detailed inventory of the treasury and "swore before God" that he had turned over the entire treasury when he was arrested at Gata. Ney "strongly doubted the sincerity of his declaration," but Pavetti seems to have confirmed the abbot's story of the letter and, after intensive investigation, assured himself of the truth of the story and the good character of the three clerics. He wrote to Masséna, "They have never manifested a marked resentment against the government, either French or Spanish, and as their monastery is situated near this town, they are left by circumstances to follow one or the other." Solis submitted a petition to Masséna, who wrote to Ney for additional information in order to respond to the abbot's petition. Masséna replied on 11 August concerning the treasury. Based on the investigation and comments of Pavetti, Solis and his colleagues apparently were given their freedom.[36] Most of the hearings before the commissioners of war were less dramatic but the results were equally rewarding. Daily collections varied from 8,580 to 121,908 réaux, and by 9 August a total of 697,753 réaux had been collected.[37]

The artillery of the army faced similar administrative, jurisdictional, and logistical problems. The very responsible but equally pessimistic artillery commander, Eblé, was instructed by Masséna to create an enlarged siege parc of 70 or 80 pieces and a vast siege train for attack on Almeida—an extraordinary request. Eblé reacted by writing directly to Berthier in Paris. The general asked him to consider "that the war in Spain does not resemble that of any other nation of Europe. Spain does not offer resources of any kind, not even those that are abundant everywhere. It is necessary to demolish the buildings to collect wood and iron that is necessary for our work. It is necessary to send great distances to obtain charcoal; finally it is necessary to create everything, and it is in this scarcity that Your Excellency would leave the artillery without arms." In order to organize and increase the siege train he requested six pieces of sixteen, four mortars, 11 caissons, 25,000 projectiles, 15,000 sandbags, and 65 ton of powder. He also appealed for 342 additional artillerymen to fill out the complement of his newly augmented siege armaments. Two weeks later he requested that the 250 artillerymen stationed at Burgos and Pancorbo be dispatched to Ciudad Rodrigo. Moreover, when he learned that two Spanish artillerymen would be sent to fill positions on his staff, he lectured Berthier, discouraging the appointments.[38]

Masséna, keenly aware of Eblé's difficulties, gave his requests first priority. He wrote directly to Berthier requesting that the "just and urgent" needs of the general be met, especially for cannon and projectiles that could not be found in the countryside. Each time Eblé requested additional resources, Masséna responded with new funds. After an inventory of the guns and munitions found in the magazines at Ciudad Rodrigo, Eblé began to organize the new siege train at the convent of San Francisco. Much of the 73 ton of powder captured at Ciudad Rodrigo was ruined, but some of the 81,000 projectiles found in the ruins of a magazine were retrieved for use with the French guns. Eblé wrote to General Auguste-Daniel Belliard, governor of Madrid, requesting three Spanish ten-pound howitzers since 6,000 shells had been found for them at Ciudad Rodrigo and he only had one such gun. At the same time orders were issued for the purchase of sandbags, fascines, gabions, and powder sacks being fabricated at Salamanca. Some of his artillerymen joined the sappers and detachments of the 6th Corps in repairing walls and fortifications of the town; others collected lumber for the construction of gun platforms, prepared fuses for the bombs and shells, stripped the iron from the fortress of La Concepción, and searched for lead. Extraordinary efforts were made over a period of several weeks to collect and send some 344 blocks of lead from León and Astorga to Ciudad Rodrigo by way of Valladolid, but by 9 August, as supplies were being moved up to Almeida, the convoy could not be located. Simultaneously, the master gunners devoted considerable time to repairing and realigning the sights on the artillery pieces. When Eblé took Pelet to see the artillery parc, seven forges were in operation and twenty-seven guns had already been mounted on their carriages. Yet, by 11 August, as siege operations were drawing near, Eblé was still complaining about the lack of large projectiles and powder. He had sent to Bayonne for both, but they could not arrive before the batteries were armed at Almeida.[39]

There were jurisdictional disputes among Eblé and the various army commanders, especially Ney. He was involved in a continual controversy with Ney over the Hanoverian Legion, which had been transferred to the siege train. When the second battalion of the Hanoverian Legion was recalled by Ney, Eblé complained bitterly to Masséna that these troops were vital for the siege train. Horses also became a point of contention between the two men. As a result of the weakened condition of his horses and draft animals and the deteriorated condition of the road from Ciudad Rodrigo to Almeida, Eblé was forced to allot two days for double teams to drag each wagon, caisson, and siege piece for 21 miles. Efforts were made to repair the foundation of the road with small stones to avoid the numerous wagon breakdowns en route and ease the load of the horses. The sappers faced serious problems concerning the safety of the stone bridge between Alameda and Gallegos when the teams dragged the heavy guns across it. This heavy work, the lack of ripe fodder, and "continual activity" claimed almost a score of horses each day and weakened those still working. By the time the siege train marched on Almeida, over 400 horses were useless, and by the end of the siege 1,400 had succumbed. Consequently, Eblé appealed to Masséna for the use of 300 horses each day from the 6th Corps. After considerable discussion it was agreed that 250 draft horses would be sent each day from both the 6th and 8th Corps and the 2d Corps would be required to provide 150 work horses. Moreover, the foot artillerymen from each corps were to be placed at the disposition of the siege train.[40]

To supplement preparations of the siege train at Ciudad Rodrigo, detachments were sent out to gather charcoal—invaluable for the artillerymen. A workshop was established in the woods between La Concepción and Aldea del Obispo to prepare and store the charcoal until needed by Eblé's men. A workshop for the fabrication of gabions and *saucissons* was also constructed in the woods nearby. Troops of the 6th Corps were sent into the woods to fell the great trees surrounding the shop, and the workers, composed of several hundred men from the Hanoverian Legion and the artillery from both Ciudad Rodrigo and the 6th Corps, constructed large quantities of fascines and other siege equipment, thanks in part to Eblé's timely shipment of 200 hatchets. Three miles east of the workshops, the large church in the village of Alameda was transformed into a munitions magazine. Powder and cannonballs were stored there until after the siege had begun. Carpenters and woodworkers from the army and throughout the Sixth Military District were employed by the artillerymen and sappers, and the butchers of the 6th Corps busied themselves collecting two ton of grease for the axles of the siege train. Clearly, Masséna and his staff were deeply committed to meeting the needs of Eblé. Nevertheless, the general was discouraged by the lack of cooperation from the various provincial governors and their staffs. He continually appealed to them for supplies, and he often sent them specific instructions on the formation of convoys and their loads en route from Salamanca.[41]

General Lazowski, working closely with Eblé, coordinated the efforts of the sappers. He also received special consideration from Masséna. Funds from the Spanish treasury, the "extraordinary contribution," and the levy on Ciudad Rodrigo were placed at his disposal to repair the breach in the walls and fortifications of Ciudad Rodrigo, as well as the two damaged bastions at La Concepción. The sappers from the 2d Corps were ordered to join him with their tools and all of their available sandbags. Yet, Lazowski was exasperated. For the lack of funds, the 20 wagons that were to follow him from Bayonne with 6,000 trenching tools never left France. Sandbags, so vital for excavation in the rocky surfaces surrounding Almeida, were in short supply, but 10,000 were being fabricated at Salamanca to augment those supplied by the 2d Corps and some 6,000 unused during the siege of Ciudad Rodrigo. Nevertheless, on 10 August, Masséna was still pleading with Berthier concerning siege equipment: "The opening of the trenches before Almeida will take place on the 15th of this month. The difficulties the sappers experience to procure wood for fascines and the *fagots de sape*, as well as several other indispensable objects, necessarily cause these delays." [42]

As the date approached for opening the trenches and beginning the siege, Eblé and Lazowski labored endlessly to complete and coordinate their final plans. Shells for the pieces of twelve and the six-pound mortars had not arrived but were expected soon from Valladolid along with cartridge paper. In the meantime, the first fifteen wagons of the siege train left the Colada gate of Ciudad Rodrigo and crossed the Roman bridge below the town walls. Following the rough road through Gallegos and Alameda to Aldea del Obispo, the teamsters unloaded the gunpowder while the succeeding convoys deposited their munitions in the church at Alameda or continued on to the vast plain east of Almeida. With a total of 65 siege pieces including 15 massive pieces of twenty-four, 10 pieces of sixteen, and 15 pieces of twelve, 12 mortars, three howitzers, and four swivel guns, Eblé had organized a formidable train. The remainder of his impressive train included 529 wagons loaded with 55,745 projectiles, 72 ton of powder, 132,901 cartridges, and 160 wagons carrying picks, shovels, axes, flints, shell casings, saltpeter, charcoal, shell fuses, torches, grenades, almost 15,000 sandbags, thousands of gabions and saucissons, and vast quantities of lumber for the batteries. [43]

With siege wagons leaving Ciudad Rodrigo each day, Masséna was anxious to transfer his headquarters to La Concepción. Although apprehensive about the defenses of the town, he instructed Eblé to "arm, repair, and place [Ciudad Rodrigo] in the best state of defense." Indeed, the general's engineers and sappers had succeeded in filling the trenches on Grand and Little Teso; they had, with the aid of the troops of the 6th Corps, repaired the breach in the walls, and the town fortifications had been partially restored. The town arsenal, the castle except for the tower, the chapel of Cerralbo, and the magazine of Tavervilla [?] were in ruins as a result of the French bombardment. Eblé, therefore, continued to use the cathedral as the town magazine. The subterranean vault of the portal was used to store up to 80,000 ton of powder, and the long nave, protected by the towering roof, was used to store the arms of the garrison. However, he was unwilling to assume the responsibility for the defenses of Ciudad Rodrigo. Only with the arrival of powder and projectiles from France could the town be put in a state of defense, but without wagons he could not retrieve the necessary supplies. He also would need a demi-company of workers, a large detachment of artillerymen, extensive funds, building materials, and a large garrison. "That is very succinctly," he wrote, "the obstacle that we face in the execution of your orders." Eblé also wrote to Berthier and the minister of war, Henri Clarke, detailing Masséna's orders; he reiterated his responses, noting that it would be utterly impossible to undertake two operations such as the siege of Almeida and the refortification of Ciudad Rodrigo simultaneously.[44]

Despite the determination and confidence with which Masséna administered the preparations for the siege of Almeida, his correspondence with Berthier reflects a sense of frustration and abandonment. Although he wrote long and voluminous letters to Berthier detailing his many problems, the "Major General" seemed more concerned with promotions, the disposition of troops, and so on. As soon as Ciudad Rodrigo fell, Masséna began to appeal for support in preparing for the siege of Almeida: "We suffer great difficulties in gathering subsistence at Ciudad Rodrigo to effect our march on Almeida and invest it." The harvest had not yet started and the lack of adequate transportation was "most embarrassing." He acknowledged the efforts of his staff, especially Lambert, but he was deeply disturbed by the impact of the dangerous guerrilla bands which "multiply and increase daily" in their war against his supply columns.[45]

Four days later Masséna again complained about the lack of transportation that brought his operation to a halt: "It is impossible to march without any type of subsistence in this very arid Portuguese country. I do everything possible, but unfortunately my intentions and those of the quartermaster general cannot change our position." Only with the coming harvest would he be able to "put the army in movement. Despite all my efforts, I am able to promise nothing."

Masséna felt that his letters did not reflect the urgency that he had hoped to convey, so on 25 July he wrote a confidential letter to Berthier: "It will be impossible for me to detail to you all of the extortion that takes place in the two corps. It exists in finance and despite all my care, disorder still exists beyond all description. I have served and commanded in the armies, but I never have seen anything similar. The contribution that His Majesty has ordered to be levied for the pay and needs of the army are, for the most part, spent in different areas. They have made a traffic in subsistence. . . . I have [implemented] all the penalties to halt it but the unfortunates who arrive in Spain are generally subject to the most shameful exactions." Masséna was forced to admit that he could not solve the chaotic financial situation. Complaining about the corruption and incompetence, he observed, "I would tell you personally what I cannot write. I am often embarrassed. I do all that is possible but I cannot begin [the siege]."[46]

Despite his pessimism, on 13 August, as he was preparing to leave Ciudad Rodrigo to take up his new quarters at the fort of La Concepción, Masséna announced that over a million rations of biscuit would be available by the end of the month. On 16 August, he left his residence at Ciudad Rodrigo and traveled to La Concepción, where his concerns for logistical problems were replaced with the tactical considerations of a fortress under siege.

Chapter 12

Preliminary Operations at Almeida

WHILE SUPPLIES were being collected and siege equipment concentrated for the advance to Almeida, the advanced guard of the army was deployed to cover the siege. Following the battle on the Côa, Ney moved to secure the left bank of the river, probe Wellington's positions, and protect the investing forces. Two battalions of the 66th Line and 200 horsemen of the 25th Dragoons crossed the Côa at 2:00 A.M. on 25 July and followed the dirt road across the plateau toward the village of Valverde. Leaving one battalion to occupy the village, they pursued a detachment of enemy cavalry to the heights before Pereiro; a few stragglers were sabered, but the exhausted dragoons could not overtake the main column until they were confronted by almost a thousand horsemen and infantry. General Gardanne immediately withdrew his column to the Côa and his men took up positions behind Cabeço Negro. Outposts were established flanking Valverde, and half a battalion of the dragoons was deployed at Aldeia Nova to observe the road to Guarda.[1]

Early the morning of 26 July, Ferey pushed several columns toward Guarda and Celorico to determine the exact location of the Allied army. One column marched for three hours along the difficult and rocky road toward Pinhel, only to find that it had been evacuated several hours earlier by Picton's division. A second column passed through Valverde in the direction of Carvalhal; Craufurd had abruptly left the latter at 2:00 A.M. and retired to Freixedas and Celorico. A third column proceeded southward toward Pinzio and Guarda. At Carvalhal they sighted a vast detachment of cavalry, perhaps 900 horsemen, retiring along the road toward Celorico. Again on 27 July, Loison sent two battalions of the 66th Line to Pinhel while another battalion of the 66th occupied Valverde in order to sustain General Lamotte's light cavalry brigade. Loison moved his headquarters to Pinhel at 4:00 A.M. and deployed his troops to resist any enemy attack "by Alverca, Freixedas, and Carvalhal, the only points by which it would be possible to attack the center of [the French] position from the left bank of the Coa." [2]

To determine the exact location and strength of Wellington's forces at Guarda, Loison sent Gardanne's column out from Valverde; marching southwest through Azinhal and Peva, they occupied Freixo on 28 July. At 9:30 the next morning they resumed their march, passing through Lavarexo, Castanheira, and Pousade. Reaching a point within six miles of the high plateau on which Guarda was situated, the detachment was confronted by 200 peasants drawn up in a line and firing their weapons in the air. Gardanne sent a proclamation to them; none of them could read but their firing ceased. After securing intelligence on the British positions, Gardanne withdrew his column through Pousade and Castanheira. By 7:00 P.M. they reached Freixo and soon after dark they arrived at Valverde. [3] Meanwhile, Lamotte advanced on Alverca only to be shadowed by a detachment of 60 Allied cavalrymen. Passing through the gutted village of Souro Pires on the road to Trancoso, this column was halted beyond Póvoa, where Allied infantry and cavalry barred its advance. From these reconnaissances, Loison learned that the British held formidable positions at Guarda and Celorico. [4]

In fact, Cole's Fourth Division and the Royal Dragoons held Guarda while the Light Division and Cotton's cavalry were in the vicinity of Celorico. "In this position," Wellington had declared confidently, "I am equally prepared for any operation that it might be in my power to undertake for the relief of Almeida, if it should be attacked; and better prepared for our retreat, if that should be necessary." At the same time he would force Masséna to endure the inconvenience of employing both of his corps for the siege since the Allied army was massed between Celorico and Pinhanços—well within four hours of concentration. [5]

Simultaneously, several of Montbrun's cavalry regiments carried

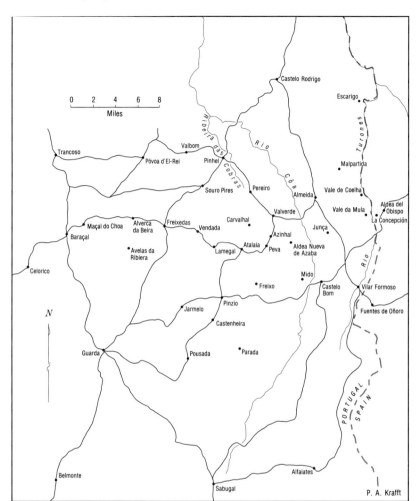

Map 10. Area between Almeida and Guarda

out reconnaissances of the Allied positions. Lorcet's cavalry advanced to Fuente Guinaldo to communicate with General Reynier's column, which was marching from the Tagus River. Other columns fanned out toward Vila Maior and along the Côa valley; each was fired upon by Portuguese ordenanza and each suffered casualties. The French were stunned to find the Portuguese peasants armed and ready

Figure 35. Road and terrain from Valverde to Pinhel

to resist. "The inhabitants in the hamlets or little villages," complained Montbrun, "gather many people to defend against the approach of our troops. I do not yet know if it is a general measure of the Portuguese, but I suppose that until now it only occurs in those villages pillaged by our soldiers." However, Montbrun was not the only officer to complain about the resistance of the Portuguese peasants. Within a week it would be clear to the French that their unexpected reception was a result of Wellington's "Proclamation to the People of Portugal." In it he exhorted them "to render the enemy's advance into their country as difficult as possible, by removing out of his way everything that is valuable, or that can contribute to his subsistence, or frustrate his progress." The weak and indolent would be forced "to make an exertion to save themselves from the danger that awaits them, and to save their country." Indeed, any person who held communications with the enemy or aided and assisted them in any way would be considered traitors; they would be "tried and punished accordingly."[6]

Some Portuguese peasants in the vicinity of Pinhel did, in fact, return to their villages. They were promised security for their families and property in return for wine, bread, and meat, but this case was an exception. When the Marquis d'Alorna went to Pinhel to make contact with his compatriots ten days later, he reported that "the English have committed horrors" by chasing the inhabitants from their homes with their swords and "pillaging the property left behind." Regretfully, he admitted, "The few inhabitants left behind all say the same, . . . that they have been mistreated by the French soldiers." Acknowledging the efforts of an officer to maintain order and respect for private property, d'Alorna claimed, "The good will of the officer is not general and much violence is committed; this will render the conquest of Portugal very arduous." On the other hand "the Portuguese resent the yoke of the English." He claimed, "The Portuguese troops detest them and the people are convinced that the English are responsible for their misfortunes."[7]

Masséna hoped to win the support of the Portuguese by issuing a conciliatory proclamation. He declared, "We enter your territory as friends, not as conquerors. We do not come to make war on you, but to fight those who force you to make it." After detailing the suffering brought on by the British, he appealed to the inhabitants to remain peacefully in their homes, continue their domestic work, and "do not regard us as your enemies as you should those who counsel you in a war in which you cannot benefit." To underscore his determination and to maintain the strictest discipline and protect the Portuguese population, he issued an Order of the Day admonishing his general officers to "punish severely soldiers convicted of marauding or pillaging." There would be no leniency! "The laws and regulations are to be executed with exemplary rigor."[8]

Despite these measures, reports continued to plague Masséna of the continued violence across the frontier and the bitter resistance exhibited by the Portuguese peasants. Another letter was sent to his corps commanders on 7 August: "Rape, pillage, and murder seem to be the order of the day [in Portugal]. Recently in a village on the Portuguese frontier some unknown soldiers raped three girls after murdering their father. Some days later a merchant following the army was stopped . . . and plundered completely. Unfortunately, I am able to cite fifty more examples [just] as revolting." He appealed to them to join him in "repressing these disorders." Each corps commander was instructed to meet with his officers and inform them that they were to be held "personally responsible for all excesses committed in their regiments, battalions, and companies." As a means of curtailing future excesses, those found guilty of such crimes would receive the "most severe" punishment. He also sent a confidential letter to Loison, whose troops were deployed in Portugal. Describing "the violence, the pillage, and murder . . . [as] too lengthy to detail," he informed Loison that he would countenance no further complaints against his division. "If His Majesty receives any complaints on your account, it will only prejudice his opinion of you," Masséna warned. Weeks later, Masséna received a dispatch from Berthier dated 15 August concerning the excesses committed by his troops: "His Majesty charges me to inform you that you are obliged to punish severely all disorder or insubordination; that you are in command and there is no modification in command; [and] that you are obliged to halt the brigandage."[9] Masséna was unable to fulfill this simple and direct order despite the severity with which he punished the guilty.

In the meantime, a formal advanced guard was organized under the command of General Ferey to provide an early warning in event of an enemy attack. This force, composed of battalions of the 15th and 32d Léger, the 66th Line, the 3d Hussars, and the 15th Chasseurs à cheval, supported by four pieces of four, was deployed in a line of posts to screen French operations at Almeida. A battalion of the 15th Léger was posted on the heights to the right of the village of Pereiro; a unit of voltigeurs and the first squadron of the hussars held the bridge and village of Pinhel and observed the roads to Celorico and Trancoso. A battalion of the 32d Léger was established to the left and behind Aldeia Nova along with the 15th Chasseurs à cheval. The second and third squadrons of the 3d Hussars were posted at Carvalhal on the left bank of the Cabras River, and a company of voltigeurs and another company of the 66th Line occupied Valverde where Loison's headquarters had been earlier. Finally, the fifth and sixth battalions of the 66th Line were camped before Gateira [?] with two pieces of four. The primary goal of Ferey's unit was to observe the routes from Guarda and Celorico and to avoid any serious contact with Wellington's forces. If the enemy were to advance in force from Celorico on Pinhel or from Guarda on Aldeia Nova, Ferey was instructed to retire across the Côa and "defend the passage of the river until the last extreme" or until he received new orders; but whatever the case, he was expected to cover the rear of the 6th Corps, which was engaged in the investment of Almeida. At the same time, Montbrun established three cavalry regiments along the Portuguese frontier from Fuentes de Oñoro through Sabugal and Atalaia to form a junction with Reynier's cavalry, deployed northward. However, the bulk of his cavalry units were deployed in the various villages between Ciudad Rodrigo and Almeida to protect the siege convoys from attack by guerrilla bands.[10]

The advanced guard occupied their assigned positions and reconnaissance columns routinely crossed into enemy territory to detect any troop movements. The monotony of post duty was occasionally interrupted by the capture of enemy patrols or the exchange of information under a flag of truce; usually topics of common interest were discussed, especially those concerned with the welfare and exchange of prisoners. On 6 August, French columns were fired upon near Freixedas and south of Aldeia Nova, but their probes continued in the directions of Celorico and Guarda. A line of allied posts was sighted near Carvalhal the next day and the 3d Hussars observed a post of eighty horsemen at Lamegal. Despite continual assurances that Wellington's positions remained unchanged, Ney was apprehensive about an attack since his artillerymen had been detached for service with the siege train. Masséna was aware of his concern but was determined to undertake the siege of Almeida utilizing all of the resources at his disposal.[11]

Opposition from the Portuguese peasants and irregulars increased in intensity each day. On 8 August, Chef de bataillon Delomme, leading five companies of infantry to reconnoiter the Douro River valley and seize any available cattle, was stopped from crossing the river by a strong peasant force. Delomme was forced to withdraw up the Douro to the Côa in order to reach the opposite bank. In approaching Vila Nova de Fozcoa he engaged a detachment of militia, forcing them back into the town, where the defenders fired artillery at his column. In accordance with his orders, Delomme withdrew, taking a herd of sheep with him. The same day Mermet sent a column toward Vila Maior but Portuguese troops had already occupied the village. Ferey led a company of voltigeurs and 50 cavalry from Carvalhal toward Lamegal, where he sighted 100 enemy horsemen; following a brief skirmish, the French withdrew. Although reconnaissance columns continued to press Wellington's posts, there was little contact for days since Craufurd's post could observe the French from their vantage point atop the heights of Jarmelo. On 11 August, however, a company of voltigeurs encountered 60 Allied cavalry at the village of Souro Pires. Another column led by Colonel Laferrière attacked an enemy post three miles beyond Carvalhal on the road to Celorico, driving back the defenders at a gallop and overrunning the second post with little difficulty. A third column of infantry and cavalry marched from Aldeia Nova but soon encountered a band of peasants under the command of retired Captain José António. When the reports of all the reconnaissance commanders were examined that night, it became obvious that there had been little change in Wellington's positions, except an increased presence before Lamegal.[12]

In addition to the intelligence gleaned from the daily reconnaissances carried out by French troops, less reliable information was collected from local peasants and captured soldiers. Deserters who came into the advanced posts almost daily, especially from the King's German Legion, provided precise details and data on the location and strength of almost every regiment in the Allied army. All reports placed the Allied army in the vicinity of Celorico and Guarda with advanced posts as far as Atalaia and Lamego, but Masséna was more interested in accounts that Wellington's army was retreating toward Coimbra and the sea. All reports confirmed that preparations were under way to withdraw both British and Portuguese armies. The baggage, artillery, and sick were reported to have been evacuated to Coimbra; the magazines had been transferred toward Lisbon; the wine ration for the army had been halted; and the women and wagons had been sent on to Lisbon or Porto to escape the French advance. "The British have not the least confidence in the Portuguese troops," wrote Ney, and, according to his intelligence reports, Wellington wanted to resist the French incursion into Portugal, but the British government had decided upon "a very formal defense with nothing serious undertaken against the French." Ney repeated these erroneous reports in almost every letter to Masséna during the first half of August. This information was even reinforced by the Marquis d'Alorna who learned from his countrymen that the road paralleling the Serra da Estrêla and the Mondego River had been repaired for the movement of artillery and wagons to Coimbra.[13]

Based on the persistent reports of Wellington's withdrawal, Ney and his staff were convinced that their attack on Almeida would be the last and perhaps least demanding operation of the campaign. They expected minimal resistance from the garrison at Almeida and a leisurely advance to Lisbon where they would assume control of the capital. These inaccurate reports undoubtedly lulled the French into a sense of false security that would be dashed at Almeida and throughout the campaign.

The British, on the other hand, expected the French to move against their army immediately, rather than to invest Almeida. Indeed, on 27 July, Wellington confided to Hill, "There is not the smallest appearance of the enemy's intention to attack Almeida; and I conclude that, as soon as they have got together their force, they will make a dash at us, and endeavor to make our retreat as difficult as possible." Two days later he confessed to Charles Stuart in Lisbon, "The enemy's operations against Almeida are so very feeble, and their intentions so little distinct" that this indecision could only benefit the Allies. Awaiting the French attack, Wellington's staff cautiously sifted through the reports of his patrols, the detailed accounts of the ordenanza officers, and the interrogation reports on the deserters, especially from the French Hanoverian Legion, to determine Masséna's intentions. Rumors of a French advance were quickly pursued to determine authenticity, and Wellington's intelligence network assured him that there would be adequate time to deploy his army against any surprise attack.[14]

While the advanced guard of the French army established secure positions on the west bank of the Côa to protect siege operations, the remaining units of Loison's division tightened their investment of Almeida. Indeed, while Loison was pursuing Craufurd's threatened division down to the bridge on the Côa on 24 July, Simon's brigade was racing across the plateau to seal off Almeida. As a result of this swift advance, hundreds of acres of grain, wagons loaded with grain, and fields of sheaved wheat were captured. Even before the French pickets had been established around Almeida, a French officer was sent to the fortress barrier under a white flag with a letter from Loison. Governor Cox happened to be in the covered way near the garrison gate; he met the Frenchman there rather than permitting his entry into the fortress. Cox refused to discuss capitulation terms, declaring that Almeida would be defended "to the last extremity." The following morning when the infantry of Simon's brigade slipped behind some field walls within range of the garrison guns, Cox opened fire on them. Surveying the size and seeming disorder of the French troops surrounding Almeida and the lack of siege artillery and equipment, Cox informed Beresford, "[The French] movements hitherto made have more the appearance of a blockade than the investiture of a place, with a serious intention of besieging it."[15]

On 26 July, Cox ordered his cannoneers to commence fire on advancing French pickets when they came within range of their guns. This firing was followed by a sortie of 600 men of the 24th Line and some militiamen supported by a detachment of horsemen of the Portuguese 11th Cavalry. Marching 400 yards from the fortress, some soldiers began to level the walls of several buildings that provided the French with cover and masked the fire of the fortress guns; others gathered the sheaves of grain standing in the nearby fields. Loison reacted immediately by deploying two companies of voltigeurs and one of grenadiers, supported by four companies of the Légion du Midi and two howitzers. The Légion, led by Captains Duplan and Boizin, attacked the infantry and charged the soldiers who were tearing down the houses; the Portuguese were driven across the plateau to the glacis of the fortress. At the same time, a small column of perhaps 40 horsemen was sent down to the convent of Nossa Senhora da Barca, situated on a knoll between the fortress and the bridge on the Côa, to maintain communications with Craufurd. They drove a small garrison out of the church, but French skirmishers soon threatened to cut them off from Almeida. As they galloped back toward the fortress, the French opened fire at point-blank range, killing and wounding a number of men and horses before they could reach the safety of the fortress guns. Masséna claimed two casualties in repelling this sortie and placed the garrison losses at 40, while Cox wrote to Beresford, "We had an officer and four or five men slightly wounded." That evening another sortie, composed of almost 400 infantry and 40 cavalry, again moved on the left flank of Marchand's position to retrieve the sheaves of grain. From these sorties, Masséna incorrectly assumed that the garrison's magazines were already low, reinforcing his belief that the defense of Almeida would be minimal.[16]

There was little action on 27 July as Simon's infantry established a line of posts just beyond the range of the fortress artillery. One French soldier of the 26th Line was killed, but there was only isolated skirmishing during the day because the French were busy harvesting the grain and collecting sheaves in the neighboring countryside. However, the following day was one of activity for both Cox and Masséna. At daybreak Cox sent a column of some 800 men to attack the French troops harvesting grain. Three companies of infantry were sufficient to force them to "return precipitously to the fort." A company of voltigeurs of the 69th Line attacked 300 Portuguese infantry, deployed in ambush, and chased them with bayonets to the glacis. Ney acknowledged two dead and three wounded while noting, "The enemy has left several men dead and a great number wounded." Later in the day, a second foray, almost as large as the first but with four field pieces, sallied out from Almeida, again to attack the harvesters working to the left of the French position. At first the four companies of the 6th Léger, according to Captain Guingret, were staggered by the Portuguese attack, but the 69th Line moved forward immediately to reinforce them. A counterattack was launched "with the greatest audacity" and Captain Neumayer and a conscript, Chevreuse, leading the 6th Léger, were able to seize several wagons and one of the guns near the glacis. At the same time a sergeant led 30 dragoons in a flanking maneuver to seize the three remaining guns, but their horses were halted by the many boulders near the glacis. Ney placed the Portuguese losses at 30 and the French at two dead and six wounded. Undaunted by their previous failures, Cox ordered a third column to advance to the left of Simon's brigade to demolish an old complex of stone walls that formed a redoubt on the reverse slope of the glacis. A company of voltigeurs of the 15th Léger repulsed the sortie without loss.[17]

While the Portuguese sorties were being repulsed, Masséna, who had spent the previous night at Ney's headquarters, carried out a preliminary reconnaissance of Almeida. Accompanied by Ney and Fririon, and followed by Generals Eblé, Lazowski, and Ruty, as well as Pelet, Masséna rode to an old stone mill within 800 yards of the fortress, a good vantage point to judge the works, although the garrison opened a brisk fire on his party. After a cursory examination of the fortress, Masséna inspected the troops of Simon and Marchand and then left for Ney's headquarters. Eblé, Ruty, and Lazowski, however, continued their reconnaissance, which was only completed late the following day. Before leaving Aldea del Obispo for his own headquarters at Ciudad Rodrigo, Masséna formally assigned Ney's 6th Corps to conduct the siege of Almeida. Masséna would have preferred to employ Junot's 8th Corps, but strategic and logistic considerations "and the force of circumstances" forced him to reject Junot's request. Much to Junot's dismay, his corps was to remain on the east bank of the Agueda. Clauzel was to deploy his division so that he could cross the Agueda at several points simultaneously between San Felices el Chico and San Felices de los Gallegos in order to reach Almeida within three hours. Junot's two cavalry regiments, the 65th Line, and

Solignac's entire division were to be ready to march in support of Clauzel at a moment's notice. These orders were put into effect the following day.[18]

As soon as Masséna had returned to Ciudad Rodrigo, he wrote to Lazowski and Eblé, "I await with much impatience the results of your reconnaissance and your plan of attack for Almeida." He asked Lazowski to provide details on the proposed trenches, a time schedule, and availability of supplies, concluding, "I am extremely anxious to commence the siege . . . and hasten the operations." Cognizant that the investing troops would "suffer much" from lack of food, inadequate siege materials, and the blistering sun, he appealed to Lazowski to complete his preparations "in the least possible time, and once begun, to continue without the slightest interruption." In a similar letter to Eblé, Masséna requested details on his preparations to establish the batteries, organize an artillery depot, and formulate a realistic timetable for the movement of the siege train to Almeida. Again he emphasized the importance of speed in establishing the batteries and beginning the bombardment: "I urge you to neglect nothing in sending what is necessary in the first convoy to establish your batteries."[19]

At Masséna's headquarters there was considerable ignorance about Portugal in general and Almeida in particular. Until Eblé's reconnaissance had been completed, Masséna and his état-major could only rely upon the information supplied by the pro-French Portuguese officers attached to the army by Napoleon. Expressing anxiety about the formidability of Almeida, Pelet turned to the Marquis d'Alorna, a former lieutenant general in the Portuguese service. Years earlier, as a commander in chief in the district, d'Alorna had established his headquarters at Almeida and directed the reconstruction of its fortifications. Pelet recalled, "He should have been able to give me exact information. . . . He was zealous, devoted, and conversed fluently on military matters or any other subject. The marquis was always ready to tell us everything except what we needed to know, and to answer any question he was not asked." Seeking information on the number of bastions at Almeida, Pelet recorded in his journal, "After counting several times on his fingers, he assured me Almeida had seven bastions and therefore seven fronts." A memorandum prepared in 1808

Figure 36. Aerial view of Almeida

by a French engineer described only six fronts at Almeida, so Pelet pressed d'Alorna for more details. "The marquis protested and assured me there were seven." However, the issue was settled in the first sentence of Eblé's reconnaissance report: "The fortress of Almeida is a hexagon." [20]

Eblé sent his eleven-page reconnaissance report to Masséna on 1 August, detailing the strengths and weaknesses of each component of the fortress defenses. Almeida was constructed in the Vauban tradition in the form of "a rather long and irregular hexagon" with six bastions augmented by six demilunes of varying sizes to cover the bastions, and enveloped by a covered way, salients, entrenchments, a ditch, and a glacis. In examining each bastion and demilune, the fortress curtain, and the terrain before each, Eblé and Ruty agreed that the profiles of the four demilunes were inadequate to protect the flanks of the adjoining bastions. One large demilune, located between the bastions of Santa Barbara and São João de Deos, was well planned and fortified. A second, called the "great demilune," was constructed to cover the flanks of the bastions of Santo António and Nossa Senhora das Santa Brotas and to defend the gate of Santo António that passed through it. The granite walls of the fortress rose as much as 40 feet above the ditch, which was well over 100 feet in width. The counterscarp was faced with granite culminating in a well-palisaded covered way. The glacis was adequately formed but rather steep, thus masking the approach of attackers. [21]

The interior of the fortress had been carefully prepared by the Portuguese with the aid of British engineers. The bastions of Santa Barbara, São Francisco, and São Pedro were dominated by massive granite towers, and south of the gate of Santo António on a slight rise stood "an immense but very old castle with four enormous towers surrounded by a moat." Considered bombproof, it was utilized as the central powder magazine and a barracks for the garrison. There were also several formidable bombproof casemates and living quarters constructed in the bastions and beneath the terreplein of the fortress. According to Pelet, "The British had apparently taken the utmost care of everything in the city for some time," since Almeida was obviously in a good state of repair in anticipation of the siege.

Despite the advanced state of the defenses of Almeida, the garri-

Figure 37. Almeida: The bastion of Santa Barbara, the curtain, escarp, ditch, counterscarp, covered way, and glacis

son and its commander, Governor Cox, dreaded the impending siege. Cox had been appointed to command Almeida in early 1809 so he was well acquainted with the problems related to its defense. For well over a year he had been engaged in efforts to enhance the fortifications, increase the armaments, establish an adequate magazine, solve the crushing financial problems, improve the living conditions of the garrison, and organize, discipline, and train the troops.

From the time of his arrival at Almeida, Cox's correspondence with the commander in chief of the Portuguese army, Beresford, and his military secretary, Major Robert Arbuthnot, revolved around the lack of resources. Soon after he arrived, Cox wrote to Beresford, "I continue to be tormented from all quarters about money; and neither the paymaster nor commissary have any." How could he feed between 8,000 and 9,000 men "without provisions, money, or authority to provide for them"? Cox faced a major crisis when a payroll shipment was temporarily delayed, reducing his troops to destitution. He complained, "They are badly fed, are almost naked, have no beds of any kind to lie on, have no allowance of wood to cook their victuals, and have now for a long time been deprived of their pay, which renders it impossible for them to purchase it or procure any other kind of comfort." Indeed, the troops had received meat only four or five times in the previous three months and a substitute of dried salt fish was "often served out to them in a state approaching to putridity." Cox sought to secure foodstuffs from the neighboring Portuguese officials, but he was at the mercy of the local village official, the *juiz de fora*, who frequently contracted to sell the produce to the agents of the British commissariat for ready cash. Even if adequate funds had been available to purchase supplies, the commissariat of the British army usually leased all available transportation in the area. This situation was to continue for almost a year. Three weeks before Almeida was invested, Cox was still complaining about supplies: "We are dreadfully off, as you know, with respect to provisions: except the small reserve of biscuit, we have not one days bread within the place; and have been obliged this day to serve out rice in lieu of it." However, the "English" magazine at Almeida contained 248,774 pounds of biscuit that Cox hoped to secure for the garrison, thereby solving part of his problem. Scarcities were not limited to food. Cox had begun requesting flints for his troops in August 1809, and a year later he was appealing for 100,000 flints and one million musket ball cartridges to assure his garrison of a 50-day supply. The same situation was faced regarding the needs of the hospital, the barracks, and the commissary.[22]

Initially the garrison of Almeida included two line regiments, the 12th and 23d Lines, and six militia regiments. Cox, with the aid of a small corps of British officers, began to instill discipline and introduce British drill into the regiments. At the end of May 1809, the 24th Line was reassigned to Almeida in place of the 23d; Cox was named colonel of the regiment, but this did not deter him from denouncing its condition. "The new regiment," he declared, "is in the most dreadful state that it is possible to imagine: they are in want of arms, clothing, accoutrements, and in short everything." He gave them the muskets of a recently disbanded militia regiment, but it was evident that the 24th Line would have to be reorganized, reequipped, and retrained. Despite Cox's requests, the 24th Line was still without accoutrements four months later. The regimental officers, both Portuguese and British, worked at length with the 12th and 24th Line, but after six months Cox admitted to Wellington, "I am sorry to say that the two regiments of this garrison have made very little progress in

Figure 38. Almeida: Staircase to bombproof casemate

discipline since you saw them . . . principally owing to the want of active and intelligent officers." They suffered severe deprivation during the winter months, and when Wellington reviewed them in January 1810, "it was so bitter cold that between 20 and 30 men and three or four officers fell down in the ranks." By spring considerable progress had been made in training the 24th Line, under Lieutenant Colonel Bernardo de Figueiredo Sarmento, but the 23d Line had been transferred from Almeida; there was dissatisfaction within the regiment as exemplified by the desertion rate—16 men within a two-day period in March. Nevertheless, by mid-June, desertions were negligible and Cox regarded the 24th Line as a "good regiment of infantry." There were also 222 artillerymen, primarily from the Portuguese 4th Artillery Regiment, as well as 100 men who had volunteered from the 23d Line in order to remain at Almeida. Cox appealed to Wellington for a company of British artillerymen and an engineer, and presently a Royal engineer was sent to Almeida. However, more useful was the arrival on 15 June of a company of the Portuguese 11th Cavalry, numbering 61 men, under the command of Captain Alexandre Pereira da Costa Cardoso.[23]

The training of the militia regiments garrisoned at Almeida was an insurmountable problem for Cox. Soon after his arrival at Almeida, Cox began preparations to disband three understaffed militia regiments. After claiming their accoutrements for the remaining units, he sent them home to Arouce, Tondella, and Viseu. However, Cox never regarded the remaining militia regiments of Guarda, Arganil, and Trancoso as more than bands of peasants serving as part-time soldiers. Five weeks before Almeida was invested he admitted candidly to Beresford, his brother-in-law: "I have very little dependence on them; and even in point of numbers, they are very incomplete; upwards of 800 of the three regiments which I have here, are still absent without leave." Local Portuguese officials were under orders to confiscate the property of deserters, but this had little noticeable effect upon the desertion rate. Recalling the role of the militia in the siege of Almeida during the Seven Years War, Cox observed, "I hope that what I have got will not serve me in the way which those who were here in the year 1762 acted." In that siege all but fifteen rank and file of the three militia regiments deserted before

Figure 39. Almeida: Gate of São Francisco

the siege ended. By the end of June, over 1,000 men from the militia regiments at Almeida were absent without leave. Cox was clearly disturbed by this situation, which reinforced his prejudice against the use of militia. He wrote to Beresford promising to resist the enemy attack for at least fifty days if two of the militia regiments could be replaced with one line regiment: "I think that the place is worth saving, and that its defence should not be entrusted to an inadequate garrison, chiefly composed of peasants who are taken from their houses and families, and shut up as [it] were in a prison, in which they are forcibly kept, and only kept from desertion by the disagreeable measure which I have now been obliged to adopt of not allowing a soldier to pass the gates." Twelve days later the gate guards carried loaded firearms to prevent desertion, and periodically executions of deserters were carried out before the assembled garrison to discourage the practice. He noted poignantly, "When it is necessary to keep troops in a garrison by such means, there is little to be expected from them."[24]

Cox regarded the forced service of peasants in the ordenanza and

Figure 40. Almeida: The demilune between the bastions of Santa Barbara and São João de Deos, the escarp, ditch, counterscarp, covered way, and glacis

militia as counterproductive. The crops rotted in the fields while the garrison and local inhabitants starved—a preposterous situation! Cox declared, "I am well convinced that the advantage to be derived from a number of peasants with unserviceable arms posted upon the passes of the Coa can never counterbalance their loss to the agriculture of the country." During the summer of 1810 the militiamen were "so clamorous to get home to cut their corn" that Cox acquiesced, fearing a mutiny. In fact, to increase the magazines of Almeida, Cox sent many of the garrison troops into the environs to harvest the corn and pick tomatoes. Yet Cox could do little about securing firearms and accoutrements for his militia regiments. Two weeks before the investment, the Trancoso militia, commanded by Colonel Bartolomeu de Aragão e Costa, had little military equipment and the regiment of Arganil, directed by Colonel José de Melo Freire Bulhões, had no accoutrements; over 100 men were without firearms. "I begin now to despair," Cox wrote to Beresford, "of our ever seeing the different articles of equipment which have been so long promised me." Even the 24th Line was still without bayonet belts, 500 caps, haversacks, canteens, greatcoats, and other necessary field articles.[25]

As contact with the French increased along the Portuguese fron-

Figure 41. Almeida: The castle ruins

tier, rumors circulated among the garrison that Nova de Avel had been occupied on the night of 17 July. Consequently, Cox experienced an "extraordinary desertion" of two companies of the Guarda regiment. Since many of the militiamen came from that village, he assumed that they had "gone off with a view of protecting their families and properties." Several parties and later officers were sent out "to bring in the deserters" but no one returned. What else could be expected, asked Cox, from this type of troops; again he declared his inability to answer for the defense of Almeida unless another line regiment was sent there.[26]

As the French drew closer to Almeida, Cox seemed to be overwhelmed by his efforts to secure additional supplies and troops. He frantically appealed to the local juiz de fora of Castelo Rodrigo for "as much grain as possible without a moments loss of time," and on 20 July he complained acrimoniously to Arbuthnot: "Never was a sufficient force placed here for the defence of the fortress since I have had the honor to command it. There never was at any one period 3,000 effective firelocks in the garrison which number . . . I consider as very inadequate." The following morning Cox seemed to panic as gunfire thundered across the plateau and French troops were detected within four miles of the fortress. The stream of pessimistic letters from Cox expressing doubt, persecution, resentment, and even despair had stunned Beresford. The harassed Cox seemed to be crumbling under the increasing pressures. Earlier he had complained about the lack of a "properly organized staff, and persons . . . in whom I can place confidence. I am obliged to attend myself to every little minutia, and my time is completely taken up in seeing and examining everybody who comes into the place, and hearing and deciding upon questions which are every moment referred to me." Upon reflection, Cox regained his composure: "I don't think that I am inclined to view things in an unfavorable light but being rather of a pensative turn of mind, I take things as they are, and reason upon them cooly and dispassionately." Perhaps to assure Beresford of his emotional stability, he concluded, "However I may contemplate misfortune at a distance, I have sufficient courage in the moment of danger, and fortitude enough to bear me up in the most trying adversity." [27]

Beresford did not respond to Cox until he heard gunfire in the direction of Almeida on 24 July. Assuming the arrival of a large food convoy, Beresford commented, "You are indeed I think now most fully stocked with provisions and I hope you will have time to eat them all, but should the fortunes of war decide otherwise, you will let as little as possible fall into the hands of the enemy, or of ammunition." Perhaps Beresford, as Cox, had some premonition of the impending disaster. "In case of ultimate necessity," he wrote, "I need not remind you to have all the public papers destroyed." Yet in an optimistic vein he announced that rumors of Napoleon's arrival in the Peninsula with reinforcements for Masséna were false: "I have therefore some hopes that you may be better off in Almeida than you expect. . . . But whatever be your fortune I beg you will rest assured that I will not forget you, . . . and should you be made a prisoner, you will I am sure have first gained your share of honor, and you will not remain long so." This was not a very comforting thought for Cox as the French skirmishers were closing in around the fortress. [28]

Besides his preoccupation with supplies, the quality of his garri-

Figure 42. Convent of Nossa Senhora da Barca

son, the advancing French, and self-doubts, Cox became engaged in a lengthy strategic controversy with Wellington. Opinionated and outspoken, his relationship with the commander in chief had been less than cordial on several occasions, as exemplified by their correspondence during the past year. Cox regarded himself as a tactician. In May he had already contemplated a possible withdrawal of the Allied army and a lengthy siege: "It would be very difficult [to aid this place,] and getting off the garrison when the place can no longer be defended is an operation I think scarcely practicable." Noting that the guns of Almeida could not cover the bridge on the Côa, he pointed out to Beresford that when the French seized the bridge the fate of his garrison would be sealed.[29]

Despite Cox's evaluation of the situation, Wellington believed it was important to the "general cause" for Cox to "adopt measures to keep open the communication between the fort and the bridge on the Coa. This may be accomplished in my opinion without much difficulty." If the old mill north of the town could be armed with a gun and fitted as a Martello tower, if the convent of Nossa Senhora da Barca could be fortified as a post for 200 men with two guns, if a formidable post for some 500 men with a gun could be established on the dominant hillock between the convent and the bridge, and small posts

placed on a line from the tower to the convent, then, according to
Wellington, "The governor would keep open the communication with
the river; and the enemy in order to mask him [Cox] must occupy both
sides [of the Côa] in strength." Wellington was convinced that these
positions could not be forced without "first breaching the mill which
would require equipment for that purpose." [30]

Irritated that Wellington's memorandum was written in the form
of suggestions or "hints," Cox realized he could not consider them "in
any other light than as positive orders." Yet he appealed to Beresford,
"As however I am ostensibly the responsible person for the safety of
the place . . . I think it necessary to express my opinion upon the
plan proposed for adoption when it is not conformable to my own
ideas, and may I think be disastrous in its consequences; this will at
least exonerate me from the blame of failure, and I am satisfied that it
shall deprive me of the merit of success." Placing the complement of
the garrison at 3,000 effective men, exclusive of the cavalry and
three artillery companies, Cox declared the force "insufficient for its
defence, particularly when I look at the description of troops of which
it is principally composed." Consequently he was adamant in his opposition to detach any part of the garrison from Almeida. The fortress
guns might cover some of the proposed posts during the day but at
night each position would be vulnerable to French attacks. Moreover,
such an operation would require his best troops, the 24th Line, while
the safety of Almeida would be entrusted to untrained and untried
militiamen. In a private letter to Beresford accompanying his official
correspondence, Cox complained, "I don't think it quite fair for a
commander in chief to give *written hints* to an officer in my situation.
. . . [The officer] becomes liable to blame if the hints are not attended
to and if adopted and fail of success they were only hints suggested
for consideration: positive instructions in such cases would be much
more satisfactory." [31]

Despite Cox's apprehension, he reluctantly began mounting a
heavy gun in the old mill north of the fortress; two pieces were established at the convent of Nossa Senhora da Barca "and one in advance
of it," although he prophesied that all would "be inevitably lost."
Wellington proposed a force of 600 soldiers to man these posts, but
Cox was inclined to reduce the number. This debate on strategy

ended in Beresford's blunt letter of 24 July: "In respect to your representations, I think you have been too pressing on them and that you mistake the nature and cause of responsibility. You cannot be exonerated because you think your garrison too small, or are you responsible should it be too little. The first is merely matter of opinion of yours, and the latter rests with us who have given that garrison. . . . Your honor," he noted, "is only committed in making the best possible defence with the means you have, which I am confident, you will do." [32] As events proved later that day, Cox was correct in his judgment. Almeida was isolated by the defeat of Craufurd, and communications with the Allied army were immediately cut when the Côa bridge was captured; the detachment that occupied the convent escaped capture only by fleeing into the fortress.

In addition to the scope of the fortifications, the quality of the garrison, the leadership of the governor, and the resources of the fortress, the configuration of the terrain surrounding Almeida was another prime consideration for the French. The small plateau on which the fortress was constructed was sloped toward the northwest where the old castle stood. Beneath the thin veneer of earth around Almeida was a substratum of granite. The terrain was irregular and enormous ledges of extremely hard granite projected above the soil, offering almost continuous cover to any attacker. These stone formations were larger in the direction of the Côa, "where they seemed to emerge from the ground as if sown in the surface, presenting a veritable image of obstacles," recalled Pelet. Consequently, trench work would be difficult in many areas, so a careful analysis of the terrain by Eblé and Lazowski was considered mandatory. Eblé admitted, "The rocks protrude and appear at a multitude of points," but he optimistically believed "that beyond the valley toward the glacis the terrain [would] be more favorable." [33]

Between the bastion of São Pedro and a slight ridge 1,100 yards to the south was a valley or depression that would permit the French to advance undetected and sheltered from the fortress fire. From the adjoining bastion of São Francisco to the demilune beyond the bastion of São João de Deos, this valley moderated, terminating in a mild slope. The terrain again formed a cavity beyond the bastion of Santa Barbara, extending to the bastion of Nossa Senhora das Brotas where it blended into the surrounding countryside. Westward, in the direction of the Côa, the ground between Nossa Senhora das Brotas and Santo António dropped rapidly to the river less than two miles away.

Based on this information, Eblé declared in his report: "It appears by these details that the point of attack is obliged to be at the segment of the wall included between bastions 1 and 3 [Santo António and Santa Barbara]; it will remain to determine if we will advance on two bastions and one demilune or on two demilunes and one bastion." Eventually the bastion of São Pedro, situated in this area, was designated as the point of attack because it invited the use of ricochet fire, was detached from the adjacent demilunes, and had favorable terrain before it. With the point of attack established, Eblé devoted the last eight pages of his report to the placement and disposition of 64 guns in 11 batteries. He detailed the movement of supplies and the lack of transportation as well as an estimate of expenses for the construction of special siege matériel—gabions, sandbags, and saucisson. Similarly, Lazowski's three-page reconnaissance report described his plans for the excavation of a vast network of trenches: "We estimate the total development of the works from the opening of the communication trench to the crowning of the covered way will be a distance of 27,000 feet and it will require more than 50,000 work days [in labor]." Lazowski also expressed apprehension about the rocky terrain and the massive stones which would force his workers to seek the questionable safety of the gabions, fascines, and sandbags. At the same time he complained about the lack of siege supplies and transportation that forced continual delays in opening the trenches.[34]

With the reports of both Eblé and Lazowski accepted by Masséna and his état-major, it was now only a matter of time until the siege would begin. As soon as the siege train and the necessary equipment had been moved to the siege site, the trenches could be opened. The Allies hoped the garrison of Almeida would resist for ninety days and the French expected a marginal defense of perhaps eight days, but both armies were stunned by the events that finally ended the siege.

Chapter 13

Trench Work before Almeida

DESPITE THE determined efforts of his administrators, the officers and men of the 6th and 8th Corps, and some of the provincial governors under his command, Masséna failed to accumulate adequate resources to meet the 9 August deadline for beginning the siege. Six additional days were required to concentrate enough matériel at Almeida to open the trenches. Masséna had expressed a desire to be present when the trenches were begun, but on 15 August he was still at Ciudad Rodrigo observing Napoleon's birthday and dictating his last orders to Lambert. With reasonable assurances that the remaining siege supplies would be forthcoming and confident in his deployment of the army, Masséna anticipated an early end to the siege. The west bank of the Côa was assured by Ferey's advanced guard; the southern flank was covered by detachments of Reynier's 2d Corps stretching from Alcántara to Penamacor and Monsanto; and in the north General Séras had deployed 10,000 troops northward from Puebla de Sanabria. Thus, his full attention could be concentrated on the siege.

The first detailed order to open the trenches was issued on 14 August by General Marchand, whose division would carry the brunt of the operations. Twenty-five hundred men of the 6th Léger and the 39th, 69th, and 76th Lines were organized into three general units by Marchand; these were subdivided into four work columns and placed under the command of chefs de bataillon drawn from the corps of engineers. The first column of 400 men was placed under Couche, whose service at Ciudad Rodrigo had been less than conspicuous; a second column of 700 infantry was commanded by Bruley; the third, totaling 700 men, was confided to Morlet; and the last column, 700 soldiers, was directed by Nempde. Each man in these units was assured of a full ration of food and drink as well as an immediate bonus of 20 centimes for nighttime duty or 75 centimes for the more dangerous daytime service.[1]

By mid-afternoon on 15 August, 2,000 troops assigned to trench duty left their packs at regimental headquarters and marched to a staging area at the engineers' camp, just behind the 26th Line. Three engineer officers were assigned to each detachment of 100 men to instruct them in their duties for the coming night. At sunset each man collected a fascine, a shovel, and a pick before advancing quietly toward the areas designated for the excavation. The workers were followed by three battalions of trench guards drawn from Marchand's division. Both Ney and Simon arrived to supervise the placement of the trench guards in order to assure the safety of the men.[2]

As darkness settled around the fortress and the workers made their way to the trench tracings, Ney sent a column of 500 men and 30 sappers under Captain Vincent down a ravine by the Alvercas River, southeast of Almeida, to begin a false attack on the bastion of São João de Deos. This move attracted the attention of the garrison, which immediately unleashed a violent three-hour bombardment and fusillade against Vincent and his men. With the diversion in progress, 2,000 workers and 120 sappers, under the close supervision of the engineers, began to open the first parallel and the two communication trenches less than 1,500 feet from the fortifications of Almeida. The French worked feverishly, thankful that the Portuguese pickets and patrols had been withdrawn earlier by Cox. The noise generated by Vincent's attack also served to muffle the noise of their picks striking the rocky soil. With the aid of a bright moon, the workers were able to open the first parallel to a depth of three feet along most of its 3,000-foot development. At several points the parallel could only be excavated to a depth of one foot because of the ledges of granite and protruding rocks, so gabions were thrown up to protect the workers. The communication trench on the right was opened up for a distance of over 900 feet; the one to the left was extended approximately 600 feet. Work might have continued in the trenches, but

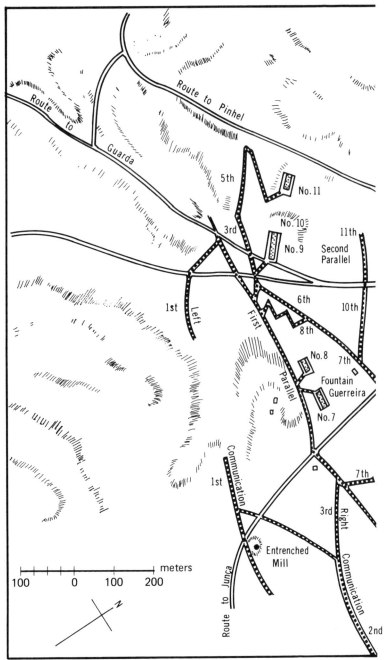

Map 11. Almeida

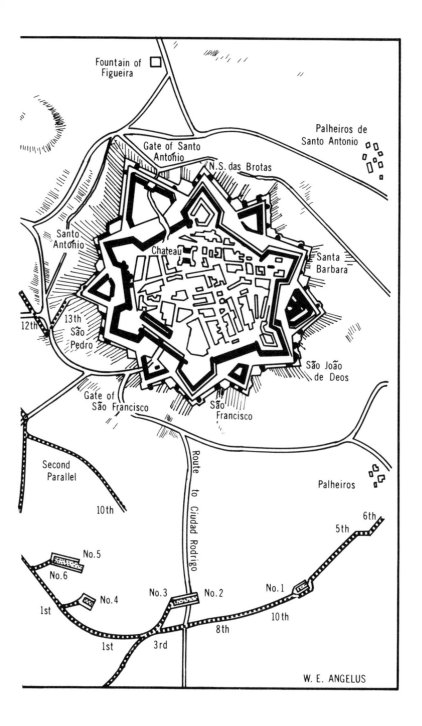

Fountain of Figueira

Palheiros de Santo Antonio

Gate of Santo Antonio

N.S. das Brotas

Santo Antonio

Chateau

Santa Barbara

12th

13th São Pedro

São João de Deos

Gate of São Francisco

São Francisco

Second Parallel

10th

Palheiros

Route to Ciudad Rodrigo

No. 5

No. 6

No. 4

No. 3

No. 2

No. 1

6th

5th

1st

1st

3rd

8th

10th

W. E. ANGELUS

the laborers were recalled at the prescribed time—3 : 00 A.M.—with an unusually low casualty list of four dead and ten wounded.[3]

During the day some 2,000 workers climbed into the parallel and communication trenches to begin extending them in both depth and width. Several sappers, using petards and canvas bags of powder, blew up the immense rocks projecting into the trenches, but the work was slow, tedious, and extremely dangerous. Soil from the excavation was thrown up before the trenches to form a parapet, and banquettes were begun so the infantry would have a ledge on which to stand when they fired out from the parallel. Masséna arrived late in the afternoon to find the parallel between six and eight feet wide and three feet deep throughout.[4]

After surveying the trenches, Masséna met with Eblé, Loison, and Ruty. There was immediate disagreement about the placement of the artillery batteries. Ruty complained that the extreme distance from the first parallel to the fortress would render the guns ineffective. The artillerymen wanted battery construction delayed until the trenches were closer to the covered way and the bastion of São Pedro. The engineers, on the other hand, proposed that the batteries be set up along the first parallel, the sooner the better, to protect their trench workers. There was also a lively disagreement over the location of the breach battery. To save time and protect the workers, the engineers pleaded for the establishment of the battery on the first parallel rather than near the covered way where Eblé and Ruty wanted it. After listening to the discussion Masséna sent first for Lazowski and then for Ney, but each was in a different segment of the trench. When Lazowski finally returned, Pelet suggested the option of placing the breach battery between the first and second parallels or before the covered way with the rationale "that we were dealing only with a rather poor fortress and a Portuguese garrison, commanded by a foreign general."[5]

No final decision was reached before Masséna left camp to make his new headquarters in the vacant lodging of the governor at Fort La Concepción. The men of his état-major moved into the bombproof casemates with their horses. Pelet took up residence in one of the casemates with two of his long-time comrades who also served on Masséna's staff, Benôit-Edouard Beaufort d'Hautpoul and François

Cavailher. There was constant activity at the fort. With the influx of administrative officers and members of the commissary, the establishment of four bake ovens and several brigades of bakers, and the posting of a garrison of three companies of Taupin's brigade, a small community began to spring up at La Concepción. A café and other service-oriented shops were opened and all types of military amusements, such as horse racing, cards, gambling, singing, and story telling, soon appeared to remind the soldiers of their homeland.[6]

Masséna was overwhelmed with innumerable duties regarding the siege, preparations for the invasion of Portugal, and maintenance of his command across the provinces of northern Spain. Yet he maintained close and direct contact with Eblé and Lazowski on the siege operations. He insisted on detailed progress reports each day from both the artillerymen and the engineers concerning the trench shifts; in addition, plans for tracing, organizing, arming, and utilizing each gun were to be forwarded to his headquarters as soon as possible. Ney was expected to send daily accounts of the siege operations in which his troops were engaged. Masséna also carried on a heavy correspondence with Lambert, who administered the vast administrative and logistical empire from army headquarters at Ciudad Rodrigo. His preoccupation with the collection of foodstuffs and financial resources is clearly reflected in these letters. The collection, processing, and shipping of army matériel from all parts of his military district to Salamanca and on to Ciudad Rodrigo was of prime importance to Masséna; his most pressing task, however, was to assure the necessary resources for his troops at Almeida to bring the siege to a speedy and successful conclusion. Again he wanted specific numbers of rations baked each day at each of the 14 ovens at Ciudad Rodrigo, the number of baker brigades available for service, of pints of brandy available and their cost, of sick and convalescing patients at each of the hospitals, of wagons and mules available to the commissariat, etc.[7]

The second night of open trenches, 16 August, the workers extended the parallel 780 feet to the left to reach the protection of a valley, but the soil was so rocky that the workers were unable to make much progress. By dawn the laborers were still working above ground, exposed to enemy gunfire, so they were quietly withdrawn. In the center of the parallel, a third communication trench was excavated toward an old entrenched windmill in the rear, but the work was slow and strenuous. The other communication trenches were enlarged without difficulty. Lazowski was not satisfied with the progress of the work; he complained to Masséna, "In general the work suffers from the lack of workers." He had requested two detachments of 1,500 men to work in each of the two shifts, but his engineers reported a deficit of 800 men. That night Lazowski faced a similar situation; he appealed to Ney for 2,500 men, but only 1,927 actually turned out for trench work. Consequently, some laborers, working an earlier shift, had only four hours of rest in twenty-four before being sent back into the trenches. This lack of manpower was a continuing problem since Ney's troops were busy harvesting the crops in the neighboring field. Lazowski's casualties for the night were not high, two dead and five wounded, but Masséna resolved to organize a corps of 150 sharpshooters under the command of Captain Palander. The first night 36 men were posted between 600 and 900 feet in advance of the parallel with instructions to fire at the Portuguese artillerymen manning the guns on the ramparts.[8]

During the daylight hours of 17 August, the first parallel was extended to a width of between nine and twelve feet, except on the extremities where 240 feet were opened to a width of only four feet because of the strata of granite. Communications trenches on both the left and the right were expanded to nine feet in width, and the central communication trench was broadened to over four feet. This progress was accomplished primarily by a corps of twenty sappers who blasted the granite out of the trenches. Very early the same day, Masséna rode from La Concepción over to the siege site to survey the progress and settle the argument between the engineers and artillerymen. Eblé, Ruty, and Lazowski discussed their project at length in Masséna's presence. After considering the various alternatives, it was agreed that the construction of the batteries would begin the next night along the first parallel. Apparently Masséna felt uninformed about the details and progress of the operation. Accordingly, he had a small hut constructed near the trenches where two of his aides-de-camp would be on duty, "always ready . . . to give him an immediate account of everything taking place." After visiting the trenches with Masséna, Pelet volunteered, "I went into the trenches and visited the works every time I could approach them. The parallel was splendid, quite improved and relatively safe from right to left, as were the communication trenches. The fortress fired a great deal and most accurately. Its shells and bombs were landing with great effectiveness." As Masséna and his staff prepared to return to La Concepción, they noted with some alarm the effect of the garrison guns on the trench workers.[9]

As dusk fell on the third night of open trenches, 17 August, the sappers directed the excavation of the parallel 260 feet on the right until it was opposite the demilune beyond the bastion of São Francisco; this excavation was four feet wide and three feet deep by the time the night shift withdrew from the trenches, but the laborers on the extreme left of the parallel were less successful, the trench being only four and one-half feet wide. Finally, the massive stone ledges in the central communication trench were removed, and it was carried to a depth of three feet and a width of three and a half feet. The artillery casualties for the night work were placed at one dead and two wounded, and Ney's chief of staff, Béchet de Léocour, acknowledged one dead and fourteen wounded among the trench workers.[10]

On the morning of 18 August, a large detachment of the trench workers was placed at the disposition of Eblé, Ruty, and Lazowski in order to trace the artillery batteries before the first parallel. Considering the location of the parallel, the configuration of the terrain, and the point of attack, they carefully traced each site and determined the type, number, and caliber of guns for each of the eleven designated batteries. The first emplacement, an enfilading battery of three six-pound howitzers, the second battery of two howitzers and two pieces of sixteen, and the third battery of a howitzer and two pieces of twelve were to be constructed along and beyond the right flank of the first parallel in order to bombard the bastion of São Francisco and the adjoining demilune. Battery No. 4 was composed of five ten-pound mortars and Battery No. 5—one of the most formidable batteries before the parallel—included three pieces of twenty-four, four pieces of sixteen, and a howitzer; they were positioned to strike directly on the point of attack—the bastion of São Pedro. Battery No. 6 was made up of a howitzer and two pieces of twelve, and Battery No. 7 had two pieces of twenty-four, two pieces of sixteen, and four pieces of twelve;

these guns were also directed to fire on São Pedro. Battery No. 8 embraced one twelve-pound mortar and three eight-pound mortars, and Battery No. 9 had one howitzer and two pieces of twelve. These two batteries were to concentrate their fire on the left salient of the bastion of São Pedro. Battery No. 10, designated as the breach battery, was composed of four pieces of sixteen, one piece of twelve, and a howitzer. As the most powerful battery in the French armaments, it was expected to pound a breach in the left salient of São Pedro and the adjoining demilune. Finally, Battery No. 11, on the extreme left of the French position, was organized as an enfilading battery with one piece of twelve and two howitzers; its cannoneers were assigned the task of battering the demilune between São Pedro and Santo António. Utilizing 52 heavy guns in 11 batteries, Eblé held nine heavy guns and four howitzers in reserve to replace damaged guns or to establish another battery. After the batteries had been traced the three generals drew up a joint letter to Masséna indicating that the armaments were "insufficient to attack a place such as Almeida with certain success." Eblé underscored their attitude by sending another letter to the Prince the following day reiterating his personal concern and apprehension.[11]

While Eblé's artillerymen were making preparations to begin the artillery emplacements later that evening, Marshal Ney came from his headquarters at Malpartida to visit the trenches. He stunned Eblé by requesting the return in ten days of some 600 Hanoverian Legionnaires who had been assigned to the siege train before the siege of Ciudad Rodrigo. Eblé had utilized the Germans as auxiliaries during the attack on Ciudad Rodrigo and was in the process of assimilating them with his cannoneers for the siege of Almeida. He was aware of their high desertion rate and their low morale as a result of their continuous service in providing the manual labor for the artillery, but he was unwilling to acquiesce to Ney's request. He wrote directly to Masséna and complained, "This measure will delay artillery operations." To improve the morale of the legion, he also proposed that at least 100 line troops "of good will" be attached to them. Before the afternoon shift of workers had returned from the trenches, the first great convoy arrived at the siege site. Twenty-five heavy guns, six mortars, several wagons with munitions, and 113 ton of gunpowder were escorted by 435 auxiliaries from the Hanoverian Legion and 54 artillerymen. [12]

On the night of 18 August, the fourth night of open trenches, as the laborers moved into the trenches, Eblé sent half of his cannoneers, the available auxiliaries of the Hanoverian Legion, and some 400 workers from the line regiments through the trenches to begin work on the battery emplacements. Working quickly in the darkness under a swift bombardment, most of the artillerymen found the soil pliable; digging three or four feet below the ground level, they were "perfectly covered" before dawn. On the extreme right of the parallel, where large granite ledges broke the surface, the artillerymen accomplished little before they were withdrawn from the site. The trench workers, meanwhile, continued to enlarge the first parallel and the communication trenches with the aid of the sappers who detonated petards throughout the night to blow large segments of the rock out of the trenches. The parallel reached a width of 12 feet except along both extremes, where it was five feet wide. The communication trenches on both the right and left were over nine feet wide, but ledges of granite in the central communication trench delayed the laborers noticeably. The banquettes were improved and the trenches were almost wide and deep enough for the passage of wagons and the siege pieces. Simon acknowledged three dead and 21 wounded among the artillery and trench workers as testimony to the accuracy of the Portuguese guns while Eblé suffered one dead and seven wounded. [13]

The following morning, 19 August, 2,000 trench workers returned to their work, but only 260 of the 400 men requested by Eblé to work on the batteries arrived at artillery headquarters. Eblé complained to Masséna who, in turn, instructed Marchand to reduce the number of trench guards from three battalions to nine companies so that the relieved companies of the 26th and 82d Lines and the Légion du Midi would be available for trench work. There was also disagreement between the engineers and artillerymen over the fate of Battery No. 1. Lazowski continually opposed the construction of the battery because of its distance from the parallel, the extra time that would be required to excavate it, "and the poor nature of the terrain." Eblé, on the other hand, claimed that it was necessary to maximize the fire on the point of attack. He argued that it was an advantageous position and would not be particularly difficult to excavate. Noting that Lazowski had initially agreed in the establishment of Battery No. 1, Eblé threatened, "If you do not share my sentiments, I beg you to request the decision from His Highness, the Prince d'Essling, so our work will not be halted." Consequently, work on the communication trench to the battery would be undertaken, and a trench 675 feet long would be opened from the first parallel to it. The results of this disagreement were not unexpected since Eblé, in fact, had quickly assumed responsibility for siege operations while Lazowski, perhaps as a result of his poor health, was relegated to a secondary role. A similar communication trench had already been started on the extreme left of the parallel to link Battery No. 11 with the trench and battery network.[14]

During the day, a piece of sixteen, a mortar, 4,919 projectiles, five ton of powder, and 2,971 sandbags reached Eblé's camp before Almeida. Eblé immediately sent 200 horses back to Ciudad Rodrigo for the next convoy of siege supplies. Ruty was also instructed to send 3,000 ten-pound mortar shells as soon as possible. Large quantities of the powder were stored in the church at São Pedro do Rio Seco. Eblé was apprehensive that flammable materials in the village might ignite the magazine, so a number of homes were torn down, resulting in unexpected violence against the inhabitants.[15]

By the night of 19 August, the fifth night of open trenches, Lazowski declared, perhaps prematurely, that both communication trenches and the first parallel were "totally completed," with the exception of some rocks projecting into the trenches. His sappers were busy blasting the rocks out of the trenches to permit the passage of wheeled vehicles. After dusk 800 workers were sent into the trenches, primarily on the extreme right of the parallel, to construct a flèche; this post was to protect 150 grenadiers assigned to defend Battery No. 1 and its howitzers. The night was difficult for the men in the trenches. The Portuguese artillery of Major Fortunato José Barreiros had a devastating effect on the French. Although 50 marksmen took up positions between the trenches and the fortress to pick off the Portuguese cannoneers, casualties among the trench workers accounted for six dead and 35 wounded while Eblé's artillerymen suffered four dead and 21 wounded.[16]

During the same evening "several rather large signal fires" illuminated the sky in the direction of Celorico and Guarda and the telegraph at Almeida "was very active." Ney immediately sent an aide-de-camp to Ferey's advanced guard to determine if an attack was under way. He was relieved to learn that Wellington's posts were inactive but he took the occasion to propose a redeployment of the army. He pointed out that a force of 10,000 or 12,000 Allied troops could advance against Ferey, driving him back across the Côa. Moreover, if Wellington were to send a column with infantry and cavalry from Guarda across the Côa, while units of cavalry, infantry, and artillery advanced from Celorico and Pinhel toward Castelo Rodrigo, Ney's corps would be in a tenuous position. In fact, if the Allies "directed a column by Castelo Bom and another by Castelo Rodrigo, [it would] expose at the same time [his] right and left" and seriously threaten the siege of Almeida. Consequently, he proposed a sweeping redeployment of the forces under Masséna's command. Ney suggested that one division of Reynier's 2d Corps could be posted between Espeja and Castelo Bom and another between Fuente Guinaldo and Castelo Branco. Junot could deploy his brigades between Barba de Puerco and La Concepción with posts at Ledesma, Salamanca, and San Felices de los Gallegos; Montbrun would be expected to post his cavalry along the Agueda and on a line from Fuentes de Oñoro to Vila Maior; Séras's infantry at Puebla de Sanabria and Mombuey would form a junction with Ney's forces; General Jean-Pierre Bonet would occupy Astorga and León; and, finally, Kellerman would send reinforcements from Valladolid. Admitting that Masséna might not be in agreement "on all these points, it seems to me," Ney cautioned, "it is of the utmost importance to unite a rather considerable army . . . to resist the enemy in case he attacks us."[17]

Masséna replied to him suggesting a meeting on 20 August at his trench hut to discuss the merits of the project. During the meeting, Lazowski, Ruty, Eblé, and the sly old Loison joined in the discussion. Despite Loison's efforts to undermine Ney's project, Masséna accepted part of the proposal. Following their conference, Masséna instructed Junot to redeploy his corps so that they could reach Almeida or Castelo Rodrigo within two hours, according to the movements of the enemy. Clauzel moved his division to Escarigo, and Solignac established his headquarters at San Felices de los Gallegos with the 69th Line and the elite regiments of Prussians and Irishmen.[18]

By the morning of 20 August, the trench workers, already digging below the surface of the ground, were relatively safe from all but a direct hit on the trenches. Working through the day and into the night, the laborers widened the left side of the parallel and the communication trench was enlarged toward the battery of howitzers on the extreme right. The artillerymen pushed ahead, constructing embrasures for the guns, but Batteries Nos. 5 and 6 were not yet completed. During the day another convoy reached the artillery camp with three eight-pound mortars, 1,720 shells, 8,000 sandbags, and 13 ton of gunpowder.[19]

Lazowski was not satisfied with the progress in the trenches and he complained in his report: "The rocks are so numerous, especially toward the left and in the center of the parallel, that the work will require several days before the communication trenches will be practicable for the artillery; moreover, the army does not have a company of miners or mining equipment and the sappers have very incomplete supplies" to remove the rocks. Lazowski was also convinced that the progress on the flèche, under construction to protect the grenadiers and Battery No. 1, was being delayed because of the lack of manpower. He had requested 150 laborers from Simon's brigade, but only 95 workers arrived for work. Lazowski complained to the état-major of the 6th Corps. Not only had his request for workers been unfulfilled, but many of those who did reach the trenches arrived late and placed themselves in completed sections of the trenches rather than inform the trench officer of their arrival; they avoided work but stood in line to collect their bonus at the end of the shift. "These problems delay[ed] the work very much," so Lazowski proposed that all trench workers be marched by a regimental officer to the trenches where they would be turned over to an engineer officer; he would guide them to a sapper for their trench assignments. If a laborer arrived late for work, he would be returned to his regiment and forfeit his bonus.[20]

Coupled with the problem of inadequate manpower, Lazowski and Eblé faced an acute and embarrassing financial problem. On 22 August, Lazowski informed Masséna, "The siege . . . will be more

costly for us than we first calculated." Indeed, there had been no
funds to pay the trench workers' bonus since 20 August. They appealed to Masséna, who sent their request to his quartermaster general, Lambert, at Ciudad Rodrigo. Initially, Masséna requested
20,000 francs to be placed at the disposal of both Lazowski and Eblé
to defray expenses. Lambert began making arrangements to transfer
funds from the Spanish treasury, but he soon found himself in an es-
calating controversy with a stubborn paymaster, M. Mallet. The paymaster refused to honor his requests, as well as one for 50,000 francs
to secure transportation for the movement of food and siege supplies
from Valladolid and Salamanca to Ciudad Rodrigo; he declared that
such expenses were unauthorized. Lambert was livid and Masséna
was noticeably irritated. Writing to Masséna, Lambert accused Mallet of "criminal" behavior: "The transports from Salamanca to Ciudad
Rodrigo, the only point where the movement of army subsistence is
assured, are paralized by his refusal to pay." By 25 August, Lambert
needed 32,000 francs for the engineers and 20,000 for Eblé's artillerymen, as well as funds for the hospitals, the siege, the army
corps, the postal system, and other logistical expenses. When Mallet
proved unwilling to cooperate, he resolved to force the issue. Consequently, Masséna complained to Berthier of the "difficulties" that
Mallet had caused in refusing "to pay the indispensable expenses for
the army matériel. If he persists in his refusal . . . for necessary
funds for the engineers and artillery, we will be obliged to suspend
operations at the siege of Almeida." He also wrote a similar letter to
the minister of the public treasury and concluded requesting "the recall of M. Mallet with whom I am very discontented."[21]

Another interrelated problem that caused Masséna some anxiety
was Ney's continual requests for provisions. Masséna was in the process of creating a massive magazine at Ciudad Rodrigo in preparation
for the invasion of Portugal. However, the demands for food from the
magazines at Ciudad Rodrigo totaled 23,500 rations each day while
the 14 ovens in operation there and at La Caridad produced only
22,500 rations a day. With an allocation of 12,000 rations of bread
for the 6th Corps, Masséna was indignant when Ney asked him "to
order the quartermaster general to promptly send aid to these troops
who, without this measure, will not be able to hold their position and

will be forced to withdraw to the left bank of the Coa." Masséna was well aware that Ferey's advanced guard was performing a valuable service for the army. By probing the enemy posts each day and sending out extensive reconnaissance columns deep into areas under enemy control, Ferey could provide invaluable information on the location and possible intentions of Wellington. Nevertheless, Masséna would not be coerced into modifying his provision allotments. He wrote sharply to Ney, "It is impossible that the quartermaster general can furnish food to Ferey's brigade. Your corps draws 12,000 rations from Ciudad Rodrigo daily." Masséna concluded by suggesting that Loison assume the responsibility of nourishing the troops of the advanced guard.[22]

Besides the logistical difficulties facing Masséna, he became increasingly alarmed by the continual violence between his troops and the Portuguese inhabitants. Each of Ferey's reconnaissance columns experienced bitter resistance from the local inhabitants. Every dispatch from Loison described attacks on French troops, followed by a casualty list. Loison's troops reacted by crushing all opposition ruthlessly. Although Masséna had issued orders of the day and made personal appeals to the corps commanders to halt these disorders, he continued to receive reports of horrible excesses. He moved decisively on 14 August to reinforce his earlier order of the day. Since leadership below the regimental structure seemed to have broken down in the enforcement of his orders, he struck with a vengeance: "All commanders of cantonments, detachments, or escorts are personally responsible for the offenses of the troops under their orders." Noncommissioned officers and corporals guilty of such conduct would be dismissed. Officers would be suspended and sent to the rear to await Berthier's reaction. The general officers were ordered to have this order of the day read at the head of each company for eight days so no one could plead ignorance. It galled Masséna to see the progress before Almeida being undermined by the slow erosion of discipline and morale as his troops became more exasperated each day by the conduct of the Portuguese peasants. Yet, his measures were clearly ineffective.[23]

After his regular visit to the trenches on 20 August, Masséna returned to La Concepción and wrote to Berthier admitting that the

British "employ a means of defense that results in the greatest misfortune to the nation. They have ordered the inhabitants to leave their homes; the women, the children, and the old are to put themselves behind the army; the men, between seventeen and fifty years of age, are to arm themselves with guns, pikes, axes, fire, etc., in order to act as partisans." He was aware that the British supplied the Portuguese with all types of military supplies and enjoined them "under the pain of death, to retire and leave nothing that would survive to provide subsistence for the French army." When inhabitants refused to conform to these orders, "the British have to lead them away by force. They pillage and devastate [Portuguese] homes . . . and commit excesses worthy of cannibals." Masséna's only consolation was the belief that "despite all these grand measures, the British army has sent its heavy equipment to Coimbra and the various ports." According to all reports, the British would fight at Viseu or Coimbra "not to prevent our conquest of Portugal but for honor and to do [their] duty in the eyes of Europe."[24]

On 21 August, the trench laborers continued work on the communication trench to Battery No. 11, where most of the large stones were located. Gabions and fascines were thrown up before the trench to cover and protect the workers so only one was killed and four wounded despite the artillery and musket fire from the garrison. As darkness settled over the trenches, two approaches were begun from the first parallel in the direction of the point of attack. Although only 933 of the 1,200 workers requested for trench duty turned out, these laborers advanced the approaches at angles in order to form a salient post 660 feet in front of the parallel. Working relatively close to the fortress and well within musket range, the sappers concealed their work from the enemy by employing fascines but still had one killed and ten wounded. At the same time, the batteries were well advanced or completed, except No. 6, despite the heavy barrage of grapeshot poured on the artillerymen, especially those on the left of the parallel, wounding four men. With the continual arrival of supplies, five gun platforms, destined for batteries on the right flank, were moved into the trenches.[25]

At seven o'clock on the morning of 22 August, 1,000 trench workers marched into the communication trenches, through the first

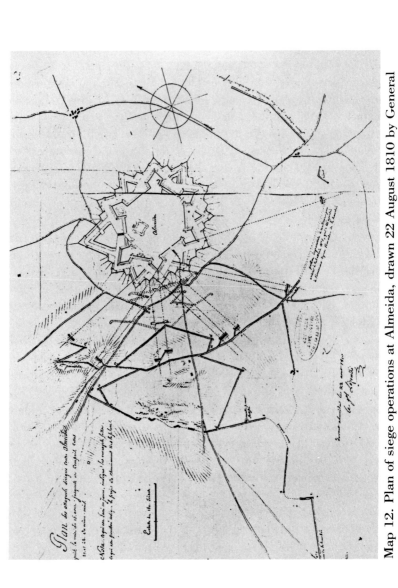

Map 12. Plan of siege operations at Almeida, drawn 22 August 1810 by General Joseph-Félix Lazowski

parallel, to their assigned positions. Most of them resumed work on
the two approaches that were extended to a width of six feet. However, after opening the approach on the left for almost 420 feet, the
sappers struck an underwater spring and water gushed into the
trench. The laborers quickly retreated and sealed off the trench, but
this delay threatened Lazowski's schedule. The communication trench
leading to Battery No. 11 was widened to almost nine feet. The sappers, meanwhile, struggling to blow up large shelves of rock still
obstructing the passage, were forced to erect extensive parapets to
protect those passing through the trenches.[26]

During the eighth night of open trenches, 22 August, 1,200
workers opened a long communication trench to Battery No. 1 on the
extreme right of the parallel. Working frantically to avoid detection
by the garrison, they excavated the trench to a depth of two and one-
half feet and a width of three feet. To replace the flooded approach on
the left, another detachment of laborers began digging a new trench
almost parallel to the inundated approach. Utilizing an inordinate
number of petards, the sappers were able to bypass the flooded area.
At the same time the artillerymen completed several batteries, and
over 100 projectiles and the gun platforms were pulled through the
trenches on wagons to the batteries on the right flank of the parallel;
the emplacements on the left were without provisions because the
trench was still impracticable for the movement of wagons. The casualties for the day and night included one artilleryman killed and five
wounded while the trench workers suffered five dead and 20 wounded.
There was doubt in Lazowski's mind that casualties would be reduced
noticeably even if his sappers could be reinforced. He appealed to
Masséna for a company of miners to be dispatched from Madrid to
clear the remaining rocks out of the trenches but his pleas went
unheeded.[27]

By seven in the morning, 23 August, a detachment of 1,200 laborers climbed into the trenches and proceeded to their assigned
work sites. They began to perfect the communication trenches to both
enfilading batteries at the extremes of the first parallel as well as in
the two approaches. The latter was carried to nine feet, and the remaining banquettes were completed along the entire length of the first
parallel. An eyewitness recalled, "The approaches were becoming

uninhabitable under the noonday sun. Movements were extremely difficult, and a terrible reflection off the sand created a suffocating heat." During the day another convoy arrived at the French camp with four mortars, five gun carriages, wagons loaded with 3,145 projectiles, and 17 ton of powder for the artillerymen.[28]

At 7:00 in the evening, 1,200 workers gathered to begin the night shift in the trenches. One thousand men returned to the parallel and the approaches, but a detachment of 200 laborers opened a trench on the extreme right of the parallel to link the enfilading battery to the network of trenches. The salient formed by the junction of the two approaches was enlarged, and earthen parapets were raised before the trenches. Banquettes were formed in the walls of the approaches, which were extended to seven feet in width. Earth-filled gabions were thrown up before the trench excavated to Battery No. 11; these were to supplement the parapets and cover the sappers still clearing away the massive rock formations obstructing the trench. At the other end of the parallel, on the extreme right, workers labored to complete the communication trench to Battery No. 1. The swift and accurate fire of the garrison overthrew the gabions and forced the workers to retreat from the trench, but not before they succeeded in linking the communication trench with the first parallel by a small trench three feet wide and two and one-half deep. Casualties included one dead and seventeen wounded.[29]

The artillerymen continued their work without respite. Ramps were constructed to roll the guns up onto the platforms, and during the night, wagons were dragged through the trenches laden with enough projectiles to arm guns in the three batteries on the extreme right. Three mortars were pulled through several hundred yards of trenches to Battery No. 4. Massive pieces of sixteen were pushed onto platforms of the breach battery, but its embrasures and revetments were still incomplete. The arrival of a small convoy laden with 4,850 projectiles and 10 ton of powder enabled the artillerymen to continue the distribution of munitions to the batteries. Considering the advanced location of the workers and the intensity of the garrison fire, the sharpshooters were moved forward toward the glacis so casualties were limited to six wounded. Perhaps to spur the workers to greater efforts, an announcement was also made that Masséna had decided to open fire on Almeida on the morning of 25 August.[30]

At dawn on 24 August, 1,200 weary trench workers were deployed throughout the trench complex to complete the remaining work and begin hauling gabions and fascines into the trenches for the anticipated opening of the second parallel. The sappers continued to blast the last of the rock ledges out of the trenches with their petards. During the day three mortars arrived along with a convoy of artillery wagons carrying 1,659 projectiles and 10 more ton of gun powder. As soon as darkness obscured the movements of the workers, they marched quickly through the first parallel and into the approaches to begin work on the second parallel. From the salient formed by the junction of the approaches, trenches were excavated in both directions at a distance of 600 feet from the fortress. Working within sight of the defenders, the French came under a violent bombardment. Shells plowed into the soft earth and ricocheted off the granite subsoil; flying rock wounded many, including Pelet's long-time comrade, Beaufort d'Hautpoul, and Vauvilliers. Before dawn the workers were withdrawn from both extremes of the second parallel to avert a possible slaughter. Work also continued on the communication trench to Battery No. 1. Losses included seven dead and 32 wounded, of whom all but three were trench workers.[31]

The artillerymen, sensing an end to their laborious duty, finished arming the three batteries on the right flank of the first parallel. There was also a controversy between Eblé and Masséna's staff about the composition of two batteries. "At last, after much debate and many pleas for the intervention of the Prince," recorded Pelet, "General Eblé, the best and most devoted man in the world and a devil of an artilleryman, consented to change the caliber of the two cannon," but not until he received direct written orders from Masséna. Battery No. 4 was augmented by two more ten-pound mortars; a piece of twelve was replaced by a piece of twenty-four in Batteries Nos. 5 and 10.[32]

By the afternoon of 25 August all the batteries were armed, provisioned with shells and powder, manned by artillerymen, and ready for the bombardment the following morning. Detailed instructions were issued by Eblé to each battery commander regarding his primary and secondary targets, his rate of fire, and his ultimate goals. In effect, each gun was assigned a particular target along the southern fortifications of Almeida from the right salient of the bastion of São Francisco to the demilune beyond the bastion of São Pedro. Each salient of the bastions, each flank of the demilunes, the covered way, the terreplein, and fortress curtain along this area were also targeted for certain guns of a specific battery. The most concentrated fire was reserved for São Pedro where the breach would ultimately be made. The mortars of Battery No. 4 would perform double service, lobbing 500 incendiary shells into the town each night in an effort to increase terror and undermine the morale of the garrison.[33]

Soon after daybreak on 25 August, 2,000 laborers entered the trench to perfect their work on the communication trench to Battery No. 1. The second parallel was also enlarged along three-fourths of its length, but its flanks were full of rock. The sappers, armed with petards, filed into the second parallel to begin clearing away the shelves of granite. "This work [was] so considerable that we had no hope of seeing the end for two days and two nights," complained La-zowski. Two thousand laborers entered the second parallel that night and continued work, but the swift fire of the fortress, which had harassed the workers all day, continued unabated throughout the night and forced the workers' recall; they claimed four dead and 23 wounded. The artillerymen and their auxiliaries suffered five wounded while finishing their preparations; before the first rays of the sun appeared in the east, they were armed and ready to begin the bombardment.[34]

As arrangements were being completed for the bombardment, Ferey was instructed to increase his reconnaissance of the Allied positions. The interrogation reports of prisoners and deserters indicated no immediate movement. Yet there were disturbing reports that the Patriarch of Lisbon, also a member of the Portuguese Regency, had just arrived at Guarda. Deserters announced that he had just returned from London with instructions for Wellington to "defend Portugal." Current rumors suggested a double envelopment by Wellington from across the Côa. Loison also reported that three British and two Portuguese regiments were below Almeida while other large detachments were preparing to advance with artillery.[35]

Based upon these intelligence reports and rumors, Masséna resolved to cover his southern flank. On 25 August, he ordered Reynier to form a junction with the troops engaged in the siege. "It is necessary," he wrote, "that you deploy yourself in a manner to be able to march on Almeida and join me on first orders." He admitted that there was no indication that Wellington was preparing to attack and raise the siege but he could not take the chance. Specifically, he ordered Reynier to move his army corps to Alfaiates and send reconnaissance columns on to Almeida to establish communication with him and "observe the enemy." Masséna cautioned, "Survey his movements; an extremely important point to observe is the bridge of Sabugal on the Coa. It is only from there that the English will be able to advance on my left flank." [36]

With the army deployed to repulse any Allied advance, the trenches well advanced, and the batteries armed and ready to commence fire, Masséna was ready to demonstrate the efficiency and the effectiveness of a French army in action. Now he would test the determination of the Portuguese and British to defend the Kingdom of Portugal. Never in his fondest hopes, however, could he have anticipated the spectacular results of his efforts.

Chapter 14

The Bombardment and Capitulation of Almeida

A T FIVE O'CLOCK on the morning of 26 August, Eblé gave orders for the bombardment to begin on the fog-shrouded silhouette of Almeida. "Although eleven batteries were firing simultaneously, the sight was not very imposing to those accustomed to genuine battles—not too much noise and little effect," recalled an observer. The first salvos of the artillery were too short; three shells fell on the second parallel and others fell to the rear, killing several trench workers. The artillerymen augmented their powder and angle of fire to increase the range of the guns. Projectiles soon began to hit the terreplein and the covered way of the fortress, but still some ricochet shots landed in the second parallel; the embarrassed cannoneers of Batteries Nos. 9 and 10 saw their projectiles plow into the parapets of the French trenches. Lazowski quickly recalled his workers from the parallel to protect them from Eblé's guns. Pelet recorded in his journal that from the first parallel the fire looked "low, short, and had little effect. . . . Nothing had been damaged, and only a few cannonballs or ricochet shots were falling in the *gazonnements* and embrasures. However, the city was firing more strongly than ever." [1]

The fire of the howitzers in the enfilading batteries (Nos. 1 and 11) was ineffective; the deployment of the guns, the distance from the fortress, and the nature of the targets required additional modification of the pieces. Batteries Nos. 9 and 10 fired swiftly but were less effective than expected because the Portuguese artillerymen of the bastion of São Pedro concentrated a withering fire on their positions. The superiority of the Portuguese fire was clearly recognized by

298

Lazowski and Masséna's aides who were standing by his hut. A direct
hit on a 50-pound powder magazine of Battery No. 2 exploded a number of charged projectiles, wounding five men. The fortress gunfire
slackened during the afternoon but increased in intensity as darkness
approached. The French, on the other hand, damaged one battery
platform and overthrew another, but the men of the Portuguese 4th
Artillery, directed by Captains Bernardo Guterres and Alberto Guer-
reiro, continued their fire against the French. Battery No. 4 ignited
two small powder magazines on the ramparts, and the batteries along
the central sections of the parallel (Nos. 5, 6, 7, and 8) pounded the
bastion of São Pedro and its gun embrasures. Orders were implemented by the men of the howitzer and mortar batteries to begin bom-
barding the town with charged shells, and soon fires broke out across
the town. The fire in the first house was extinguished, but it was unre-
alistic to expect the exhausted men on the ramparts to fight the fires.
The flames spread to several houses in an area already evacuated by
the inhabitants. Eblé described the general effect of the bombardment
as "satisfactory," but he must have been disappointed by the lack of
visible progress. He acknowledged one killed and 20 wounded and
that the consumption of munitions was high—6,177 projectiles and
nine ton of powder. Only 84 projectiles and 10 ton of powder reached
the French camp that day.[2]

Earlier in the day Cox had visited the great magazine in the castle; he recalled, "Everything was well arranged and I gave strict orders respecting the necessary precautions and what should be done
when the arsenal was opened." Between nine and ten in the morning
he went to the governor's house to take "some refreshments. Finding
it very much exposed to fire, shells, and bombs that had already
passed through it, [he] left for a small casemate within the arcade
. . . as a place of security and safety, where [he] could rest a few
hours." Returning to the walls he observed the fortress gunfire and
that of the French; he walked to the castle, repeated his orders about
the arsenal, and reassured himself that all was ready for the coming
night.[3]

The French bombardment continued throughout the day without
abatement. A thousand men labored in the trenches, primarily in the
second parallel, but the massive rock formations forced them to throw

up fascines along two-thirds of its length. Fascines and gabions were dragged through the network of trenches into the second parallel in preparation for opening a new approach in the direction of the bastion of São Pedro. As the sappers exploded their petards and the laborers shoveled rock out of the parallel, they were unnerved by the shells of the French guns whizzing overhead and often landing in their trenches; after a number had been killed or wounded, the men were withdrawn by Lazowski.[4]

As dusk approached, activity increased on the ramparts of Almeida. The garrison transferred powder and projectiles from the central magazine in the castle to the small expense magazines on the ramparts. At approximately 7:00 P.M. one or perhaps two charged bombs from Eblé's Battery No. 4 landed in the courtyard before the castle. According to a Portuguese artillery officer, 30 artillerymen were working in the magazine to transfer barrels of powder to the expense magazines on the ramparts so the great doors of the castle were open. The charged bomb rolled down the steps of the building into a subsidiary magazine and ignited 4,000 charged projectiles, which instantly ignited 150,000 pounds of gunpowder and over a million infantry cartridges. A variation of this account was repeated by a French artillery chef de bataillon, Bouvier, who inventoried the remains of the magazine; he claimed that the French bomb ignited a trail of powder, spilled from a faulty barrel being transported from the magazine to the ramparts. Another artillery officer, João de Sousa Moreira, claimed that a "chance" French bomb ignited a barrel of powder in the courtyard which spread quickly to the central magazine. Yet, no eyewitness survived to give an exact account of the explosion. Cox theorized, "The most probable explanation is that a bomb of great calibre crashed through the gate into the entrance [of the castle] despite the precautions that I had taken to cover it with massive wood timbers." He discounted the claim that the door had been deliberately left open, and he assured Liverpool that no carts loaded with powder had been left in the courtyard as the French declared.[5]

The entire building erupted in a spectacular explosion. The abruptness of the detonation and its volcanic appearance stunned both the defenders and the besiegers. According to Cox, after he returned to his casemate, "I hardly sat down when I felt a violent shock similar to an earthquake which had a tremendous boom and a white column of air burst into the middle of the gallery." Cox rushed out to determine the cause of the explosion and found "general terror and confusion." Some horrified citizens told him the castle had blown up; others said the French had fired a mine, that the laboratory had exploded, or that an expense magazine on the ramparts had been ignited. There were "a few moments of great silence," recalled Cox. "Not one shot was fired from the enemy batteries or the trenches." Cox rushed to the castle immediately, "climbing over a mountain of rubble in the street" to reach the arsenal. "I could clearly tell that the whole building was a jagged mass of stone and it was entirely demolished. . . . The principal powder magazine of 2,500 barrels of gunpowder and two subsidiary magazines in the castle which had been full of charged projectiles and musket cartridges had been completely destroyed," Cox declared. "I climbed over the ruins of the castle to determine visually that the great arsenal had blown up. I reflected for a moment on what I should do." Since it was possible or even probable that the French would attempt an assault "during the terror and consternation of the explosion," Cox ordered those of his garrison still alive to return to the ramparts and maintain as heavy a fire as possible in order to hide the true situation from the enemy. He went to the walls, and, aided by one artillery officer, he fired all the loaded guns and then maintained a sporadic fire throughout the night. Cox also attempted, in vain, to induce "a single person to go out and inform the army what had happened. I could not find anyone who could perform this essential service."[6]

According to Ney's chief of staff, "The explosion was dreadful but the effect was even greater. Massive blocks of stone were thrown into our trenches, killing and wounding some men there. Cannon of large caliber were blown off the ramparts and thrown far across the countryside. . . . A great part of the town disappeared and the remainder was in rubble." Debris from the castle had been scattered throughout the town and in the fields adjoining the fortress. The cathedral and homes in the vicinity of the castle were reduced to ruins, entombing hundreds of soldiers and citizens. Captain Jacques-Louis Hulot, at Ney's headquarters three miles away, later recorded in his journal, "The disaster was terrible and the spectacle unbelievable. . . . This immense and horrible column of blood, iron, and stone" had a sober-ing effect on him. The same can be said of Ney's aide-de-camp, Sprünglin; after riding around the fortress with Ney, the two sat down on a hill to watch the bombardment. Sprünglin recalled that the ex-plosion "resembled the eruption of a volcano and the memory [had] not diminished after twenty-six years."[7] However, the fortification of Almeida seemed to have suffered little significant damage. The French and Portuguese cannoneers continued firing irregularly after the ex-plosion, but Lazowski's workers noticed that the garrison was re-sponding primarily with musket fire. Indeed, rather than combat the conflagrations raging through the fortress, Cox, fearing a French as-sault, had ordered the infantry to return to the walls and maintain a heavy fusillade on the French workers. With the bright sky the work-ers made excellent targets. Lazowski and Eblé suffered 32 casualties during the night.[8]

After the explosion the 900 trench laborers had to be forced to continue work in the trenches. Instructions had been issued to open a new approach from the second parallel in the direction of the glacis and the covered way, but after the explosion the workers began to re-move the immense rocks strewn in the parallels. The workers on the right flank of the first parallel continued enlarging the communication trench to Battery No. 1 to facilitate the passage of wagons and supplies.[9]

With the first rays of the sun, the French sought to gain a glimpse of Almeida. When the fog had dissipated, they were astonished to see that the castle and the cathedral nearby had been demolished. Cox and the garrison were dismayed by what they found at dawn. Those in the fortress were overwhelmed "with the most horrible spectacle that can be imagined." Almeida was in ruins and not one house had been spared damage by the explosion or the bombardment. Many buildings were in flames and "the roads and the walls were full of bodies, many of the dead were terribly mutilated." The dazed soldiers and citizens were apprehensive, but Cox insisted that the surviving artillerymen continue to man their guns. The fortress walls were intact except for a few cracks. All the munitions, with the exception of 39 barrels of powder stored in the laboratory and a few barrels stored in the ex-pense magazine, had gone up in the explosion. As many as 600 infantrymen and over 200 artillerymen who had mounted the ramparts that morning were killed either by the blast or by the rain of stones and debris following the eruption. Some soldiers in the barracks survived the catastrophe, but those billeted or working in the castle had been killed. Perhaps 1,000 citizens had refused to heed Cox's plea to evacuate the town before the investment. When the explosion occurred, many of them had taken refuge in bombproof casemates opposite the point of attack, but as many as 500 remained in their homes and were either crushed by collapsing buildings or died seeking safety in the castle itself.[10]

While the French officers were surveying the damage to Almeida, the trench workers entered the second parallel and continued to clear out the immense rocks. The gun batteries continued their fire on the bastion of São Pedro and its adjoining demilune. Soon thereafter, Masséna rode up to his hut behind the first parallel, accompanied by Pelet and followed by the Marquis d'Alorna and Adjutant Commander Rippert. The garrison was not firing. Pelet recorded in his journal, "We could not see the tower, the church, or the castle. Everything appeared turned upside down." Masséna carefully examined the results of the explosion and decided to summon the garrison. At 9:00 A.M. the workers were withdrawn from the trenches and the artillery batteries were silenced.[11]

Pelet had already been to the trenches where he saw General Fririon, Masséna's chief of staff, and learned that Simon was preparing to send an ultimatum on his own initiative to the governor.[12] Returning to Masséna, he was instructed to accompany Captain Gama, a Portuguese officer on d'Alorna's staff, and Captain Sprünglin of the 6th Corps, to arrange for discussions with Cox. Pelet remained at the fortress barrier since only two officers were allowed to enter. After a lengthy wait, Pelet sent several notes to the officers to expedite the discussion; finally Masséna dispatched two notes to his officers prompting their immediate return. With the preliminaries completed, he sent Pelet to deliver the ultimatum, accompanied by Captain Gama. After waiting for a considerable length of time at the fortress barrier, Pelet and Gama were blindfolded and led through the fortress before entering the passage to the governor's casemate. When their blindfolds were removed, Pelet and Gama were ushered into the governor's presence. Cox appeared to be in his mid-thirties, according to Pelet, who described him as "tall, noble, a handsome figure with the shrewdness of self-discipline, the appearance of a strong character— in all, *un bel anglais*." Pelet presented Masséna's ultimatum to the governor: "The town of Almeida is burning. All of my siege artillery is in its batteries, and it is impossible for your allies to come to your aid. Render yourself to the generosity of the armies of His Majesty, the Emperor and King." Masséna offered "honourable conditions" with the reminder that he should remember the unfortunate fate of Ciudad Rodrigo and the suffering that would attend a prolonged defense of Almeida.[13]

As soon as the explosion occurred, it was evident to Cox that Almeida was indefensible. His only hope rested with the Allied army although Wellington had "never expressed his specific intention in this respect." Aware that the Allied army was only a day's march away, Cox realized that Wellington's strategy would have to determine the fate of Almeida. Soon after the explosion, Cox discussed the grim situation with Lieutenant Colonel Francisco Bernardo da Costa e Almeida, lieutenant governor of the fortress. The Portuguese officer was also overwhelmed by the enormity of the catastrophe and its possible consequences. Cox instructed him to examine and determine the state of the fortress. An hour before Pelet arrived at the governor's quarters with Gama to present Masséna's ultimatum, Cox received the report from Costa declaring he should "capitulate because the fortress is in such a state that it could capitulate with honor." Considering this report as "urging [him] strongly to surrender," Cox rejected the recommendation "absolutely," declaring the town would be defended "to give the army time to relieve it." While Cox was negotiating with Pelet and Gama, Costa and a few officers came to the governor's quarters to speak with him. They asked Major Manoel Roballo Caldeira, posted at the door, to express their opinion to the governor that a council of war should be called before any decision was made on the French proposals. Later Cox would claim that he had intended to speak with each of the officers separately about a possible surrender, but the officers' request for a council of war could not be denied at this juncture. The governor ordered Major Caldeira to convene a council of war quickly in a nearby casemate where the officers often congregated. Apparently, while Pelet and Gama waited, Cox joined Costa and the other officers to discuss the tense situation. Costa had already described the dismal conditions of the fortress and the morale of the inhabitants to a few officers. Major Fortunato Barreiros was the first of the officers to express his opinion. The members of the council felt an outright rejection of the French ultimatum might lead to an assault and the death of the garrison. Moreover, the inhabitants of the town, who included both women and children of the officers' families, might suffer a fate even more cruel. Cox and Costa did not cast votes, but the council was in agreement in recommending the surrender of the fortress. Although the vote could not be binding on the governor, Cox was obviously discouraged by the attitude of the Portuguese officers, especially Costa who had "acted with much zeal and propriety" and was the only survivor of a unit of thirteen men working on the bastion of São João de Deos when the castle erupted. It was agreed that Cox would prolong negotiations with the French, at least until the next day, hoping Wellington might march to relieve the town.[14]

Pelet presented Masséna's ultimatum, but the governor was unwilling to accept it. "The conversation began on a serious note, then became pleasant, then light, and was always carried on in an agreeable way." Sanguine in his comments, Pelet "told him the truth about the state of affairs," and soon he sent Gama with a note for Masséna. Cox discussed the capitulation with Pelet and then presented his response. He wrote to Masséna, "Since I do not find myself reduced to the last extremity, I desire to know the terms of this proposition beforehand. I have decided to simply enter into negotiations, if conditions are advantageous to us." In awaiting Masséna's response, he suspended operations and assumed the French would do likewise. Before Pelet left the governor's casemate, Cox appointed Major Barreiros, commander of the fortress artillery, and Captain Pedro de Mello of his staff to accompany Pelet to Masséna's headquarters as parliamentarians. They were given the "necessary powers . . . to conclude a definitive treaty of capitulation," within his guidelines, that is, to refuse any surrender before noon of the following day, and to insist that the men of the garrison be freed to return to their homes. Without a blindfold, Pelet rode out of Almeida with the two Portuguese negotiators and through the French lines to the old mill where Masséna, Ney, and their staffs were waiting.[15]

During negotiations at Almeida between Masséna's representatives and Cox, events seemed to outdistance the parliamentarians. D'Alorna rode up to the walls of the fortress on horseback with General Manuel Ignácio Martins Pamplona and several of his Portuguese staff. When recognized by the troops on the ramparts, many shouted, "Long live Marquis d'Alorna." With a familiar face in the enemy camp, many of the soldiers adopted a congenial attitude and conversed freely with him and the other Portuguese officers.[16]

Meanwhile, Masséna was engaged in negotiations with Barreiros and Mello. The Portuguese insisted on freedom for the entire garrison and the opportunity to rejoin the Allied army with all of their equipment. Masséna categorically refused. In the course of the discussions, Barreiros, apparently without Mello's knowledge, divulged the actual state of the fortress to Masséna. He admitted that all of the shells and bombs and all but 39 barrels of gunpowder had been lost in the explosion and that the officers and troops of the garrison were anxious to capitulate. This information reaffirmed Masséna's decision to grant no further concessions. Barreiros signed the capitulation although Mello still insisted that the garrison be freed.[17]

Once the capitulation had been signed, Mello and Pelet returned to the fortress. Pelet was made to wait, apparently outside the governor's quarters, for over an hour. Rippert joined him with another copy of the capitulation before he was finally permitted to talk to Cox. The governor seemed "worried and preoccupied." Pelet reported Masséna's precise words—"to allow the garrison to return home if they desired, but to insist on the rest of the capitulation terms." Pelet assured Cox that if the town surrendered under the terms of the capitulation, the whole garrison would be free to return home. Masséna had authorized Pelet to make this offer at their initial meeting, but he could not guarantee it in writing; after the surrender he would announce this condition as a sign of magnanimity. This was, in fact, what Cox was requesting with minor modifications: "That the garrison would be free to go home on their word of honor, that the British would be allowed to return to England on the same terms, and that the doors would not be opened until the next day at noon." Pelet wanted to consider each article separately, but the governor wanted to discuss them as an entity. Pelet insisted that the French occupy one gate immediately, but the governor refused. Cox, in turn, offered his word of honor and some hostages at the moment the capitulation was signed by him, but he wanted to wait until noon the next day. After some heated discussion, calmed by a glass of Porto wine, Pelet became convinced that Cox was attempting to extend negotiations so Wellington would have time to concentrate his army and march to raise the siege. The parley was cut short.[18]

After leaving a copy of the capitulation with the governor, Pelet and Rippert left the fortress. Upon their return to Masséna's post, they described the governor's rejection of the capitulation. Masséna refused Cox's request at once and prepared to resume siege operations. However, to avoid additional bloodshed on both sides and to enter the town as soon as possible, he sent another officer an hour later with an uncompromising letter. "I am sorry that you have not accepted the honorable terms of capitulation that I have offered you," he wrote. Cox was advised that the gunfire would begin and continue until his terms were accepted: "Consider your options. You have one-half hour to decide." Masséna also linked a prompt surrender with the return of the English officers to Britain, and he asked the governor to sign and return the copy that had been left by Pelet. When Masséna's aide left Almeida, Cox requested the return of Major Barreiros. Masséna sent another aide-de-camp with a final offer granting freedom to the militia to return to their homes if the fortress surrendered. Before this officer could return with Cox's reply, French guns recommenced fire at 8:00 P.M. Cox was stunned; he could only attribute it to the confusion of the moment.[19]

The artillery fire proved very effective, thanks to the aid of Major Barreiros who had decided to remain with the French army. He aided Eblé's men in aiming their guns on remaining magazines in Almeida. Meanwhile, the telegraph at Almeida continued to signal Wellington's advanced posts as it had all day, but it had become evident that the Allied army would not march to aid the garrison. The Portuguese officers and men had already decided not to sacrifice themselves for a useless cause. There was no alternative. Therefore, Cox sent the French officer, stranded at Almeida during the bombardment, back to

Masséna with a Portuguese officer and a trumpeter. Just after dawn the French howitzer and mortars ceased fire, and the Portuguese officer returned to Cox announcing that Masséna had accepted capitulation at around 3:00 A.M.[20]

Early the morning of 28 August, General Fririon arrived at the fortress to ensure the conditions of the surrender would be fulfilled. According to the capitulation articles, the troops would march out of Almeida, deposit their arms on the glacis and surrender to Simon's infantry. The men of the 24th Line would be made prisoners of war, but the men of the three militia regiments would be given their freedom and marched to the interior of Portugal. According to the agreement, the Portuguese and British officers would retain their swords and baggage and the soldiers would keep their sacks. The inhabitants of the town would maintain their property and be free from persecution. The munitions of war and the artillery would be transferred to the French army. The treasury and magazine would be placed under the French commissioner of war and plans relating to the fortifications of Almeida would be given to Lazowski. Finally, the responsibility for the British and Portuguese sick in the hospital would be assumed by the French medical staff until the patients could follow their regiments to prison.[21]

Fririon found Cox hesitant because he had not been given a signed copy of the capitulation. When Masséna learned of the governor's delay, he reacted decisively. Orders were issued for the troops of Marchand's division to prepare for an assault. Eblé and Lazowski were to make preparations to blow in the fortress gate and "put the garrison to the sword, with the governor, if these difficulties [were] renewed." This threat ended the governor's objections. The garrison marched out of the gate at mid-morning after depositing their arms on the esplanade near the glacis. Despite the exaggerated claims by the French regarding the size of the garrison, approximately 3,000 Portuguese troops and three British officers surrendered to the 6th Corps. Their losses included some 200 artillerymen and more than 600 infantry; as many as 500 inhabitants of the town perished in the explosion and the bombardment. Considering the duration and intensity of the siege, French losses were surprisingly low—58 dead and 320 wounded.[22]

Orders were drawn up for the return of the militia to their homes and the transfer of the 24th Line and the British officers to La Concepción, but these arrangements were altered after the troops met with the Marquis d'Alorna: "They were wildly enthusiastic about the return of their old general in chief. . . . They received the marquis as their savior and proclaimed him the defender and the avenger of the country." According to Pelet, "They asked his help and swore to assist in breaking the chains of the British who had just abandoned them so infamously." Masséna was amazed by the tumultuous welcome accorded d'Alorna, who appealed to him for permission to organize a Portuguese unit for service with the French army. Masséna and several of his staff officers were apprehensive about such an arrangement, but the advantages could not be denied. If he could detach the Portuguese army from the British cause, success would be assured and the war would end with the "least possible bloodshed."[23]

Masséna granted d'Alorna permission to organize a Portuguese unit of pioneers to serve primarily with the engineers of the army. Six officers and 200 men, chosen from each of the three militia regiments, swore allegiance to Napoleon and were sent to La Concepción. The French claimed that these "men of good will" were volunteers, but Cox was appalled by the entire affair; later he declared they were taken "against all their desires and in direct violation of the expressed articles of the capitulation." The remaining militiamen, however, were organized into three columns and marched on three separate days toward the Allied lines.[24]

Preparations were made to send the men of the 24th Line to La Concepción as prisoners of war. On the assumption that Masséna would free the prisoners, Cox later complained to Liverpool that despite the "verbal promise to send all the garrison to their homes, it was denied that I ever had heard this." Cox, two British officers serving in the 24th Line, Major Hewitt and Captain Foley, and one Portuguese officer who refused service with the French were sent to La Concepción. From there Cox wrote Masséna offering his word of honor that neither he nor his officers would serve against France until exchanged. Continuing to Paris, Cox anticipated an immediate return to Britain. However, Masséna apparently neglected to write to the French minister of war about his promise, so the three British officers were dispatched to Verdun where they remained until their exchange could be arranged. However, the fate of the 24th Line was very different. Before Lieutenant Colonel Figueiredo moved the regiment to Aldea del Obispo for the march to France, several officers and men approached d'Alorna. They expressed a desire to serve with the French army, apparently hoping for an opportunity to escape. The men of the 24th Line took the oath to Napoleon. They were rearmed and placed under the command of the Portuguese general, Pamplona. The 112 men of the 4th Artillery Regiment requested service with France and were placed under Eblé's command; 60 men of the 11th Cavalry were attached to the French cavalry.[25]

As soon as the Portuguese had evacuated Almeida, two battalions of Simon's infantry, commanded by Antoine François Brenier de Montmorand, the new governor, marched into the town. They were shocked to see the havoc and devastation. Every house either had been demolished or had suffered serious damage, and only the granite foundation remained of the castle. Few houses had roofs and massive stones littered the streets and obstructed passage. After administering to the wounded and securing the magazines, the troops began clearing the streets. Since Masséna had designated the fortress as a depot for the army, reconstruction work was begun immediately. Under the direction of the engineers and sappers, new roofs were raised on the public buildings. Shelters were constructed to protect the soldiers, the powder magazines, and the supplies of the army. Lacking wood, tile, and sandstone, Bernier sent his troops into the countryside to dismantle buildings in neighboring villages in order to secure the necessary construction materials. To repair the cracked arches of the casemates and eliminate the rainwater dripping into the powder magazines, he sent troops as far as Fuente Guinaldo to haul back suitable sandstone for the repairs.[26]

On 29 August, Masséna ordered 300 Portuguese pioneers into the fortress under the direction of the engineers to continue cleanup operations. They were cautioned to use extreme care to avoid further explosions. Four hundred soldiers of the 39th, 69th, and 76th Lines were ordered by Marchand to begin filling in the trenches, working from the third parallel outward from the fortress. Reynier was also instructed to send 190 men to Almeida to join in the work. At the same time Chef de bataillon Bouvier compiled an inventory of the fortress armaments. The French captured 172 guns of all calibers, 605,695 cartridges, and 2,885 small arms, but only 39 barrels of powder. Six flags from the Portuguese militia regiments and the 24th Line were brought into Masséna's headquarters as trophies of war.[27]

Brenier posted guards outside the food magazines upon his arrival in the town and they remained closed on Masséna's personal instructions until the commissariat officers arrived to inventory the provisions. They found 300,000 rations of biscuit, 10,000 rations of salted meat, 24 ton of wheat, 25 of rice, 80 of maize, two of beans, 80 of barley, 34 barrels of wine, and 150 ton of straw. With this vast reserve of food, it was obvious that the garrison might have continued the defense of Almeida for several months if the powder magazine had not blown up.[28]

French operations at Almeida had proved to be remarkably successful. Masséna could not contain himself when he wrote to Berthier following the capitulation: "By a remarkable turn of fortune beyond all of our hopes, an important fortress that might have cost us dearly and delayed us for many days yet, and obliged us to crown the covered way in order to pound a breach in the foot of the ramparts, has been delivered to us almost without loss of men and little use of our military depot for the expedition to Portugal." In an atmosphere of elation, he observed, "The capture will influence the success of this campaign because of the strong reputation it enjoyed among the Portuguese who regarded it as an impregnable bulwark on this frontier, and they will not pardon Lord Wellington for abandoning it." He also expressed satisfaction with the successful efforts of Lazowski and Eblé; he applauded "the courage, perseverance, and indefatigable activity of the line troops: generals, officers, and soldiers all merit great praise; all of them have manifested the same devotion already demonstrated during the siege of Ciudad Rodrigo."[29]

For the second time in two months, Masséna's army had succeeded in capturing a formidable fortress within a day's march of the Allied army. Siege operations had been planned and implemented more effectively than those at Ciudad Rodrigo. After 11 days of open trenches and 30 hours of bombardment the engineers had reached the glacis and the artillery bombardment had destroyed much of the town. Mars had smiled on *l'enfant chéri de la victoire* in an extraordinary fashion and he had fulfilled his master's seemingly impossible timetable for the subjugation of Almeida. Napoleon had wanted Almeida to be in French possession "towards the end of August"; Masséna announced to Berthier on 28 August, "Almeida is in the power of His Imperial Majesty, the Emperor, and King."[30]

Wellington was shocked by the unexpected announcement that the French had occupied Almeida. He had written confidently to his brother, Henry, "If we cannot relieve Almeida, it will, I hope, make a stout defence: The Governor is an obstinate fellow, and talks of a siege of ninety days." When the guns of Almeida fell silent at 8:15 P.M. on 26 August, he wrote to Hill, "I am sorry to tell you that the enemy are in possession of Almeida." The next morning, still in a state of shock, he wrote again to Hill, "I cannot express how much I am disappointed at this fatal event, which I cannot account for in any manner. The place could not have been breached." Considering the supplies at Almeida, he was dismayed to think that "the remaining 350,000 [rations] will enable the enemy to invade Portugal." Almost unwilling to accept the loss of Almeida which was crucial in the defense of the Kingdom, Wellington expressed his sense of disbelief to Liverpool: "The manner in which the garrison was supplied with all the necessities for the defence of the fort, to the respectable state of the works and to the good spirit which I understood from the Governor that the garrison maintained, I had hoped that the place would hold out to the last extremity . . . [and] would have detained the enemy till a late period in the season."[31]

When Wellington learned more details of the explosion from captured Frenchmen the day following the capitulation, he hoped the accounts were "correct in all material points." He declared, "It will give me great satisfaction to find that the loss of Almeida . . . [has] not been occasioned by any fault of the Governor or of the garrison." Despite the reported activity of the French in the fortress, Wellington confessed to his brother, "The loss of Almeida is a great misfortune, but I do not lose all hopes yet." On 31 August a large detachment of militia from Arganil, freed by Masséna, arrived at the Allied posts. The regimental colonel, José de Melo Freire Bulhões, described the explosion and the events leading to the capitulation. Reassured by this information, Wellington wrote to Stuart, "The garrison, till the accident, had sustained no loss, and was in the best order and spirits, and had not thoughts of surrender, and expected to hold the place for two months." Descriptions of the damage suffered at Almeida were exaggerated every time they were repeated, and within a day Wellington was writing to Hill: "The magazine at Almeida was blown up . . . and all the ammunition destroyed; a breach made in the place; the guns, excepting three, blown into the ditch, and nearly all the artillerymen killed or wounded. The whole town was destroyed." Indeed, he even announced the death of 40 French trench workers as a result of the shower of stones following the explosions. If there were any positive result of this catastrophe for the Allies, it was the realization that the Portuguese troops at Almeida had performed effectively from the investment on 24 July until the explosion destroyed any hope of further defense.[32]

Disbelief and resentment about the capitulation of Almeida was directed toward Wellington. Although his force was comparable in size to Masséna's army, he had remained inactive rather than attempt to relieve Almeida. Few in his own army and even fewer among the Portuguese understood or appreciated his strategy for the mobilization of Portugal. As a result he was denounced by the Portuguese and questioned by some of his own soldiers for abandoning his ally. A Portuguese general was reputed to have said to Wellington, "If you are unable to defend us, why do you stimulate our resistance and cover our unfortunate country with blood and ruins? If you are in force, deliver battle; if you are too weak and cannot obtain reinforcements, retire and leave us to compromise with the conquerors." Two members of the Regency, the Principal Sousa and the Patriarch, attacked his policies, passionately claiming that he should have contested the French at Almeida and along the frontier rather than permitting Masséna's troops to turn central Portugal into a wasteland. In a rather ingenuous letter to Forjaz, the Regency secretary, Wellington lamented that the "melancholy and unexpected news of the loss of Almeida . . . had prevented [his] moving to succour the place." In fact, he had no intention of relieving Almeida. Despite the demands of the Regency and the "anxiety of the public" after the fall of Almeida, Wellington refused to renounce his plans, pointing out that he would fail in his duty to his sovereign and the Prince Regent "if I should permit public clamor or panic to induce me to change, in the smallest degree, the system and plan of the operations which I have adopted." Impatient with the changes in the Regency's attitude toward his strategy, which had been supported for twelve months, Wellington wrote to Stuart in Lisbon, "It appears the Government have lately discovered we are all wrong, they have become impatient for the defeat of the enemy." He was firm in his resolution, declaring, "I will not lose the only chance which remains of saving the cause, by paying the smallest attention to the senseless suggestions of the Portuguese Government." The fall of Almeida might serve as a catalyst to those opposing his strategy, but he would carry out his plans or he was determined to quit the army. "If I find the Government hesitating upon this subject, and alarmed by the mob of Lisbon . . . I shall forthwith embark the army . . . and the Portuguese nation will have the satisfaction of losing itself, and the Peninsula." [33]

The Portuguese government attempted to make the best of an unfortunate situation. In a document issued by the Regency, the Marquess Monteiro Mor minimized the loss: "Although the disastrous loss of the fort of Almeida has little effect on the great cause and salvation of the country, it is unfortunate because of the death of some of the glorious defenders and the captivity of the others by the enemy." Referring to the French army as "highwaymen," and Wellington as the "son of victory," he called upon the faithful people to remain loyal to the course of the Prince Regent and the country against the "army of slaves." Beresford was equally anxious to reassure the army of his confidence. Extolling the defense of the garrison as "worthy of the Portuguese character," he took particular pleasure in noting "the brilliant behavior" of the militia regiments. On the contrary, he admitted the defection of the 24th Line. The enlisted men who "lacked education" were excused, but he could not "forgive the officers for behavior so vile and indignant to the name of Portuguese officers," even if their action was only a means to return to their colors. The loss of the regiment could easily be remedied with the induction of new conscripts, but "the 15 or 20 days" lost by the unexpected surrender of Almeida were more difficult to rationalize. Yet he concluded confidently by pointing out that "the Kingdom had never been . . . in such a good state since the war began."[34]

Until the fall of Almeida, Wellington's preparations for the defense of Portugal had made significant progress. The skillful deployment of his army from Guarda to Celorico and Trancoso had forced Masséna to waste precious time and resources in deploying his army to protect the besiegers. At the same time, his troops, both British and Portuguese, had improved in discipline and experience and his vast plans for the mobilization continued determinedly. However, when Almeida fell, the time for preparations was drawing to an end and the time to test the validity of his strategy was about to begin. No doubt, if the mobilization had been more advanced, the failure of Masséna's expedition would have been more immediate and decisive, sparing Portugal from the suffering, and deprivations occasioned by an occupying army. The time lost by the surrender of Almeida might have been regained, according to Pelet. He cogently pointed out, "The harm done could have been repaired with thirty wagons of powder" if Wellington had felt that Almeida was worth saving and had been willing to maneuver on the flanks of the French army.[35]

Governor Cox's role in the loss of Almeida is less clear but not without responsibility. For over a year he had demonstrated an uncommon commitment in preparing the fortress defenses. His personal courage, composure, and determination in defending Almeida before and after the explosion were above reproach. However, it is abundantly clear that he committed a monumental blunder by establishing the great powder magazines in the castle of the town. In considering the consequences of his decision, both Portuguese and French artillery officers condemned him for concentrating the entire powder magazine in one building. It is also noteworthy that despite the size of his garrison, Cox did not attempt a single sortie to obstruct the workers once the trenches had been opened. This failure probably reflected his lack of confidence in the militia and his belief that he could not risk the loss of any part of the 24th Line in a sortie. With the destruction of the powder magazine, Cox had no alternative but to surrender or risk an assault and the death of the garrison.[36]

Ignoring Cox's lack of foresight in preparing the magazines, both

Wellington and Beresford came to Cox's defense after the capitulation. Beresford wrote to Wellington that the Portuguese garrison "unanimously state their Governor's conduct inspired them with [the highest spirit], as every officer and man gives the highest applause to his unremitting zeal and activity, encouraging all by his own example." Wellington repeated this praise to Liverpool, declaring, "It was impossible to expect that Col. Cox should continue the defense of the place after the unfortunate occurrence." Blame had to be assessed for the catastrophe, so it was shifted to the treason of Barreiros and the alleged cowardice of Costa, although their actions had little to do with the ultimate defense or surrender of Almeida. Very little time would have been gained by continued resistance while the lives of the garrison would have been in serious jeopardy for no purpose, because Wellington was not about to alter his strategy.[37]

In the meantime, an event occurred a few days after the surrender that marred the French victory and caused widespread skepticism, disgust, and resentment among the soldiers and officers of the French army. It took four days to rearm, organize, and attach the 24th Line, the artillerymen, and the cavalry to the appropriate French units. "They had taken an oath of obedience and fidelity to France" but Masséna was apprehensive about their loyalty. He did not want to embarrass d'Alorna and the other Portuguese officers on his staff, but he confided to Berthier, "I shall be careful in watching these troops and place them in less important positions." Masséna's suspicions were not unfounded; within a few days large numbers of pioneers working along the road to Pinhel slipped out of camp and deserted. Soon some of the 24th Line began to leave camp at opportune moments and, by 7 September, 17 officers and 500 men had rejoined Wellington with all their equipment while others had headed toward Bragança. In fact, within another week the regiment, with the exception of some 200 men, had returned to Portuguese colors. Several Portuguese officers, including cavalry, visited Masséna to reiterate their oath but within a few days most of them had left camp. During the second week of September, the cavalrymen walked out of camp early one morning. Masséna reacted bitterly by disarming the remaining troops; only 300 men of the original 3,000 prisoners remained, and they were sent to France as prisoners of war.[38]

Masséna was embarrassed by the turn of events, but he was more depressed by his inability to form the nucleus of a pro-French Portuguese army. With this force he might have induced others in Wellington's army to join his forces, especially when the British army reached the sea and prepared to embark. "Nothing equaled the confusion and chagrin of our poor Portuguese generals who had counseled the Prince on this measure and guaranteed its success," wrote Pelet. The officers and men of the French army expressed dismay as a result of Masséna's decision and apparent lack of judgment. Some suggested that the Portuguese prisoners might have been exchanged for Frenchmen held by the British, while others lashed out at the Portuguese officers, especially d'Alorna, claiming that he was an adventurer without honor.[39]

Upon the return of the impressed militia, Wellington sent them home since Masséna had already sent almost 1,500 to their homes as the capitulation required. However, when some of the 24th Line reached Beresford's headquarters, Wellington had serious reservations about the immediate return of the officers to active service. Despite the planned desertion, their oath to France had a great impact upon his own officers as well as British officers in the Portuguese service. He wanted to emphasize "the principles of men of honor, and the sentiments officers and gentlemen ought to induce them to do on similar occasions." The Portuguese government, however, decided to minimize the circumstances concerning their escape to freedom and acknowledge their honorable service to the nation. They claimed the oath to serve the French had been negated when Masséna violated the capitulation terms by incorporating 600 militia into the French army. Ironically, two months later a battalion of the 24th Line was active in driving French pickets back into Almeida and masking the fortress.[40] Thus ended a rather bizarre episode in Masséna's spectacular capture of Almeida. The fruits of victory were partially nullified by his generous treatment of the prisoners and his poor judgment in accepting the advice of his Portuguese advisors. These actions had little direct effect upon the campaign but did undermine the confidence of his men who were about to embark upon a crucial campaign for the domination of the Peninsula.

Chapter 15

Conclusions

EIGHTEEN DAYS after the fall of Almeida, Masséna set his army in motion. Led by Ney's 6th Corps, the army marched across the bridge on the Côa and pushed into the Portuguese hinterland. Advancing through Viseu toward Coimbra, the French army marched 126 miles in ten days. By the night of 25 September the advanced guard of the army stood at the foot of the Serra de Bussaco observing the Allied army deployed along its eight-mile crest. Wellington had drawn up his army on one of the most dominant positions in Portugal, ready to contest Masséna's advance.

Despite the various claims, Wellington's final decision to fight was predicated on his belief that Masséna could be halted. He wrote confidently to Stuart in Lisbon, "I shall do every thing in my power to stop the enemy here." Obviously, if he were successful, the heartland of Portugal would be spared the devastation of an invading army. On the contrary, if he were driven off the mountain, those who clamored for battle to halt the French invasion would be appeased. Moreover, the British commitment to the Portuguese cause would be demonstrated; the Portuguese troops would gain experience and confidence; and at least some of the time lost by the unexpected capitulation of Almeida would be recouped, thereby securing additional time to complete the vital Lines of Torres Vedras.[1]

On 27 September, Masséna's army attacked Wellington's positions along the skyline of the Serra de Bussaco. In spite of the determined attack of the corps of Ney and Reynier, they were repulsed by the Allied army with 5,000 casualties. Rather than risk the fate of the

campaign on the uncertain success of another attack, Masséna followed the road to Boialvo, thereby outflanking the Anglo-Portuguese
position. Wellington reacted by ordering an immediate retreat of the
army. He had lost 1,252 men, but he had achieved several of his
goals as well as gaining five additional days for the men laboring to
complete the lines before Lisbon.[2]

The French occupied Coimbra on 1 October and three days later
they continued the pursuit of the Allied army. Pressing Wellington's
rear guard, Montbrun's cavalry engaged in periodic skirmishes with
the horsemen of the British 16th Light Dragoons until they reached
Rio Maior on 8 October. As the Allies recoiled before the French
advance, Wellington was still unswerving in the determination to
carry out his strategy. He wrote confidently to Liverpool, "The enemy
suffer great distress. The inhabitants of the country have fled from
their houses universally, carrying with them every thing they could
take away which could be deemed useful to the enemy." Once the
French had passed Rio Maior, the resistance of the Allied rear guard
became more stubborn. A bitter action took place between Sainte-
Croix's cavalry and the British horsemen at Alquentre and again at
Moinho Cubo. On 10 October, Taupin's troops were confronted by the
Light Division at Alenquer, but Craufurd fell back slowly toward Sobral. The next day French cavalry columns, pushing down the two
main roads toward Lisbon, halted abruptly when they reached Alhandra and Sobral; as far as the eye could see, a line of strategically
located fortified positions stretched toward the ocean. For two days
the French attempted to resume their advance only to be repulsed by
large elements of Wellington's army, supported by artillery on the
heights behind them.[3]

Masséna had first heard talk of the fortified lines on 9 October,
two days before his army reached them. On the twelfth he rode up to
the lines, accompanied by Pelet and several members of his staff, to
reconnoiter the positions for himself. It was only following his own
observations and the reports of his état-major that he gradually began
to realize the implications of his delays before the fortresses of
Ciudad Rodrigo and Almeida. He continued to probe the lines for
almost a month. However, as his army exhausted the terrain before
the lines and the reinforced Allied army became more threatening,

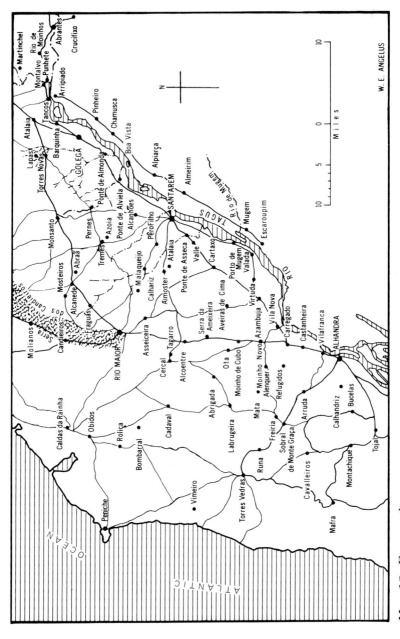

Map 13. Estremadura

Masséna decided to withdraw to Santarém, 30 miles northeast of the lines. He had no alternative but to appeal directly to Napoleon for reinforcements and a siege train.

While Masséna undertook the sieges of Ciudad Rodrigo and Almeida during the summer of 1810, the British and Portuguese engineers pushed their Portuguese workers relentlessly, aware that the lines would have to be completed before the enemy reached them. After the ill-timed surrender of Almeida, Wellington encouraged Colonel Fletcher, commanding the engineers, to complete the lines as quickly as possible. The lines surrounding the evacuation enclave at São Julião had yet to be completed, and Captain John T. Jones, in charge of actual site construction, was dissatisfied with the first line and the fortifications before the lines. He wanted to transform the advanced positions into another line so there would be three lines of defense. This would take more time and some adjustments in plans for the defense of the entire network of fortifications. He began work on the modifications after writing to Fletcher, "Alhandra . . . does not altogether satisfy me as a position; I should fear that an enemy acting with a very superior force would penetrate by the hills on the left." While this new work was being undertaken, Wellington ordered trees cut, abatis arranged, and the bridges mined; by mid-September the work was finished. When the French were within 100 miles of the lines, Fletcher wrote confidentially to Jones, "Present circumstances seem to render it necessary that every precaution should be taken at or near our works for their being immediately occupied and defended." Hand grenades and water were distributed to each redoubt. Yet four days before the French reached the lines, Jones was writing, "It is lucky we commenced dressing off so soon, for now everything is in confusion: the people are all running away. . . . No one will believe that the army will halt till it reaches St. Julian's, and all authority and order is beginning to be lost." Indeed, the lines were not yet completed. Only 126 of the 152 redoubts had been completed and 427 of the 534 guns were ready for action.[4]

The first contingent of the Allied army began to arrive at the lines on 7 October, and despite the misdirection of several divisions the entire force was behind the lines within three days, closely pursued by the French. Once the troops were deployed, Wellington ordered the immediate construction of three redoubts above Runa while other troops labored to barricade the road from Sobral to Ribaldeira and arrange abatis in the valleys behind Gosundeira and Zibreira.[5]

Based on the course of events before the Lines of Torres Vedras, it became increasingly evident that the time afforded to Wellington's engineers by the defenses of Ciudad Rodrigo and Almeida was of major significance. Without the three months gained by the defenders of the fortresses, Masséna's army would have been before the gates of Lisbon long before the lines were completed; an attack at that juncture would have had considerable chance of success. In fact, years later, Wellington's second in command, General Sir Rowland Hill, is reputed to have said that if the French had attacked within the first ten days of their arrival, they could easily have breached the incomplete fortifications.[6]

In any case, the Lines of Torres Vedras discouraged any further French advance. Masséna sent several officers to appeal personally to Napoleon for support. Napoleon made some effort to send aid, but less than 7,000 troops and almost no supplies reached Masséna's forces. By the first of March, Masséna's starving army, reduced by 25,000 men, totaled less than 42,000, while the Allied army was increasing in strength with the arrival of each transport in Lisbon harbor.[7] With munitions and powder almost exhausted and only a minimal magazine left to feed the retreating army, Masséna ordered a withdrawal on 5 March. Attempts to halt the retreat and remain in Portugal were made, but several bitter rearguard actions convinced Masséna that his only safety rested with the fortresses of Almeida and Ciudad Rodrigo. By the first of April the Army of Portugal had been forced back into Spain. The French were still in possession of Almeida, but it was besieged by Wellington's forces. In an effort to relieve the garrison of Almeida during the first week of May, Masséna reentered Portugal to fight what became his last battle. Wellington was waiting for him at Fuentes de Oñoro. In two days of bitter fighting, the French army was decisively repulsed. Masséna fell back to Ciudad Rodrigo, defeated, broken in health, and abandoned, ending the illustrious career of one of the greatest soldiers to serve under French colors. Brenier and his garrison finally were able to slip out of Almeida and join Masséna; but with this withdrawal, Napoleon's hopes for the subjugation of Portugal and the expulsion of the British were shattered.

Ciudad Rodrigo remained under French control until it was besieged in January 1812 by Wellington; he ordered a rather premature but successful assault on the town before French reinforcements arrived. It fell after a bloody attack marked by pillage, rape, and fire. Allied control of the city was never again challenged by a French army. From Ciudad Rodrigo, Wellington launched his great offensive in the spring of 1813 that carried the victorious Allied armies across northern Spain. In July, King Joseph's army was overwhelmed at Vitoria, and before the end of the year Wellington was leading his army into France—his strategy for Iberia fully justified.

In assessing the significance of the twin sieges, their impact on Masséna's invasion of Portugal, and the ultimate defeat of the French, it is clear that they became vital in Wellington's overall strategy for Iberia. The sieges prepared the French for the victories that failed to materialize at Bussaco and before the Lines of Torres Vedras, undermining French morale and confidence. The time lost by the French army before Ciudad Rodrigo and Almeida was never regained and the Lines of Torres Vedras were sufficiently completed to halt their advance. Yet, it is difficult to fault Masséna's overall action, limited as he was by Napoleon's constraints. If Masséna had been free to mask the fortresses, invade Portugal, and march on Lisbon, the history of the campaign might have been quite different. The same is true of Wellington who opted to abandon the fortresses for the ultimate victory at Torres Vedras. He capitalized on Napoleon's faulty strategy and made the French pay dearly for his mistake. If responsibility for the French failure must be assigned, Napoleon must share the blame since he issued the orders that spelled victory for his enemy and failure for his own army.

The Allied victory in Iberia was the result of a combination of factors: the uprising of the Spanish and Portuguese people; the inability of the French to overcome their staggering administrative, logistic, geographic, and strategic problems; the resistance of the Spanish guerrillas; the mobilization of Portugal; the intervention of Great Britain under Wellington's leadership; and Napoleon's failure to grasp the true nature of the struggle. The impact of the sieges of

Ciudad Rodrigo and Almeida was reflected to some degree in each of these factors. However, in the mobilization of Portugal and the strategy of Wellington, the twin sieges were of major importance to the Allied cause. Indeed, it was from the sanctuary behind the Lines of Torres Vedras that the Allies began the great counteroffensive that swept through Portugal, across Spain, and into France, culminating in the battle of Toulouse—the last major battle fought by French troops during the First Empire.

Notes

Chapter 1. *The Spanish Quagmire*

1. Donald D. Horward, *The Battle of Bussaco: Masséna vs Wellington*, pp. 1–5; Donald D. Horward, "Portuguese Neutrality and Mobilization, 1801–1810."
2. Napoleon Bonaparte, *Correspondance de Napoléon Ier publiée par ordre de l'Empereur Napoléon III*, No. 13861, Napoleon to Junot, 11 May 1808, XVII, 115; Alphonse Grasset, *La guerre d'Espagne (1807–1813)*, II, 259–60; Julio de Ramon Laca, *El General Pérez de Herrasti, Heroe de Ciudad Rodrigo*, pp. 75–76.
3. Maximilien Foy, *History of the War in the Peninsula, under Napoleon*, II, 429, 436–37, 538; Paul Charles Thiébault, *Relation de l'expedition du Portugal, faite en 1807 et 1808*, pp. 112, 147–53; France, Archives de la guerre, Service historique de l'armée, Chateau de Vincennes, MSS, Correspondance: Armée de Portugal, Junot to Thiébault, 22 May 1809; Junot to Loison, 7 June 1809, Carton C^7 16.
4. Correspondance: Armée de Portugal, Junot to Kellermann, 31 May 1809, Carton C^7 16; Foy, *War in the Peninsula*, II, 538, 604.
5. Joseph Bonaparte, *Mémoires et correspondance politique et militaire du roi Joseph*, Jourdan to Soult, 22 July 1809, VI, 278–80; Joseph to Napoleon, 29, 31 July, 7, 9 August 1809, VI, 282–86, 300–301, 307–8; Soult to Joseph, 6 August 1809, VI, 296–98; Soult to Jourdan, 18 August 1809, VI, 346–48; Soult to Clarke, 23 August 1809, VI, 363–66; *Correspondance de Napoléon Ier*, No. 15594, Napoleon to Clarke, 29 July 1809, XIX, 338; Henri Bonnal, *La vie militaire du maréchal Ney, duc d'Elchingen, prince de la Moskowa*, Ney to Joseph,

18 August 1808, III, 244–47; Ney to Soult, 19 May 1808, III, 250–51.

6. Bonnal, *Vie militaire du maréchal Ney*, Ney to Joseph, 16 December 1808, III, 286.

7. *Correspondance du roi Joseph*, Soult to Berthier, 1 January 1810, VII, 196–98.

8. Ibid., Soult to Berthier, 1, 3 January 1810, VII, 202–3, 206–8.

9. Bonnal, *Vie militaire du maréchal Ney*, III, 288; Emmanuel-Frédéric Sprünglin, *Souvenirs, Revue Hispanique*, p. 398.

10. *Correspondance de Napoléon Ier*, No. 16132, Napoleon to Berthier, 11 January 1810, XX, 136–40.

11. Ibid., No. 16131, Napoleon to Berthier, 11 January 1810, XX, 133–36; Bonnal, *Vie militaire du maréchal Ney*, Ney to Soult, 6, 7 February 1810, III, 291; Sprünglin, *Souvenirs*, pp. 400–402.

12. *Gazeta de Lisboa*, No. 63, 14 March 1810; "Extract of the Official Reports of Events of February 11, 12 and 13 at Ciudad Rodrigo;" Sprünglin, *Souvenirs*, p. 402.

13. Jacques Vital Belmas, *Journaux des siéges faits ou soutenus par les français dans la péninsule, de 1807 à 1814*, Ney to Herrasti, 12 February 1810, III, 268–69; Great Britain, Public Record Office, London, MSS (hereafter cited as P.R.O.), 30/43/51, Ellis to Cole, 12 February 1810. See also Belmas, *Journaux des siéges*, Herrasti to Ney, 12 February 1810, III, 270.

14. Bonnal, *Vie militaire du maréchal Ney*, Ney to Soult, 16 February 1810, III, 293; P.R.O. 30/43/54, Ruman to Cox(?), 13 February 1810; *Gazeta de Lisboa*, No. 63, 14 March 1810, "Extract . . . at Ciudad Rodrigo;" P.R.O., 30/43/51, Cox to Cole, 14 February 1810.

15. Sprünglin, *Souvenirs*, pp. 402–3; P.R.O., 30/43/51, Cox to Cole, 14 February 1810; 30/43/54, Numan to Cox, 13 February 1810.

16. *Gazeta de Lisboa*, No. 63, 14 March 1810, "Extract . . . at Ciudad Rodrigo."

17. Bonnal, *Vie militaire du maréchal Ney*, Ney to Soult, 16 February 1810, III, 293.

18. Sprünglin, *Souvenirs*, p. 404; *Correspondance de Napoléon Ier*, No. 16190, Napoleon to Berthier, 31 January 1810, XX, 191–93.

19. *Correspondance de Napoleon Ier*, No. 16230, Napoleon to Berthier, 8 February 1810, XX, 226; Bonnal, *Vie militaire du maréchal Ney*, Ney to Berthier, 21 February 1810, III, 289–90; Sprünglin, *Souvenirs*, pp. 405–6. The province of Salamanca was assessed six million réaux;

Toro and Zamora were to contribute a total of 12 million réaux while León would collect 10 million réaux for the 6th Corps.

20. Ibid., Nos. 15909, 16021, Napoleon to Clarke, 7 October, 23 November 1809, XIX, 648−49, XX, 49−50; No. 16028, Napoleon to Berthier, 28 November 1809, XX, 54; No. 16031; "Discours, A l'Ouverture de la Session du Corps Legislatif," 3 December 1809, XX, 56−58.

21. Ibid., Nos. 16032, 16051, Napoleon to Clarke, 5, 15 December 1809; Nos. 16040, 16047, 16048, 16055, 16059, 16060−62, 16091, 16152, 16245, Napoleon to Berthier, 9, 13, 14, 15, 17, 28 December 1809, 20 January 1810, 12 February 1810, XX, 56 ff. See Charles Oman, *A History of the Peninsular War*, III, 198−99. Oman questioned Napoleon's intention to go to Spain, labeling it a "ruse de guerre." The foregoing letters clearly reflect Napoleon's intentions.

22. Bonnal, *Vie militaire du maréchal Ney*, Ney to Berthier, 23 February 1810, III, 295−96; Sprünglin, *Souvenirs*, pp. 404−6.

23. Ibid., Soult to Ney, 18 February 1810, III, 297.

24. Sprünglin, *Souvenirs*, pp. 401−13.

25. Bonnal, *Vie militaire de maréchal Ney*, Junot to Ney, 8 March 1810; Ney to Junot, 11, 17 March 1810, III, 296−97.

26. Sprünglin, *Souvenirs*, p. 413.

27. P.R.O., 30/43/51, Cox to Cole, 16, 26 February, 3 March 1810; *Gazeta de Lisboa*, No. 61, 26 March, "Report from Almeida, February 26, 1810."

28. Bonnal, *Vie militaire du maréchal Ney*, Ney to Soult, 17 March 1810, III, 297−98; Sprünglin, *Souvenirs*, p. 411; P.R.O., 30/43/51, Cox to Cole, 9, 10 March 1810; John Burgoyne, *Life and Correspondence of Field Marshal Sir John Burgoyne*, I, 67−68; Despite this action both Oman and Fortescue make no mention of it. Oman wrote, "The first test of the efficiency of Craufurd's outpost system was made on the night of March 19−20." *Peninsular War*, III, 238. Fortescue stated, "Once only the French ventured to test the merit of Craufurd's dispositions . . . on the night of the 19th of March." John Fortescue, *A History of the British Army*, VII, 495.

29. P.R.O. 30/43/51, Cox to Cole, 3, 10, 14 March 1810. Despite the laudatory complements by Oman and Fortescue regarding the effectiveness of Craufurd's outpost system, two senior officers were skeptical of his actions. See Fortescue, *British Army*, VII, 463−65; Oman, *Peninsular War*, III, 237−38. See also P.R.O., 30/43/51, Cox to Cole, 18 April 1810. Cox also complained, "General Craufurd is now, *I believe*,

at Villar de Ciervo, but he moves about without acquainting either his own troops, or those who have to correspond with him, where he is to be found."

30. Bonnal, *Vie militaire du maréchal Ney*, Ney to Junot, 23 March 1810, III, 304–5.

31. John Kincaid, *Random Shots from a Rifleman*, p. 197. George Simmons, *A British Rifle Man: The Journals and Correspondence of Major George Simmons, Rifle Brigade, during the Peninsular War*, pp. 52–55; P.R.O. 30/43/51, Cox to Cole, 20 March 1810; Jonathan Leach, *Rough Sketches of the Life of an Old Soldier*, pp. 127–28.

32. Portugal, Arquivo Nacional da Torre do Tombo, Palacio de São Bento, Lisbon, MSS, Ministério dos Negócios Estrangeiros (Hereafter cited as M.N.E.), Maço 168 (1), Cox to Beresford, 21 March 1810; P.R.O., 30/43/51, Cox to Cole, 20 March 1810. British eyewitnesses generally agree on the number of losses suffered by both British and French. See: Simmons, *British Rifle Man*, p. 55; Leach, *Rough Sketches*, p. 129; Burgoyne, *Life and Correspondence*, I, 69; Charles Boutflower, *The Journal of an Army Surgeon during the Peninsular War*, p. 43; Arthur Wellesley, Duke of Wellington, *The Dispatches of Field Marshal the Duke of Wellington*, Wellington to Liverpool, 28 March 1810, V, 604–6. However, Ney estimated British losses at 120. See France, Archives Nationales, AF IV, Carton 1626, Plaq. 4[1], "Affaires d'Espagne, Armée du Portugal, 2e 6e 8e Corps, 1810," Ney to Berthier, 23 March 1810. This manuscript collection is located in the Archives Nationales in Paris.

33. Ibid.; Simmons, *British Rifle Man*, p. 55.

34. Bonnal, *Vie militaire du maréchal Ney*, Ney to Berthier, 23 March 1810, III, 304–5. Ney also learned the number, position, and health of the Allied army as well as the fact that the Portuguese army, composed of 24 infantry regiments, 12 cavalry regiments, 4 regiments of *Chasseurs à pied*, and 4 regiments of artillery, were trained and commanded by British officers.

35. *Wellington's Dispatches*, Wellington to Hill, 2 April 1810, VI, 6; Bonnal, *Vie militaire du maréchal Ney*, Ney to Soult, 27 March 1810, III, 305–6.

36. Bonnal, *Vie militaire du maréchal Ney*, Ney to Soult, 17 March 1810, III, 297–98.

37. Sprünglin, *Souvenirs*, pp. 415–16; François-Nicholas Fririon, *Journal historique de la campagne de Portugal*, p. 14.

38. Bonnal, *Vie militaire du maréchal Ney*, Ney to Soult, 29 March 1810, III, 308–9.
39. Ibid., Junot to Ney, 5 April 1810, III, 312.
40. *Correspondance de Napoléon Ier*, No. 16343, Napoleon to Berthier, 16 March 1810, XX, 313–14; *Correspondance du roi Joseph*, Napoleon to Berthier, 9 April 1810, VII, 271; Joseph to Napoleon, 30 April 1810, VII, 271, 278–79; Sprünglin, *Souvenirs*, pp. 416–17.
41. Bonnal, *Vie militaire du maréchal Ney*, Soult to Ney, 14 April 1810; Ney to Berthier, 18 April 1810, III, 310–13. Benjamin D'Urban, *The Peninsular Journal of Major-General Sir Benjamin D'Urban, 1808–1817*, p. 97. D'Urban confirmed Ney's situation stating, "Tis difficult to bring one'self to believe that Marshal Ney dares to undertake this Siege with 22,000 Men, under the very nose of Lord Wellington." See also *Wellington's Dispatches*, Wellington to Craufurd, 9, 15, 20, 29 April, 2 May 1810, VI, 28 ff.
42. Ibid., Ney to Berthier, 18 April 1810, III, 310–12.
43. Sprünglin, *Souvenirs*, p. 419; Bonnal, *Vie militaire du maréchal Ney*, III, 314.
44. Jean Baptiste Frédéric Koch, *Mémoires de Masséna*, VII, 26 ff; Fririon, *Journal historique*, Masséna to Berthier, 5 June 1810, p. 16; Belmas, *Journaux des siéges*, III, 217.
45. Bonnal, *Vie militaire du maréchal Ney*, Soult to Ney, 18 February (19, 22 March, reference in Ney's letter of 4 April), 14 April 1810; Ney to Soult, 17, 29 March, 4 April 1810; Ney to Berthier, 30 March, 18 April 1810, III, 297–311.

Chapter 2. *Wellington's Peninsular Strategy: The Role of Ciudad Rodrigo and Almeida*

1. Donald D. Horward, "British Seapower and its Influence upon the Peninsular War (1808–1814)"; *Wellington's Dispatches*, Wellington to Beresford, 23 January, 19 February 1810, V, 436–37, 505–6; Wellington to Hill, 17, 27 February 1810, V, 431–32, 528; Wellington to Leite, 28 February 1810, V, 529–30; Wellington to Wilson, 18 February 1810, V, 503–4; Wellington to Bacellar, 26 January 1810, V, 457–58; Wellington to Stuart, 19 February 1810, V, 507–8; Memorandum for Lieut. Colonel Fletcher, 20 October 1809, V, 234–39.
2. *Wellington's Dispatches*, Wellington to Bacellar, 26 January 1810, V,

457–58; Wellington to Hill, 27 February 1810, V, 528. See also Wellington to Leite, 28 February 1810, V, 529–30; Wellington to Sherbrooke, 31 January 1810, V, 74–76.

3. Ibid., Wellington to Leite, 28 February 1810, V, 529–30. See also Andrew Halliday, *Observations on the Present State of the Portuguese Army, as organized by Lieutenant-General Sir William Carr Beresford*, pp. 52–56.

4. Ibid., Wellington to Bacellar, 1 March 1810, V, 534–36.

5. Ibid., Wellington to Liverpool, 4 January, 22 February 1810, V, 411, 517–18; Wellington to Frere, 30 January 1810, V, 467–68; Arthur Wellesley, Duke of Wellington, *Supplementary Despatches and Memoranda of Field Marshal Arthur Duke of Wellington*, Wellington to Villiers, 4 January 1810, VI, 466.

6. *Wellington's Supplementary Despatches*, General Orders, 22 February 1810, VI, 485–86; *Wellington's Dispatches*, Wellington to Sherbrooke, 31 January, V, 474–76; Simão José da Luz Soriano, *Historia da guerra civil e do estabelecimento do governo parlamentar em Portugal, 1777–1834*, Segunda Epocha, III, 48–49.

7. *Wellington's Dispatches*, Wellington to Villiers, 14 January 1810, V, 424–26; Wellington to Liverpool, 14 November 1809, V, 280–82.

8. Donald D. Horward, "Economics at War: The Transformation of the Portuguese economy and social structure during the Peninsular War"; P.R.O., Foreign Office (hereafter cited as F.O.), 342/18, Stuart to Marquess Wellesley, 18 February 1810; *Wellington's Dispatches*, Wellington to Liverpool, 14 March 1810, V, 572.

9. *Wellington's Supplementary Despatches*, Marquess Wellesley to Villiers, 5 January 1810; Villiers to Wellington, 23 January 1810, VI, 476–80; *Wellington's Dispatches*, Wellington to Liverpool, 20 March 1810, V, 581–83; P.R.O., War Office (hereafter cited as W.O.), 6/50, Liverpool to Wellington, 24 April 1810.

10. *Wellington's Dispatches*, Wellington to Liverpool, 24 January, 20 March 1810, V, 446–49, 581–83.

11. Ibid., Wellington to Liverpool, 1 March 1810, V, 538–42; P.R.O., W.O., 6/50, Liverpool to Wellington, 3 January 1810.

12. *Wellington's Supplementary Despatches*, Liverpool to Wellington, 13 March 1810, VI, 493–94.

13. *Wellington's Dispatches*, Wellington to Forjaz, 8 March 1810, V, 556–59.

14. Ibid., Wellington to Stuart, 1 March 1810, V, 536–38. See also Wel-

lington to Liverpool, 24, 31 January 1810, V, 446–49, 482–84; Wellington to Stuart, 10 March 1810, V, 561–64; Wellington to Berkeley, 21 March 1810, V, 583–85; P.R.O., F.O., 342/18, Stuart to Marquess Wellesley, 24 February 1810. Stuart indicated 24,000 ton of shipping would be sufficient to evacuate the British army; with 40,000 ton the Portuguese army could also be embarked and another 10,000 ton would be adequate "for such other persons as will be desirous to move, together with their property."

15. Ibid., Wellington to Liverpool, 2 April 1810, VI, 5–10.
16. P.R.O., W.O., 6/50, Liverpool to Wellington, 6 March 1810.
17. *Wellington's Dispatches*, Wellington to Berkeley, 24 January 1810, V, 442–43; Wellington to Stuart, 6 May 1810, VI, 93–94.
18. Ibid., Wellington to Liverpool, 2 April 1810, VI, 5–10; Wellington to Berkeley, 7 April 1810, VI, 21–22.
19. *Wellington's Supplementary Despatches*, Taylor to Liverpool, 15 April 1810, V, 515; Liverpool to Wellington, n.d. April 1810, VI, 517.
20. P.R.O., F.O., 342/18, Stuart to Marquess Wellesley, 4 April 1810; *Wellington's Dispatches*, Wellington to Stuart, 8 April, 24 June 1810, VI, 25–26, 225.
21. *Wellington's Dispatches*, Wellington to Henry Wellesley, 29 April 1810, VI, 66–71. See also Oman, *Peninsular War*, III, 195. Oman indicted Portugal for attempting to take advantage of Spain's weakness but Wellington's correspondence indicated the Spanish were attempting to further their interests at the expense of Portugal.
22. P.R.O., 30/43/54. This collection of correspondence included the intelligence reports of Captain Ruman of the 97th Line between 31 January and 25 July 1810. See also *Wellington's Dispatches*, Wellington to Ruman, 25 January 1810, V, 450–51; Wellington to LeCor, 18 February 1810, V, 503; Wellington to Wilson, 18 February 1810, V, 503–4; Torre do Tombo, M.N.E., Maço 168 (1–2).
23. *Wellington's Dispatches*, Wellington to Liverpool, 15 January, 21 February 1810, V, 429–30, 511–14; Wellington to Beresford, 15 February 1810, V, 500–501; Wellington to Craufurd, 8 March 1810, V, 553–54; P.R.O., F.O., 342/18, Stuart to Marquess Wellesley, 25 February 1810; P.R.O., 30/43/51, Cox to Cole, 16 March 1810. Cox believed Junot would attack Portugal from Galicia while Mortier advanced from Alentejo and Ney advanced on Almeida.
24. Ibid., Wellington to Craufurd, 11 March 1810, V, 565; Memorandum to Picton, Cole, Craufurd, 11 March 1810, V, 566; P.R.O., 30/43/52, Craufurd to Cole, 14 March 1810; P.R.O., 30/43/51, Cox to Cole, 14

March 1810; *Wellington's Dispatches*, Wellington to Torrens, 31 March 1810, V, 610−11.

25. Ibid., Wellington to Villiers, 14 January 1810, 6 December 1809, V, 424−26, 335−38; P.R.O., W.O., 6/50, Liverpool to Wellington, 1 January, 6 March, 24 April 1810; *Wellington's Dispatches*, Wellington to Stuart, 5 February 1810, V, 487; Wellington to Berkeley, 5 February 1810, V, 487−88.

26. Ibid., Wellington to Craufurd, 9 April 1810, VI, 28−29; *Wellington's Supplementary Despatches*, Wellington to Liverpool, 26 April 1810, VI, 516; Luz Soriano, *Guerra civil*, Segunda Epocha, III, 25−26.

27. Ibid., Wellington to Henry Wellesley, 15 April 1810, VI, 40−42; Wellington to Craufurd, 20 April, 2 May 1810, VI, 50−51, 80−81; P.R.O., 30/43/51, Cox to Cole, 22 April 1810.

28. P.R.O., F.O., 342/19, Stuart to Marquess Wellesley, 20 April 1810; *Wellington's Dispatches*, Wellington to Hill, 27 April 1810, VI, 60; Wellington to Stuart, 27 April 1810, VI, 60; Wellington to Liverpool, 2 May 1810, VI, 80−82; P.R.O., 30/43/51, Cox to Cole, 26 April 1810.

29. Torre do Tombo, M.N.E., Maço 168 (1), Cox to Beresford, 19, 29 November, 3, 6, 8, 17 December 1809; *Wellington's Dispatches*, Wellington to Liverpool, 27 January 1810, V, 461−64.

30. *Wellington's Dispatches*, Wellington to Frere, 30 January 1810, V, 467−68; Wellington to Craufurd, 20 March, 23 April 1810, V, 579, VI, 54−55; Wellington to Cox, 1 May 1810, VI, 74.

31. Ibid., Wellington to Herrasti, 7 May 1810, VI, 94−95.

Chapter 3.   *Masséna Assumes Command*

1. *Wellington's Dispatches*, Wellington to Liverpool, 2 April 1810, VI, 5−10.

2. Donald D. Horward, "Education and the Commander: Marshal André Masséna." For details of Masséna's early career see: Pierre Sabor, *Masséna et sa famille*; Koch, *Mémoires de Masséna*; August Amic, *Histoire de Masséna*; James Marshall-Cornwall, *Marshal Massena*.

3. Edouard Gachot, "Masséna en Portugal, 1810−1811," LXI, 19.

4. Ibid., Clarke to Masséna, 16 April 1810; Archives de Masséna, MSS, Berthier to Masséna, 18 April 1810, LII, 8−10. This manuscript collection is in the possession of Victor André Masséna, the 7th Prince d'Essling. *Correspondance de Napoléon Ier*, No. 16385, Imperial Decree, 17 April 1810, XX, 338.

5. Koch, *Mémoires de Masséna*, VII, 18; Archives de Masséna, Instructions for Masséna, LII, 8–10.
6. Ibid., VII, 19–21. See also Gachot, "Masséna en Portugal," Masséna to Napoleon, 20 April 1810, LXI, 18–19. Gachot rejects this conversation between Napoleon and Masséna by citing a farewell letter from Masséna dated 20 April (Archives Nationales, MSS, AF IV 1626) which he interpreted as evidence that they did not meet. This author could not locate this letter in AF IV 1626, plaq. 4[1] during a recent examination of the carton.
7. Archives de Masséna, Napoleon to Masséna, 18 April 1810, LII, 8–10.
8. Bonnal, *Vie militaire du maréchal Ney*, Masséna to Ney, 20 April 1810, III, 316. For variation see Archives de Masséna, Masséna to Ney, 21 April 1810, LI, 133; *Correspondance de Napoléon Ier*, No. 15987, Napoleon to Clarke, 30 October 1809, XX, 26–27; Bonnal, *Vie militaire du maréchal Ney*, Ney to Berthier, 7 May 1810, III, 316.
9. Archives de Masséna, Ney to Masséna, 7 May 1810, LII, 100.
10. In addition to the nameless women linked romantically with Masséna, Signora Sylvia Cepolini was his mistress from 1798 until 1802 when she proved unfaithful. At the age of 45 Masséna became enamored with a 17-year-old girl in the ballet troop of the Paris opera. She was later replaced by her younger sister, Henriette, who was married to a cavalry officer named Leberton. Her brother served in Masséna's état-major in Spain and Portugal. For more details see Augustin Thierry, *Masséna, l'enfant gâte de la victoire*, pp. 42–50; René Valentin, *Le maréchal Masséna (1758–1818)*, pp. 312–15.
11. Bonnal, *Vie militaire du maréchal Ney*, Ney to Soult, 2 May 1810, III, 315.
12. Sprünglin, *Souvenirs*, pp. 423–24.
13. Belmas, *Journaux des siéges*, Mermet to Herrasti, 12 May 1810, III, 272–74; Andrés Pérez de Herrasti, *Relacion histórica y circunstanciada de los sucesos del sitio de la plaza de Ciudad-Rodrigo en el año de 1810*, pp. 78–81, 18–19.
14. Bonnal, *Vie militaire du maréchal Ney*, Ney to Soult, 10 May 1810, III, 317–18.
15. Archives de Masséna, Ney to Masséna, 10, 11 May 1810, LII, 101–2, 133.
16. Donald D. Horward, *The French Campaign in Portugal, 1810–1811: An Account by Jean Jacques Pelet*, pp. 18–20.
17. Jean-Baptiste Marbot, *Mémoires du général baron de Marbot*, II, 332.

18. Laure Permon Junot, Duchesse d'Abrantès, *Mémoires de madame la duchesse d'Abrantès ou souvenirs historique sur Napoléon*, XIII, 63–67; Marbot, *Mémoires*, II, 332–35. The accounts of both Marbot and the Duchesse d'Abrantès are probably gross exaggerations since both had reputations of being scandalmongers with little sympathy for Masséna. It should also be noted that several contemporaries claimed Masséna would accept command of the Army of Portugal only if his mistress were permitted to accompany him. See also François C. Cranrobert, *Le maréchal Cranrobert, souvenirs d'un siècle*, I, 105.
19. Archives de Masséna, Ordre du jour, 12 May 1810, LI, 5; Fririon, *Journal historique*, p. 13.
20. Horward, *Pelet*, pp. 22–23, 33.
21. Archives de Masséna, Masséna to Joseph, 17 May 1810, LI, 121.
22. Horward, *Pelet*, p. 34.
23. Archives de Masséna, Ney to Masséna, 18, 20 May 1810, LII, 192–93, 201.
24. Ibid., Masséna to Ney, 19, 21 May 1810, LI, 133–34.
25. Sprünglin, *Souvenirs*, pp. 425–26; France, Archives de la guerre, Service historique de l'armée, Chateau de Vincennes, Correspondance: Armée de Portugal, Registre de correspondance du général Loison, MSS, Loison to Ney, 25 May 1810, Carton C⁷ 20; Archives de Masséna, Ney to Masséna, 30 May 1810, LII, 257; Fririon, *Journal historique*, p. 15. Fririon maintained the magazines of the 6th Corps had six days' ration and 19 days' forage.
26. Archives de Masséna, Ney to Masséna, 25 May 1810, LII, 226–27; Horward, *Pelet*, p. 49.

Chapter 4. *The Allied Army in Beira*

1. *Wellington's Dispatches*, Wellington to Berkeley, 8 May 1810, VI, 98; Wellington to Liverpool, 9 May 1810, VI, 98–99; Wellington to Stuart, 6 May 1810, VI, 93–94; P.R.O., 30/43/51, Cox to Cole, 20 May 1810.
2. Ibid., Memorandum to Picton, Cole, and Craufurd, 28 May 1810, VI, 149–50; Simmons, *British Rifle Man*, p. 68; Leach, *Rough Sketches*, pp. 131–32; D'Urban, *Peninsular Journal*, p. 102.
3. *Wellington's Dispatches*, Wellington to Craufurd, 5, 8 May 1810, VI, 89–91, 96–97.
4. Ibid., Wellington to Stuart, 1, 11 May 1810, VI, 76–77, 102–04. See

also P.R.O., F.O., 342/19, Stuart to Marquess Wellesley, 19 May 1810; D'Urban, *Peninsular Journal*, pp. 106–7.

5. P.R.O., F.O., 342/19, Luis António de Araujo Amorim to Forjaz, 29 April 1810; Torre do Tombo, M.N.E., Maço 167 (1), Cox to Beresford, 12, 16, 20 May 1810; Cox to Wellington, 16 May 1810; *Wellington's Dispatches*, Wellington to Cox, 14, 17 May 1810, VI, 113–14, 126.

6. Ibid., Stuart to Marquess Wellesley, 19, 26 May 1810; *Wellington's Dispatches*, Wellington to Stuart, 11 June 1810, VI, 184–85.

7. Ibid., Stuart to Marquess Wellesley, 19 May 1810; *Wellington's Dispatches*, Wellington to Stuart, 13 May 1810, VI, 109–10. See also D'Urban, *Peninsular Journal*, p. 104. D'Urban declared, "Both [forage] and provisions are certainly very scarce, to the Portuguese army, whose wretched system of procuring supplies must of necessity fail." For details concerning the Portuguese commissariat see Francisco de la Fuente, "Dom Miguel Pereira Forjaz: His Early Career and Role in the Mobilization and Defense of Portugal during the Peninsular War, 1807–1814," pp. 250–71.

8. D'Urban, *Peninsular Journal*, p. 105; P.R.O., F.O., 342/19, "Mappa geral dos transportes do Exercito Portuguez em Abril, 1810."

9. P.R.O., F.O., 342/19, Stuart to Hamilton, 29 April 1810; Stuart to Marquess Wellesley, 26 May 1810; *Wellington's Dispatches*, Wellington to Stuart, 2, 13 May 1810, VI, 82, 110–11. For text of Stuart's proclamation, Wellington's modifications, and the published version, see P.R.O., 342/19, Proclamation (private), 29 April 1810; Os Governadores do Reino, 1 June 1810.

10. Of the 24 line regiments the British government subsidized all but the 5th, 17th and 23d Line. In a second archival document the 3d, 8th, and 15th Line were included in this group. See P.R.O., F.O., 342/19, 5 May 1810. In addition to pay, "the clothing, arms, and accoutrements for that portion of the army subsidized by His Majesty" were also provided. See *Wellington's Dispatches*, Wellington to Liverpool, 16, 23, 29 May, 6 June 1810, VI, 121–23, 146–47, 157–58, 174.

11. P.R.O., W.O., 6/50, Liverpool to Wellington, 26 June, 3 July 1810. The shipment from Portsmouth was increased to 560,000 dollars by 3 July 1810.

12. *Wellington's Dispatches*, Wellington to Henry Wellesley, 11 May 1810, VI, 104–5; Wellington to Liverpool, 17 May 1810, VI, 120; William Warre, *Letters from the Peninsula, 1808–1812*, 130–32; D'Urban, *Peninsular Journal*, p. 106; P.R.O., 30/43/52, Cox to Cole, 20 May 1810; 30/43/54, Ruman to Cole (?), 28 May 1810; P.R.O., F.O., Stuart

to Marquess Wellesley, 19, 26 May, 2 June 1810; *Gazeta de Lisboa*, No. 128, "Notices of Almeida, 20 May 1810;" Torre do Tombo, M.N.E., Maço 167 (1), Cox to Beresford, 18 May 1810.

13. P.R.O., F.O., 342/19, Stuart to Marquess Wellesley, 2 June 1810.

14. Edward Costello, *The Peninsular and Waterloo Campaigns*, p. 32; Warre, *Letters*, p. 141; Horward, *Pelet*, p. 112. The author spent 12 August 1972, 1 October 1976, and 11 July 1982 carefully examining and photographing La Concepción. On 27 October 1978 he surveyed the fortress in great detail with 1st Sergeant Manuel Agustino and Manuel Ramus Rodrigues of the Guarda Fiscal of Vale da Mula. Although the fortress is partially in ruins today and often used by local sheep herders and gun enthusiasts, it is still one of the most remarkable and beautifully proportioned fortifications in the Peninsula. The curtains and bastions have been partially restored but a gaping hole and breach exist in the front curtain, and several of its demilunes are in semi-ruin; the caponier and the massive blockhouse are likewise in ruin. Nevertheless, it is possible to climb up the front gate, pass through the front casemate, cross the esplanade, and follow the ramp up to the ramparts for a spectacular view of the surrounding countryside. Because of its secluded location in Spain and the lack of information on Spanish military, provincial, and commercial maps, very few know of its existence. Moreover on a visit in 1982, the road to the fortress was cut; barbed wire was strung in the fields surrounding it, thereby forcing the visitor to go over and under several fences. Yet it is still worth the effort to see La Concepción.

15. *Wellington's Dispatches*, Wellington to Cox, 27, 28 May 1810, VI, 148–49, 151; Wellington to Commander of Fort La Concepción, 28 May 1810, VI, 150; D'Urban, *Peninsular Journal*, pp. 108–10; Burgoyne, *Life and Correspondence*, I, 76–94; John T. Jones, *Journals of Sieges carried on . . . in Spain, during the years 1811 to 1814*, III, 102–8.

16. Ibid., Wellington to Villiers, 5 June 1810, VI, 170.

17. P.R.O., F.O., 342/19, "Mappa geral em rezumo da força armada em todo o Reino em mez do Abril de 1810;" *Wellington's Dispatches*, Wellington to Villiers, 5 June 1810, VI, 170.

18. *Wellington's Dispatches*, Wellington to Liverpool, 2 May 1810, VI, 82–84; Wellington to Doyle, 3 May 1810, VI, 87–88; Wellington to Henry Wellesley, 14 May 1810, VI, 115.

19. Torre do Tombo, M.N.E., Maço 167 (1), Cox to Arbuthnot, 18 May 1810; Cox to Beresford, 28 May 1810; *Wellington's Dispatches*, Welling-

ton to Beresford, 13, 14 May 1810, VI, 107, 111–12; Wellington to Cox, 17 May 1810, VI, 126.
20. *Wellington's Dispatches*, Wellington to Herrasti, 6 June 1810, VI, 171–72.

Chapter 5. *The Investment of Ciudad Rodrigo*

1. Horward, *Pelet*, p. 43.
2. P.R.O., 30/43/54, Ruman to Cox (?), 28 May 1810; Archives de Masséna, Ney to Masséna, 25, 28 May 1810, LII, 226–27, 255–56; "Rapport des mouvement du parc de siège," signed by Ruty, 4 June 1810, LIII, 70; Correspondance: Armée de Portugal, Ruty to Masséna, 8 June 1810, Carton C⁷ 8; Horward, *Pelet*, p. 48.
3. Archives de Masséna, "Rapport des mouvement du parc de siège," signed by Ruty, 4 June 1810, LIII, 70; Sprünglin, *Souvenirs*, p. 427; Gachot, "Masséna en Portugal," LXII, 40; D'Urban, *Peninsular Journal*, p. 103.
4. The monastery of La Caridad is now in the process of restoration, thanks to the dedicated efforts of the Uhagón-Foxá family. Several apartments, the great halls, the kitchen, the grand staircase, and the central courtyard have been restored. Work continues daily and on 3 February each year the monastery is opened to the citizens of Ciudad Rodrigo for the annual St. Blaise celebration. The author is indebted to the family for their warm hospitality. He has spent many memorable days at the monastery examining and photographing the entire complex in 1978, 1980, and 1982.
5. Archives de Masséna, Ney to Masséna, 31 May 1810, LII, 255–56.
6. The description of Ciudad Rodrigo and its defenses are based upon notes made by the author in June 1965, May 1967, August 1972, October 1976, October 1978, July 1980, and July 1982. See also: Horward, *Pelet*, pp. 44–46, 52–54; Belmas, *Journaux de siéges*, III, 214–16; Koch, *Mémoires de Masséna*, VII, 50–52; José Gómez de Arteche y Moro, *Guerra de la Independencia. Historia militar de España de 1808 á 1814*, VIII, 357–60; Archives de Masséna, "Reconnaissance de la place de Ciudad Rodrigo pour servir à déterminer le front d'attaque," signed by Ruty and Couche, 6 June 1810, LIII, 81 *bis.*, 87–88; Correspondance: Armée de Portugal, Ruty to Masséna, 8 June 1810, Carton C⁷ 8.

7. Herrasti, *Relacion histórica*, pp. 4–6.
8. Ibid., pp. 5–10; Horward, *Pelet*, p. 45.
9. Ibid., pp. 13–15; Gachot, "Masséna en Portugal," LXII, 51. Gachot placed the garrison at 6,721 men. See also: "Estado que manifiesta la fuerza efectiva que tenian los cuerpos que componian la guarnicion de la plaza de Ciudad Rodrigo el 25 de abril del año 1810, en que fué atacada por los franceses; y los muertos y heridos de todas clases tuvieron en el sitio," in Herrasti, *Relacion histórica*, p. 130. This document places the garrison at 5,510, excluding Sánchez's cavalry; Arteche y Moro, *Guerra de la Independencia*, VIII, 360. Arteche stated the garrison included 5,879 men of whom 340 were Sánchez's cavalry.
10. Ibid., pp. 9–12; Gachot, "Masséna en Portugal," LXII, 49–50.
11. Horward, *Pelet*, p. 48. With little charity for the clergy, Pelet complained that the garrison and inhabitants did not share the enthusiasm of the junta to defend the city: "We were told that the Junta was composed primarily of priests, hiding in cellars sheltered from all dangers; they ordered people to brave death and fight to the end."
12. Gachot, "Masséna en Portugal," LXII, 40. Cited from Archivo Histórico Nacional, Madrid, Liste 34, Series F.
13. Correspondance: Armée de Portugal, Ruty to Masséna, 8 June 1810, C⁷ 8; Archives de Masséna, "Reconnaissance de la place de Ciudad Rodrigo pour servir à détérminer le point d'attaque," signed by Couche, 6 June 1810, LIII, 81 *bis.*, 87–88; Ney to Masséna, 28 May 1810, LII, 255–56.
14. Ibid., Nos. 424, 430, Loison to Ney, 2, 7 June, 1810, Carton C⁷ 20; Archives de Masséna, Ney to Masséna, 1, 4, 6 June 1810, LIII, 31, 69, 80; Masséna to Ney, 5 June 1810, LI, 135; Sprünglin, *Souvenirs*, p. 428; *Wellington's Dispatches*, Wellington to Craufurd, 8 June 1810, VI, 177; D'Urban, *Peninsular Journal*, p. 111; Burgoyne, *Life and Correspondence*, II, 82.
15. Archives de Masséna, Ney to Masséna, 31 May 1810, LII, 261–62.
16. Correspondance: Armée de Portugal, No. 424, Loison to Ney, 1 June 1810, Carton C⁷ 20; Archives de Masséna, Ney to Masséna, 4 June 1810, LIII, 69. In Ney's correspondence to Masséna he claimed that these sorties took place on 2 June but Loison, who commanded the operations, described them in his letter of 1 June.
17. Archives de Masséna, Ney to Masséna, 31 May 1810, LII, 261–62.
18. Horward, *Pelet*, pp. 51–54.
19. Ibid., pp. 49–50.
20. Correspondance: Armée de Portugal, Masséna to Berthier, 5 June

1810, Carton C⁷ 8. Masséna wrote to Berthier again on 9 June complaining, "Our troops suffer much. I repeat it to Your Highness, le maréchal d'Elchingen s'est trop pressé."

21. Ibid., Ney to Junot, 6 June 1810, Carton C⁷ 8. Several sentences of the manuscript have been underlined; it is impossible to determine when this was done. There are also several minor variations in the text. See Bonnal, *Vie militaire du maréchal Ney*, III, 336–37.

22. Ibid., No. 425, Loison to Ney, 3 June 1810, Carton C⁷20.

23. Ibid.

24. Archives de Masséna, Ruty to Ney, 5 June 1810, LIII, 72.

25. Correspondance: Armée de Portugal, Nos. 425, 426, Loison to Ney, 3, 4 June 1810, Carton C⁷ 20; Gachot, "Masséna en Portugal," LXII, 51; Archives de Masséna, Ney to Masséna, 6 June 1810, LIII, 80.

26. Archives de Masséna, Ney to Masséna, 6 June 1810; Correspondance: Armée de Portugal, No. 427, Loison to Ney, 5 June 1810, Carton C⁷ 20. For details of Krauchenberg's operations see: Burgoyne, *Life and Correspondence*, I, 80. After the skirmish Krauchenberg's dog followed the French troops back to their positions. On 12 June, when one of Ney's officers delivered letters to Wellington and his compliments to Craufurd, a message was given to Krauchenberg "saying his dog is safe, and shall be returned by the first opportunity."

27. Gachot, "Masséna en Portugal," LXII, 51; Archives de Masséna, Ney to Masséna, 6 June 1810, LIII, 80; Correspondance: Armée de Portugal, No. 427, Loison to Ney, 5 June 1810, Carton C⁷ 20. Gachot claimed that Montbrun took part in this reconnaissance but it was impossible since Masséna wrote to Ney on 5 June 1810: "General Montbrun will leave the day after tomorrow [from Salamanca] to go to your headquarters." See Archives de Masséna, Masséna to Ney, 5 June 1810, LI, 135.

28. Correspondance: Armée de Portugal, No. 429, Loison to Ney, 6 June 1810, Carton C⁷ 20.

29. Detailed accounts of these sorties can be found in the following: Archives de Masséna, Ney to Masséna, 7 June 1810, LIII, 104–5; Correspondence: Armée de Portugal, No. 429, Loison to Ney, 6 June 1810, Carton C⁷ 20. See also Herrasti, *Relacion histórica*, p. 26. The governor wrote of one sortie of 400 men led by Lieutenant Colonel Don Luis Minayo of the Minorca regiment. Horward, *Pelet*, p. 62; Sprünglin, *Souvenirs*, pp. 429–30. Sprünglin placed the French losses at 10 dead and 34 wounded and the enemy at more than 50 dead while Koch placed the French casualties at 18 dead and 40 wounded and the Span-

ish at 30 dead and 100 wounded. Koch, *Mémoires de Masséna*, VII, 57; Belmas, *Journaux des siéges*, III, 222. Belmas's account is inaccurate and misleading.

30. Correspondance: Armée de Portugal, No. 429, Loison to Ney, 6 June 1810, Carton C⁷ 20.

31. Ibid.

32. Archives de Masséna, Ney to Masséna, 7, 9, 10, 12 June 1810, LIII, 104, 120, 122−23, 191; Correspondance: Armée de Portugal, Nos. 430, 431, 435, Loison to Ney, 7, 8, 11 June 1810, Carton C⁷ 20.

33. Ibid., Ney to Masséna, 10 June 1810, LIII, 122−23; Correspondance: Armée de Portugal, No. 435, Loison to Ney, 11 June 1810, Carton C⁷ 20; Archives de Masséna, Ney to Masséna, 12 June 1810, LIII, 191.

34. Horward, *Pelet*, p. 61; Archives de Masséna, Michaux to Masséna, 20 May 1810, LII, 205−13.

35. Archives de Masséna, Ney to Masséna, 31 May 1810, LII, 261−62; Correspondance: Armée de Portugal, No. 432, Loison to Ney, 9 June 1810, Carton C⁷ 20. See also Bonnal, *Vie militaire du maréchal Ney*, Ney to Fririon, 9 June 1810. In fact, numerous villages paid their contributions in specie rather than food because they did not have the available grain. Subsistence was then purchased at villages where produce was in abundance.

36. Ibid., Michaux to Masséna, 3, 5 June 1810, LIII, 47, 65; Correspondance: Armée de Portugal, Masséna to Kellermann, 10 June 1810, Carton C⁷ 8.

37. Ibid,. Masséna to Ney, 5, 12 June 1810, LI, 135, 137; Michaux to Masséna, 3, 5, 8 June 1810, LIII, 47, 74−75, 108, 110; Masséna to Lambert, 7 June 1810, LI, 135. Masséna could promise Ney this because Michaux had guaranteed to collect at Salamanca, within 15 days, enough bread for the entire army for a month.

38. Ibid., Michaux to Masséna (two letters), 1 June 1810, LIII, 57−58; Daultane to Masséna, 11 June 1810, LIII, 133. This letter was based on a letter written by Governor Hugo of Avila on 9 June 1810, complaining about Michaux's conduct. See Hugo to Daultane, 9 June 1810, LIII, 135. For additional complaints about Michaux see Lambert to Masséna, 21 June 1810, LIV, 3; Michaux to Masséna, 1, 5 June, LIII, 60, 75−76.

39. Ibid., Lambert to Masséna, 12 June 1810, LIII, 182.

40. Ibid., "Rapport des mouvement et operation du parc d'artillerie de siège," signed by Ruty, 8 June 1810, LIII, 107; Ney to Masséna, 10 June 1810, LIII, 122−23; Michaux to Masséna, 8 June 1810, LIII,

108; Eblé to Masséna, 1 June 1810, LIII, 30; Lambert to Masséna, 8 June 1810, LIII, 111.

41. Correspondance: Armée de Portugal, Nos. 87, 95, Eblé to Masséna, 8, 11 June 1810, Carton C^{7}23; Masséna to Berthier, 11 June 1810, Carton C^{7}8; Clarke to Berthier, 9 June 1810, Carton C^{7}8; Archives de Masséna, Masséna to Eblé, 12 June 1810, LI, 136.

42. Archives de Masséna, Masséna to Eblé, 7 June 1810, LII, 134; Masséna to Ney, 8 June 1810, LII, 134; Correspondance: Armée de Portugal, Ruty to Masséna, 8 June 1810, Carton C^{7}8.

43. Ibid., Masséna to Ney, 5 June 1810, LI, 135; Masséna to Junot, 9 June 1810, LI, 135.

44. Ibid., Kellermann to Masséna, 8, 10 (two letters), 11 June 1810, LIII, 113, 127–30, 144, 166–67; Junot to Masséna, 10, 11 June 1810, LIII, 126, 155–56; Lauberdière to Masséna, 10, 11, 14 June 1810, LIII, 162–65, 168–69; Masséna to Junot, 10 June 1810, LI, 136; Masséna to Berthier, 9, 12, May 1810, LI, 37–38; Masséna to Ney, 10, 12 June 1810, LI, 136–37.

45. Ibid., Masséna to Junot, 14 June 1810, LI, 137; Masséna to Junot, 9 June 1810, LI, 135.

46. Fririon, *Journal historique*, p. 11; Koch, *Mémoires de Masséna*, VII, 35–36, 63; Archives Nationales, AF IV, 1626 Plaq. 4^{11}, Junot to Napoleon, 14 June 1810.

47. *Correspondance de Napoleon Ier*, 16504, Napoleon to Berthier, 27 May 1810, XX, 438–39. This dispatch was a direct reversal of a letter sent earlier the same day to Berthier. See *The Confidential Correspondence of Napoleon Bonaparte with His Brother Joseph, sometime King of Spain*, II, 119. This letter, not included in the *Correspondance de Napoleon Ier*, instructed Reynier to advance on Alcántara while Mortier's 5th Corps marched toward Badajoz, forming a three pronged attack on Portugal. In the letter quoted in text, Mortier was ordered to remain in Andalusia under Soult.

48. Ibid., No. 16519, Napoleon to Berthier, 29 May 1810, XX, 447–49. In a second letter the same day, Napoleon limited Masséna's jurisdiction by placing the area around Burgos under the command of General Jean-Marie Dorsenne, commanding 16,000 Imperial Guard. See also No. 16520, Napoleon to Berthier, 29 May 1810, XX, 449–50; Archives de Masséna, Berthier to Masséna, 30, 31 May 1810, mentioned in Masséna to Berthier, 11, 12 June 1810, LIII, 37.

49. Leach, *Rough Sketches*, p. 134.

50. *Wellington's Dispatches*, Wellington to Craufurd, 9, 12, 14 June 1810,

VI, 178, 188–89, 194; Wellington to Liverpool, 6 June 1810, VI, 172–73.
51. Ibid., Wellington to Henry Wellesley, 11 June 1810, VI, 186–88.
52. Ibid., Wellington to Hill, 15 June 1810, VI, 195–96; Wellington to Stuart, 15 June 1810, VI, 197–98. See also Wellington to Berkeley, 15 June 1810, VI, 196–97.

Chapter 6. *Open Trenches at Ciudad Rodrigo*

1. Correspondance: Armée de Portugal, Ruty to Masséna, 8 June 1810, Carton C⁷ 8; Archives de Masséna, "Reconnaissance de la place de Ciudad Rodrigo pour servir à détérminer le point d'attaque," signed by Couche, 6 June 1810, LIII, 81 *bis*, 87–88. The author is pleased to recognize the interest and aid of Don José Enrique de Uhagón-Foxá and his most gracious wife Angelica, as well as Don Bienvenido Calvarro Martin, on 28–29 October 1978 in examining Grand Teso, the ruins of the trenches, the various mills and fords on the Agueda, the remains of the convent of San Francisco, Santo Domingo, etc. This topographic research was invaluable in understanding the siege operations.
2. Bonnal, *Vie militaire du maréchal Ney*, Ney to Loison, 8 June 1810, III, 339.
3. Archives de Masséna, Ney to Masséna, 11 June 1810, LIII, 175; Horward, *Pelet*, p. 60.
4. Ibid., Ney to Masséna, 14 June 1810, LIII, 201–2; Correspondance: Armée de Portugal, Loison to Ney, 13 June 1810, Carton C⁷ 20. For additional details see this letter.
5. Ibid., 15 June 1810, LIII, 210.
6. Ibid., Michaux to Masséna, 8 June 1810, LIII, 108; Lazowski to Masséna, 15 June 1810, LIII, 216; "Rapport du movement en operations du parc d'artillerie de siége," 8 June 1810, LIII, 107. Correspondance: Armée de Portugal, Dejean to Berthier, 28 June 1810, Carton C⁷ 8.
7. The reorganization of the various divisional units in the Army of Portugal was detailed in Napoleon's correspondance to Berthier, dated 29 May 1810. Based on this, Masséna made the necessary arrangements to dissolve Lagrange's division and assign his regiments to the units indicated in Berthier's correspondence. Four battalions of the 46th Line would be assigned to Clauzel's division; the four battalions of the 65th Line would be attached to Solignac's division. The 2d, 4th and 12th

Léger as well as the 32d and 58th Line would be attached to Jean-Mathieu Séras's division; the 3d Hussars and 15th Chasseurs would serve with the 6th Corps; the 1st, 2d, and 3d Provisional Dragoons would be detached to Junot's Corps; the 15th, 25th, 6th, 10th, and 11th Dragoons would be formed into the reserve cavalry division under the command of General Montbrun for service with the Army of Portugal; and finally, the 3d and 4th Dragoon brigades (6th, 7th, 8th, 9th, and 10th Provisional Dragoons) would be divided between Generals Kellermann and Séras so the division of General Lagrange would no longer exist. *Correspondance de Napoléon Ier*, No. 16519, Napoléon to Berthier, 19 May 1810, XX, 447–49; Archives de Masséna, Masséna to Ney, Junot, and Montbrun, 11 June 1810, LI, 136–37; Masséna to Berthier, 12, 16 June 1810, LI, 37–39; Correspondance: Armée de Portugal, Masséna to Junot, 14 June 1810, Masséna to Ney, 17 June 1810, Carton C^7 8.

8. Archives de Masséna, Masséna to Eblé, 14 June 1810, L, 137; Masséna to Ney, 14 June 1810, L, 137.

9. The first detachment of 400 men would be commanded by engineer Captain Audoy; the second of 200 men would be held in reserve; the third of 300 men would be under engineer Captain Lablanc; the fourth of 300 men would be directed by Captain Treussart; the fifth of 300 soldiers would be directed by Captain Vincent; the sixth of 300 workers would be under Captain Cathala; and the seventh of 400 troops would be supervised by Captain Meltzen. Both the third and fourth detachments would be protected by two battalions of grenadiers each, and the fifth, sixth, and seventh detachments would be protected by five battalions of grenadiers. Archives de Masséna, "Dipositif pour l'ouverture de la tranchée sous Ciudad Rodrigo, 14 June 1810," signed by Ney, LIII, 203–6. See also Correspondance: Armée de Portugal, C^7 8. A second set of instructions with minor variations is included in the Correspondance: Armée de Portugal entitled "Instructions sur la disposition et le nombre de troupes à employer pour la garde et le travail de la tranchée, 14 June 1810," signed by Ney.

10. Ibid.

11. Ibid., Ney to Masséna, 16, 17 June 1810, LIII, 213, 232; Masséna to Berthier, 19 June 1810, LI, 39. "Dipositif pour l'ouverture de la tranchée. . . 14 June 1810," signed by Ney, LIII, 203–6.

12. Ibid., Ney to Masséna, 18 June 1810, LIII, 239; Ney to Masséna, 19 June 1810, LIII, 245.

13. Ibid., Ney to Masséna, 18 June 1810, LIII, 239; Masséna to Berthier, 19 June 1810, LI, 39; "Rapport du 17 juin 1810. Travaux de la tranchée principale attaque," signed by Couche, LIII, 231.

14. Ibid., "Travaux de la tranchée, Rapport du 18 juin 1810," LIII, 240; Ney to Masséna, 19 June 1810, LIII, 244−45; Correspondance: Armée du Portugal, Masséna to Berthier, 21 June 1810, Carton C^7 8; "Rapport sur la tranchée du 18 à 8 heure du matin jusqu'au 19 à la même heure," signed by Couche, 19 June 1810, LIII, 235; Masséna to Berthier, 21 June 1810, LI, 39−40.

15. Ibid., Eblé to Masséna, 16, 18, 20 June 1810, LIII, 214, 242, 253. The first battery had four howitzers, the second had ten mortars, the third included six pieces of twelve, the fourth had seven pieces of sixteen, the fifth encompassed nine pieces of twenty-four and was designated as the breach battery, and the sixth included six pieces of twelve and four howitzers. For specific details of the targets of each battery see Belmas, *Journaux des siéges*, III, 226−27.

16. Ibid., Ney to Masséna, 18 June, 11:00 A.M., 20 June, 7:00 P.M., 21, 22 June 1810, LIII, 239, 252; LIV, 8, 18−19; Masséna to Berthier, 23 June 1810, LI, 40−41; Correspondance: Armée de Portugal, Loison to Ney, 19, 21 June 1810, Carton C^7 20.

17. Ibid.

18. Ibid., Ney to Masséna, 9:00 P.M., 22 June 1810, LIV, 20; Bonnal, *Vie militaire du maréchal Ney*, Ney to Loison, 22 June 1810, III, 342. According to Bonnal, Ney also wrote to Fririon offering to take command of the 6th and 8th Corps to attack Wellington.

19. Horward, *Pelet*, p. 59.

20. Archives de Masséna, Loison to Ney, 18 June 1810, LIII, 234. (Initially Clauzel was instructed to post one brigade at San Felices de los Gallegos.) Ney to Masséna, 11:30 A.M., 19 June 1810, LIII, 250; Masséna to Ney, 18 June 1810, LI, 138; Masséna to Lambert, 20 June 1810, LI, 138; Masséna to Ney, 21 June 1810, LI, 138; Lambert to Masséna, 21 June 1810, LIII, 261; Loison to Ney [?], 13 June 1810, Carton C^7 20. Finally, on 21 June 1810, Lambert did issue orders for the construction of ovens at San Felices de los Gallegos for Clauzel's division.

21. Ibid., Masséna to Lambert, 15 June 1810, LI, 137.

22. Horward, *Pelet*, p. 61.

23. Archives de Masséna, "Etat des envoie faites au 6e Corps les 18, 19, et 20 juin," signed by Lambert, LIII, 109. Moreover, by 8 June 1810 the magazine at Salamanca included 54,640 rations of grain, 113,060 ra-

tions of flour, 15,166 rations of bread, 3,370 rations of barley, etc. See "Situation du magasin des vivres de la place le 18 juin an 1810," signed by Michaux, LIII, 211.

24. Ibid., Masséna to Junot, 22 June 1810, LI, 139. To strengthen the 8th Corps, Masséna resolved to transfer the Prussian and Irish regiments from the 8th Corps to garrison Salamanca and replace them with battalions of the 46th and 65th Line. See Archives de Masséna, 15 June 1810, LI, 137.

25. Ibid., Ney to Masséna, 22 June, 9:00 P.M., 24 June 1810, LIV, 18–20; Masséna to Berthier, 23 June 1810, LI, 41; Koch, *Mémoires de Masséna*, VII, 77.

26. Ibid., Ney to Masséna, 23 June 1810, LIV, 36-37; Masséna to Berthier, 26 June 1810, LI, 41; Ney to Masséna, 4:00 P.M., 24 June 1810, LIV, 46.

27. Herrasti, *Relacion histórica*, pp. 34–35; Archives de Masséna, Ney to Masséna, 10:00 A.M., 23 June 1810, LIV, 36–37; Ney to Masséna, 4:00 P.M., 24 June 1810, LIV, 46. There is some dispute about the number of troops who escaped with Sánchez. On 27 June, Wellington claimed that Sánchez escaped with 195 men but the next day he indicated that only 90 had slipped out of Ciudad Rodrigo. See *Wellington's Dispatches*, Wellington to Liverpool, 27 June 1810, VI, 227–29; Wellington to Henry Wellesley, 28 June 1810, VI, 231–32.

28. Archives de Masséna, Ney to Masséna, 4:00 A.M., 24 June 1810, LIV, 46–47; Masséna to Berthier, 26 June 1810, LI, 41–42.

29. Correspondance: Armée de Portugal, Loison to Ney, 24 June 1810, Carton C⁷ 20; Archives de Masséna, Ney to Masséna, 4:00 A.M., 24 June 1810, LIV, 46–47; Masséna to Berthier, 26 June 1810, LI, 41–42. For minor variations see: Koch, *Mémoires de Masséna*, VII, 74–75; Belmas, *Journaux des siéges*, III, 230–32; Herrasti, *Relacion histórica*, pp. 36–38; Arteche y Moro, *Guerra de la Independencia*, VIII, 381–83. In his report Rocherond claimed success for his expedition and described his success in exploding a mine against the convent wall but Loison discounted his statements as a complete fabrication.

30. Ibid.; Herrasti, *Relacion histórica*, pp. 38–39. For additional details on the attack at Santa Cruz see Don Angel Castellano y Estrada, "Defensa de Santa Cruz," pp. 101–112. This author places the French losses at 153 killed and 45 wounded.

31. Archives de Masséna, Ney to Masséna, 4:00 P.M., 24 June, 5:00 P.M., 25 June 1810, LIV, 46–47, 49–50; Masséna to Berthier, 26 June 1810, LI, 41.

32. Ibid., "Etat général des réquisitions en nature frappés par l'Intendant général sur les provinces et arrondissements occupés par l'Armée depuis le 8 jusqu'au 19 juin 1810," signed by Lambert, LIII, 259–60; Lambert to Masséna, 21, 22, 23 June 1810, LIV, 7, 14, 32, 38.
33. Ibid.
34. Ibid., Lambert to Masséna, 25 June 1810, LIX, 59; Correspondance: Armée de Portugal, [?] to Berthier, 26 June 1810, Carton C⁷ 8.
35. Ibid., Lambert to Masséna, 24, 25, 27 June 1810, LIV, 48, 62–63, 77; Correspondance: Armée de Portugal, Lambert to Kellermann, 25 July 1810, Carton C⁷ 8.
36. Correspondance: Armée de Portugal, Masséna to Berthier, 23 June 1810, Carton C⁷ 8.

Chapter 7. *The Bombardment and Supporting Operations at Ciudad Rodrigo*

1. Archives de Masséna, Eblé to Masséna, 20 June 1810, LIII, 253. According to Eblé's letter, "The fire will commence the 25th or the 26th." See Horward, *Pelet*, p. 65.
2. Horward, *Pelet*, p. 65.
3. Archives de Masséna, Ney to Masséna, 5:00 P.M., 25 June, 6:00 P.M., 26 June 1810, LIV, 49–50, 68–69. Masséna to Berthier, 26 June 1810, LI, 40–41. Torre do Tombo, M.N.E., Maço 167 (1), Cox to Beresford, 16 June 1810.
4. Correspondance: Armée de Portugal, Loison to Gardanne, 24 June 1810; Loison to Ney, 25 June 1810, Carton C⁷ 20; Archives de Masséna, Ney to Masséna, 10:00 P.M., 25 June, LIV, 49–50.
5. Archives de Masséna, Masséna to Berthier, 27 June 1810, LI, 42; Ney to Masséna, 6:00 P.M., 26 June 1810, LIV, 68–69.
6. Ibid., Masséna to Eblé, 9:30 P.M., 26 June 1810, LI, 140; Horward, *Pelet*, p. 65.
7. Ibid., Ney to Masséna, 9:00 P.M., 27 June 1810, LIV, 72–74.
8. Correspondance: Armée de Portugal, Masséna to Berthier, 27 June 1810, Carton C⁷ 8; Archives de Masséna, Ney to Masséna, 9:00 P.M., 27 June, 28 June 1810, LIV, 72–74, 83. See also Belmas, *Journaux des siéges*, III, 235.
9. Archives de Masséna, Masséna to Berthier, 11:30 P.M., 29 June 1810, LI, 42; "Rapport de artillerie de siège du 27 juin, 1810," and

"Rapport de la nuit du 26 au 27," signed by Eblé, LIV, 74, 76; Ney to Masséna, 9:00 P.M., 27 June, 10:00 P.M., 28 June 1810, LIV, 72–73, 83–84.

10. Ibid., "Rapport de l'artillerie de siège journée du 28 juin, 1810," signed by Eblé, LIV, 85. Ney to Masséna, 10:00 P.M., 28 June, LIV, 83–84. Bonnal, *Vie militaire du maréchal Ney*, Ruty to Ney, 28 June 1810, III, 349.

11. Ibid., Ney to Herrasti, 28 June 1810, LIV, 81. For variations in this document see Correspondance: Armée de Portugal, Carton C⁷8.

12. Herrasti, *Relacion histórica*, pp. 43–44, 84. Correspondance: Armée de Portugal, Herrasti to Ney, 28 June 1810, Carton C⁷ 8. Herrasti concluded his letter requesting permission to send a dispatch to Wellington concerning the French summons. If the British responded in the affirmative, Herrasti would reconsider the French offer. This was apparently based on an offer by Esmenard but Ney would have no part of it.

13. Archives de Masséna, Ney to Masséna, 8:00 P.M., 28 June 1810, LIV, 80.

14. Ibid., Ney to Masséna, 10:00 P.M., 28 June 1810, LIV, 83–84. It should be noted that Ney used Ruty's arguments in his letter to Masséna to counter any suggestion that the summons had been premature. See Bonnal, *Vie militaire du maréchal Ney*, Ruty to Ney, 28 June 1810, III, 349.

15. Herrasti, *Relacion histórica*, pp. 40–41, 43, 58–59. The shell marks are still visible on the tower and the balustrades of the cathedral are partially in ruin today, testifying to the destruction wrought by the French artillery.

16. Correspondance: Armée de Portugal, Loison to Ney, 28 June 1810, Carton C⁷ 20; Archives de Masséna, Ney to Masséna, 10:00 P.M., 28 June, 11:00 P.M., 28 June, 29 June 1810, LIV, 83–84, 87.

17. Archives de Masséna, Ney to Masséna, 29 June, 11:00 P.M., 29 June 1810, LIV, 87, 96; Masséna to Berthier, 1 July 1810, LI, 43.

18. Horward, *Pelet*, p. 68.

19. Archives de Masséna, Ruty and Couche to Ney, 29 June 1810, LIV, 97–98. See also Ney to Masséna, 29 June 1810, LIV, 96; Horward, *Pelet*, pp. 53–54.

20. Horward, *Pelet*, p. 68.

21. Correspondance: Armée de Portugal, Ruty to Masséna, 8 June 1810, Carton C⁷ 8.

22. Abrantès, *Mémoires*, XIII, 86–91. According to Madame Junot, Valazé was a close personal friend of her husband; he introduced Valazé to

Masséna hoping his protégé might be given some chance to win the
"glories of advancement." Masséna sent Valazé to Ney's headquarters to
take command of the siege. Ney was furious and refused to employ him
in the siege. Two days later Valazé was back at Masséna's headquarters
repeating Ney's comments, "The Prince d'Essling, all prince that he is,
is not going to upset my staff. . . . I do not want the Duc d'Abrantès to
trouble me with his protégés. If they are good, let him keep them himself." The indignant Masséna sent Valazé back to Ney with orders to
assume direction of the siege. In a few days the young engineer had
returned to Masséna with the following letter which Madame Junot
claimed to have copied: "Monsieur le Maréchal, I am a Duke and a
Marshal of the Empire like you; as for your title the Prince d'Essling, it
is not important outside the Tuileries. You tell me that you are the commander in chief of the Army of Portugal. I know it only too well. So
when you tell Michel Ney to lead his troops against the enemy, you will
see how he obeys you. But when it pleases you to disarrange the staff of
the army, appointed by the Prince de Neufchâtel [Berthier], you must
understand that I will no more listen to you than I fear your threats.
. . . I esteem you and you know it. You esteem me and I know it. But
why the devil create discord between us over a mere caprice? For after
all, how are you to know that your little man can throw a bomb better
than my old veteran, who is, I assure you, a reliable man. They say
your man dances nicely, all the better for him; but that does not prove
he can make those mad Spanish dance, and that is what we want. I
remain, Monsieur le Maréchal, Maréchal Ney."

According to Madame Junot, Masséna was outraged by Ney's insubordination and he shouted to Junot, "Am I only the commander in chief
in appearance. I want this young man to conduct the siege, and by the
devil in hell, Monsieur Ney shall bend the knee before my will, or my
name is not Masséna." The letter above is reputed to be a copy of the
original copied by Madame Junot, but the original no longer exists.
This document has been quoted extensively in several biographies devoted to Ney's career. See Andrew Hilliard Atteridge, *The Bravest of the
Brave, Michel Ney, Marshal of France, Duke of Elchingen, Prince of the
Moskowa, 1769–1815*, pp. 191–92; Legette Blythe, *Marshal Ney: A
Dual Life*, pp. 101–2. Nevertheless, this letter is a forgery. See Bonnal, *Vie militaire du maréchal Ney*, III, 327–28. Bonnal correctly
noted the following inconsistencies: rather than employ the expression
"Monsieur le Maréchal," Ney always used the word "Prince"; Ney, as a
native of Saarlouis, was never disposed to engage in superficial pleas-

antries; and after 1808, his signature was always "Le maréchal duc d'Elchingen," never Maréchal Ney. Bonnal hypothesizes this letter was fabricated by someone working in the Archives of War. See also Louis Garros, *Ney, le brave des brave*, p. 126. Garros, archivist at the Service historique de l'armée at Vincennes, wrote of this controversial letter, "La duchesse d'Abrantès affirme qu'elle a copie cette lettre sur l'original. Faut il la croire? C'est bien invraisemblable."

23. Horward, *Pelet*, pp. 68–69.
24. Archives de Masséna, Ney to Masséna, 11:00 P.M., 30 June, 11:00 P.M., 1 July 1810, LIV, 100–101, 138–39; Correspondance: Armée de Portugal, Masséna to Berthier, 11:30 P.M., 1 July 1810, Carton C[7] 8.
25. Belmas, *Journaux des siéges*, Valazé to Masséna, 1 July 1810, III, 243.
26. Ibid., III, 244. If the breach battery had been constructed on the steep pitch of the glacis, it would have been exposed to grenade bombardment from the ramparts while the defenders, on the contrary, would be protected by a high parapet.
27. For variations of this letter, see Correspondance: Armée de Portugal, Masséna to Berthier, 2 July 1810, Carton C[7] 8; Belmas, *Journaux des siéges*, III, 290–92.
28. Ibid.
29. Archives de Masséna, Lambert to Masséna, 27, 28, 29 June 1810, LIV, 78, 79, 88.
30. *Wellington's Dispatches*, Wellington to Stuart, 15 June 1810, VI, 197–98; Wellington to Berkeley, 15 June 1810, VI, 196–97.
31. Torre do Tombo, M.N.E., Maço 169 (1), Cox to Beresford, 17 June 1810; *Wellington's Dispatches*, Wellington to Herrasti, 19 June 1810, VI, 203–4. For letters to which Wellington referred see: Wellington to Herrasti, 7 May, 6 June 1810, VI, 94–95, 171–72; Wellington to Craufurd, 19 June 1810, VI, 202–3.
32. *Wellington's Dispatches*, Wellington to Henry Wellesley, 20 June 1810, VI, 212–14; Wellington to Liverpool, 20 June 1810, VI, 215–16; Wellington to Craufurd, 21 June 1810, VI, 218. See also John Severn, *A Wellesley Affair, Richard Marquess Wellesley and the Conduct of Anglo-Spanish Diplomacy, 1809–1812.*
33. Archives de Masséna, Ney to Masséna, 14 June 1810, LIII, 201–2; "Rapport d'un emissarie," LIV, 11–12; Ney to Masséna, 18, 20, 21, 22 June, 10:00 P.M., 23 June 1810, LIII, 239, 252; LIV, 8, 18–20, 36–37.

34. *Wellington's Dispatches*, Wellington to Craufurd, 22, 24 June 1810, VI, 219, 221–23.
35. Ibid., Wellington to Craufurd, 4:30 P.M., 25 June, 7:00 P.M., 26 June 1810, VI, 225–26; Archives de Masséna, Ney to Masséna, 5:00 P.M., 25 June 1810, LIV, 49–50; Masséna to Berthier, 26 June 1810, LI, 41.
36. Ibid., Wellington to Craufurd, 26, 28 June 1810, VI, 226, 230–31.
37. Ibid., Wellington to Henry Wellesley, 28 June 1810, VI, 231–32; Wellington to Liverpool, 27 June 1810, VI, 227–29.
38. Ibid., Memorandum for the 14th Light Dragoons, 29 June 1810, VI, 232–33; Wellington to Craufurd, 29 June 1810, VI, 233; "Correspondence of Colonel Ernest von Linsingen" in North Ludlow Beamish, *History of the King's German Legion*, I, 273.
39. Archives de Masséna, Ney to Masséna, 10:00 P.M., 11:00 P.M., 30 June, LIV, 100–01, 106–7. According to a deserter who came into the French camp early on 1 July, rather than attempt to escape from the fortress, the garrison labored to clear away the debris that had accumulated at the foot of the breach. See Ney to Masséna, 9:00 A.M., 1 July 1810, LIV, 137; *Wellington's Dispatches*, Wellington to Cole, 6:30 P.M., 30 June 1810, VI, 234; Wellington to Craufurd, 1 July 1810, VI, 234–35.
40. Herrasti, *Relacion histórica*, Sebastián Gallardo to Agapito Gallardo, 4 July 1810, pp. 48–49; Archives de Masséna, Ney to Masséna, 11:00 P.M., 1 July 1810, LIV, 138–39.
41. Horward, *Pelet*, pp. 71–74.
42. Sebastián Gallardo successfully escaped into the countryside and survived the French occupation. The author is pleased to acknowledge the kind hospitality of His Excellency Demetrio Mansilla Reoyo, Bishop of Ciudad Rodrigo in receiving him on 27 October 1978. Given access to the Episcopal Archives in the cathedral, the author examined the cathedral registry—Volume XXII (1804–1808) and XXIII (1811–1814); although material did not exist for the period of the French occupation, an entry dated 6 July 1812 was signed by Gallardo, confirming his almost miraculous survival.
43. Herrasti, *Relacion histórica*, pp. 50–51.
44. These columns included a company of voltigeurs and carabineers of the Légion du Midi, 40 voltigeurs of the 32d Léger, 60 grenadiers each from the fourth battalion of the 26th and 82d Lines, and 200 soldiers from the other regiments of Simon's brigade.
45. Archives de Masséna, Loison to Ney, 2 July 1810, LIV, 177 *bis*; Corre-

spondance: Armée de Portugal, Loison to Ney, 2 July 1810, Carton C⁷ 20. The volunteers mentioned in Loison's letter included: Rossi, Lavetta, Roatis, Arietti, and Louison, all of the Légion du Midi.

46. Ibid. These documents are substantially the same with a few minor variations. See also Ney to Masséna, 10:00 P.M., 2 July 1810, LIV, 148–49; Masséna to Berthier, 11:00 A.M., 2 July 1810, LI, 44–45; Gachot, "Masséna en Portugal," LXII, 53; Belmas, *Journaux des siéges*, III, 247.

47. Ibid., Ney to Masséna, 10:00 P.M., 2 July, 11:00 P.M. 3 July 1810, LIV, 148–49, 166–67; Masséna to Berthier, 2 July, 11:00 P.M., 3 July 1810, LI, 44–45.

48. Ibid., Ney to Masséna, 11:00 P.M., 3 July 1810, LIV, 166–67; Masséna to Berthier, 11:00 P.M., 3 July 1810, LI, 45.

49. Ibid., Rippert to Masséna, 2 July 1810, LIV, 156–58; Correspondance: Armée de Portugal, Masséna to Junot, 1 July 1810, Carton C⁷ 8.

50. Ibid., Masséna to Junot, 9:30 P.M., 2 July 1810, LI, 140; Trelliard to Junot, 3 July 1810, LIV, 164–65; Ney to Masséna, 11:00 P.M., 3 July 1810, LIV, 166–67.

51. Ibid., Masséna to Junot, 7:30 P.M., 3 July 1810, LI, 140–41; Junot to Masséna, 5 July 1810, LIV, 168–69.

52. William Tomkinson, *The Diary of a Cavalry Officer in the Peninsular and Waterloo Campaigns, 1809–1815*, p. 28; Archives de Masséna, Junot to Masséna, 5 July 1810, LIV, 168–69; Fririon, *Journal historique*, p. 22. Junot claimed the enemy had seven squadrons of hussars and light cavalry, three battalions of infantry, and four pieces of artillery, but this was excessive. For details of the British defense, see "Journal of Major Cordemann" in Beamish, *King's German Legion*, I, 275–78.

53. The British account of this battle is based primarily on the eyewitness accounts of Tomkinson, Charles Napier, Cordemann, and Shaw-Kennedy. See: Tomkinson, *Diary*, pp. 28–30; William Francis Patrick Napier, *The Life and Opinions of General Sir Charles James Napier*, I, 131–32; James Shaw-Kennedy, *A Private Journal of General Craufurd's Out-Post Operations on the Coa and Agueda in 1810*, in Frederick Fitzclarence, *A Manual of Out-Post Duties*, pp. 215–19; "Journal of Major Cordemann" in Beamish, *King's German Legion*, I, 274–78.

54. Regarding this skirmishing on 4 July the English historian Fortescue wrote, "The whole affair was admirably handled." This supports the view of Oman who declared, "The Light Division maneuvered with its

customary intelligence and alertness all day." See Oman, *Peninsular War*, III, 251, and Fortescue, *British Army*, VI, 471−72. However, Charles Napier, an eyewitness, claimed that the 16th Light Dragoons were mismanaged and the 3d Caçadores fired on British horsemen. See also Torre do Tombo, M.N.E., Maço 166 (1), Cox to Beresford, 4 July 1810.

55. Archives de Masséna, Junot to Masséna, 5 July 1810, LIV, 168−69. Junot claimed the French suffered 11 wounded and four dead while Fririon set the figure at 20 wounded and four dead. Fririon, *Journal historique*, p. 22. British losses according to Beamish totaled four wounded while Tomkinson listed two dead and three wounded. Shaw-Kennedy placed the British casualties at five wounded. See Beamish, *King's German Legion*, I, 277; Tomkinson, *Diary*, p. 29; Shaw-Kennedy, *Private Journal*, p. 219. Junot claimed Craufurd had confronted him with eleven infantry battalions and eight cavalry squadrons supported by seven guns, but Pelet wrote that although Junot estimated the enemy force at ten battalions of infantry and twelve squadrons of cavalry, "Adjutant Commander Rippert went there at the order of the Prince, and he saw nothing more than confusion." See Horward, *Pelet*, p. 73.

56. Ibid., Ney to Masséna, 4 June 1810, LIV, 181; Junot to Masséna, 5 June 1810, LIV, 168−69; Correspondance: Armée de Portugal, Loison to Ney, 4, 5 June 1810, Carton C⁷ 20; Horward, *Pelet*, p. 75.

57. Ibid., Ney to Masséna, 5 July 1810, LIV, 188−89; "Rapport de l'artillerie," signed by Eblé, 4, 5 July 1810, LIV, 173, 186; Koch, *Mémoires de Masséna*, VII, 93. Belmas, *Journaux des siéges*, III, 248.

58. Ibid., Ney to Masséna, 5, 6 July 1810, LIV, 188−89, 195−96; "Rapport de l'artillerie," signed by Eblé, 6 July 1810, LIV, 191. Koch, *Mémoires de Masséna*, VII, 94.

59. Ibid., Lambert to Masséna, 29, 30 June 1810, LIV, 88, 105.

60. Ibid., Lambert to Ney, 1 July, 4:00 P.M., 2 July, 2 (two letters) July 1810, LIV, 141, 142, 150−51, 155.

61. Ibid., Masséna to Lambert, 2 July 1810, LI, 140. An indication of Masséna's attitude toward the shipment of requisitions is exemplified by Fririon's letter which was delivered by Fontenilles on 2 July 1810. See Lambert to Masséna, 2 July 1810, LIV, 150.

62. Ibid., Lambert to Masséna, 3 July 1810, LIV, 170; Masséna to Lambert, 3 July 1810, L, 140; Masséna to Berthier, 3 July 1810, LI, 45; Lambert to Masséna, 24 June, 2 July 1810, LIV, 48, 154; Lambert to Masséna, 4 (two letters) July 1810, LIV, 183, 184. In these letters there is some variation in the amounts of food shipped.

63. Ibid., Masséna to Lambert, 4 July 1810, LI, 141.
64. Ibid., Lambert to Masséna, 2, 5 July 1810, LIV, 153, 190; Ney to Masséna, 5 July 1810, LIV, 188–89.
65. Ibid., Lambert to Masséna, 7 July 1810, LIV, 203.
66. Ibid., Ney to Masséna, 6 July 1810, LIV, 195–96; Correspondance: Armée de Portugal, Masséna to Berthier, 7 July 1810, Carton C⁷8.
67. Horward, *Pelet*, p. 75.
68. Battery No. 1 was eliminated and three pieces of twelve were sent to Battery No. 3 and one to Battery No. 4. Battery No. 2 was completely dismantled and its seven mortars were used to arm Battery No. 12. Two howitzers from Battery No. 3 were transferred to Battery No. 4 which in turn sent two pieces of sixteen to Battery No. 5; it now included four pieces of twenty-four, two pieces of sixteen, and one piece of twelve. See Archives de Masséna, Ney to Masséna, 7 July 1810, LIV, 204–5; "Rapport de l'artillerie," signed by Eblé, 7 July 1810, LIV, 206. Correspondance: Armée de Portugal, Masséna to Berthier, 7 July 1810, Carton C⁷8.
69. Horward, *Pelet*, p. 75.
70. Ibid.; Archives de Masséna, "Rapport de l'artillerie," signed by Eblé, 8 July 1810, LIV, 220; Ney to Masséna, 8 July 1810, LIV, 221–22.
71. Archives de Masséna, Ney to Masséna, 8 July 1810, LIV, 221–22.
72. Sprünglin, *Souvenirs*, p. 436; Archives de Masséna, Ney to Masséna, 8, 9 July 1810, LIV, 221–22, 226–27; "Rapporte de trois déserteurs Espagnole sortie de Ciudad Rodrigo hier 9 juillet à 11 heures du matin," LIV, 234. Sprünglin claimed there were two sorties and they numbered 500 and 1,000 men respectively.
73. Archives de Masséna, "Rapport de l'artillerie de siège," signed by Eblé, 9 July 1810, LIV, 223. For more specifics see this "Rapport."
74. Ibid., Ney to Masséna, 9 July 1810, LIV, 226–27.
75. Horward, *Pelet*, p. 77; Belmas, *Journaux des siéges*, III, 253.
76. Herrasti, *Relacion histórica*, "Copia del segundo parte . . . al señor Secretario de la Guerra el dia 30 de Julio próxîmo pasado," signed by Herrasti, 29 August 1810, pp. 91–101.
77. Archives de Masséna, Trelliard to Masséna, 10 July 1810, p. 229; "Relation du siége de Ciudad Rodrigo fait en juin et juillet 1810," signed by Couche, 12 July 1810, LIV, 278–86; Horward, *Pelet*, pp. 77–78; Correspondance: Armée de Portugal, Loison to Ney, 10 July 1810, Carton C⁷8; Belmas, *Journaux des siéges*, Valazé to Masséna, 10 [?] July 1810, III, 254–55.

Chapter 8. *The Assault and Capitulation of Ciudad Rodrigo*

1. For specific assignments of each gun see Koch, *Mémoires de Masséna*, VII, 99–100.
2. Horward, *Pelet*, pp. 78–79; Archives de Masséna, Ney to Masséna, 11 July 1810, LIV, 252–54.
3. Archives de Masséna, "Dispositions général pour l'assault de Ciudad Rodrigo," signed by Ney, 10 July 1810, LIV, 232–33.
4. Ibid.
5. Horward, *Pelet*, p. 76.
6. Archives de Masséna, Masséna to Berthier, 6, 8, 10 July 1810, LI, 46–47. In the letter of 6 June, Koch's text does not conform with the material in the Archives de Masséna although this was his source. See Koch, *Mémoires de Masséna*, VII, 96. On 9 July, three Spanish deserters came in from the fortress announcing that the junta had been meeting for the past six days. In a vote of the members, five voted to surrender while two others held out since the citizens were afraid that they would be put to the sword if they capitulated. See Archives de Masséna, "Rapporte de trois déserteurs espagnole sortie de Ciudad Rodrigo hier 9 juillet à 11 heures du matin," LIV, 234.
7. Horward, *Pelet*, p. 76; Archives de Masséna, Masséna to Joseph, 8 July 1810, LI, 123.
8. Ibid., pp. 76, 78–79; Archives de Masséna, Ney to Masséna, 11 July 1810, LIV, 252–53. Correspondance: Armée de Portugal, Masséna to Berthier, 12 July 1810, Carton C^7 8. Apparently Constantin represented Ruty on this reconnaissance. Pelet's judgment regarding the defenses at the breach was reinforced by the report of the three deserters who had come into the French camp at 11:00 A.M. on 9 July 1810.
9. Ibid., pp. 79–80; Archives de Masséna, Ney to Masséna, 11 July 1810, LIV, 252–53; "Relation du siége de Ciudad Rodrigo fait en juin et juillet 1810," signed by Couche, 12 July 1810, LIV, 278–86; Fririon, *Journal historique*, pp. 18–19; P.R.O., 30/43/51, Cox to Campbell, 11 July 1810. Cox declared the French entered the fortress at 6:00 P.M.
10. Herrasti, *Relacion histórica*, p. 53; "Copia del primer parte dado desde Hermani al señor Secretario de al Guerra el dia 30 de julio próxîmo pasado," signed by Herrasti, 25 August 1810; "Copia del segundo parte . . . al señor Secretario de la Guerra," signed by Herrasti, 30 September 1810, pp. 86–101. Initially Herrasti claimed that 36,000

shells and 40,000 bombs were fired on the fortress but he later changed this figure to 65,000 cannon shots and two million musket or rifle shots.

11. Ibid., Herrasti to Ney, 6:00 P.M., 10 July 1810, p. 86.

12. Jacques Louis Hulot, *Souvenirs militaires du baron Hulot, général d'artillerie, 1773−1843*, p. 310. Hulot claimed that Ney said, "Monsieur le gouverneur, after such a brilliant defense, you should not be afraid to wear your uniform; you honor it as much as it honors you." Pelet recalled that Ney put his hat back on after greeting Herrasti and the Spaniard did likewise, retaining much of his dignity. Horward, *Pelet*, p. 80. Another variation is proposed by Atteridge who claimed that Ney said, "Monsieur le Gouverneur, you have made too good use of it [sword], for us to think of taking it from you." Atteridge, *The Bravest of the Brave*, p. 192.

13. Herrasti, *Relacion histórica*, p. 53; "Copia del segundo parte . . . al señor Secretario de la Guerra," signed by Herrasti, 29 August 1810, pp. 91−101. See also Charles William Vane, Marquess of Londonderry, *Narrative of the Peninsular War from 1808 to 1813*, I, 480. Although there seems to be no substantiating evidence, Londonderry claimed that Ney refused to grant Herrasti conditions other than unconditional surrender, but Masséna modified the agreement and extended conditions to the governor.

14. Hulot, *Souvenirs*, p. 310; Herrasti, *Relacion histórica*, "Copia del segundo parte . . . al señor Secretario de la Guerra," signed by Herrasti, 29 August 1810, pp. 91−101.

15. Archives de Masséna, Ney to Masséna, 11 July 1810, LIV, 252−54; Masséna to Berthier, 12 July 1810, LI, 48−49; Correspondance: Armée de Portugal, Loison to Ney, 10 July 1810, Carton C⁷ 20. Oman stated, "Accordingly the garrison marched out next morning about 4,000 strong, laid down its arms below the glacis, and was marched off to Bayonne." See Oman, *Peninsular War*, III, 253. Oman's account differs markedly from the original documents.

16. Horward, *Pelet*, pp. 80−82. Pelet blamed these excesses on the fortress authorities. They only surrendered when the French were about to make themselves masters of the breach and subject the city "to the terrible laws of war." As a result the soldiers were denied the plunder that they had expected. He concluded, "With troops other than French ones, the garrison would have paid dearly for their unreasonable passion." There is some truth in this statement for after General Picton's Third Division of the Allied Army captured Ciudad Rodrigo on 19

January 1812, an uncontrollable orgy of looting and destruction broke out; large sections of the city were burned by their allies and many Spanish were put to the sword. On the other hand, Herrasti complimented the French on the establishment of strict orders against any excesses and pillaging; according to him several soldiers were shot for pillaging. See Herrasti, *Relacion histórica*, pp. 56—57.

17. Archives de Masséna, Masséna to Ney, 11 July 1810, LI, 141. Oman states, "Masséna showed his ill-temper, when all was over, by sending the civilian members of the Junta as prisoners to France." Oman, *Peninsular War*, III, 254. On the contrary, in his letters to Berthier dated 12 July 1810, Masséna expresses satisfaction and pleasure with the results of the siege. Archives de Masséna, Masséna to Berthier, 12 (two letters) July 1810, LI, 49—51.

18. Herrasti, *Relacion histórica*, "Copia del primer parte . . . al señor Secretario de la Guerra," signed by Herrasti, 25 August 1810, pp. 86—91; "Copia del segundo parte . . . al señor Secretario de la Guerra," signed by Herrasti, 30 August 1810, pp. 91—102. The author is indebted to the kindness of the former mayor of Ciudad Rodrigo, Don Leonardo Dorado Martinez, who spent much of 29—30 October 1978 pointing out the scars that remain today on the various buildings from the siege. He also provided valuable information about the siege and showed the author many artifacts of the siege including Russian coins found on the recently uncovered remains of French soldiers.

19. Horward, *Pelet*, pp. 80—83. Pelet wrote, "The defense ended at the very point where that of Saragossa had started, but the ardor of those old days was long gone. All that remained was some subdued bravado."

20. Herrasti, *Relacion histórica*, "Copia del primer parte . . . al señor Secretario de la Guerra," signed by Herrasti, 25 August 1810, pp. 86—91.

21. Belmas, *Journaux des siéges*, "Etat des consummations faites par l'artillerie pour le siége de Ciudad Rodrigo . . . le 10 juillet, époque de la reddition de la place," signed by Eblé, 10 July 1810, III, 309; Herrasti listed 461 dead and 994 wounded from among the garrison but it is impossible to determine the number of inhabitants killed in the siege. Herrasti told Loison that over 1,000 were killed during the siege but Pelet records that on 9 July 300 deaths occurred in the fortress. Spanish records stated, "Two thousand people, made up equally of garrison and inhabitants, perished." See Herrasti, *Relacion histórica*, "Estado que manifesta la fuerza efectiva que tenian los cuerpos que componian la guarnicion de la plaza de Ciudad-Rodrigo el 25 de abril de año 1810, en que fué atacada por los franceses; y los muertos y heridos de

todas clases que tuvieron en el sitio"; Correspondance: Armée de Portugal, Loison to Ney, 10 July 1810, Carton C⁷8; Archives de Masséna, Ney to Masséna, 11 July 1810, LIV, 252—54; Horward, *Pelet*, p. 84.

22. Herrasti, *Relacion histórica*, "Copia del premier parte . . . al señor Secretario de la Guerra," signed by Herrasti, 25 August 1810, pp. 86—91; Correspondance: Armée de Portugal, Masséna to Berthier, 12 July 1810, Carton C⁷8.

23. Archives de Masséna, "Inventaire général des bouches à feu, munitions et attirails d'artillerie trouvés dans la dite place après sa reddition le 10 juillet, 1810," signed by Eblé and Husson, 12 July 1810, LIV, 237—46. See also Belmas, *Journaux des siéges*, "Inventaire des principaux objects d'artillerie de la place de Ciudad Rodrigo à l'epoque de la capitulation, le 10 juillet 1810," signed by Husson, 20 July 1810, III, 310—11; Archives de Masséna, Ney to Masséna, 12 July 1810, LV, 4; "Rapporte sur les établissement et magasin trouve à Ciudad Rodrigo," signed by Montemuy, 12 July 1810, LV, 6—7.

24. Ibid., Ney to Masséna, 12 July 1810, LV, 4.

25. Ibid., Lambert to Masséna, 8, 9, 10, 11 July 1810, LV, 70; LIV, 228, 249, 265.

26. Ibid., Montemuy to Masséna, 10 July 1810, LIV, 6—7; Masséna to Eblé, 12 July 1810, LI, 142; Horward, *Pelet*, p. 84.

27. Belmas, *Journaux des siéges*, "Suite de l'état nominatif des officiers tués ou blessés pendant le siége de Ciudad Rodrigo," signed by Béchet de Léocour, 15 July 1810, III, 307; "Etat sommaire des sous-officiers et soldats tués et blessés pendant le siége de Ciudad Rodrigo," signed by Béchet de Léocour, 15 July 1810, III, 308.

28. Correspondance: Armée de Portugal, Masséna to Berthier, 12 July 1810, Carton C⁷8; Archives de Masséna, Masséna to Berthier, 12 July 1810, LI, 50—51. This letter is based on Pelet's "Rapport sommaire du siège de Ciudad Rodrigo." See Archives de Masséna, 12 July 1810, LV, 12—16. Pelet complained that "the engineers of the 6th Corps gave all of the credit to the Marshal and only indifferent mention to the Prince. . . . The Prince did not learn anything about that report." See Horward, *Pelet*, p. 85.

29. Horward, *Pelet*, p. 83.

30. Archives de Masséna, Ney to Masséna, 11 July 1810, LIV, 252—53; Loison to Ney, 10 July 1810, Carton C⁷20. Actually this statement was made by Loison who talked with Herrasti.

31. Torre do Tombo, M.N.E., Maço 167 (1), Cox to Beresford, 16 May 1810; Burgoyne, *Life and Correspondence*, I, 83; D'Urban, *Peninsular*

Journal, p. 126; W.F.P. Napier, *Life and Opinions of . . . Charles James Napier*, I, 127—31.

32. *Wellington's Dispatches*, Wellington to Liverpool, 25 July 1810, VI, 295—96.
33. Herrasti, *Relacion histórica*, pp. 112—13.

Chapter 9. *The Action at Villar de Puerco and the Fall of Fort La Concepción*

1. Archives de Masséna, "Rapport général du 22eme regt. de ligne du 10 au 11 juillet 1810," Armand to Godart, 12 July 1810, LIV, 256—57; Correspondance: Armée de Portugal, Masséna to Berthier, 12 July 1810, Carton C⁷8.
2. *Wellington's Dispatches*, Craufurd to Wellington, 12 July 1810, VI, 262—63; Wellington to Liverpool, 13 July 1810, VI, 262—64; Simmons, *British Rifle Man*, pp. 73—74; Costello, *Campaigns*, pp. 30—31; Tomkinson, *Diary*, p. 31; Stapleton Cotton, *Memoirs and Correspondence of Field-Marshal Viscount Combermere, G.C.B.*, Cocks to Cotton, 12, 17 July 1810, I, 142—44, 148—51; Shaw-Kennedy, *Private Journal*, pp. 224—25; Burgoyne, *Life and Correspondence*, I, 91—92; Alexander H. Craufurd, *General Craufurd and his Light Division*, pp. 111—20.
3. Shaw-Kennedy, *Private Journal*, pp. 225—26; "Correspondence of Colonel Ernest von Linsingen" in Beamish, *King's German Legion*, I, 280—81; Cotton, *Memoirs and Correspondence*, Cocks to Cotton, 12 July 1810, I, 142—44.
4. Archives de Masséna, "Rapport général du 22eme regt. de ligne du 10 au 11 juillet 1810," Armand to Godart, 12 July 1810, LIV, 256—57; Correspondance: Armée de Portugal, Masséna to Berthier, 12 July 1810, Carton C⁷8; *Wellington's Dispatches*, Craufurd to Wellington, 12 July 1810, VI, 262—63; Cotton, *Memoirs and Correspondence*, Cocks to Cotton, 12, 17 July 1810, I, 142—44, 148—51; Henry B. Hamilton, *Historical Record of the 14th (King's) Hussars*, "T.W. Brotherton Manuscript," pp. 68—69.
5. Cotton, *Memoirs and Correspondence*, Cocks to Cotton, 12 July 1810, I, 142—44; "T.W. Brotherton Manuscript," pp. 67—68; Archives de Masséna, "Rapport général de 22eme regt. de ligne du 10 au 11 juillet

1810," Armand to Godart, 12 July 1810, LIV, 256–57; W.F.P. Napier, *Life and Opinions of . . . Charles James Napier*, I, 133.

6. Costello, *Campaigns*, p. 31.

7. *Wellington's Dispatches*, Craufurd to Wellington, 13 July 1810, VI, 262–63; Cotton, *Memoirs and Correspondence*, Cocks to Cotton, 12, 17 July 1810; Cotton to Cole, 15 July 1810, I, 142–51. For minor variations in the number of casualties suffered by the contending forces see the sources cited in footnotes 1 and 2 of this chapter. Regarding the final resting place of Talbot, Costello described his grave near the chapel of Villar de Puerco while Cotton places him on the glacis at La Concepción. Brotherton claimed he actually buried Talbot on the glacis of La Concepción. See Costello, *Campaigns*, p. 31; Cotton, *Memoirs and Correspondence*, I, 155; "T. W. Brotherton Manuscript," p. 68.

8. Cotton, *Memoirs and Correspondence*, Cotton to Cole, 15 July 1810, I, 145–47; *Wellington's Dispatches*, Wellington to Cotton, 14 July 1810, VI, 267; Wellington to Craufurd, 23 July 1810, VI, 286–87.

9. Londonderry, *Narrative of the Peninsular War*, I, 483; Craufurd, *Craufurd and his Light Division*, p. 116; Simmons, *British Rifle Man*, p. 74; Tomkinson, *Diary*, p. 31; *Supplementary Despatches of Wellington*, Wellington to William Wellesley-Pole, 31 July 1810, VI, 561–64.

10. Archives de Masséna, Masséna to Ney, 12 July 1810, LI, 142; Correspondance: Armée de Portugal, Loison to Ney, 14 July 1810, Carton C[7] 20. The map by Tomas Lopez, entitled *Atlas Geográfico de España que comprehende el mapa general del Reyno de los particulares de sus Provincias*, was published between 1778 and 1804. The eight sections concerning Portugal were based primarily upon local civil and ecclesiastical maps, "Roteiro Terrestre de Portugal" (1748) and "Mappa de Portugal" (1762) by P. Juan Bautista de Castro, and a map by an Englishman named Thomas Jefferys. For additional examples of the unreliability of the map see Horward, *Pelet*, pp. 67, 135, 174, 251, 448, 452.

11. Ibid., "Disposition des troupes du 6e Corps, pour les 14 juillet 1810," signed by Ney, LV, 43–44; Ney to Masséna, 15 July 1810, LV, 56–57; Correspondance: Armée de Portugal, Loison to Ney, 14 July 1810, Carton C[7] 20.

12. Ibid. Mermet would also send two companies of fusiliers to Sancti Spiritus, a company to San Muñoz, and another company to Alba de Yeltes. Marchand maintained troops for a post at Pedrotoro.

13. Ibid., Masséna to Junot, 12 July 1810, LI, 142.

14. Correspondance: Armée de Portugal, Loison to Ney, 15 July 1810, Carton C⁷ 20; Archives de Masséna, Ney to Masséna, 16 July 1810, LV, 66–68.

15. Archives de Masséna, Ney to Masséna, 16 July 1810, LV, 66–68; Correspondance: Armée de Portugal, Loison to Ney, 15 July 1810, Carton C⁷ 20. Another reason for Napier's visit to the French camp was to assure Ney that he had been exchanged for two French ensigns. Ney had asked the previous day, "Why Major Napier was in the field without having been exchanged?" See W.F.P. Napier, *Life and Opinions of . . . Charles James Napier*, I, 133.

16. Correspondance: Armée de Portugal, Loison to Ney, 17 July 1810, Carton C⁷ 20.

17. Ibid., Loison to Ney, 19 July 1810, Carton C⁷ 20; Burgoyne, *Life and Correspondence*, I, 93. Burgoyne also mentioned this specific incident of the French infantryman deserting to the British.

18. Ibid., Loison to Ney, 20 July 1810, Carton C⁷ 20; Archives de Masséna, Masséna to Ney, 21 July 1810, LI, 145–46.

19. Ibid., Loison to Ney, 22 July 1810, Carton C⁷ 20; Archives de Masséna, Ney to Masséna, 1:00 A.M., 23 July 1810, LV, 184–85, 188–89.

20. *Wellington's Dispatches*, Wellington to Commander of La Concepción, 28 May 1810, VI, 150; Burgoyne, *Life and Correspondence*, I, 76–77.

21. Ibid., Wellington to Craufurd, 19, 22 June 1810, VI, 202–3, 220. See also Wellington to Craufurd, 24, 25 June, 11, 16 July 1810, VI, 221–22, 225–26, 254, 275.

22. Jones, *Journal of the Sieges*, III, 110–14; Costello, *Campaigns*, pp. 31–32; Burgoyne, *Life and Correspondence*, I, 75–95.

23. "T.W. Brotherton Manuscript," pp. 68–69; Burgoyne, *Life and Correspondence*, I, 94; Correspondance: Armée de Portugal, Loison to Ney, 22 July 1810, Carton C⁷ 20. It should be noted that in this letter to Ney, Loison requested an engineer to defuse the three mines. In Ney's letter to Masséna on 21 July, he described the explosion as having "almost entirely ruined this beautiful fortress" but in another letter, dated 23 July 1810, he noted that three mines had not exploded and the fort had been only partially destroyed. See Archives de Masséna, Ney to Masséna, 21, 23 July 1810, LV, 142, 184–85.

24. Correspondance: Armée de Portugal, Loison to Ney, 22 July 1810, Carton C⁷ 20; Archives de Masséna, Ney to Masséna, 1:00 A.M., 23 July 1810, LV, 184–85, 188–89; Shaw-Kennedy, *Private Journal*, p. 231; William H. Cope, *The History of the Rifle Brigade*, p. 55.

25. Shaw-Kennedy, *Private Journal*, pp. 231–32; Correspondance: Armée de Portugal, Loison to Ney, 22 July 1810, Carton C⁷ 20; W.F.P. Napier, *Life and Opinions of . . . Charles James Napier*, I, 136. Napier claimed that during this action the British had two men and seven or eight horses wounded. Correspondance: Armée de Portugal, Loison to Ney, 22 July 1810, Carton C⁷ 20. Loison described Craufurd's three columns as having three battalions of infantry, three guns, and 1,800 cavalry.
26. Archives de Masséna, Ney to Masséna, 1:00 A.M., 23 July 1810, LV, 184–85, 188–89. Lamotte's headquarters was established at Aldea del Obispo; Trelliard and Loison set up their headquarters at Barquilla; and Ferey and Gardanne occupied Villar de Puerco for the night.
27. *Wellington's Dispatches*, Wellington to Stuart, 23 July 1810, VI, 288; Simmons, *British Rifle Man*, p. 75.

Chapter 10. *The Battle on the Côa*

1. Correspondance: Armée de Portugal, Loison to Ney, 23 July 1810, Carton C⁷ 20; Archives de Masséna, Masséna to Ney, 22 July 1810, LI, 145–46.
2. Archives de Masséna, Ney to Masséna, 10:00 A.M., 23 July 1810, LV, 181 *bis*; Correspondance: Armée de Portugal, Loison to Ney, 23 July 1810, Carton C⁷ 20; Shaw-Kennedy, *Private Journal*, p. 232.
3. *Wellington's Dispatches*, Wellington to Picton, Cole, Slade, Campbell, and Craufurd, 2 July 1810, VI, 238–40; Wellington to Craufurd, 7:30 P.M., 11, 16, 22 July 1810, VI, 258–59, 275, 285–86. For a labored justification of Craufurd's decisions and actions see his grandson's book. Craufurd, *Craufurd and his Light Division*, pp. 123–51.
4. Costello, *Campaigns*, p. 32; Simmons, *British Rifle Man*, p. 76; Horward, *Pelet*, p. 87.
5. Archives de Masséna, Ney to Masséna, 2:00 P.M., 24 July 1810, LV, 198–99; Correspondance: Armée de Portugal, Loison to Ney, morning, 26 July 1810, Carton C⁷ 20. *The Royal Military Chronicle or, The British Officer's Monthly Register, Chronicle and Military Mentor*, "Official Documents," "Action near Almeida," signed by Craufurd, [?] November 1810, pp. 196–99. This letter also appeared in the London *Times*, 21 November 1810.
6. Correspondance: Armée de Portugal, Loison to Ney, morning, 26 July

1810, Carton C⁷ 20; Archives de Masséna, Montbrun to Masséna, 25 July 1810; Ney to Masséna, 2:00 P.M., 24 July 1810, LV, 212–13, 198–99; *Royal Military Chronicle*, "Action near Almeida," pp. 196–99; W.F.P. Napier, *Life and Opinions of . . . Charles James Napier*, I, 137; William Francis Patrick Napier, *History of the War in the Peninsula and in the south of France, from A.D. 1807 to A.D. 1814*, II, 180; Willoughby Verner, *History and Campaigns of the Rifle Brigade*, II, 112–13; William Scarth Moorsom, *Historical Record of the Fifty-second Regiment*, p. 120; Costello, *Campaigns*, p. 32; Simmons, *British Rifle Man*, p. 77.

7. Ibid., Loison to Ney, morning, 26 July 1810, Carton C⁷ 20; Costello, *Campaigns*, pp. 32–33; Simmons, *British Rifle Man*, p. 77; Verner, *Rifle Brigade*, II, 122–23; Archives de Masséna, Montbrun to Masséna, 26 July 1810, LV, 212–13; Correspondance, Armée de Portugal, Loison to Ney, morning, 25 July 1810, Carton C⁷ 20; Simmons, *British Rifle Man*, p. 77.

8. *Wellington's Supplementary Despatches*, Wellington to William Wellesley-Pole, 31 July 1810, VI, 561–63; *Royal Military Chronicle*, "Action near Almeida," pp. 196–99; Luz Soriano, *Guerra civil*, Segunda Epocha, III, 56–58. The complement of the Light Division is based primarily upon Craufurd's own statements and Luz Soriano. Ney estimated the Light Division at 8,000 infantry and 2,000 cavalry and Montburn placed the figure at almost 10,000 infantry and cavalry. Therefore, contrary to Oman's charges that Masséna doubled the size of Craufurd's force, he only repeated the figures of Ney and Montbrun in his report to Berthier. Archives de Masséna, Ney to Masséna, 2:00 P.M., 24 July 1810; Montbrun to Masséna, 25 July 1810, LV, 198–99, 212–13; Masséna to Berthier, 29 July 1810, LI, 55–56; Charles W. Oman, *Peninsular War*, III, 264; Moorsom, *Record of the Fifty-second Regiment*, p. 122.

9. Archives de Masséna, Ney to Masséna, 2:00 P.M., 24 July 1810, LV, 198–99.

10. W.F.P. Napier, *Life and Opinions of . . . Charles James Napier*, I, 137; *Royal Military Chronicle*, "Action near Almeida," pp. 196–99. Major McLeod took command of the 43d early in the fighting when Lieutenant Colonel Edward Hull, arriving the previous night to assume command of the regiment, was shot in the chest and head and instantly killed. *Wellington's Dispatches*, Wellington to Beresford, 29 July 1810, VI, 306–7; Luz Soriano, *Guerra civil*, Segunda Epocha, III, 58; William Warre, *Letters*, pp. 154–55.

11. Warre, *Letters*, pp. 154–55. There were numerous complaints about the conduct of the 1st Caçadores in crossing the Côa. Accordingly, Wellington sent Captain William Warre to investigate the charges. Before beginning his inquiry, Warre wrote to his father, "I am sorry I cannot add as much for the 1st [Caçadores] who did not behave so well [as the 3d Caçadores] and ran off at the very beginning." However, once the investigation had been completed a week later, Wellington wrote that their conduct had "been the cause of the unfavorable impression which has been created respecting them in the affair; but they had no orders to halt on the right of the Côa when they were ordered to retire, and they saw the artillery and cavalry crossing." See *Wellington's Dispatches*, Wellington to Beresford, 29 July 1810, VI, 306–7; William Carr Beresford, *Collecção das Ordens do Dia do illustrissimo e excellentissimo Senhor Guilherme Carr Beresford*, "Ordems do Dia," 3 August 1810, pp. 139–40. Concern was even voiced at the Horse Guards when Lieutenant Colonel Henry Torrens, on first report of the conduct of the Portuguese soldiers, wrote, "The only thing I don't like in the news with regard to our ultimate prospects is that a Portuguese regiment after the first shot being fired ran off and dispersed all over the country." P.R.O., W.O., 3/597, Torrens to William Wellesley-Pole, 11 August 1810, pp. 199–200.

12. *Royal Military Chronicle*, "Action near Almeida," pp. 196–99; W.F.P. Napier, *Life and Opinions of . . . Charles James Napier*, I, 137–38. A new highway is presently under construction from Almeida westward and a new ultra-modern bridge is being erected, unfortunately less than 25 yards from the old bridge.

13. W.F.P. Napier, *War in the Peninsula*, II, 378; *Royal Military Chronicle*, "Action near Almeida," pp. 196–99. The author has carefully examined and photographed the terrain and road between Almeida and the Côa River in 1967, 1972, 1976, 1978, and 1982. He also spent considerable time conferring with the late William R. Johnston who also surveyed the terrain in great detail in an attempt to understand the problems encountered by both armies maneuvering there.

14. Archives de Masséna, Ney to Masséna, 2:00 P.M., 24 July 1810, LV, 198–99.

15. *Royal Military Chronicle*, "Action near Almeida," pp. 196–99; Beresford, *Ordens do Dia, 1810*, 3 August 1810, pp. 139–40; Portugal, Arquivo Histórico Militar, Caixa 11, No. 55, Wellington to Forjaz, 25 July 1810.

16. W.F.P. Napier, *War in the Peninsula*, II, 379; Leach, *Rough Sketches*,

pp. 149−50; W.F.P. Napier, *Life and Opinions of . . . Charles James Napier*, I, 138−39; Correspondance: Armée de Portugal, Loison to Ney, morning, 26 July 1810, Carton C⁷ 20; Simmons, *British Rifle Man*, p. 93.

17. Verner, *Rifle Brigade*, II, 125. Verner cited Leach's MSS *Journal* which is somewhat different from his *Rough Sketches*. W.F.P. Napier, *War in the Peninsula*, II, 379; Correspondance: Armée de Portugal, Loison to Ney, morning, 26 July 1810, Carton C⁷ 20; George T. Napier, *Passages in the Early Military Life of General Sir George T. Napier*, p. 115.

18. Correspondance: Armée de Portugal, Loison to Ney, morning, 26 July 1810, Carton C⁷ 20; Simmons, *British Rifle Man*, p. 79; Harry George Smith, *The Autobiography of Lieutenant General Sir Harry Smith, Baronet of Aliwal on the Sultej*, I, 31; W.F.P. Napier, *War in the Peninsula*, II, 380; W.F.P. Napier, *Life and Opinions of . . . Charles James Napier*, I, 138−39.

19. Smith, *Autobiography*, I, 31; W.F.P. Napier, *War in the Peninsula*, II, 380.

20. Sprünglin, *Souvenirs*, pp. 145−46. Sprünglin's narrative of the attack on the bridge, repeated by Oman, is incorrect in listing his losses, in indicating the time of the attack as "midi" (Ney announced some 50 casualties at 2:00 P.M. so Sprünglin could not have led his attack on the bridge yet), in the claim that he succeeded in capturing the bridge, etc. On the other hand, the account in the text is based primarily upon the original letters from Loison, Ney, and Masséna. See Correspondance: Armée de Portugal, Loison to Ney, morning, 26 July 1810, Carton C⁷ 20; Archives de Masséna, Ney to Masséna, 2:00 P.M., 24 July 1810, LV, 198−99.

21. Correspondance: Armée de Portugal, Loison to Ney, morning, 26 July 1810, Carton C⁷ 20; Burgoyne, *Life and Correspondence*, I, 95; George Napier, *Military Life*, p. 115−16.

22. Simmons, *British Rifle Man*, p. 80; W.F.P. Napier, *War in the Peninsula*, II, 380; Burgoyne, *Life and Correspondence*, I, 96. See also Loison who claimed an English officer proposed a cessation of gunfire in order to administer to the wounded and bury the dead. Correspondance: Armée de Portugal, Loison to Ney, morning, 26 July 1810, Carton C⁷ 20; Costello, *Campaigns*, p. 34.

23. Archives de Masséna, Sergeant Robert Grant to John Gordon, soldier, in care of Peter Stuart, West Elchies, Aberdeur by Nortlach, Great Britain, 11:00 A.M., 25 July 1810, LV, 222−23. This manuscript has

been left unedited, as Grant declared in his postscript, "I have not time to correct the errors therefore correct them yourself."

24. Ibid., Ney to Masséna, 2:00 P.M., 24, 25 July 1810, LV, 198–99, 224–25; Correspondance: Armée de Portugal, Loison to Ney, morning, 26 July 1810, Carton C⁷ 20.

25. Correspondance: Armée de Portugal, Loison to Ney, morning, 26 July, evening, 26 July 1810, Carton C⁷ 20; Archives de Masséna, Montbrun to Masséna, 25 July 1810; Ney to Masséna, 2:00 P.M., 24 July 1810, LV, 212–13, 198–99; P.R.O., W.O., 1/245, "Return of the number of Killed, Wounded, and Missing, of a Division of the Army, under the command of His Excellency, Lieutenant General, Lord, Viscount Wellington, K.G., in Action with the French Army, near Almeida, on the 24th July 1810, Headquarters Alverca, 25 July 1810," pp. 189–90; *Wellington's Dispatches*, Wellington to Liverpool, 25 July 1810, VI, 294–95; Wellington placed his losses at 317 but Oman increased this figure to 332 by adding 15 wounded from the 52d Foot. Most other English writers accept this general figure. See Oman, *Peninsular War*, III, 544, 265; W.F.P. Napier, *War in the Peninsula*, II, 380–81.

26. Oman, *Peninsular War*, III, 264–66 n., 485–87; Fortescue, *British Army*, VII, 485–86; Correspondance: Armée de Portugal, Loison to Ney, morning, 26 July, evening, 26 July 1810, Carton C⁷ 20; Archives de Masséna, Ney to Masséna, 2:00 P.M., 24, 25, 26, 27 July 1810, LV, 198–99, 224, 242, 254–55; Montbrun to Masséna, 25 July 1810, LV, 212–13; Grant to Gordon, 25 July 1810; James M. Milne to his father, 11:00 A.M., 25 July 1810, LV, 220–23; Masséna to Berthier, 29 July 1810, LI; 55–56; *Le Moniteur* cited in Belmas, *Journaux des siéges*, Masséna to Berthier, 29 July 1810, III, 375–80. See also Jean Baptiste Koch, *Mémoires de Masséna*, VII, 118–19. Koch who also utilized the Archives de Masséna apparently based his figures on some sources other than those examined by the author; he placed French casualties at 527. Archives de Masséna, Ney to Masséna, 29 July 1810, LV, 291–92.

27. W.F.P. Napier, *War in the Peninsula*, Campbell to Napier, 13 November 1835, V, 416–17; Shaw-Kennedy to Napier, 7 November 1835, V, 416. For Picton's justification see Thomas Picton, *Memoirs of Lieutenant General Sir Thomas Picton*, I, 286–97; *Wellington's Dispatches*, Wellington to Craufurd, 8 March 1810, V, 553–54; Wellington to Picton, Cole, and Craufurd, 28 May 1810; Wellington to Picton, Cole, Slade, Campbell, and Craufurd, 2 July 1810; Wellington to Craufurd,

7:30 P.M., 11 July 1810, VI, 149–50, 238–40, 258–59; Craufurd, *Craufurd and his Light Division*, Picton to Craufurd, 4 July 1810, p. 121.

28. *Wellington's Supplementary Despatches*, Wellington to William Wellesley-Pole, 31 July 1810, VI, 561–64. See also W.F.P. Napier, *Life and Opinions of . . . Charles James Napier*, I, 136–40; Leach, *Rough Sketches*, pp. 152–53; Warre, *Letters*, p. 154; Smith, *Autobiography*, I, 30–31.

29. P.R.O., W.O., 3/597, Torrens to Bathurst, 3 August 1810, pp. 174–77; Torrens to Gordon, 4 August 1810, p. 183; Torrens to William Wellesley-Pole, 11 August 1810, pp. 199–200; Torrens to Bathurst, 14 August 1810, pp. 209–11; P.R.O., W.O., 6/50, Liverpool to Wellington, 21 August 1810, pp. 119–20.

30. Horward, *Pelet*, pp. 86–87, 90–91.

31. Archives de Masséna, Junot to Masséna, 26 July 1810, LV, 233–34; Horward, *Pelet*, pp. 91–94; Correspondance: Armée de Portugal, Masséna to Junot, 27 July 1810, Carton C⁷ 8. Masséna apologized to Junot declaring circumstances forced him to give the siege to Ney and the 6th Corps.

32. Correspondance: Armée de Portugal, Loison to Ney, morning, 26 July 1810, Carton C⁷ 20; Archives de Masséna, Montbrun to Masséna, 25 July 1810, LV, 212–13. W.F.P. Napier claimed that Montbrun, exercising independent command, refused to fulfill Ney's orders since Masséna had not sanctioned the battle. Similarly, Sprünglin claimed Montbrun would not carry out Ney's orders because Masséna was not present. In fact, Montbrun's cavalry, heavily committed to the battle, suffered heavy casualties; they sabered 810 men and captured 200 prisoners according to Montbrun, but the rocky terrain prohibited all but the most foolhardy horsemen from pursuing the enemy. See W.F.P. Napier, *War in the Peninsula*, II, 387; Sprünglin, *Souvenirs*, p. 145.

33. P.R.O., W.O., 6/50, Liverpool to Wellington, 21 August 1810, pp. 119–20.

34. *Royal Military Chronicle*, "Action near Almeida," pp. 196–99; Koch, *Mémoires de Masséna*, "Situation de l'armée de Portugal au moment de l'invasion (15 Septembre 1810)," VII, 568–70. Oman placed the complement of Ferey's infantry and Montbrun's cavalry at 3,926 and 2,975, respectively, on 15 September 1810. Oman, *Peninsular War*, III, 540–45.

35. P.R.O., W.O., 3/597, Torrens to Beresford, 30 August 1810, pp.

269–72; P.R.O., W.O., 6/50, Liverpool to Wellington, 21 August 1810, pp. 119–20.

Chapter 11. *The War of Logistics*

1. Horward, *Pelet*, pp. 88–89; Archives de Masséna, Lambert to Masséna, 10 July 1810, LIV, 250; Ney to Masséna, 12 July 1810, LV, 4.
2. Archives de Masséna, Lambert to Masséna, 14 July 1810, LV, 49; Correspondance: Armée de Portugal, Etat des expedition faites de Salamanque sur le 8ᵉ Corps/6ᵉ Corps, 14 July 1810; Carton C⁷ 8; Michaux to Junot, 14 July 1810, Carton C⁷ 8; Michaux to Lambert, 14 July 1810; Carton C⁷ 8; Michaux to Clapier, 14 July 1810, Carton C⁷ 8. (It should be noted the 6th Corps was larger than the 8th Corps and directly engaged in the siege so few of its men were available for forage duty.)
3. Correspondance: Armée de Portugal, Lambert to Michaux, 15 July 1810, Carton C⁷ 8; Archives de Masséna, Junot to Masséna, 17 July 1810, LV, 69; Masséna to Junot, 17 July 1810, LI, 144; Junot to Masséna, 19 July 1810, LV, 87.
4. Archives de Masséna, Ney to Masséna, 20 July 1810, LV, 125; Masséna to Ney, 21 July 1810, LI, 145.
5. Ibid., Lambert to Masséna, 13 July 1810, LV, 32–34. Less than 40 percent of the flour, 25 percent of the barley, and 50 percent of the wine, cattle, and sheep had been collected.
6. Ibid., Lambert to Masséna, 10, 12 July 1810, LIV, 151, LV, 29; Kellermann to Fririon, 12 July 1810, LV, 31–32.
7. Correspondance: Armée de Portugal, Lambert to Kellermann, 13 July 1810, Carton C⁷ 8; Archives de Masséna, Cautair to Lambert, 13 July 1810, LV, 37–38.
8. Archives de Masséna, Lambert to Masséna, n.d., July 1810, LV, 39; Masséna to Lambert, 14 (two letters) July 1810, LI, 142–43.
9. Ibid., Masséna to Kellermann, 14 July 1810, LI, 245.
10. Ibid., Lambert to Masséna, 15 July 1810, LV, 52; Masséna to Kellermann, 15 July 1810, LI, 246.
11. Ibid., Kellermann to Masséna, 17 July 1810, LV, 71–72.
12. Ibid., Kellermann to Masséna, 19 July 1810, LV, 82; Masséna to Kellermann, 20 July 1810, LI, 247.
13. Correspondance: Armée de Portugal, Lambert to Kellermann, 16, 23

July 1810, Carton C⁷8. The danger of escort duty is exemplified by the loss of 18 of the 37 escort troops on 18 July.

14. Archives de Masséna, Lambert to Masséna, 27, 28 (two letters), 29, 30 July 1810, LV, 257, 262–63, 266, 289, 302; Correspondance: Armée de Portugal, Dorsenne to Masséna, 22 July 1810 (reference to Masséna's letter to Dorsenne of 14 July 1810), Carton C⁷8; Lambert to Kellermann, 27 July 1810, Carton C⁷8.

15. Ibid., Masséna to Lambert, 27, 29 July 1810, LI, 146–47; Masséna to Dorsenne, 29 July 1810, LI, 249; Masséna to Lambert, 2, 8 August 1810, LI, 150, 153–54; Clapier to Masséna, 28 July 1810, LV, 273; Correspondance: Armée de Portugal, Dorsenne to Masséna, 22 July 1810, Carton C⁷8.

16. Ibid., Legarde to Masséna, 29 July 1810, LV, 256; Masséna to Lambert, 22, 23 July 1810, LI, 145–46; Clapier to Masséna, 28 July 1810, LV, 271–72.

17. Ibid., Masséna to Lambert, 31 July, 8 August 1810, LI, 148, 153; Clapier to Masséna, 30 July 1810, LV, 294–95; Clapier "Rapport," 3 August 1810, LVI, 54; Masséna to Ney, 3 August 1810, LI, 151; Lambert to Masséna, 4, 7, 9 August 1810, LVI, 76, 128, 156, 198; Horward, *Pelet*, pp. 98–99;

18. Ibid., "Note de l'envoy parti le 2 août 1810," signed by Lambert, 2 August 1810, LVI, 27.

19. Ibid., Masséna to Ney, 1, 3 August 1810, LI, 149, 150; Ney to Masséna, 4 August 1810, LV, 72–74; Horward, *Pelet*, p. 99.

20. Ibid., "Envoi parti le 3 août au matin," signed by Lambert, 3 August 1810, LVI, 46; "Note de l'envoy expédié le 4 août," signed by Lambert, 4 August 1810, LVI, 69; "Note de l'envoi parti le 4 du matin," signed by Lambert, 4 August 1810, LVI, 71.

21. Ibid., Kellermann to Masséna, 25 July 1810, LV, 214–15; "Extrait des minutes de la Sécrétairerie d'Etat," signed by Maret, 8 February 1810, LVI, 185–88; Berthier to Kellermann, 13 July 1810, LVI, 183; Masséna to Berthier, 3 August 1810, LI, 58; "Ordre du Jour," signed by Kellermann, 26 July 1810, LV, 240.

22. Ibid., Masséna to Kellermann, 6 August 1810, LI, 251; Lambert to Masséna, 7 August 1810, LVI, 158–59; Masséna to Berthier, 14 September 1810, LI, 29–30; Kellermann to Masséna, 8 August 1810, LVI, 181–82.

23. Ibid., Cautair to Lambert, 2 August 1810, LVI, 35; Lambert to Masséna, 7 August 1810, LVI, 158–59; Masséna to Berthier, 7 August

1810, LI, 58–59; General Kellermann was the son of Marshal François-Christophe Kellermann, the Duc de Valmey.

24. Ibid., Masséna to Kellermann, 8 August, 6, 11 September 1810, LI, 252, 257, 258; Masséna to Berthier, 14 September 1810, LI, 29–30. King Joseph encountered similar difficulties with Kellermann and appealed directly to Napoleon for his recall. See *Correspondance du roi Joseph*, Joseph to Napoleon, 25 January, 25 August 1810, VII, 236, 321–22. General Jean-Baptiste Drouet also experienced Kellermann's recalcitrance when he occupied Valladolid in October, 1810. Finally, Marshal Jean-Baptiste Bessières was given supreme command of northern Spain in January 1811; he apparently brought Kellermann under control. In April of the same year, a Council of State considered Kellermann's conduct; he was recalled in June and although he was not condemned, he remained without a command until 1813. For more details on Kellermann's role in the Peninsula see Terry E. Gordon, "The Early Life and Career of General François-Etienne Kellermann," pp. 218–258. For Rouyer's removal, see Archives de Masséna, Masséna to Rouyer, 19, 20 August 1810, LI, 246–47; Koch, *Mémoires de Masséna*, VII, 124.

25. Ibid., "Note de l'envoi parti le 7 au matin," signed by Lambert, 7 August 1810, LVI, 124; "Note de l'envoi parti le 8 août 1810," signed by Lambert, 8 August 1810, LVI, 167.

26. Ibid., Masséna to Lambert, 8, 15 August 1810, LI, 153–54, 157.

27. Ibid., Lambert to Masséna, 6, 7, 9 August 1810, LVI, 105, 131, 198–99; Masséna to Lambert, 7, 8, 15 August 1810, LI, 153, 154, 157.

28. Ibid., "Note de l'envoi parti le 9 août," signed by Lambert, 9 August 1810, LVI, 191; "Note de l'envoy 2eme parti le 9 aôut au soir," signed by Lambert, 9 August 1810, LVI, 193; "Note de l'envoi parti le 10 aôut," signed by Lambert, 10 August 1810, LVI, 349; "Envoi parti le 11 aôut," signed by Lambert, 11 August 1810, LVI, 245.

29. Ibid., "Note de l'envoi en chargement le 12," signed by Lambert, 12 August 1810, LVI, 286; "Situation du magazine," signed by [?], 11 August 1810, LVI, 289.

30. Ibid., Lambert to Masséna, 19 (two letters), 22 July 1810, LV, 89, 91, 165–67; Masséna to General Governors of Salamanca, Zamora, Toro, and Avila, 1 July 1810, LI, 244; Masséna to Kellermann, 19 July 1810, LI, 246; Kellermann to Masséna, 23 July 1810, LV, 193; Masséna to Kellermann, 25 July 1810, LI, 248; Masséna to Kellermann,

Dorsenne, Rouyer, and Lagrange, 19 July 1810, LI, 246. Napoleon was also aware of such practices among his commanders in Spain so he had Berthier issue a circular which reached Masséna on 9 August but this problem had already been solved. See Berthier to Masséna, 22 July 1810, LV, 205. During the summer of 1810 the exchange rate was 3.75 réaux to one franc.

31. Ibid., Masséna to Kellermann, 24, 25 July 1810, LV, 248; Kellermann to Masséna, 23, 27 July 1810, LV, 127, 250—51; Koch, *Mémoires de Masséna*, VII, 127.

32. Ibid., Lagrange to Masséna, 27 July 1810, LV, 256; Lambert to Masséna, 1 August 1810, LVI, 13; Masséna to Berthier, 13 August, 14 September 1810, LI, 29—30, 61; Ney to Masséna, 7 August 1810, LVI, 132.

33. Ibid., Lambert to Masséna, 14, 15 July, 11 August 1810, LV, 40, 53, 258; Masséna to Berthier, 1 August 1810, LI, 57; Masséna to Lazowski, 12, 17 August 1810, LI, 156, 158; Masséna to Eblé, 17 August 1810, LI, 158. The funds drawn from the Spanish treasury came under Chapter 7, *Budget du ministère de la guerre*, and Chapters 11 and 18, *Budget de l'administration de la guerre*.

34. The five provinces mentioned above were Avila, Palencia, Salamanca, Zamora, and León. For documents concerning salary see: Archives de Masséna, "Situation sommaire du payeur général de l'armée au 3 aôut," signed by Maury, 3 August 1810, LVI, 49; Lambert to Masséna, 22 July, 3 August 1810, LV, 163, LVI, 51; Koch, *Mémoires de Masséna*, VII, 126.

35. Archives de Masséna, Lambert to Masséna, 22 July 1810, LV, 149; Masséna to Lambert, 17, 22 July 1810, LI, 144, 145; Clapier to Masséna, 29 July 1810, LV, 286; Casa Seca to Masséna, 19 July 1810, LV, 88; *Procès Verbaux*, 30 July 1810, LVI, 258 ff.

36. Ibid., Pavetti to Masséna, 7 August 1810, LVI, 133—34; Solis to Governor, 23, 25, 26 July, 6, 12 August 1810, LVI, 135—42; Masséna to Ney, 3 August 1810, LI, 151; Masséna to Pavetti, 12 August 1810, LI, 253.

37. Ibid., Clapier to Masséna, 10 August 1810, LVI, 231. For daily returns of contributions see Clapier to Masséna in volumes LV and LVI.

38. Ibid., Masséna to Eblé, 12 July 1810, LI, 142; Correspondance: Armée de Portugal, Nos. 260, 261, 382, Eblé to Berthier, 19 July, 2 August 1810; No. 259, Eblé to Masséna, 19 July 1810, Carton C⁷23. The officers were Colonels Corda and Neigre. See also Archives de Masséna, Masséna to Eblé, 14 July 1810, LI, 142.

39. Ibid., Masséna to Berthier, 25 July, 1 August 1810, LI, 54, 57; Eblé to Masséna, 19 July 1810, LV, 145–46; Correspondance: Armée de Portugal, "Inventaire des principaux objects d'artillerie de la place de Ciudad Rodrigo . . . le 10 juillet 1810," signed by Husson, 20 July 1810, Carton C⁷ 8; Nos. 240, 284, Eblé to Masséna, 16, 22 July 1810; No. 373, Eblé to Fririon, 2 August 1810; No. 354, Eblé to Charbonnel, 31 July 1810, Carton C⁷ 23; Horward, *Pelet*, p. 97.
40. Correspondance: Armée de Portugal, Nos. 291, 399, Eblé to Ruty, 23 July, 4 August 1810; Nos. 241, 313, 389, 438, Eblé to Masséna, 16, 26, July, 1, 11 August, 1810; No. 361, Eblé to Berthier, 1 August 1810; No. 395, Eblé to Foucher, 4 August 1810; No. 396, Eblé to Charbonnel, 4 August 1810; No. 397; Eblé to Ney, 4 July 1810; No. 398, Eblé to Junot, 4 July 1810, Carton C⁷ 23.
41. Ibid., Nos. 296, 332, 345, 384, Eblé to Ruty, 24, 30, 31 July, 2 August 1810; No. 346, Eblé to Charbonnel, 31 July 1810; No. 321, Eblé to Guérard, 27 July 1810, Carton C⁷ 23; Archives de Masséna, Lambert to Masséna, 4 August 1810, LVI, 76; Clapier to Masséna, 27 July 1810, LV, 253.
42. Ibid., Lazowski to Reynier, 25 July 1810, Carton C⁷ 8; Archives de Masséna, Masséna to Berthier, 25 July, 1 August 1810, LI, 54, 59; Lazowski to Masséna, 9 August 1810, LVI, 207; Belmas, *Journaux des sièges*, III, 340.
43. Ibid., No. 434, Eblé to Masséna, 10 August 1810, Carton C⁷ 23; Archives de Masséna, "Artillerie parc de siège," signed by Eblé, 11 August 1810, LVI, 222–24.
44. Archives de Masséna, Masséna to Eblé, 9 August 1810, LI, 154; Correspondance: Armée de Portugal, No. 343, Eblé to Fririon, 31 July 1810; "Mémoire succinct sur la place de Ciudad Rodrigo," signed by Eblé, 8 August 1810; No. 425, Eblé to Masséna, 9 August 1810; Nos. 441, 442, Eblé to Berthier and Clarke, 11 August 1810, Carton C⁷ 23.
45. Ibid., Masséna to Berthier, 17 July 1810, LI, 53.
46. Ibid., Masséna to Berthier, 21, 25, 29 July, 2, 13 August 1810, LI, 53, 54, 56, 57, 61.

Chapter 12. *Preliminary Operations at Almeida*

1. Archives de Masséna, Ney to Masséna, 27 July 1810, LV, 254.
2. Correspondance: Armée de Portugal, Loison to Ney, 26, 27 July 1810,

Carton C⁷ 20; Archives de Masséna, Ney to Masséna, 27, 28 July 1810, LV, 254, 260; *Wellington's Dispatches*, Wellington to Cole, 26 July 1810, VI, 297.

3. Archives de Masséna, Ney to Masséna, 30 July 1810, LV, 304; Correspondance: Armée de Portugal, Loison to Ney, 30 July 1810, Carton C⁷ 20; *Wellington's Dispatches*, Wellington to Craufurd, 27 July 1810, VI, 299–300; Wellington to Cole, 27 July 1810, VI, 300.

4. Correspondance: Armée de Portugal, Loison to Ney, 30 July 1810, Carton C⁷ 20.

5. *Wellington's Dispatches*, Wellington to Stuart, 29 July 1810, VI, 306; Wellington to Craufurd, 26 July 1810, VI, 299.

6. Archives de Masséna, Montbrun to Masséna, 31 July 1810, LV, 312; Ney to Masséna, 15 August 1810, LVI, 336–7; *Wellington's Dispatches*, Wellington to Cotton, 7 August 1810, VI, 333; "Proclamation to the People of Portugal," 4 August 1810, VI, 329–30.

7. Correspondance: Armée de Portugal, Loison to Ferey, 3 August 1810, Carton C⁷ 20; Archives de Masséna, d'Alorna to Masséna, 14 August 1810, LVI, 327–28; *Wellington's Dispatches*, Wellington to Cotton, 6 August 1810, VI, 332; Horward, *Pelet*, pp. 99–100. Wellington, in fact, complained about the conduct of the troops of the King's German Legion toward the Portuguese. "It has gone so far," he wrote, that the Portuguese "have inquired whether they might kill the Germans in our service, as well as in the service of the French."

8. Archives de Masséna, "Proclamation aux Portugais," 1 August 1810, LI, 5; Ordre du Jour, 1 August 1810, LI, 5.

9. Ibid., Masséna to Ney and Junot, 7 August 1810, LI, 153; Masséna to Loison, 8 August 1810, LI, 29; Berthier to Masséna, 15 August 1810, LVI, 338; Horward, *Pelet*, p. 110.

10. Correspondance: Armée de Portugal, Loison to Ferey, 3 August 1810, Carton C⁷ 20; Archives de Masséna, Ney to Masséna, 2 August 1810, LVI, 38–40.

11. Archives de Masséna, Ney to Masséna, 30 July, 2, 6, 8 August 1810, LV, 304, LVI, 38–39, 93–94, 163–64; Correspondance: Armée de Portugal, Loison to Ney, 8 August 1810, Carton C⁷ 20; *Wellington's Dispatches*, Wellington to Cotton, 31 July, 1, 5 August 1810, VI, 311, 313, 331.

12. Ibid., Ney to Masséna, 8, 13, 15 August 1810, LVI, 165, 314, 336–37; Correspondance: Armée de Portugal, Loison to Ney, 10, 12 August 1810, Carton C⁷ 20; *Wellington's Dispatches*, Wellington to Cotton, 8 August 1810, VI, 225.

13. Ibid., Ney to Masséna, 2, 8, 15 (two letters) August 1810, LVI, 38–39, 164–65, 336–37, 347; d'Alorna to Masséna, 14 August 1810, LVI, 327–28.

14. *Wellington's Dispatches*, Wellington to Hill, 27 July 1810, VI, 300–302; Wellington to Stuart, 29 July 1810, VI, 306; Wellington to Craufurd, 27 July 1810, VI, 299–300; Wellington to Cotton, 30 July, 15 August 1810, VI, 309–10, 357–58; Wellington to Doyle, 3 May 1810, VI, 87–88; Wellington to Liverpool, 2 June 1810, VI, 167–69. It is curious to note that the French gathered much valuable information from the deserters of the King's German Legion while the German troops in the French Hanoverian Legion frequently deserted to the Allies. No doubt this was caused primarily by their assignment to the difficult work of the siege train. However, Wellington's proclamation to deserters, promising them good treatment, new clothing, and twenty dollars for each enlistment, provided strong incentive.

15. Torre do Tombo, M.N.E., Maço 166 (1), Cox to Beresford, 25 July 1810.

16. Correspondance: Armée de Portugal, Loison to Ney, 27 July 1810, Carton C⁷20; Torre do Tombo, M.N.E., Maço 166 (1), Cox to Beresford, 26 July 1810; Archives de Masséna, Masséna to Berthier, 29 July 1810, LI, 55–56.

17. Ibid., Loison to Ney, 28 July 1810, Carton C⁷20; Archives de Masséna, Ney to Masséna, 29 July 1810, LV, 291; Captain Guingret, *Relation historique et militaire de la campagne de Portugal*, pp. 25–26.

18. Horward, *Pelet*, pp. 91–94; Archives de Masséna, Masséna to Junot, 30 (two letters) July 1810, LI, 147. The fifth battalion of Junot's 15th, 47th, and 86th Lines, along with the fourth and fifth battalions of the 70th Line, were detached for the garrison duty at Ciudad Rodrigo.

19. Archives de Masséna, Masséna to Eblé, 31 July 1810, LI, 148; Masséna to Lazowski, 31 July 1810, LI, 147–48.

20. Horward, *Pelet*, pp. 94–96; Archives de Masséna, "Reconnaissance d'Almeyda, et projet d'attaque contre cette place," signed by Eblé, 1 August 1810, LVI, 15–20. Ney was even more demonstrative in his attitude toward the marquis. When Masséna ordered d'Alorna to make contact with the leading Portuguese of Pinhel, Ney refused to permit his passage through the lines of the 6th Corps, despite Masséna's instructions. D'Alorna responded, "The Emperor honored me with a certain degree of confidence; then he sent me to the Army of Portugal with orders to strive to be useful to my country and the French Army." Ney still refused to permit d'Alorna's passage. The marquis invoked Masséna's authority and detailed his qualifications, but Ney responded, "*malgre*

celle." D'Alorna abandoned his plans and returned to headquarters until Masséna issued precise instructions to Ney about the marquis's mission. See Archives de Masséna, d'Alorna to Masséna, 3 August 1810, LVI, 48.

21. Ibid. This description of Almeida and its environs is based primarily upon Eblé's reconnaissance report, Pelet's journal, and the author's topographic research at Almeida on 30 July 1960, 26–27 May 1967, 30 September, 3 October 1976, 27 October 1978, and 11 July 1982. He would like to take this opportunity to acknowledge the aid of Senhor Eduardo Rodriguez of Almeida who spent several hours on 26 May 1967 and again on 3 October 1976 guiding him around the walls of the fortress and through the various casemates, the prison, the casemate of Governor Cox, and into the demilune before Santa Barbara.

22. Torre do Tombo, M.N.E., Maço 170 (2), Cox to Beresford, 16, 26 May 1809; Maço 161 (1), Cox to Beresford, 23 August 1809; Maço 169 (1), Cox to Arbuthnot, 10 September 1809; Maço 167 (1), Cox to Beresford, 11, 16 May 1810; Maço 166 (1), Cox to Beresford, 4, 8, 12 July 1810.

23. Ibid., Maço 170 (2), Cox to Beresford, 21, 30 May 1809; Cox to Arbuthnot, 28 May 1810; Maço 166 (1), Cox to Beresford, 25 October 1810; Maço 170 (2), Cox to Beresford, 19 January 1810; Maço 168 (1), Cox to Beresford, 18 March 1810; Cox to Wellington, 8 March 1810; Maço 169 (1), Cox to Beresford, 15 June 1810; Maço 166 (1), Cox to Beresford, 19 July 1810.

24. Ibid., Maço 170 (2), Cox to Beresford, 12 May 1809; Maço 169 (1), Beresford to Cox, 15 June 1810; Cox to Wellington, 26 June 1810; Maço 166 (1), Cox to Beresford, 8, 18 July 1810; Cox to Arbuthnot, 20 July 1810.

25. Ibid., Maço 166 (1), Cox to Beresford, 8, 9, 11 July 1810.

26. Ibid., Maço 166 (1), Cox to Beresford, 18 July 1810.

27. Ibid., Maço 166 (1), Cox to Beresford, 18, 21 July 1810; Cox to Arbuthnot, 20 July 1810; Maço 169 (1), Cox to Beresford, 18 June 1810.

28. Ibid., Maço 166 (1), Beresford to Cox, 24 July 1810.

29. Ibid., Maço 169 (1), Cox to Beresford, 24 May 1810.

30. Ibid., Maço 169 (1), Wellington's "Memorandum," 29 June 1810.

31. Ibid., Maço 168 (2), Cox to Beresford, 1 (two letters) July 1810.

32. Ibid., Maço 168 (2), Cox to Beresford, 4 July 1810; Beresford to Cox, 24 July 1810.

33. Horward, *Pelet*, p. 96; Archives de Masséna, "Reconnaissance d'Al-

meyda, et projet d'attaque contre cette place," signed by Eblé, 1 August 1810, LVI, 15–20.

34. Archives de Masséna, "Reconnaissance d'Almeyda, et projet d'attaque contre cette place," signed by Eblé, 1 August 1810, LVI, 15–20; Lazowski to Masséna, 2 August 1810, LVI, 36–37.

Chapter 13. *Trench Work before Almeida*

1. Correspondance: Armée de Portugal, "Disposition pour l'ouverture de la tranchée devant Almeyda," signed by Marchand, 15 August 1810; "Dispositions générales," signed by Marchand, 14 August 1810; "Ordre de la division," signed by Marchand, 15 August 1810, Carton C⁷9.
2. Archives de Masséna, "Rapport de l'ouverture de la tranchée devant Almeida, du 15 au 16 août 1810," signed by Lazowski, 16 August 1810, LVIII, 12.
3. Guingret, *Relation historique*, pp. 26–27; Archives de Masséna, Masséna to Berthier, 17 August 1810, LI, 63; "Rapport de l'ouverture de la tranchée devant Almeida, du 15 au 16 août 1810," signed by Lazowski, 16 August 1810, LVIII, 13.
4. Ibid., "Rapport de la tranchée devant Almeida pendant le journée du 16 août et pendant la nuit du 16 au 17," signed by Lazowski, 17 August 1810, LVIII, 11. There is a variation of this letter signed by Béchet de Léocour, n.d., LVIII, 8.
5. Horward, *Pelet*, pp. 110–11.
6. Ibid., p. 113; Archives de Masséna, Masséna to Lambert, 15 August 1810, LI, 157; Lambert to Masséna, 19 August 1810, LVIII, 80.
7. Correspondance: Armée de Portugal, No. 499, Eblé to Ruty, 19 August 1810, Carton C⁷23; Archives de Masséna, Masséna to Ney, 17 August 1810, LI, 158; Masséna to Eblé and Lazowski, 19 August 1810, LI, 158; Lambert to Masséna, 17 (three letters), 19, 20 (three letters) August 1810, LVIII, 29, 30–31, 33, 80, 84, 103; Masséna to Lambert, 15, 17 August 1810, LI, 157–58.
8. Archives de Masséna, "Rapport de la tranchée devant Almeida pendant la journée du 16 août et pendant la nuit du 16 au 17," signed by Lazowski, 17 August 1810, LVIII, 11. There is a variation of this report signed by Béchet de Léocour, n.d., LVIII, 8.
9. Ibid., "Rapport de la tranchée devant Almeida pendant la journée du

17 août et de la nuit du 17 au 18," signed by Lazowski, n.d., LVIII, 17. There is a variation of this letter signed by Béchet de Léocour, LVIII, 20. Horward, *Pelet*, p. 114.

10. Ibid.

11. Ibid., "Projet pour l'emplacement et l'armement des batteries . . . ," signed by Eblé, Lazowski, Ruty, 18 August 1810, LVIII, 58; "Consignes données aux batteries," signed by Eblé, n.d., LVIII, 67–72; Eblé to Masséna, 19 August 1810, LVIII, 57.

12. Ibid., Eblé to Masséna, 18, 21 August 1810, LVIII, 39–40; "Rapport du 18 au 19 août 1810," signed by Eblé, n.d., LVIII, 75. See also Correspondance: Armée de Portugal, No. 515, Eblé to Masséna, 22 August 1810, Carton C⁷23.

13. Ibid., "Rapport du 18 au 19 août 1810," signed by Eblé, n.d., LVIII, 75; "Rapport de la tranchée devant Almeyda, du 18 août et de la nuit du 18 au 19," signed by Béchet de Léocour, n.d., LVIII, 73. There is a variation of this letter signed by Lazowski, LVIII, 78.

14. Ibid., "Rapport de la tranchée devant Almeyda, du 18 au 19 août 1810," signed by Béchet de Léocour, n.d., LVIII, 73; Sprünglin, *Souvenirs*, pp. 443–44; Correspondance: Armée de Portugal, Nos. 504, 510, Eblé to Lazowski, 20, 22 August 1810, Carton C⁷23; Archives de Masséna, "Rapport de la tranchée devant Almeyda, de la journée du 19 août et de la nuit du 19 au 20," signed by Béchet de Léocour, n.d., LVIII, 74; Lazowski to Masséna, 22, 28 August 1810, LVIII, 129–30, 234.

15. Ibid., "Rapport du 19 au 20 août," signed by Eblé, LVIII, 76; Correspondance: Armée de Portugal, No. 480, Eblé to Masséna, 15 August 1810; No. 502, Eblé to Charbonnel, 20 August 1810; No. 503, Eblé to Ruty, 21 August 1810, Carton C⁷ 23.

16. Ibid., "Rapport de la tranchée devant Almeyda, de la journée du 19 août et de la nuit du 19 au 20," signed by Lazowski, n.d., LVIII, 77. There is a variation of this letter signed by Béchet de Léocour, n.d., LVIII, 74. "Rapport du 19 au 20 août," signed by Eblé, 20 August 1810, LVIII, 76.

17. Ibid., Ney to Masséna, 19 August 1810, LVIII, 60–63.

18. Horward, *Pelet*, p. 115; Archives de Masséna, Masséna to Junot, 21 August 1810, LI, 159–60. A regiment of the 8th Corps garrisoned Ciudad Rodrigo, three companies of Taupin's brigade replaced Ney's troops at La Concepción, and several detachments held Ledesma.

19. Archives de Masséna, "Rapport de la tranchée devant Almeyda pendant le journée du 20 août et le nuit du 20 au 21," signed by Lazowski,

n.d., LVIII, 304. There is a variation of this letter signed by Béchet de Léocour, n.d., LVIII, 305. "Rapport journée du 20 et nuit du 20 au 21," signed by Eblé, 21 August 1810, LVIII, 306.

20. Ibid., "Rapport de la tranchée devant Almeyda pendant la journée du 20 août et le nuit de 20 au 21," signed by Lazowski, n.d., LVIII, 304.

21. Ibid., Lazowski to Masséna, 22 August 1810, LVIII, 129–30; Masséna to Lazowski and Eblé, 17, 22 August 1810, LI, 158, 160; Eblé to Masséna, 24 (two letters) August 1810, LVIII, 144, 163; Lambert to Masséna, 24, 25 (two letters) August 1810, LVIII, 150, 154, 155–56; Masséna to Berthier, 26 August 1810, LI, 69; Masséna to Public Treasurer, 26 August 1810, LI, 70.

22. Ibid., Lambert to Masséna, 17, 23 August 1810, LVIII, 30–31, 133–34; Ney to Masséna, 24 August 1810, LVIII, 161–62; Masséna to Lambert, 19 August 1810, LI, 158; Masséna to Ney, 25 August 1810, LI, 162. Of the 23,500 rations utilized each day, 6,000 went to the hospital, 2,500 for Taupin's troops at La Concepción, 3,000 for the general headquarters at La Concepción, and 12,000 for the 6th Corps. In reserve there were 148,000 rations at Ciudad Rodrigo, 420,000 at Segovia, and 244,600 at Salamanca, for a total of 812,600 rations at the disposal of the army. It should be noted that Ney's request for food was motivated by a letter from Loison declaring, "General Ferey has absolutely no food for his troops." Correspondance: Armée de Portugal, Loison to Ney, 24 August 1810, Carton C[7] 20.

23. Correspondance: Armée de Portugal, Loison to Ney, 15, 16, 18 August 1810, Carton C[7] 20; "Ordre du jour," No. 35, 14 August 1810, Carton C[7] 9.

24. Archives de Masséna, Masséna to Berthier, 20 August 1810, LI, 64–65.

25. Ibid., "Rapport de la tranchée devant Almeida, pendant la journée du 21 août et la nuit du 21 au 22 août," signed by Eblé, 22 August 1810, LVIII, 308.

26. Ibid., "Rapport de la tranchée devant Almeyda pendant la journée du 22 août et la nuit du 22 au 23," signed by Lazowski, n.d., LVIII, 309. There is a variation of this report signed by Béchet de Léocour, n.d., LVIII, 310.

27. Ibid., "Rapport de la tranchée devant Almeida pendant le journée du 22 août et de nuit du 22 au 23," signed by Béchet de Léocour, n.d., LVIII, 310. There is a variation of this report signed by Lazowski, n.d., LVIII, 309. "Rapport du 22 au 23 août," signed by Eblé, 23 August 1810, LVIII, 315; Lazowski to Masséna, 22 August 1810, LVIII, 128.

28. Ibid., "Rapport de la tranchée devant Almeida, pendant la journée du 23 et la nuit du 23 au 24," signed by Béchet de Léocour, n.d., LVIII, 312. There is a variation of this report signed by Lazowski, n.d., LVIII, 311. "Rapport du 23 au 24 août," signed by Eblé, 24 August 1810, LVIII, 314; Horward, *Pelet*, p. 117.

29. Ibid.

30. Ibid., "Rapport du 23 au 24 août," signed by Eblé, 24 August 1810, LVIII, 314.

31. Fririon, *Journal historique*, p. 30; Archives de Masséna, "Rapport de la tranchée devant Almeyda pendant la journée du 24 et la nuit du 24 au 25 août 1810," signed by Lazowski, n.d., LVIII, 316. There is a more extensive version of this letter signed by Béchet de Léocour, n.d., LVIII, 317–18. "Rapport du 24 au 25," signed by Eblé, n.d., LVIII, 319.

32. Correspondance: Armée de Portugal, No. 516, Eblé to Masséna, 24 August 1810, Carton C⁷23; Horward, *Pelet*, p. 117; Archives de Masséna, "Rapport de la tranchée devant Almeida, pendant la journée du 24 et la nuit du 24 au 25 août 1810," signed by Béchet de Léocour, n.d., LVIII, 317–18.

33. Archives de Masséna, "Consignes données au batteries," signed by Eblé, n.d., LVIII, 67–72; Koch, *Mémoires de Masséna*, VII, 150–52.

34. Ibid., "Rapport de la tranchée devant Almeida, pendant la journée du 25 et la nuit du 25 au 26 août 1810," signed by Lazowski, n.d., LVIII, 320. A variation of this report has been signed by Béchet de Léocour, n.d., LVIII, 321. "Rapport du 25 au 26 août," signed by Eblé, 26 August 1810, LVIII, 322. An additional 345 projectiles arrived on 25 August.

35. Correspondance: Armée de Portugal, Loison to Ney, 24 August 1810, Carton C⁷20; Archives de Masséna, Ney to Masséna, 24 August 1810, LVIII, 159; "Rapport de la tranchée devant Almeida, pendant la journée du 24 et la nuit du 24 au 25 août 1810," signed by Béchet de Léocour, n.d., LVIII, 317–18.

36. Archives de Masséna, Masséna to Reynier, 25, 10:00 P.M., 25 August 1810, LI, 161–63.

Chapter 14. *The Bombardment and Capitulation of Almeida*

1. Horward, *Pelet*, p. 120; Archives de Masséna, "Rapport sur la tir et l'effet des batteries depuis six heures du matin qu'elles ont commence

se feu, jusqu'à onze heures," signed by Lazowski, dated 26 August 1810, LVII, 324.

2. Archives de Masséna, "Rapport du 26 au 27," signed by Eblé, 27 August 1810, LVIII, 325–26; "Rapport sur la tir . . . jusqu'à onze heures," signed by Lazowski, dated 26 August 1810, LVII, 324.

3. Christovam Ayres de Magalhães Sepúlveda, *História orgânica e politica do exército portuguêz*, "Narração das circunstancias que concorreram para a entrega da Praça de Almeida," signed by Cox, [27 November 1810], X, 188–94.

4. Archives de Masséna, "Rapport de la tranchée devant Almeyda pendant la journée du 26 et la nuit du 26 au 27 août 1810," signed by Lazowski, n.d., LVII, 323.

5. Horward, *Pelet*, p. 129; Hulot, *Souvenirs militaire*, p. 317; Luz Soriano, *Guerra Civil*, Segunda Epocha, III, 73n; Sepúlveda, *História orgânica*, Cox to Liverpool, 27 November 1810; "Narração," signed by Cox, [27 November 1810], X, 186–94; José Cezar Ferreira Gil, *A infantaria Portuguesa na Guerra da Peninsula*, Segunda Parte, p. 285n. See also Carlos de Passos, *Beresford e o Tenente-rei da Praça d'Almeida*, p. 13. Passos claimed that the Portuguese artillery commander, Fortunato José Barreiros, who later committed treason, permitted open barrels and charged bombs to be left lying in the castle courtyard.

6. Sepúlveda, *História orgânica*, "Narração," signed by Cox, [27 November 1810], X, 188–94.

7. Archives de Masséna, "Journal du siége d'Almeyda fait par les troupes de 6ᵉ corps," signed by Béchet de Léocour, n.d., LVII, 227–31; Hulot, *Souvenirs militaire*, p. 316; Sprünglin, *Souvenirs*, p. 445; Jean Nicolas Noël, *Souvenirs militaires d'un officier du premier empire, 1765–1832*, p. 107; Claudio de Chaby, *Excerptos Historicos Collecção de documentos relativos á guerra denominada da Peninsula*, Wellington to Forjaz, 29 August 1810, VI, 150–52; William Carr Beresford, *Collecção das Ordens do Dia*, "Ordem do dia," signed by Mosinho, 6 September 1810, 159–62.

8. Ibid., "Journal . . . du 6ᵉ corps," signed by Béchet de Léocour, n.d., LVII, 227–31; Sepúlveda, *História orgânica*, "Narração," signed by Cox, [27 November 1810], X, 188–94.

9. Ibid., "Rapport de la tranchée devant Almeyda pendant la journée du 26 et la nuit du 26 au 27 août 1810," signed by Lazowski, n.d., LVII, 323; Noël, *Souvenirs militaire*, p. 197.

10. Sepúlveda, *História orgânica*, "Narração," signed by Cox [27 November 1810], X, 188–94; Torre do Tombo, M.N.E., Maço 166 (1), Cox to Beresford, 9 July 1810.

11. Horward, *Pelet*, pp. 121–22.
12. Fririon, *Journal historique*, pp. 31–32. Fririon claimed he was sent by Masséna as the parliamentarian to deliver the ultimatum. He committed the unconscionable act of fabricating a conversation between Cox and himself, and including it in his *Journal*. Although many historians have relied on Fririon's account, it is contradicted directly by the three participants—Masséna, Cox, and Pelet. When Fririon's son published his father's journal in the *Spectateur militaire* during 1841, Pelet, then Director of the *Depôt de la guerre*, responded to the journal editor, "The details [of 27 August] given in the *Journal historique* are incorrect. The first summons addressed to the governor was delivered by Portuguese commander Gama. I carried the articles of capitulation that were later adopted to Governor William Cox. All the meetings on this day were between the English general and me." Archives de Masséna, Masséna to Berthier, 30 August 1810, LI, 72–74; Sepúlveda, *História orgânica*, "Narração," signed by Cox [27 November 1810], X, 188–94; Service historique de la armée, Mémoires historique, "Lettre à M. le directeur du *Spectateur militaire*," signed by Pelet, 4 May 1841, Carton 916.
13. Horward, *Pelet*, pp. 122–23; Archives de Masséna, Masséna to Cox, 27 August 1810, LVII, 210. There is a variation of this letter in Belmas, *Journaux des siéges*, pp. 382–83. It should be noted that later in the nineteenth century the casemate was used as a prison and it can still be visited today. It is curious that Sprünglin claimed he accompanied "Colonel Pelet" in this mission but the latter mentions only Gama. See Sprünglin, *Souvenirs*, p. 445.
14. Sepúlveda, *História orgânica*, "Narração," signed by Cox [27 November 1810]; Cox to Liverpool, 27 November 1810, X, 186–94; William Carr Beresford, *Collecção das Ordens do Dia*, "Ordem do dia," signed by Beresford, 12 August 1812, pp. 133–35; Arquivo Histórico Militar, Caixa 11, Wellington to Forjaz, 5 September 1810; William Carr Beresford, *Refutation of Colonel Napier's Justification of his Third Volume*, "Order of the Day," signed by Beresford, 12 August 1812; *Wellington's Dispatches* (1852 edition), Cox to Beresford, 30 August 1810, IV, 257–58; William Francis Patrick Napier, *Colonel Napier's Justification of his Third Volume*, p. 3; William Francis Patrick Napier, *A Letter to General Viscount Beresford, being an answer to His Lordship's assumed refutation of Colonel Napier's Justification of his Third Volume*, pp. 10–11; Passos, *Beresford e o Tenente-rei*, p. 35–53; João da Silva Mendes, *Memoira biographica do coronel Francisco Bernardo da Costa e Al-*

meida, Tenente-rei da praça de Almeida em 1810, Testimony of Manoel Roballo Caldeira, 10 October 1810, pp. 253–54. Cox initially complained to Beresford on 30 August about the conduct of Costa which was amplified in his letter of 27 November 1810 to Liverpool. He accused Costa of undermining his authority. This treasonous activity led to the collapse of Portuguese morale and the surrender of the fortress. In the court martial report published with the Order of the Day, dated 12 August 1812, it was noted that, "by the influence which he is proved to have exercised over the officers of the garrison—by refusing to support the authority, and the opinion of the governor, as was his duty, but on the contrary, withdrawing from the governor his legitimate influence . . . [Costa] succeeded in obliging the governor to capitulate." However, it is curious to note that Costa was convicted by a court martial on the basis of Items 4 and 5 of the Articles of War; that is, cowardice and fear led him to neglect his duty.

15. Archives de Masséna, Cox to Masséna, 27 (two letters) August 1810, LVII, 213, 217; Horward, *Pelet*, pp. 123–24. Cox's decision to send Barreiros as a parliamentarian was inappropriate since the Portuguese officer had been accused of French sympathies for his role as governor of the fort of Santa Luzia at Elvas. He commanded the French garrison there until September 1808 when it was restored to the Portuguese. It was claimed he ordered French soldiers to fire on the Portuguese but when he was tried before a court martial there were few witnesses and no affidavits to support the charges. See Sepúlveda, *História orgânica*, X, 198–220.

16. Horward, *Pelet*, p. 123; Archives de Masséna, Masséna to Berthier, 28, 30 August 1810, LI, 70, 72–74.

17. Passos, *Beresford e o Tenente-rei*, p. 16; Sepúlveda, *História orgânica*, Cox to Liverpool, 27 November 1810; "Narração," signed by Cox [27 November 1810], X, 186–94; *Wellington's Dispatches* (1852 edition), Cox to Beresford, 30 August 1810; Beresford to Wellington, 4 September 1810; Wellington to Liverpool, 5 September 1810, III, 257–58; Horward, *Pelet*, pp. 123–24. For Barreiros's justification of his conduct see *Exposição veridica e sincera das razões e impossibilidades que provam a sua alteza real, o principe regente de Portugal, e a toda a naçaõ, a falsidade do facto, e depoimento das testemunhas que juraram contra Fortunato José Barreiros* . . Offerecido a nação portugueza por F. J. B.

18. Horward, *Pelet*, p. 124; Sepúlveda, *História orgânica*, "Narração," signed by Cox, [27 November 1810], X, 188–94. The accounts of Pelet and Cox were remarkably similar, even in language, but in several in-

stances, events described by one at the first meeting were mentioned by the other at the second meeting.

19. Sepúlveda, *História orgânica*, Masséna to Cox, 27 August 1810, X, 190; "Narração," signed by Cox, [27 November 1810], X, 188–94. Archives de Masséna, Masséna to Berthier, 28 August 1810, LI, 71.

20. Archives de Masséna, "Journal . . . du 6ᵉ corps," signed by Béchet de Léocour, n.d., LVII, 227–31; "Rapport du 27 au 28 août," signed by Eblé, 28 August 1810, LVII, 328; Sepúlveda, *História orgânica*, "Narração," signed by Cox, [27 November 1810], X, 188–94. Eblé declared the firing recommenced at 9:00 P.M. *Wellington's Dispatches*, Wellington to Stuart, 31 August 1810; Wellington to Liverpool, 5 September, VI, 396–97, 404. Wellington claimed that Masséna promoted Barreiros to the rank of colonel because of his treachery. However, contrary to Cox's claim, Costa remained in the Portuguese army until he was court martialed and shot.

21. Archives de Masséna, "Capitulation pour la reddition de la place d'Almeyda aux armée de sa Majeste l'Empereur des français," signed by Masséna to Cox, 27 August 1810, LVII, 215, 219, 221.

22. Horward, *Pelet*, p. 126; Bonnal, *La vie militaire du maréchal Ney*, Fririon to Ney, 28 August 1810, III, 366; Sepúlveda, *História orgânica*, "Narração," signed by Cox, [27 November 1810], X, 188–94. It has proved impossible to determine the exact loss of Portuguese troops and inhabitants at Almeida. French losses during the siege are not exact. Fririon and Koch placed the French dead at 62 and the wounded at 377. (Koch apparently erred combining the number of dead and wounded to reach his total of 439 wounded); Belmas's figures are included in the text. Fririon, *Journal historique*, p. 32; Koch, *Mémoires de Masséna*, VIII, 156; Belmas, *Journaux des siéges*, III, 357.

23. Ibid., pp. 126–28; Archives de Masséna, Masséna to Berthier, 28, 30 August 1810, LI, 70, 72–74.

24. Arquivo Histórico Militar, Caixa 11, No. 72, Beresford to Wellington, 4 September 1810; Caixa 93, No. 106, Beresford to Forjaz, 4 September 1810; Sepúlveda, *História orgânica*, "Narração," signed by Cox, [27 November 1810], X, 188–94; Correspondance: Armée de Portugal, Masséna to Eblé, 29 August 1810; Carton C⁷ 9.

25. Sepúlveda, *História orgânica*, "Narração," signed by Cox, [27 November 1810], X, 186–94; *Wellington's Dispatches* (1852 edition), Cox to Beresford, 30 August 1810, IV, 257–58; Beresford, *Collecção das Ordens do Dia*, "Ordem do dia," signed by Beresford, 11 September 1810, pp. 163–65; Correspondance: Armée de Portugal, Masséna to

Eblé, 29 August 1810, Carton C⁷9; Archives de Masséna, Masséna to Berthier, 30 August 1810, LI, 72; Cox to Masséna, 30 August 1810, LVII, 251 *bis*; *Wellington's Dispatches*, Wellington to Stuart, 31 August 1810, VI, 396–97. Wellington regarded the plan to desert as "well enough for the private soldiers, but is highly disgraceful to the character of the officers."

26. Belmas, *Journaux des siéges*, Brenier to Berthier, 17 October 1810, III, 397–98. The foundation of the castle can still be seen today.

27. Correspondance: Armée de Portugal, Masséna to Eblé, 29 August 1810; [Dispositions général], signed by Marchand, 29 August 1810; Fririon to Reynier, 30 August 1810, Carton C⁷9; Belmas, *Journaux des siéges*, "Etat des bouches à feu et munitions de guerre existant dans la place d'Almeida, à l'époque du 27 août 1810, jour de sa reddition," signed by Bouvier, 28 [?] 1810, III, 393–94. Bouvier's inventory included 80 large-caliber bronze guns, 22 large-caliber iron guns, 27 pieces of light artillery, six mountain guns, 26 mortars, eight howitzers, and three swivel guns. Bouvier erred in his addition listing 174 instead of 172 pieces. Other eyewitnesses listed a total of anywhere from 105 to 150 guns but Bouvier actually inventoried the armaments of Almeida.

28. Correspondance: Armée de Portugal, "Note des approvisionnemens trouvés dans la place d'Almeyda," n.n., n.d.; Lambert to Berthier, 31 August 1810, Carton C⁷9.

29. Archives de Masséna, Masséna to Berthier, 30 August 1810, LI, 72–74.

30. Ibid., Berthier to Masséna, 29 July 1810, LVI, 290; Correspondance: Armée de Portugal, Masséna to Berthier, 28 August 1810, Carton C⁷9.

31. *Wellington's Dispatches*, Wellington to Henry Wellesley, 20 August 1810, VI, 373–75; Wellington to Hill, 8:15 P.M., 27, 28 August 1810, 385–86, 386–87; Wellington to Liverpool, 29 August 1810, VI, 389–92.

32. Ibid., Wellington to Liverpool, 29 August 1810, VI, 389–92; Wellington to Henry Wellesley, 30 August 1810, VI, 394–95; Wellington to Stuart, 31 August 1810, VI, 396–97; Wellington to Hill, 1 September 1810, VI, 399–400; Arquivo Histórico Militar, Caixa 20, No. 9, Beresford to Forjaz, 31 August 1810.

33. Fririon, *Journal historique*, p. 34; *Wellington's Dispatches*, Wellington to Forjaz, 6 September 1810, VI, 408–9; Wellington to Stuart, 7, 9, 11 September 1810, VI, 412–13, 422–24, 427–30; Wellington to Liverpool, 13 September 1810, VI, 434–37. When the fall of Almeida was announced in Lisbon the men of two Portuguese regiments, expressing the view that the British would embark, proposed to occupy the forts of

the city to prevent the British embarkation. Wellington responded by ordering both units to the front to demonstrate their "warlike" qualities.

34. Portugal, Academia de Ciências de Lisboa, "Colleção da Academia das Sciências de Lisboa," Decree signed by Monteiro Mor, 6 September 1810; Beresford, *Collecção das Ordens do Dia*, "Ordem do Dia," signed by Beresford, 6 September 1810, pp. 159—62.

35. Horward, *Pelet*, p. 130.

36. Hulot, *Souvenirs militaire*, p. 317—19; Passos, *Beresford e o Tenente-rei*, p. 53.

37. *Wellington's Dispatches* (1852 edition), Beresford to Wellington, 4 September 1810; Wellington to Liverpool, 5 September 1810, IV, 257—58. Despite Cox's "unremitting zeal," when he was recommended for a command in the Portuguese army in 1815, it was denied by the Portuguese government. After the surrender of the fortress, Costa remained a prisoner at Almeida for a month. According to his testimony, he was temporarily released to seek medical attention but he fled with his wife and made his way to Moncorvo. At an official inquiry convened by Beresford to consider the conduct of the officers serving at Almeida, Costa was adjudged innocent of any wrongdoing by General Francisco Silveira. He was also exonerated at Coimbra by General Manuel Pinto de Morais Bacelar for his behavior there. Anxious to return to the army, he slipped through French lines at Cartaxo to rejoin his unit. Beresford had him arrested immediately. For seventeen months he remained in prison until he was brought before a court martial in April of 1812. Instead of being convicted of treasonous activity, he was accused and convicted of cowardice for seeking shelter in one of the bastions during the bombardment. He was condemned to death and despite objections by many Portuguese, Beresford confirmed the sentence on 15 June. He was taken to the Campo do Ourique and executed on 22 August before a firing squad but this was not the end of the case. There were strong feelings among the Portuguese that Costa had been sacrificed as a scapegoat by Beresford to protect his brother-in-law, Cox. If, as Beresford claimed, Almeida had not been reduced to the last extreme when it surrendered, many Portuguese felt Cox should have been tried and not Costa. In 1815 Beresford reopened the case but the conviction was reaffirmed. Napier raised the case in 1832 and in 1852 J.A. Carvalho e Oliveira wrote an article questioning Costa's guilt. W.F.P. Napier, *War in the Peninsula*, II, 389; W.F.P. Napier, *Colonel Napier's Justification*, p. 3; W.F.P. Napier, *A Letter to General Lord Viscount Beresford*, pp. 10—11. J.A. Carvalho e Oliveira, "A praça d'Almeida em 1810." For

details of the charges, testimony, cross-examination, decision of the 1812 court martial, and eloquent defenses of Costa see: Passos, *Beresford e o Tenente-rei* and Silva Mendes, *Memoria biographica*.

38. Guingret, *Relation historique*, pp. 33–34; Hulot, *Souvenirs militaires*, pp. 320–21; Correspondance: Armée de Portugal, Masséna to Eblé, 29 August 1810, Carton C⁷ 9; Horward, *Pelet*, p. 131; Archives de Masséna, Masséna to Berthier, 30 August 1810, LI, 72; "Etat du regiment No. 24 le 2 September 1810," signed by Pamplona, 2 September 1810, LVIII, 41. Pamplona certified that there were 21 officers and 623 men on the active rolls and 63 in the hospital at Almeida on 2 September. *Wellington's Dispatches*, Wellington to Henry Wellesley, 7 September 1810, VI, 413–14; Wellington to Liverpool, 13 September 1810, VI, 437–38. In this letter Wellington indicated that all but 200 men of the 24th Line returned to the Allied lines.

39. Horward, *Pelet*, p. 131; Guingret, *Relation historique*, pp. 33–34; *Wellington's Dispatches*, Wellington to Hill, 8 September 1810, VI, 416. Wellington regarded d'Alorna as a traitor seeking to undermine Portuguese resistance. "It is extraordinary that any man in his senses should act this part, which is, after all, only that of the jackal." He attributed d'Alorna's conduct to "extreme folly and inordinate vanity and ambition."

40. *Wellington's Dispatches*, Wellington to Stuart, 11 September 1810, VI, 427–30; Wellington to Masséna, 24 September 1810, VI, 464–65; Wellington to Liverpool, 10 November 1810, VI, 604–5; Chaby, *Collecção de documentos*, "Ordem do dia," 6, 11 September, 28 December 1810, VI, 154–60.

Chapter 15. *Conclusions*

1. *Wellington's Dispatches*, Wellington to Stuart, 24 September 1810, VI, 466–67; Horward, *Bussaco*, pp. 142–43; Horward, *Pelet*, p. 196n.
2. Horward, *Bussaco*, pp. 172–75.
3. Fririon, *Journal historique*, pp. 77–79; Tomkinson, *Diary*, pp. 50–54; W.F.P. Napier, *Peninsular War*, II, 414.
4. Jones, *Journal of Sieges*, Fletcher to Jones, 31 August, 3 October 1810; Jones to Fletcher, *circa* 29 August 1810; III, 231, 242–43, 234, 252–53, 94–100.
5. *Wellington's Dispatches*, Wellington to Hill, 8 October 1810, VI,

499–501; Wellington to Spencer, 11 October 1810, VI, 505–6; Wellington to Stuart, 12 October 1810, VI, 506; Jones, *Journal of Sieges*, III, 33–34.

6. Marbot, *Mémoires*, II, 410.

7. Koch, *Mémoires de Masséna*, "Situation au 1er Avril 1811," VII, 579–83.

Bibliography

Manuscripts

THERE WERE many valuable manuscript collections utilized in the completion of this study, but the most important was located in the Archives de Masséna. For examining the day-to-day operations of the French army at Almeida and Ciudad Rodrigo from May through August, this collection was unequaled. Volume LI of the collection provided a registry of all of Masséna's correspondence with Napoleon's chief of staff, Alexandre Berthier, and the minister of war, General Henri Clarke. Moreover, it included his letters to the corps commanders, Ney, Junot, and Reynier; the quartermaster general, Lambert; the ordonnateurs and paymasters; the artillery and engineer commanders, Eblé and Lazowski respectively; and the provisional governors under his jurisdiction as Kellermann, Rouyer, and Dorsenne. Additional letters to Napoleon and King Joseph, orders of the day, instructions for the movement of the army, and Masséna's secret correspondence were also found in this volume. Volumes LII through LVIII included several thousand letters written to Masséna by his corps commanders, quartermaster general, artillery and engineer commanders, provisional governors, specially assigned officers, and even Spanish officials in the service of France. A significant number of letters written by Napoleon, King Joseph, and Berthier were also found within these volumes. In all, this collection presented a comprehensive and yet highly detailed view of the army under Masséna's command, much of which has been untapped to the present.

The Correspondence of the Army of Portugal, located in the collection of the Service historique de l'armée at the Archives de la Guerre in the Chateau de Vincennes outside of Paris, was also of immense value. Again, there were actually thousands of letters and documents relative to the operations of the Army of Portugal between April and August of 1810 (Carton C⁷ 7–9). Although there was some duplication between these documents and the Archives de Masséna, a considerable number of documents concerning Reynier's 2d Corps were included in the cartons of the Army of Portugal. Also in this collection was the letter registry of General Loison (Carton C⁷ 20), divisional commander of Ney's 6th Corps; it provided details on the operation of his unit not available in the more general letters of Ney and Masséna. This was also true of Eblé's letter registry (Carton C⁷ 23) which reduced artillery operations to the most basic level. His correspondence with various subordinate artillery commanders presented insights into daily operations that have long been ignored. Pelet's role in the negotiations at Almeida can be found in a carton labeled "Guerre d'Espagne, 1808–1812" from the vast collection designated as "Mémoires historique" (916). Other French manuscript collections pertinent to Masséna's operations against Almeida and Ciudad Rodrigo were located in the Archives Nationales in Paris. In the series designated "Secrétairerie d'Etat, Imperial, Empire" (AF IV), important documents entitled "Rapport de Berthier sur l'armée de Portugal, mars-decembre 1810" (AF IV 1628) proved highly useful.

In Portugal there were also a number of extremely valuable collections related to the siege of Almeida. The manuscripts deposited at the Arquivo Nacional da Torre do Tombo, located at the Palacio de São Bento, were indispensable in this study. In the collection titled Ministerio dos Negoçios Extrangeiros (Maço 166–170) thousands of documents related to the Peninsular War were catalogued. More specifically, most of Governor Cox's correspondence with Marshal Beresford and Lord Wellington was found in this collection; it provided new and at times highly personal material about the governor and his efforts to prepare Almeida for the siege. Located at the Arquivo Histórico Militar were several caixa, among their extensive collection of Peninsular War material, related to the Anglo-Portuguese army and the siege of Almeida. Beresford's correspondence with Forjaz in 1810 (Caixa 19–20, 95), Forjaz's correspondence with Beresford and Wellington in 1810 (Caixa 38–39, 175, 270), and Wellington's correspondence with Forjaz in 1810 (Caixa 10–11) were available in these archives, located at the Museu Militar at Largo dos Caminho de Ferro in Lisbon. The Biblioteca Nacional, now located near Campo Grande at the University of Lisbon, also had significant material relevant to Beresford, Forjaz, and the siege of Almeida in the Arquivo Almada e Lencastre (Pacote 66, 74, and 115). At the Academia de Ciências in Lisbon, the manuscripts in the Colleção da Academia das Sciências de Lisboa proved useful in considering the impact of the fall of Almeida upon the civilian population of the country.

In Great Britain the most valuable manuscript collection relative to the operations of the British army and the sieges of Almeida and Ciudad Rodrigo were housed in the Public Record Office at Kew Gardens, outside of London. The letters of General Craufurd, Colonel Cox, and superspy Captain Louis Ruman (P.R.O., 30/43/51–54) provided valuable insights into British operations during the spring and summer of 1810. The collection of Foreign Office documents, especially the Stuart de Rothesay papers (P.R.O., F.O., 342/19–20) was vital for understanding Wellington's relationship with the Portuguese Regency during the summer of 1810. In addition, the collection of Lord Liverpool's correspondence to Wellington in the War Office (P.R.O., W.O., 6/34, 6/50) presented insights into Wellington's financial problems with the British and Portuguese governments. A number of letters concerning the surrender of Almeida and its impact upon the British, signed by Alexis Roveira, were located in the manuscript collection at The Royal United Service Institute.

In Spain there were several manuscript collections related to the siege of Ciudad Rodrigo. A useful collection of documents at the Archivo Histórico Nacional was found in the papers of the Central Junta (Legajo 34), and at the Servicio Histórico Militar pertinent documents were located in the Colección Documental de Fraile.

Published Correspondence, Memoirs, Diaries

Abrantès, Laure Permon Junot, Duchesse d'. *Mémoires de madame la duchesse d'Abrantès ou souvenirs historique sur Napoléon, la Révolution, le Directoire, le Consulat, l'Empire et la Restauration*. 18 vols. Paris: Mame-Delauney, 1831–33.

Barreiros, Fortunato José. *Exposição veridica e sincera das razões e impossibilidades que provam a sua alteza real, o principe regente de Portugal, e a toda a nação, a falsidade do facto, e depoimento das testemunhas que juraram contra Fortunato José Barreiros . . . Offerecido a nação portugueza por F.J.B*. Bourges: Souchois, 1815.

Beamish, North Ludlow. *History of the King's German Legion*. 2 vols. London: Thomas and William Boone, 1832.

Belmas, Jacques Vital. *Journaux des siéges faits ou soutenus par les français dans la péninsule, de 1807 à 1814*. 4 vols. Paris: Firmin Didot, 1836–37.

Beresford, William Carr. *Collecção das Ordens do Dia do illustrissimo e ex-*

cellentissimo Senhor Guilherme Carr Beresford. 9 vols. Lisbon: António
Nunes dos Santos, 1809–15.

————. *Refutation of Colonel Napier's Justification of his Third Volume.*
London: John Murray, 1834.

Bonaparte, Joseph. *Mémoires et correspondance politique et militaire du roi
Joseph.* Edited by Albert Du Casse. 10 vols. Paris: Perrotin, 1855.

Bonaparte, Napoleon. *The Confidential Correspondence of Napoleon Bonaparte with his Brother Joseph, sometime King of Spain.* 2 vols. London: John Murray, 1855.

————. *Correspondance de Napoléon 1ᵉʳ publiée par ordre de l'Empereur
Napoléon III.* 32 vols. Paris: Imprimerie Impériale, 1858–69.

————. *Lettres inédites de Napoléon 1ᵉʳ (An VIII-1815).* Edited by Léon
Lecestre. 2 vols. Paris: E. Plon, Nourrit, 1897.

Bonnal, Henri. *La vie militaire du maréchal Ney, duc d'Elchingen, prince de
la Moskowa.* 3 vols. Paris: Chapelot, 1910–14.

Boutflower, Charles. *The Journal of an Army Surgeon during the Peninsular
War.* Manchester: Private Printing, n.d.

Burgoyne, John. *Life and Correspondence of Field Marshal Sir John Burgoyne.* Edited by George Wrottesley. 2 vols. London: Richard Bentley,
1873.

Chaby, Claudio de. *Excerptos Historicos e Collecção de Documentos relativos
á guerra denominada da Peninsula . . . .* 6 vols. Lisbon: Imprensa Nacional, 1863–85.

Combermere, Mary Wooley Gibbings Cotton, Viscountess. *Memoirs and
Correspondence of Field-Marshal Viscount Combermere, G.C.B., etc.
from his family papers.* Edited by the Right Hon. Mary, Viscountess
Combermere, and Capt. W. W. Knollys. 2 vols. London: Hurst and
Blackett, 1866.

Costello, Edward. *The Peninsular and Waterloo Campaigns.* Edited by An-
tony Brett-James. London: Longmans, 1967.

Cotton, Stapleton. *See* Combermere.

Cranrobert, François C. *Le maréchal Cranrobert, souvenirs d'un siecle.*
Edited by Germain Bapst. 6 vols. Paris: E. Plon, Nourrit, 1914.

Craufurd, Alexander Henry. *General Craufurd and his Light Division with
many anecdotes, a paper and letters by Sir John Moore, and also letters
from the Right Hon. W. Windham, the Duke of Wellington, Lord Londonderry, and others.* London: Griffith, Farran, Okeden & Welsh [1891].

D'Urban, Benjamin. *The Peninsular Journal of Major-General Sir Benjamin
D'Urban, 1808–1817.* Edited by I.J. Rousseau. London: Longmans,
Green, 1930.

Fitzclarence, Frederick. *A Manual of Out-Post Duties.* Part 3. *A Private Journal of General Craufurd's Out-Post Operations on the Coa and Agueda in 1810,* by James Shaw-Kennedy. London: Parker, Furnivall, and Parker, 1851.

Foy, Maximilien Sébastien. *History of the War in the Peninsula, under Napoleon: to which is prefixed a view of the political and military state of the four belligerent powers.* 2 vols. London: Treuttel and Würtz, 1827.

Fririon, François-Nicolas. *Journal historique de la campagne de Portugal, entreprise par les français, sous les ordre du maréchal Masséna, prince d'Essling, du 15 septembre 1810 au 2 mai 1811.* Paris: Leneveu, 1841.

Guingret, Captain. *Relation historique et militaire de la campagne de Portugal, sous le maréchal Masséna, prince d'Essling.* Limoges: Bargeas, 1817.

Halliday, Andrew. *Observations on the Present State of the Portuguese Army, as organised by Lieutenant-General Sir William Carr Beresford.* London: John Murray, 1811.

Herrasti. *See* Pérez de Herrasti.

Horward, Donald D. *The French Campaign in Portugal, 1810–1811: An Account by Jean Jacques Pelet.* Edited, annotated, and translated. Minneapolis: University of Minnesota Press, 1973.

Hulot, Jacques Louis. *Souvenirs militaires du baron Hulot, général d'artillerie, 1773–1843.* Paris: Spectateur militaire, 1886.

Jones, Sir John Thomas, bart. *Journals of Sieges carried on by the Army under the Duke of Wellington, in Spain, during the years 1811 to 1814; with notes and additions; also Memoranda Relative to the Lines thrown up to cover Lisbon in 1810.* Edited by H.D. Jones. 3 vols. 3d ed. London: J. Weale, 1846.

Kincaid, John. *Adventures in the Rifle Brigade and Random Shots of a Rifleman.* London: Macaren and Company, n.d.

———. *Random Shots from a Rifleman.* London: T. and W. Boone, 1847.

Koch, Jean Baptiste. *Mémoires de Masséna rédigés d'après les documents qu'il a laissés et sur ceux du dépôt de la guerre et du dépôt des fortifications.* 7 vols. Paris: Paulin and Lechevalier, 1848–50.

Leach, Jonathan. *Rough Sketches of the Life of an Old Soldier.* London: Longman, Rees, Orme, Brown, and Green, 1831.

Londonderry, Charles William Vane, Marquess of. *Narrative of the Peninsular War from 1808 to 1813.* 2 vols. 3d ed. London: Henry Colburn, 1829.

Marbot, Jean-Baptiste. *Mémoires du général baron de Marbot.* 3 vols. 5th ed. Paris: E. Plon, Nourrit, 1891.

Napier, George T. *Passages in the Early Military Life of General Sir George T. Napier.* Edited by W. C. E. Napier. 2d ed. London: John Murray, 1886.

Napier, William Francis Patrick. *Colonel Napier's Justification of his Third Volume; Forming a sequel to his reply to various opponents, and containing some new and curious facts relative to the battle of Albuera.* London: Thomas and William Boone, 1833.

———. *History of the War in the Peninsula and in the South of France from A.D. 1807 to A.D. 1814.* 5 vols. New York: W. J. Widdleton, 1864.

———. *A Letter to General Lord Viscount Beresford, being an answer to his Lordship's assumed refutation of Colonel Napier's Justification of his Third Volume.* London: Thomas and William Boone, 1834.

———. *The Life and Opinions of General Sir Charles James Napier, G.C.B.* 4 vols. London: Murray, 1857.

Noël, Jean Nicolas Auguste. *Souvenirs militaires d'un officier du premier empire, 1765–1832.* Paris: Berger-Levrault, 1895.

Pelet, Jean Jacques. "Coup-D'Oeil Militaire sur le Portugal." *Le Spectateur militaire* II(1827):413–45.

———. "Notes sur la campagne de Portugal en 1810 et 1811." *Victoires, conquêtes, désastres, revers et guerres civiles des français, de 1792 à 1815,* XXVII (1821): 314–44.

Pérez de Herrasti, Andrés. *Relacion histórica y circunstanciada de los sucesos del sitio de la plaza de Ciudad-Rodrigo en el eño de 1810.* Madrid: Repullés, 1814.

Picton, Thomas. *Memoirs of Lieutenant General Sir Thomas Picton.* 2 vols. Edited by Heaton B. Robinson. London: Richard Bentley, 1836.

The Royal Military Chronicle or, The British Officer's Monthly Register, Chronicle, and Military Mentor. London: J. Davis, 1810.

Shaw-Kennedy. *See* Fitzclarence.

Simmons, George. *A British Rifle Man: The Journals and Correspondence of Major George Simmons, Rifle Brigade, during the Peninsular War and the Campaign of Waterloo.* Edited by Willoughby Verner. London: A. C. Black, 1899.

Smith, Sir Harry George Wakelyn. *The Autobiography of Lieutenant General Sir Harry Smith, Baronet of Aliwal on the Sutlej.* Edited with the addition of some supplementary chapters by G. C. Moore Smith. 2 vols. London: J. Murray, 1901.

Sprünglin, Emmanuel-Frédéric. *Souvenirs, Revue Hispanique.* Paris: Klincksieck, 1904.

Thiébault, Paul Charles. *Relation de l'expédition du Portugal, faite en 1807* *et 1808, par le Ier corps d'observation de la Gironde, devenu armée de Portugal.* Paris: Margimel, Anselin, and Pochard, 1817.

Tomkinson, William. *The Diary of a Cavalry Officer in the Peninsular and Waterloo Campaigns, 1809–1815.* Edited by James Tomkinson. London: Swan Sonnenschein, 1894.

Verner, Willoughby. *History and Campaigns of the Rifle Brigade.* 2 vols. London: John Bale, Sons and Danielsson, Ltd., 1919.

Warre, Lt. Gen. Sir William. *Letters from the Peninsula, 1808–1812.* Edited by his nephew, Edward Warre, Jr. London: John Murray, 1909.

Wellington, Arthur Wellesley, Duke of. *The Dispatches of Field Marshal the Duke of Wellington, during His Various Campaigns in India, Denmark, Portugal, Spain, the Low Countries, and France, from 1799 to 1818.* Edited by John Gurwood. 13 vols. London: John Murray, 1835–38; 8 vols. London: John Murray, 1852.

———. *Supplementary Despatches and Memoranda of Field Marshal Arthur Duke of Wellington, K.G.* Edited by his son, the Duke of Wellington. 15 vols. London: Murray, 1857–72.

Secondary Sources

Amic, Auguste. *Histoire de Masséna.* Paris: E. Dentu, 1864.

Atteridge, Andrew Hilliard. *The Bravest of the Brave, Michel Ney, Marshal of France, Duke of Elchingen, Prince of the Moskowa, 1769–1815.* New York: Brentano, 1912.

Ayres de Magalhães Sepúlveda, Christovam. *História orgânica e politica do excército portuguêz.* 17 vols. in 21. Lisbon: Imprensa Nacional, 1896–1932.

Blythe, Legette. *Marshal Ney: A Dual Life.* London: Jarrolds, 1937.

Carvalho e Oliveira, J.A. "A praça d'Almeida em 1810." *Revista Universal Lisbonense* (1852): 137ff.

Castello y Estrada, Don Angel. "Defensa de Santa Cruz." *Tierra Charra.* Ciudad Rodrigo, n.d., 101–112.

Cope, William H., bart. *The History of the Rifle Brigade (the Prince Consort's Own), formerly the 95th.* London: Chatto and Windus, 1877.

De la Fuente, Francisco A. "Dom Miguel Pereira Forjaz: His Early Career and Role in the Mobilization and Defense of Portugal during the Peninsular War, 1807–1814." Ph.D. dissertation, Florida State University, 1980.

Faria de Morais, Alberto. "O Cerco de Almeida em 1762." *Boletim do Arquivo Histórico Militar* XX (1950): 5–50.

Fortescue, John W. *A History of the British Army.* 20 vols. London: Macmillan, 1910–30.

Gachot, Edouard. "Masséna en Portugal, 1810–1811." *Revue de la société des amis du musée de l'armée* LXI-LXIII(1958–60): 19–22, 49–54, 45–50.

Garros, Louis. *Ney, le brave des braves.* Paris: Amiot-Dupont, 1955.

Gil, José Cezar Ferreira. *A infantaria Portuguêsa na Guerra da Peninsula.* 2 vols. Lisbon: Tipografia da Cooperativa Militar, 1912–13.

Gómez de Arteche y Moro, José. *Guerra de la Independencia. Historia militar de España de 1808 à 1814.* 14 vols. Madrid: Depósito de la Guerra, 1866–1903.

Gordon, Terry E. "The Early Life and Career of General François-Etienne Kellermann." M.A. thesis, Florida State University, 1979.

Grasset, Alphonse Louis. *La guerre d'Espagne (1807–1813).* 3 vols. Paris: Berger-Levrault, 1914–32.

Hamilton, Henry B. *Historical Record of the 14th (King's) Hussars from A.D. 1715 to A.D. 1900.* London, New York, and Bombay: Longmans, Green, and Co., 1901.

Horward, Donald D. *The Battle of Bussaco: Masséna vs. Wellington.* Tallahassee: Florida State University, 1965.

———. "British Seapower and its Influence upon the Peninsular War (1808–1814)." *Naval War College Review* XXI(1978): 54–71.

———. "'The Dreadful Day': Wellington and Masséna on the Côa, 1810." *Military Affairs* XLIV (1980): 163–170.

———. "Economics at War: The Transformation of the Portuguese economy and social structure during the Peninsular War." Unpublished paper presented at the Eighth International Congress of Economic History, 16–22 August 1982, Budapest, Hungary.

———. "Education and the Commander: Marshal André Masséna." *The Consortium on Revolutionary Europe, Proceedings.* Athens: University of Georgia, 1983.

———. "Um Episodio da Guerra Peninsular." *Boletim do Arquivo Histórico Militar* L (1980): 39–73.

———. "The French Invasion of Portugal, 1810–1811." Ph.D. dissertation, University of Minnesota, 1962.

———. "Portuguese Neutrality and Mobilization, 1801–1810." *Revue International d'Histoire Militaire* Acta 3 (1978): 275–79.

López, Juan Priego. *Guerra de la Independencia, 1808–1814.* 5- vols. Madrid: San Martin, 1972-.

Luz Soriano, Simão José da. *Historia da guerra civil e do estabelecimento do governo parlamentar em Portugal, 1777–1834.* 19 vols. Lisbon: Imprensa Nacional, 1866–90.

Marshall-Cornwall, James. *Marshal Masséna.* London: Oxford University Press, 1965.

Moorsom, William Scarth, ed. *Historical Record of the Fifty-second Regiment (Oxfordshire light infantry) from the year 1755 to the year 1858.* Compiled under direction of the committee and edited by W. S. Moorsom. 2d ed. London: Bentley, 1860.

Oman, Charles. *A History of the Peninsular War.* 7 vols. Oxford: Clarendon Press, 1902–30.

Passos, Carlos de. *Beresford e o Tenente-rei da Praça d'Almeida. Ressurreição d'uma victima do jugo Inglez do temp da Guerra Peninsular.* Com uma carta-prefacio de Maximiano d'Aragão. Porto: Eduardo Tavares Martins, 1924.

Ramon Laca, Julio de. *El General Pérez de Herrasti, Heroe de Ciudad Rodrigo.* Madrid: Raycar Sa Impressores Matilde, 1967.

"Reprodução de Documentos Histórico-Militares." *Boletim do Arquivo Histórico Militar* II (1931): 3–201.

"Reprodução de Documentos Históricos Existentes no Arquivo Histórico Militar." *Boletim do Arquivo Histórico Militar* III(1933): 153–246.

Sabor, Pierre. *Masséna et sa famille.* Aix-en-Provence: Editions du "Feu", 1926.

Sepúlveda. *See* Ayres de Magalhães Sepúlveda.

Severn, John Kenneth. *A Wellesley Affair: Richard Marquess Wellesley and the Conduct of Anglo-Spanish Diplomacy, 1809–1812.* Tallahassee: Florida State University Press, 1981.

Silva Mendes, João da. *Memoria biographica do coronel Francisco Bernardo da Costa e Almeida, Tenente rei da praça de Almeida em 1810.* Porto: Silva Teixeira, 1883.

Thierry, Augustin. *Masséna, l'enfant gâté de la victoire.* Paris: A. Michel [1947].

Tuetey, Louis. *Catalogue général des manuscrits des bibliothèques publiques de France: archives de la guerre.* 3 vols. Paris: E. Plon, Nourrit, 1912.

Valentin, René. *Le maréchal Masséna (1758–1817).* Paris: Charles-Lavauzelle [1960].

Wyld, James, ed. *Maps and Plans of the Principal Movements, Battles, and*

Sieges in which the British Army was engaged during the War from 1808 to 1814 in the Spanish Peninsula and the South of France. London: James Wyld, [1841].

Newspapers

Gazeta da Lisboa (Lisbon).
Le Moniteur (Paris).
The Times (London).

Recent Works

Barrios, Colonel. "Andrés Pérez de Herrasti, Héro de Ciudad Rodrigo." Unpublished paper, Congreso International sobre la Guerra de la Independencia, 2 August 1984.

Brotherton, Thomas. *A Hawk at War: The Peninsular War Reminiscences of General Sir Thomas Brotherton, CB.* Edited by Bryan Perrett. Chippenham, UK: Picton, 1986.

Carvalho, José Vilhena de. *Almeida subsidos para a sua história.* n.n., 1974.

Cuesta, Josefina. "Una figura de Guerrillero: Don Julián Sánchez, El Charro." Unpublished paper, Congreso International sobre la Guerra de la Independencia, 3 August 1984.

D'Urban, Benjamin. *The Peninsular Journal, 1808–1817.* Edited by I.J. Rousseau. London: Longmans Green, 1930; Greenhill, 1988.

Flor, Fernando R. de la. "Las fortificationes de Ciudad Rodrigo y La Concepción." Unpublished paper, Congreso International sobre la Guerra de la Independencia, 3 August 1984.

Fuente, Francisco de la. "Tenente-Rei Francisco Bernardo da Costa e Almeida y la liberación de Almeida." Unpublished paper, Congreso International sobre la Guerra de la Independencia, 4 August 1984.

Gash, Norman. *Wellington: Studies in the Military and Political Career of the first Duke of Wellington*: Manchester, UK, 1990.

Gates, David. *The Spanish Ulcer: A History of the Peninsular War.* London: Allen and Unwin, 1986.

Grattan, William. *Adventures with the Connaught Rangers, 1809–1814.* Edited by Charles Oman. London: Edward Arnold, 1902; Greenhill, 1989.

Horward, Donald D. "Masséna and the Siege of Ciudad Rodrigo." Unpublished paper, Congreso International sobre la Guerra de la Independencia, 3 August 1984.

———. "Wellington's Peninsular Strategy, Portugal, and the Lines of Torres Vedras." *Portuguese Studies Review* 2 (1993): 46–59.

Jones, Lieutenant Rice. *An Engineer Officer under Wellington in the Peninsula.* Edited by H.V. Shore. Cambridge, UK: Trotman, 1986.

Marbot, Jean-Baptiste. *The Memoirs of Baron de Marbot.* 2 vols. Translated by Arthur John Butler. London: Longmans Green, 1892; Greenhill, 1988.

Oman, Charles. *Wellington's Army, 1809–1814.* London: Edward Arnold, 1913; Greenhill, 1986, 1993.

Page, Julia. *Intelligence Officer in the Peninsula: Letters and Diaries of Major the Hon. Edward Charles Cocks, 1786–1812.* Tunbridge Wells: Spellmount; New York: Hippocrene, 1986.

Raeuber, Charles-Alphonse. *Les Renseignements, La réconnaissance et les transmissions militaires du temps de Napoléon: l'example de la troisième invasion du Portugal.* Lisbon: Comissâo Portuguesa da História, 1993.

Rodriguez, Nicolas Horta. *D. Julián Sánchez "El Charro" guerrillero y brigadier.* Ciudad Rodrigo: Gráficas Ortega, 1986.

Simmons, George. *A British Rifleman.* Edited by Willoughby Verner. London: A. & C. Black, 1899; Greenhill, 1986.

Uhagón de Foxá, José Enrique. "La Caridad durante la Guerra de la Independencia." Unpublished paper, Congreso International sobre la Guerra de la Independencia, 3 August 1984.

Vicente, António Pedro. *Le génie français au Portugal sous l'empire.* Lisbon, 1984

———. "Massena in Portugal," *The British Historical Society of Portugal* 17 (1990): 57–84.

———. "Vision de la Almeida del Siglio XIX en la Guerra Peninsular." Unpublished paper, Congreso International sobre la Guerra de la Independencia, 43 August 1984.

Weller, Jac. *Wellington in the Peninsula 1808–1814.* London: Nicholas Vane, 1962; Greenhill, 1992.

Glossary

Abatis A military entrenchment made of large tree limbs or entire trees placed side by side with the branches pointing toward the enemy; they were arranged in a ditch a short distance from the parapets of a fieldwork.

Approaches Trenches, at least ten feet in depth and width, extending from the parallels and leading toward the point under attack. Because of the appearance of their excavations, they were often referred to as zigzags, *cheminements*, saps, or *boyaux*. They served as communication trenches for the passage of wagons and guns to more advanced positions.

Arsenal A depot or magazine for military stores, usually established in the most secure building or site in a town.

Artillery parc An encampment for an artillery train, equipment, animals, and munitions not in immediate use. The term also refers to an artillery train attached to an army in the field.

Balustrade A parapet or low screen consisting of a coping rail supported on balusters and organized in groups.

Banquette A small mound of earth three or four feet wide, running along the inside of and four or five feet below the top of the parapet of a trench, on which men stood to fire at the enemy.

Barrier A strong fencelike obstruction formed at a gate or in a street to block and prevent an enemy from rushing it.

Bastion A projecting part of an internal enclosure of a fortification, consisting of two faces meeting at angles; it was extended by two flanks set at angles to the faces. The flanks of the two adjacent bastions were connected by a straight section of wall called a curtain. The bastion was constructed so it could be effectively covered by flanking fire from other parts of the works.

Berm A narow ledge or shelf two or three feet wide, formed along the exterior slope of a parapet to prevent any of it from falling into the ditch below when hit by enemy fire.

Breach An opening or gap, blasted in a wall or rampart by a mine or cannon fire, wide enough for a body of troops to enter the works or fortress. A practical breach was made when a soldier could climb up through the breach into the fortification without difficulty.

Breastwork A parapet, perhaps four or five feet in height, erected to protect soldiers from enemy fire.

Bridgehead A fortification, often referred to as a *tête de pont*, designed to cover the passage of one or both banks of a river; formed by a semicircle of field works, houses, villages, etc., established above and below a site where a bridge was to be established. Its function was to protect and defend the approaches to the bridge from enemy attack.

Caçadores Portuguese light infantry organized into battalions and brigaded with British infantry battalions or regiments; they were among the most effective fighting men in the army.

Caisson Ammunition wagon of various lengths and with two or four wheels.

Caponier A protected passage from the main fort to an outwork, frequently ten or twelve feet wide and five or six feet deep, covered on each side by a parapet up to seven feet high; extending from a fortress wall to the gorge of a detached work, it was faced with stone and had banquettes along its length.

Casemate A bombproof cellar or vault built under a rampart and usually designed to quarter cannoneers or the garrison. Loopholes existed along the exterior wall for artillery.

Chasseurs à cheval French light cavalry armed with carbines, sabers, and pistols. *Chasseurs à pied* were light infantry armed with the usual 1777 Charleville musket.

Chef de bataillon The commander of a battalion of up to 840 men. Although equal to the British rank of major, the duties of this rank corresponded more closely to those of a lieutenant colonel, nonexistent in the Napoleonic armies. Three battalions constituted a regiment of 2,500 men, commanded by a colonel. French regiments did include a major but he was a staff officer and his duties were concerned primarily with the administration of a regiment.

Counterscarp The outer slope or side of a ditch, opposite the fortress wall, usually faced with stone or brick to make the besiegers' descent into the ditch more difficult.

Coup de main A sudden and vigorous attack designed to surprise an enemy and seize his fortification or position.

Covered way or road An area up to thirty feet in width between the counterscarp and the crest of the glacis, completely surrounding the fortress and its outworks. It was usually covered by a parapet, banquettes, and palisades.

Curtain The portion of a fortress wall between two adjacent bastions and often protected by a demilune.

Defile A narrow passage that forced a column to string out in passing through it. Troops were vulnerable in emerging from the defile if enemy troops were present.

Demilune A work, usually triangular in construction, positioned to protect a wall of a fort and the flanks of the adjoining bastion. A ravelin was another term for this fortification.

Detached work A fortification so far removed from the main work that it could receive no direct aid from it.

Ditch or moat A large trench, often sixteen feet deep and from 80 to 130 feet wide, encircling the rampart of a fort. The term *moat* applied to a ditch filled with water. The two slopes of the ditch were termed the escarp and the counterscarp. When the ditch was excavated, the earth was utilized to form the parapets and ramparts of the fort.

Earthwork A temporary field fortification of various forms and sizes. The essential segment consisted of sheltered trenches covered by parapets and protected against enfilading fire.

Echelon A formation of troops in which each unit maneuvered slightly to the left or right of the unit ahead of it. It was the most expeditious way for large units of troops to advance or retreat.

Embrasure An opening in a fortress parapet or artillery emplacement through which artillery pieces were fired.

Enceinte The principal wall enclosing a fortified town, consisting of bastions, ditch, covered way, etc.

Enfilade Gunfire directed from the flanks of a position in order to sweep the length of any line of works or troops.

Epaulement A barricade of earth raised beside a battery to cover the troops behind it from enfilading fire. Fascines and gabions were often utilized in its construction.

Escarp The slope or side of a ditch adjoining the rampart; faced with stone or brick it was called a revêtment if of permanent construction.

Esplanade A vast expanse or parade ground of a fortified place set apart for garrison drill or exercise.

Etat-major A corps of officers of various grades who formed a kind of council to serve a brigade, division, corps, or army commander. Under the leadership of a *chef de l'état-major* they would carry out administrative operations of the unit, handle dispatches and correspondence, prepare reports and determine troop movements, transmit orders quickly to the various units of the command, provide cartographic information and maps, give advice and suggestions to the commander in chief, and be ready to carry out his orders without hesitation.

Expense magazine An auxiliary magazine established at various sites throughout a fort, but usually on or near the ramparts for use by the artillerymen.

False attack A feint attack made to deceive or divert the attention of an enemy away from the actual point of attack.

Fascines A bundle of twigs, small branches, or brushwood, often ten feet long and one foot thick, tied together with rope. They were used in field fortifications as facing on the interior of parapets or on the sides of embrasures.

Faussebraie A lower wall erected several yards outside the main fortress wall. It provided shelter for riflemen or artillerymen firing against the besiegers before they entered the ditch, but once captured, it served as a means to scale the fortress walls: it might also provide additional protection for the main wall in a bombardment and force the besiegers to pound a breach in both walls.

Field fortifications or fieldworks Temporary fortifications of various shapes and styles, including open, enclosed, or partially closed earthenworks for the protection of more important works.

Flèche A simple temporary fieldwork consisting of two faces forming a salient angle; easily constructed for the defense of a position, they varied in size and had parapets and ditches.

Flying column An independent detachment of considerable strength, organized for rapid movement and complete in equipment and supplies; it often included infantry, cavalry, and light artillery.

Fraise Rows of stakes up to eight feet in length and five inches in diameter, pointed at one end and anchored into a thick beam. Arranged to face an enemy at a height of between four and five feet.

Gabions Hollow, cylindrical, bottomless baskets, usually three or four feet high and two or three feet in diameter, made of wickerwork or twigs and used in the construction of earthworks. When filled with earth, gabions formed effective facing for fieldworks in the construction of batteries, and in the excavation of parallels and approaches.

Gallery A covered passage, dug into the earth and used for a simple communication in areas threatened by enemy fire; also a tunnel-like structure utilized to place a mine alongside and blow up the counterscarp.

Gazonnement Wedge-shaped pieces of fresh sod about a foot in length and half a foot thick. They were used to cover the ramparts, parapets, banquettes, etc., to absorb enemy shell fire.

Glacis The downward slope of a rampart of a covered way, extending gradually into the surrounding terrain within a distance of about 200 feet.

Gorge The entrance into a bastion or other outwork of a fortress.

Grapeshot A combination of small shot, from one and one half ounces to four pounds, tightly tied in a thick canvas bag to form a kind of cylinder adaptable to a cannon barrel; it was highly effective against infantry at close range.

Grenade Hollow balls or shells of iron about two and one half inches in diameter charged with white powder. With a small fuse they were lit by soldiers and thrown up to thirty yards, primarily at besiegers approaching a breach or working close to the fortress walls.

Grenadiers Usually 5'8" in height and among the strongest soldiers in an infantry regiment, they were formed into companies and deployed to lead attacks or serve on the right flank of a battalion.

Honors of war Any unusual privilege granted under certain circumstances to an army or garrison that capitulated; arms, standards, baggage, or even freedom might be retained by the surrendering force.

Howitzer A short mobile cannon used for indirect or high-angle fire to drop shells behind the enemy lines or into a town. It differed from a mortar in that it was on trunions and pivoted from the middle rather than near the base of the barrel.

Invest Initial actions in besieging a town by securing all roads and avenues leading to it and by capturing the commanding positions surrounding it. The investing force was to prevent the besieged force from receiving assistance or supplies and to contain the garrison until the siege train could be brought forward.

Léger French light infantry regiment, often the elite troops, attached to each infantry division; they proved valuable in skirmish and reconnaissance duty.

Limber The forward section of a traveling gun carriage drawn by horses. When brought into action the gun was unhitched from the limber and employed alone.

Line regiment Regular French infantry regiments armed with 1777 Charleville muskets; they were the backbone of the Napoleonic armies.

Loopholes Small square openings, similar in use to the embrasures, but located in the walls of a fortification or casemate.

Lunette A field work consisting of a simple salient with flanks; usually constructed to strengthen a demilune or the wall of a fortification.

Magazine Usually a bombproof building or site where stores, arms, ammunition, and provisions were kept. Also applied to an arsenal where powder and shot were stored.

Mine A subterranean passage excavated from the lines of the besiegers to a point under the rampart of a fortification in order to blow it up with gunpowder.

Mortar A short cannon with large bore, made of cast iron or brass, and mounted for fire at an elevation of between forty-five and seventy degrees; particularly effective in throwing hollow shells containing combustible material to set fires, overthrow works, and kill enemy troops.

Ordonnateur Administrative official of the French army authorized to issue warrants of payment on the purchase of army supplies.

Palisades Rows of firm stakes, six or seven inches in diameter and eight or ten feet long, sharpened at one end. They were planted vertically in the ground at a depth of three feet and at intervals of three inches; parallel to the crest of the glacis, they prevented a surprise attack on the fort.

Parallels Deep wide trenches, at least twelve feet wide and ten feet deep, roughly parallel to the point of attack. Generally two or three in number, connected by a series of approaches, they made possible the safe approach of wagons, artillery, and troops toward the point of attack without coming under the fire of the enemy.

Parapet A mound of earth, eighteen or twenty feet wide, raised six or seven feet above the crest of the rampart; it served to protect the troops defending a fortress or a fieldwork.

Petard A metal container attached to a square board with an iron hook. The container was filled with up to ten pound of gunpowder and detonated to destroy the object on which it was placed or attached. Leather and canvas bags were also employed to hold the powder.

Pickets Small detachments of infantry or cavalry established at an outpost to guard against a surprise attack by the enemy. Pickets in turn sent out vedettes to observe enemy movements.

Pioneer Soldiers employed to work with various tools or instruments such as picks, shovels, hatchets, saws, etc. They were assigned work on the roads, repairing fortifications and field works, clearing forests, and general construction work.

Platform A floor, usually of timber, on which the cannon were placed; it was anchored behind embrasures in artillery batteries.

Pontoniers Officers and soldiers attached to a unit responsible for the construction of temporary bridges.

Ramp A runway extending from the interior of a fort up to the rampart; it permitted troops to reach their pieces on the ramparts quickly without climbing stairs.

Rampart A broad embankment or wall of earth ten or fifteen feet high, generally lined with stone or brick, surrounding a fortified place and forming its main defense; it was often called an enciente.

Ravelin A detached work composed of two faces forming a salient angle and raised before the counterscarp.

Réaux Spanish currency with an exchange rate of 3.5 to one French franc.

Reconnaissance A survey carried on by small detachments or large columns of several hundred men, depending on their mission. Some reconnaissances were carried out to secure topographical information to create or correct maps, while others were sent to acquire details about the enemy's positions, movements, strength, and intentions.

Redans A series of indentations in the wall of a fortress, flanking each other, and generally constructed in front of a bastion.

Redoubt A small detached work without bastions placed at some distance from a fortification to guard a vital position or obstruct the progress of an enemy in a given direction. Redoubts generally had ditches, parapets, some means of providing flanking fire, and a shelter for the garrison.

Return The section of an approach of a trench in which the direction is reversed creating a zigzag effect.

Reverse The back side or part of a trench, abutment, position, etc.

Revêtment A strong exterior wall or facing of stone or brick, supporting the front of a rampart and extending down to the ditch.

Ricochet fire The trajectory of a round projectile after striking in front of a target at an especially low angle. The smaller the angle of fall and the harder the surface struck, the more effective the ricochet in causing havoc among the enemy fortifications or troops as it skipped along the ground.

Rideau A small elevation of ground serving to cover or mask a camp, a post, or an approach. Also a screen or ridge hiding troops in open country.

Salient The segment of a fortification, trench, parapet, etc., that protruded farthest toward the enemy.

Sandbags Bags of earth employed in the repair of breaches and embrasures. In rocky terrain they were utilized to protect the workers and artillerymen working above ground.

Sap A covered trench or an approach utilized as the besiegers drew near the fortress and the garrison concentrated fire on the sappers.

Sapper A soldier trained to work in the saps and given extra pay for this dangerous duty. A brigade of sappers, with their heavy breastplate and helmet, included eight men working in teams of four.

Saucisson A bundle of fascines.

Skirmish An irregular engagement between small parties sent forward to engage the enemy in order to conceal an army's actual movements, or to bring on a general battle. Also referred to the exchange of gunfire between patrols or reconnaissance columns of enemy armies.

Square A formation into which infantry were drawn, especially to resist an enemy cavalry attack. As long as it remained unbroken and its volleys were carefully controlled by ranks so no side of the square was without some loaded muskets, the square could survive. Often organized in two lines with bayonets attached while those in remaining lines loaded and prepared to replace the first two lines.

Talus Similar to a berm, a ledge formed on the inside or outside of a slope to prevent earth or debris from falling into a ditch or other structure below.

Telegraph A structure erected on a high hill and composed of a mast and yardarms from which balls or flags were suspended. Varying arrangements of the balls or flags indicated specific letters or phrases to the next telegraph post.

Terreplein The upper or horizontal surfaces of a rampart behind the parapet where the artillery pieces were located. Casemates were usually situated beneath it.

Tête de sape Usually a narrow trench excavated from a parallel or approach, and pushed forward toward the point of attack very quickly using gabions to cover the workers. Advancing as far as 150 feet within a twenty-four hour period, the sappers were exposed to the full fury of the enemy guns.

Tirailleur Originally, a "poor shot"; later, a soldier who fired at will, hence a skirmisher or marksman. Utilized to distract or delay an enemy's advance.

Trace The outline or plan on which a fortress was laid out. In tracing trenches and batteries, the engineers and artillerymen laid out with tape the exact locations to be excavated.

Traverse Usually, a parapet eight to ten feet in thickness, constructed of earth to cover an entrance or breach as well as part of a fort against enfilade or reverse fire.

Trous de loup Literally, "wolf holes," dug six feet deep and four feet in circumference in the form of an inverted cone; a sharpened stake six feet long was planted in the bottom to impale advancing infantrymen.

Vedette Cavalry outposts established on high ground and along all avenues of approach to enable them to observe an enemy advance and give early notice of their movements.

Voltigeurs Units composed of men of small stature formed into elite companies of infantry who served as skirmishers or marksmen; voltigeurs were expected to run beside cavalry or leap up onto the horse behind the rider when quick movement was required.

Index

Abrantès, Duc d'. *See* Junot

Abrantes, fortress, 29

"Afrancesados," 4

Agueda River, 15, 83; British along, 40–41, 65, 116; French bridges on, 91, 97, 99–100, 104–5, 107; French across or along, 11, 18–19, 119, 122, 137, 152, 287; relation to Ciudad Rodrigo, 26, 84, 91, 93, 121

Alameda, village, 152, 162–63, 195–97, 201, 236, 244; church of, 245–46

Alba de Tormes, town, 8, 26, 45

Alba de Yeltes, village, 81, 110, 123, 194, 359 n. 12

Alcántara, town, 115, 276, 341 n. 47

Alcanzas, village, 71

Aldea del Obispo, village, 40, 73–74, 201, 233, 245–46, 310; Ney's headquarters, 220–21, 260; seized by French, 197

Aldea Nueva de Azaba, village, 192, 195

Aldeia Nova, village, 249, 255–56

Alenquer, village, 319

Alentejo, province, 333 n. 23

Alfaiates, village, 41, 297

Algarve, province, 2

Alhandra, village, 321

Almeida, fortress, 3, 5, 40, 178, 196, 200, 221, 244, 250, 257; anticipated resistance of, 268, 275, 312, 314; castle of, 263, 299–303, 310; casualties, 303, 308; description of, 263; difficult terrain around, 274–75, 277–78, 282–283, 285–86, 288, 291, 293–96; effects of explosion, 300–303, 308, 310, 383 n. 33; investment of, 208, 258; magazines of, 264–65, 269–71, 311; siege preparations, 232, 263–74; sorties of, 258–60; illustr., 262, 264, 266, 268, 269, 270

—French artillery at: armed, 293–95; breach battery, 280, 284; effectiveness of, 298–300; embrasures, 288; emplacements, 285; enfilading batteries, 283–84, 293–94; flèches, 286; organization, 242–45; platforms, 291; traced, 283

—French siege work at: approaches, 291, 293–95, 302; communication trenches, 277, 280–83, 285, 288, 291, 293, 295–96, 302; first parallel, 277–78, 280–83, 285, 288, 291, 295, 302; lack of manpower, 282, 285, 288, 291; point of attack, 263; second parallel, 295–96, 199, 302–3; third parallel, 310

—garrison: casualties, 302–3, 308, 382 n. 22; complement, 265, 267; deserts French, 316–17; surrenders to French, 308–9

Alorna, Dom Pedro de Almeida, marquis d', 253, 257, 303; denounced by Wellington and French, 317, 385 n. 39; embarrassed by desertions, 316; misinformation from, 261–62; organizes Por-